VIRTUAL STORAGE REDEFINED

VIRTUAL STORAGE REDEFINED

TECHNOLOGIES AND APPLICATIONS FOR STORAGE VIRTUALIZATION

Paul Massiglia

with

Frank Bunn

Production Manager: Leslie Austin
Copy Editor: Anna Reynolds Trabucco
Proofreader: Martha Ghent
Interior Designer: Chris Schabow
Artists: George Kupfer, Peter Phinney, Bob Santiago and Charlie Van Meter
Compositor: The Left Coast Group
Cover Concept and Design: Nelson Carnicelli
Indexer: Kathy Pitcoff

Cataloging-in-Publication

Massiglia, Paul.
Virtual storage redefined : technologies and applications for storage virtualization : using storage virtualization to get more from enterprise data storage assets / Paul Massiglia with Frank Bunn.
p. cm.
ISBN 0-9729022-0-1

1. Virtual storage (Computer science) I. Bunn, Frank. II. Title.

QA76.9.V5M38 2003 004.5
QBI03-200287

Printed in the United States of America.

VERITAS Software Corporation
350 Ellis Street
Mountain View, CA 94043

ISBN: 0-972-9022-0-1
1 2 3 4 5 6 7 8 9 10—CDS—07 06 05 04 03
www.VERITAS.com

Contents

Foreword *xiii*

Acknowledgments *xv*

Chapter 1: Introduction to Virtualization 1

Storage Virtualization Defined *2*

Storage Virtualization: Why *3*

Storage Virtualization: What *7*

Storage Virtualization: Where and How *8*

PART 1: TECHNOLOGY 17

Chapter 2: Disk Virtualization 19

Why Virtualize a Disk? *19*

Disk Drive Data Layout *21*

Disk Virtualization: Logical Block Addressing *22*

Chapter 3: RAID: Performance and Availability in Virtual Block Storage 28

Resilient Virtual Storage with RAID *28*

A Brief History of RAID *30*

The Two Fundamental RAID-Based Virtualization Concepts *33*

Chapter 4: Failure Tolerance in Virtual Block Storage 37

Mirroring for Failure Tolerance *37*

Parity RAID Redundancy *42*

Limitations Parity RAID Arrays *45*

Chapter 5: Virtual Storage Availability 50

Components of Data Availability *51*

Examples *56*

Chapter 6: Making Virtual Storage Systems Highly Available 62

Making Virtual Storage Highly Available 63

Virtual Storage and Data Availability 65

What Mirroring and RAID Don't Do 68

Chapter 7: Locating User Data on Virtual Block Storage 71

Larger Virtual Devices: Concatenation 72

Smaller Virtual Devices: Partitioning 76

Block Address Striping 77

Applications for Array with Striped Block Addressing 80

Block Address Striping and Parity RAID 80

Chapter 8: Performance of Virtual Block Storage 85

Application I/O Performance Characteristics 86

Block Address Striping and I/O Performance 86

Parity RAID and I/O Performance 93

Striping with Mirroring 98

PART 2: IMPLEMENTATIONS 103

Chapter 9: Conventional Block Storage Virtualization 105

Block Storage Virtualization Implementations 106

RAID System Virtualization 109

Server-Based Virtualization 113

Chapter 10: Block Storage Virtualization in Storage Networks 120

Server-Centric Storage Virtualization 120

Storage Networks and Management Cost 122

In-Band Storage Network Virtualization 125

Out-of-Band Storage Network Virtualization 132

Chapter 11: Storage Virtualization in Shared Data Clusters 138

Clustering, Storage, and Data 139

Storage Virtualization for Shared Data Clusters 144

Chapter 12: Data Replication 151

Getting Data to Remote Locations 152

Forms of Replication 153

Block Storage Replication Implementation Alternatives 160

Using Replicated Data for Disaster Recovery 165

Chapter 13: Characteristics of Virtual Device Replication 168

Virtual Storage Device Replication and Application Performance 168

Failures, Disasters, and Data Integrity 173

Getting Virtual Device Replication Started 177

PART 3: APPLICATIONS 183

Chapter 14: Backup and Virtual Block Storage 185

Contemporary Backup Issues 185

Backup Windows and Block Storage Virtualization 188

Other Techniques for Minimizing Backup Windows 195

Tape Drive Virtualization 196

Chapter 15: Files and Virtual Storage 199

Virtual Storage and File Systems 200

Virtual Storage and Cluster File Systems 205

Chapter 16: Databases and Virtual Storage 212

Databases 212

Database Backup and Virtual Storage 217

Incremental Database Backup 221

Recovering Databases from Backups 222

Protecting Online Databases' Data 223

Databases and Virtual Storage Replication 226

PART 4: NETWORKS 231

Chapter 17: Interconnects for Virtual Storage 233
Storage Networks and Fibre Channel 234
Fibre Channel Storage Network Topologies 235
Storage Network Configuration Considerations 239

Chapter 18: Moving Virtual Data over Long Distances 243
Network Convergence 243
Wide Area Communications 246
Dense Wave Division Multiplexing 247
Wide Area Storage Networks 250
Integrated Network Examples 252

Chapter 19: Another Type of Virtual Storage: HSM 256
Storage Hierarchies and HSM 256
How HSM Works 260
HSM Capabilities and Implementations 261

PART 5: THE FUTURE 267

Chapter 20: Challenges for Enterprise Storage 269
Complexity: Today's Enterprise Storage Challenge 270
Dealing with Storage System Complexity 275
Storage Virtualization and Complexity 277

Chapter 21: Virtual Storage for the Future 279
The Popularity of Block Storage Virtualization 279
Objects: The Future of Virtual Storage? 283
Using Objects to Reduce Storage Complexity 289

APPENDIXES 295

Appendix A: A Summary of Block Storage Virtualization Techniques and Implementations 297

Appendix B: Other Forms of RAID 300

Appendix C: Gather Writing and Scatter Reading 302

Appendix D: A Brief Overview of File Systems 304

Appendix E: Developments in Storage Network Technology 318

Appendix F: The Nature of Availability 322

Glossary of Terminology 329

Index 349

Foreword

Technology is like fish. The longer it stays on the shelf, the less desirable it becomes.

—ANDREW HELLER, IBM Executive

As authors Paul Massiglia and Frank Bunn observe in their introduction, "virtual" may be the first official buzzword of the third millennium. The term is widely used, in computing, and in other facets of life. But it's not all about the buzz. The fact is that virtualization is an extraordinarily useful and universal concept. Wherever we look, there are examples of well-understood behavior—we expect a car to react in a certain way when we turn the wheel, step on the gas, and hit the brake. We understand what it means when we make a call and the distant telephone rings. We react to colored dots on a monitor screen as if they really were "windows." All of these are virtual devices.

A virtual device behaves like some ideal model of a useful real device with which we are familiar. Virtualization *hides* the makeup of the virtual device, which may be quite different than the mental model we form by observing its behavior and interacting with it. Thus, the car's controls may be hydraulic, or even computer assisted, and the moves we make may be only indirectly related to wheels turning or fuel being fed to the engine. The remote ringing we hear is almost certainly synthesized, and has no connection to the distant telephone. What we perceive as windows into that which we can type or forms we can fill out are nothing more than user-friendly feedback about keystrokes and mouse clicks. All of these virtualizations hide the complexity that makes things work, and free designers to innovate to improve device performance, resiliency, and function.

Virtualization has become strongly entrenched in enterprise computing—we have virtual memory, virtual machines, virtual private networks, and, of course, virtual storage. Computer data storage fits the virtualization model particularly well. Storage devices follow a simple, well-understood behavioral model that is essentially ubiquitous in computing. But physically, storage devices leave a lot to be desired. They don't perform as well as we'd like. They have some annoying limitations, like limited capacity. And above all, they fail at the worst times.

Virtualization improves the properties of storage devices without changing the behavioral model. By combining several disk drives and virtualizing them as one, throughput can be aggregated. Mirroring and RAID keep virtual devices humming, even if their components break down. Physical storage capacity in the form of additional disk drives can be added to a virtual device, in some implementations, while the virtual device is in use. None of this changes the basic storage device behavioral model. For enterprise applications, the properties of virtual storage devices are far more desirable than those of the "real" article.

These storage virtualization techniques have been known for years, which makes one wonder why all the interest in storage virtualization now. The answer is simple—storage networks have enabled the construction of potentially more functional and flexible enterprise computing environments. Connecting storage devices and the servers that use it conjures up visions of being able to redeploy storage to where it is needed, of improving performance by adding devices, and of adjusting device capacity to meet changing needs, all in a dynamic, "24×7" environment. The buzz around storage virtualization isn't so much about what it does, but about where and how it can be implemented and managed, and how it can be used to improve the computing environment.

How virtual storage is implemented and the applications that make it compelling are precisely what Massiglia and Bunn deal with in this book. Starting with the basics of the technology, the authors proceed to a comparison of different implementations, and explore the extension of virtual storage through replication to support disaster recoverability. Significant coverage is given to the principal "storage applications"—backup, file systems, and databases—illustrating how they can use the advanced properties of virtual storage to advantage. Finally, the authors discuss the local and remote storage network technologies that make the topic "hot", and close with a look at the next inhibitor to progress in computing—complexity—and suggest possible breakthroughs.

The main body of the book is written in the abstract. Vendors and products that implement the technologies are not mentioned.

Throughout the text, however, sidebars illustrate how VERITAS Software Corporation's technologies implement or support the concepts described in the main text.

The audience for this book is the information technology planner who develops enterprise information processing architectures, the system administrator who manages a data center, the application manager who must specify storage that meets requirements, the database administrator who negotiates storage quality of service appropriate for the value of data, and the CIO who signs the checks. The authors have struck a balance between technology and implementation, between detail and overview, and between abstract and concrete. Understanding the subject matter is essential for everyone who works in information technology infrastructure.

John Colgrove
VERITAS Fellow
Mountain View, California
April, 2003

Acknowledgments

This book is the first of what is to become a series of technology "drill-downs" on topics overviewed in *The Resilient Enterprise,* published by VERITAS Software Corporation in April 2002. Like *The Resilient Enterprise,* this volume owes a lot to the insights of several brilliant and articulate people. In particular, I single out Mark Erickson, who contributed the original material that led to Chapter 19 on Hierarchical Storage Management, David Lai for his contribution to the database material in Chapter 16, Greg Schulz of Inrange Technologies for the networking material on which Chapter 17 and Chapter 18 are based, and Evan Marcus for his insights on the subject of availability, which are reflected in Chapter 5 and elsewhere.

In addition to these contributors, Mike Dutch, Paul Czarnik, and Melissa Stein all reviewed various versions of the manuscript, and their insights focused and strengthened it greatly.

I was blessed in this project with three indefatigable technical reviewers from VERITAS—Dilip Ranade, Bob Rader, and especially my co-author, Frank Bunn, who in addition to writing all 53 of the VERITAS-specific sidebars that appear in the book, reviewed the main text painstakingly, and in particular, made many helpful suggestions to improve readability for international audiences.

Almost on a lark, I called Professor Greg Ganger at Carnegie Mellon University, and asked if he had a graduate student who would be interested in reviewing the manuscript from an outside-the-industry perspective. Doctoral candidate John Linwood Griffin agreed to do the review. His detailed and insightful "commentaries from hell" made me pause and think about what I was trying to say and to whom, and led to several extensive revisions of the manuscript that improved its accuracy and completeness, and left me somewhat wondering how someone so young could be so wise. I came away from the experience more impressed than ever at the versatility and maturity of Carnegie Mellon's Parallel Data Laboratory students. Thanks, John!

Finally, I wish to thank the production team who transformed the raw manuscript into a finished book. In particular, production manager Leslie Austin; copyeditor Anna Reynolds Trabucco; proofreader Martha Ghent; interior book designer Chris Schabow; artists Charlie Van Meter, Bob Santiago, and George Kupfer; the compositors of The Left Coast Group; and Nelson Carnicelli, who did double duty as VERITAS project manager and cover designer. All made notable contributions.

If in spite of the efforts of all these talented people, flaws, inaccuracies, and omissions remain, the fault can be laid at my door.

PAUL MASSIGLIA
Silverthorne, Colorado
January, 2003

CHAPTER 1

vir·tu·al (vûr'cho͞o-əl) *adj. 1. Existing or resulting in essence or effect though not in actual fact, form, or name.*

—THE AMERICAN HERITAGE DICTIONARY

Introduction to Virtualization

In this chapter . . .

- Storage virtualization defined
- Using virtualization to improve four fundamental measures of storage system quality
- Where virtualization is implemented and why

"Virtual" is certainly one of the third millennium's favorite adjectives. We have virtual reality, virtual hospitals,[1] virtual libraries,[2] and virtual universities.[3] There are virtual florists,[4] virtual museums,[5] and one global travel company even styles its Web service as *Virtually There.*[6]

Data storage was one of the earliest information technology areas to embrace the concept of virtualization. For a decade or more, storage systems have been described as implementing **virtual disk drives.**[7] More recently, systems that virtualize tape drives and tape media have been delivered. As our subject is the virtualization of online storage, it seems useful to start by exploring what the term means and why it's a useful concept for data storage technology.

1. http://www.vh.org/
2. http://icom.museum/vlmp/
3. http://vu.org/
4. http://www.virtualflowers.com/
5. http://archive.comlab.ox.ac.uk/other/museums/computing.html
6. http://www.virtuallythere.com/
7. Bold terms are defined in the "Glossary of Terminology" at the rear of this book.

STORAGE VIRTUALIZATION DEFINED

As the definition quoted at the beginning of this chapter suggests, the virtualization of an object is the creation of another object that has the important characteristics of the original object, but that is not the original object. Thus, a virtual library, for example, would typically have the important characteristics of a "real" library—it would house documents in some form useful for browsing or loan by authorized patrons—but it might lack the inessential characteristics of a physical library—having, for example, no buildings, shelves, or paper books.

Although they are marvels of complex technology, electronic data storage devices are conceptually simple—disk drives, tape drives, and tapes. The essential properties of data storage devices are the ability to store data **persistently**[8] and to deliver it to clients on request. Nonessential characteristics include device size, power consumption, performance, and storage capacity. These characteristics vary from device to device without changing the fundamental nature of what a storage device *is*. Thus, any coordinated collection of objects that is capable of storing data persistently and delivering it to clients on request might fairly be called a virtual storage device. In fact, virtual storage devices typically include aggregates of physical storage devices under common control.

Virtual storage devices don't really exist. They are simply representations of the behavior of physical devices of the same type. These representations are made by the devices' clients (usually application programs) in the form of responses to I/O requests. If these responses are sufficiently like those of the actual devices, clients need not be aware that the devices are not "real." This simple but powerful concept is what makes storage virtualization work—no application changes are required to reap its benefits. Any application or system software that can use disk drives, tape drives, libraries, or file systems can use equivalent virtual devices without being specifically adapted to do so.

Forms of Storage Virtualization

Any type of computer storage or data object can be virtualized. Figure 1–1 illustrates a taxonomy of commonly virtualized storage and data objects that was developed by the Storage Networking Industry Association (SNIA) to help organize thinking about the subject. The top row of

---

8. Data is said to be stored *persistently* if it doesn't disappear when the lights go out. Data held in a computer's memory is typically not persistent, while data stored on disk or tape media is persistent.

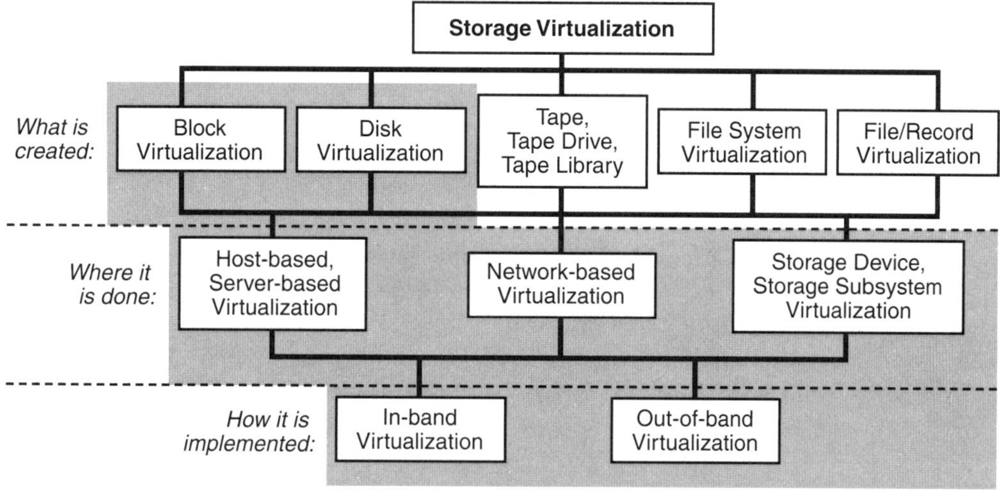

▼ **FIGURE 1–1** *The Storage Networking Industry Association Virtualization Taxonomy*[9]

the diagram in Figure 1–1 represents the virtualized objects, the middle row represents the location in a system at which virtualization occurs, and the bottom row represents virtualization techniques. This book covers what the SNIA refers to as **block** and **disk virtualization.** The types of virtualization that form its principal subject matter are those within the shaded polygon in Figure 1–1.

STORAGE VIRTUALIZATION: *WHY*

Data storage devices are simple devices with simple measures of quality, or "goodness." A storage device is perceived as good if it performs well, doesn't break (is highly available), doesn't cost much, and is easy to manage. Virtualization can be used to improve all four of these basic storage quality metrics:

9. Adapted and used by permission of the Storage Networking Industry Association.

- ***I/O Performance:*** More and more, data access and delivery speed determines the viability of applications. As an extreme example, if data cannot be delivered at the rate required by video players, a video-on-demand application is not viable. Less dramatically (but perhaps more important to most people), if credit card databases cannot be updated fast enough, queues of disgruntled customers develop at checkout lines.

  Virtualization can ***stripe*** data addresses across several storage devices to increase I/O performance as observed by applications. Chapter 7 discusses data striping.
- ***Availability:*** As society goes increasingly online, tolerance for unavailable computer systems is decreasing. Consumers don't want to hear that they can't buy meals or fill their gas tanks because "the computer is down." Energy utilities, transportation systems, public safety, and entertainment all depend on data processing systems and their data being "there" when they're needed. Data can only be "there" if data storage is equally "there."

  Virtualization can **mirror** identical data on two or more disk drives to insulate against disk and other failures and increase availability. Chapter 4 discusses mirroring and other techniques for increasing data availability.
- ***Cost of capacity:*** Disk storage prices are decreasing at a dizzying rate, which in part accounts for equally dizzying increases in storage consumption. Virtualization, in the form of mirroring and remote replication, increases consumption still further. Thus, the cost of delivered storage capacity remains a factor. Enterprises can exploit lower storage costs either as reduced information technology spending or as increased application capability for a constant spending level.

  Virtualization can **aggregate** the storage capacity of multiple devices, or **redeploy** unused capacity to other servers where it is needed, in either case enabling additional storage purchases to be deferred. Block storage capacity cost is discussed throughout the book.
- ***Manageability:*** Today's conventional information technology wisdom holds that management of system components and capabilities is the most rapidly increasing cost of processing electronic data. Every analyst has a favored estimate, but there seems to be general agreement that managing storage costs five to ten times as much as purchasing it. Management cost is therefore an important measure of storage quality. Storage purchasers eagerly seek out solutions that enable more bytes to be managed by a single administrator.

  Virtualization can ***combine*** smaller devices into larger ones, reducing the number of "things" to be managed. By increasing failure tolerance, it reduces downtime, and therefore, recovery management effort. Storage management is discussed in some form in most of the later chapters.

The case for storage virtualization is simple. It improves these basic measures of storage quality, thereby increasing the value that an enterprise can derive from its storage and data assets. The chapters that follow describe the block storage virtualization techniques and implementations that lead to improvements in these quality measures, as well as the storage applications that use them.

STORAGE VIRTUALIZATION: *WHAT*

The techniques of storage virtualization vary, depending on the objects being virtualized and the desired results. Technology exists to virtualize disk drives, tape drives, tapes, data files, and entire file systems. All of these are useful in some way. Some of them, such as disk drive virtualization and file system virtualization, are frequently integrated within a single system to enhance the beneficial effect. The following sections describe the most common forms of storage virtualization found in commercial computing environments.

Disk and Block Virtualization

Perhaps the most prevalent form of storage virtualization in use today, and the principal focus of this book, is block storage device virtualization (called "Block Virtualization" in the SNIA taxonomy shown in Figure 1–1[10]). Disk drive virtualization is accomplished by firmware within a physical disk drive. Block storage devices are disk drive-like virtual devices created by control software that manages the operation of one or more disk drives. The control software coordinates the disk drives' operations and presents *virtual block devices* to clients. Block virtualization technology has been common in both RAID systems and as **virtual volumes** created and managed by server-based **volume managers** for over a decade. More recently, it has become available in network **storage appliances.**

10. This book uses the terms *virtual block storage device, virtual block device,* and *virtual device* to denote devices that implement the SNIA's block virtualization concept.

Like a disk drive, a virtual block device contains numbered blocks, to which data can be read or written individually or in a consecutive sequence. But the virtual block device doesn't really exist; instead its control software behaves like a disk from the application point of view. Responses to application read and write requests are the same as those a disk might give. The control software mimics disk drive behavior so well that applications are unaffected by the fact that the disk on which they are storing data is not "real." This is what has made block virtualization so popular—no application modification is required to use it. Any software that can use disk drives can use virtual block devices without being specifically adapted to do so.

File System Virtualization

Entire file systems can be virtualized in at least two ways. Remote file servers run file systems that are perceived by client applications as running on the client computers. More recently, technology that aggregates multiple file systems into a single large file store has appeared. In both cases, applications access files without regard for their physical locations, while system administrators reap the management benefits of consolidated file storage for multiple applications running on multiple (possibly diverse) servers.

File Virtualization

Hierarchical storage management (**HSM**) software virtualizes files within a file system by transparently **migrating** them to low-cost offline storage, thereby reducing online capacity requirements and improving various aspects of backup and file management. Chapter 19 discusses file virtualization using HSM techniques.

Tape Media Virtualization

Because tape media can only be read and written sequentially, there are inherent challenges to tape storage. For example, deleting the second of three files on a tape creates a largely unusable gap. In consequence, some software that writes data on tape media will only store a single data set on any given tape.

To overcome this limitation, some bulk storage products use online storage capacity as a kind of cache, and emulate libraries of tape media to backup and other tape applications. Disk caching of tape data enables optimal media utilization and removes tape mount, dismount, and repo-

VERITAS and Virtualization

In its role as a leading provider of storage management software, VERITAS delivers storage virtualization of almost all types as defined in the SNIA Storage Virtualization Taxonomy. The exception is disk virtualization, which is controlled by disk firmware from disk drive manufacturers.

VERITAS delivers multiple solutions for block, tape storage, file system, and file virtualization. Perhaps the best known of these is in the area of block virtualization. VERITAS includes this solution in VERITAS™ Volume Manager (VxVM), NAS, and SAN application-based software available through VERITAS' Powered™ partners.

sitioning times from the application execution path. Better media utilization reduces tape drive hardware and media requirements (and therefore cost) and simplifies management.

Tape media virtualization also makes backup performance more predictable. The greatest vulnerability of many backup strategies is the data stream-dependent performance of tape drives. Backups that normally run well can become impossibly slow if network loading interrupts the steady flow of data and forces tape drives to stop and "reposition." Using disk storage as an intermediate buffer provides predictable backup performance that is largely independent of data stream uniformity.

Tape Drive Virtualization

With the adoption of storage networks, tape drive virtualization has become possible. At its simplest, tape drive virtualization allows a set of tape drives to be "shared" among a set of servers. This is beneficial because any given server tends to use tape drives only for the relatively brief periods during which it is actually backing up its data. Tape drives connected directly to a server tend to be idle most of the time—a poor use of assets. If backups can be staggered, however, tape drives connected to a storage network can be logically "passed" from one server to another. Tape drives stay busy, and asset utilization improves. This type of tape drive virtualization is implemented both in distributed software that runs in backup servers and in specialized storage network switches. The latter devices take tape drive virtualization one step further—they are able to pool tape drives of different types, and represent one type of drive as another, increasing flexibility and asset utilization.

Another form of tape drive virtualization is similar to block device virtualization. **Arrays** of two or more tape drives are controlled by software that represents them to clients as a single drive. Like block storage devices, tape drives are virtualized in this way to improve I/O performance and data availability. When part of the storage capacity in such arrays is used to hold redundant data for improved failure tolerance, the array is sometimes referred to as a **redundant array of independent tapes (RAIT).**

Tape Library Virtualization

Even more recently, the changing relationship between disk and tape prices (the per-byte storage costs of the two are converging) has resulted in the introduction of disk-based systems that combine tape media virtualization and tape drive virtualization to mimic the behavior of entire tape libraries. Data backed up on these devices (which hold multiple terabytes) can be spun off to actual tapes for vaulting and long-term retention during periods of low system activity.

STORAGE VIRTUALIZATION: *WHERE* AND *HOW*

This book is primarily about block storage device virtualization (the forms of storage virtualization represented by the shaded area in Figure 1–1). Virtual block storage devices are created by software that controls one or more physical storage devices. The software coordinates device operations and mimics a storage device or file system when interacting with clients. Today, most software that virtualizes disk drives runs either on dedicated specialized processors in RAID systems or on application servers, in the form of volume management software.

Implementing Block Storage Device Virtualization in the RAID System

The processors in RAID controllers have the advantages of being highly optimized for their purpose and of having access to specialized auxiliary hardware for boosting performance. Most enterprise RAID systems can connect and provide storage services to more than one application server, either through multiple parallel SCSI server ports or by connecting to a storage network.

Implementing Block Storage Device Virtualization in the Application Server

Server-based volume managers have neither of the abovementioned advantages, but they are available for most computers at lower intrinsic cost than RAID system storage. Volume managers typically support aggregation and virtualization of devices of different types. Virtual block devices presented by RAID systems as logical units (**LUN**s) are often further virtualized by volume managers. These capabilities can be exploited to improve I/O performance and data availability, for example, by striping or mirroring data between two RAID systems, or by making a virtual device available via two access paths (network connections) for protection against path failure.

VERITAS Virtualization Implementations

Virtualization is not new. For nearly a decade, VERITAS has been the leader in block storage virtualization. VERITAS is a major supplier for logical volume management for all Solaris, AIX, HP-UX, Linux, and Windows platforms.

The growing acceptance of storage networking has changed the enterprise storage landscape profoundly, requiring expansion of the virtualization concept into the storage network. VERITAS has therefore expanded its solution set to include network-based virtualization for both NAS and SAN infrastructures with appliance-based software running on conventional servers dedicated to storage virtualization. This concept is readily extensible to provide virtualization capabilities for the emerging generation of intelligent fabric switches.

Implementing Block Storage Device Virtualization in the Storage Network

As storage networks become more common, it is natural to think in terms of using storage network infrastructure components that are neither part of a storage system nor part of a server to virtualize storage. So-called *storage appliances* have already been used for this purpose, and storage network switches are another potential implementation site for this functionality. A storage network-based virtualizer can virtualize any storage devices and present virtual devices to any servers, although implementations limit what is actually supported. Network block storage virtualization devices may operate either **in-band,** with the virtualization device in the data path between client and physical storage, or **out-of-band,** cooperating with client-based virtualization components that communicate directly with storage devices. Chapter 10 discusses in-band and out-of-band network storage virtualization.

Implementing Tape Drive Virtualization

Tape drives have been virtualized both by special-purpose hardware components and by distributed software that runs in servers connected to a storage network. In the former case, the hardware presents a single tape drive on different network addresses at different times. Each network address is associated with a single application server, so each application server "thinks" it has dedicated tape drives. As long as backup or other tape access applications do not run concurrently on more servers than there are tape drives, the tape virtualization hardware can convert the virtual tape drive network addresses used by servers to physical tape drive addresses and send read and write commands to them. If a server attempts to access "its" tape drive, and no physical drive is available, the virtual drive reports that it is busy, and application I/O recovery procedures are invoked.

Software tape virtualization behaves similarly. In a typical implementation, such as the VERITAS NetBackup *Shared Storage Option,* software running in each server that accesses tape drives cooperates to allocate tape drives to servers that request them. The software blocks applications' attempts to access tape drives that are *not* allocated to the servers on which the applications are running.

Implementing Tape Library Virtualization

Virtual tape libraries that use disk storage to emulate tapes drives and media handlers typically have hardware architecture very similar to that of RAID systems. A control processor directs the operation of several disk drives as well as interfaces to a storage network or directly to application servers. The control processor organizes the storage capacity of the disk drives, providing any RAID or mirroring capabilities, and presents the resulting net capacity as tape cartridges in a library. In addition, it uses the storage network or I/O bus to emulate one or more tape drives and media loaders. The latter capability allows a virtual tape library to "slide in" to a distributed system, replacing a physical library of the type it emulates, without requiring reconfiguration of, or otherwise disturbing, any backup software.

Implementing File System Virtualization

File systems organize the raw storage capacity of virtual block devices or disk drives and present it using an interface that is "friendlier" to applications. Applications can freely create, use, and delete arbitrary numbers of files of arbitrary size according to their requirements. Table 1–1 summarizes the differences between block storage device and file access characteristics.

Conceptually, a file system runs on a server along with the applications that access data in it. In the late 1980s, **network file access protocols** were introduced. These protocols[11] convert application file access

11. There are two network file access protocols in common use: the *Network File System,* or NFS, protocol commonly used by UNIX systems and the *Common Internet File System,* or CIFS, protocol, commonly used by Windows systems.

▼ **TABLE 1–1** *Comparison of Disk and File Access Characteristics*

	Block Storage Characteristic	File and File System Characteristic
Storage objects	Disk drives and other block access storage devices of fixed capacity	Files, directories
Object persistence	Indefinite; changed by system or virtual device reconfiguration	Application-controlled by create and delete file operations
Object size	**Disk drive:** fixed at installation **Block device:** fixed at system or device reconfiguration Both addressed as numbered, fixed-size (typically 512 bytes) blocks	Arbitrary; controlled by application up to file system maximum capacity or application space quota *File objects can grow and shrink under application control*
Object operations	**Administrative:** import, export **Application:** read, write	**Administrative:** mount, unmount **Application:** create, extend, truncate, delete, read, write
Object organization	"Flat"—one "space" of consecutively numbered blocks per disk or block device	Typically hierarchical, or tree-structured, with nested directories containing other directories or files. Leaf nodes are files.

requests into messages that are sent to **file servers** that receive and act on them, absorbing data from or delivering it over the network. File access protocols are structured for **client-server architecture,** with the client making data access requests, and the server accessing an actual file system to satisfy them. File access protocols provide two primary benefits:

- ***Remote data access:*** Because a file server is essentially a software component, it can run on any system. Any system on a network can make its data files accessible by any other. The obvious advantage of this is that data required by an application can always be made accessible to that application, no matter where it runs, by making the system that controls the required data into a file server.
- ***Data sharing:*** File server software typically allows multiple clients to access data in a file system simultaneously. One obvious use of this capability is the connection of a large number of personal computers to a single large file server located in a secure data center and configured to optimize file access. This allows enterprises to centralize valuable data assets for protection and administration without unduly

In-Band or Out-of-Band?

The merits of in-band and out-of-band storage virtualization have spawned lively public debate between proponents of the two. Unfortunately, the debate contributes little to the clarity that end users need to make informed storage strategy decisions. VERITAS believes that both approaches have unique merits that suit them to different installed storage infrastructures and future requirements. The company offers both server-based and network-based in-band and out-of-band virtualization solutions today, and continues active development of both approaches for the future.

restricting access by the people and applications that need them. Because most server platforms implement both CIFS and NFS file access protocols, a single file server can make data available to a **heterogeneous** set of clients. Thus, not only is data never in the wrong place, it is also never inaccessible because the computer that needs it is of the wrong type.[12]

File access protocols virtualize files in much the same way that volume managers and RAID systems virtualize block storage devices. To applications, it appears that file access requests are satisfied by a local file system. Network file access protocols allow a file system to be separated from applications that access files in it. Network file servers have a variety of nonessential characteristics, including performance assists, capacity, robustness (e.g., through clustering), and so forth, while retaining the "look and feel" of locally connected files. It is even feasible for a file server to be replaced by another without disturbing the clients that access it.

More recent file system virtualization technology takes the concept a step further by combining the file access paradigm with the concepts of block storage virtualization and out-of-band control of metadata.[13] Perhaps the best-known example of this technology is IBM Corporation's Storage Tank.[14] This technology incorporates dedicated **metadata servers** that control file system structures, and **file access clients** (software components) in application servers that use metadata obtained from the metadata server to convert application file access requests into virtual block I/O operations. This file system virtualization architecture, illustrated in Figure 1–2, centralizes file system metadata on behalf of multiple application servers.

12. Within broad limits. There are computing platforms that are incapable of acting as either CIFS or NFS clients, but fortunately these are seldom found in enterprise information processing operations.
13. The concept of out-of-band block storage virtualization is discussed further in Chapter 10.
14. IBM Storage Tank is a trademark of the International Business Machines Corporation.

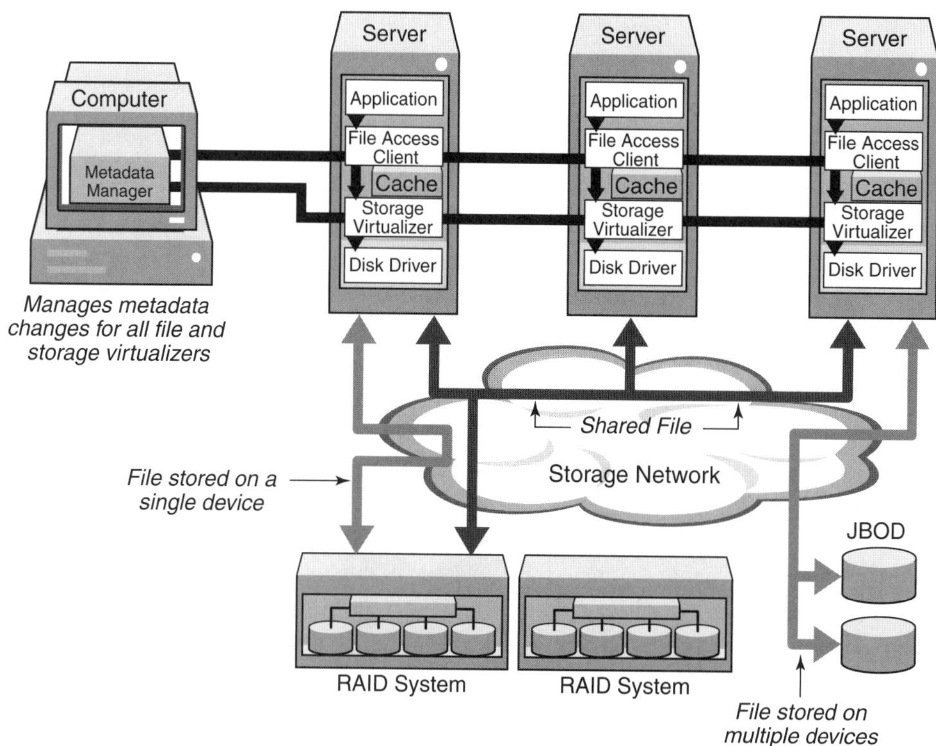

▼ **FIGURE 1–2** *Distributed File System Virtualizer*

In the architecture illustrated in Figure 1–2, applications make their file access requests to local file access clients (virtualizers). These file access clients request file access metadata (in particular, data block locations) from the central metadata server. The block location metadata enables the file access clients to satisfy application requests from a pool of virtualized block storage, instantiated in part by **storage virtualizers** that also run in the application servers.

As Figure 1–2 suggests, this architecture enables data center-wide sharing of a single pool of storage that might consist of both disk drives and LUNs presented by RAID systems. A file's data blocks may be stored on a single device or on multiple devices, as the figure indicates. With suitable concurrent access controls, this architecture makes it possible for multiple applications running in different servers to access a single file concurrently. This file system virtualization architecture offers three main advantages over conventional file servers:

- ***Data sharing:*** It enables multiple application servers of different architectures to share access to a single file system that stores data in a pool of virtualized storage. A single file system address space simplifies data management (e.g., backup can be run on behalf of an entire data center) and storage management (since all servers allocate from the same pool of storage, as long as the data center has any free capacity, any server can meet storage requirements).
- ***Short I/O path:*** This architecture shortens the I/O path between application and data. Unlike conventional file server architectures, this architecture transfers data directly between storage device and application server (without passing through an intermediate file server).
- ***Scaling:*** Because it has no single data movement bottleneck, this architecture enables a data center-wide "data farm" to scale to meet steadily growing or unpredictable application needs for data storage.

In addition to the short I/O path, this file system virtualization architecture achieves its performance through extensive caching of data in participating application servers. It is well suited to data centers that run heterogeneous servers, and need higher performance access to their data than a conventional file server can deliver.

CHAPTER SUMMARY

- Storage virtualization is the presentation of combinations of storage hardware and software components as virtual objects. The essential characteristics of these combinations are identical to those of the objects they represent. Their nonessential characteristics are determined by how the components are combined, and in general are superior to those of the virtualized objects.
- Storage is virtualized to improve one or more of its four fundamental properties—I/O performance, data availability, capacity cost, and manageability.
- Storage is virtualized by placing one or more physical devices under common software control. Storage virtualization software may run in a RAID or tape controller, an application server, or in one or more components of the storage network itself. Each implementation site results in different properties for the virtualized storage.
- Disk drives, tape drives and libraries, tape media, file systems and files can all be virtualized. This book concentrates primarily on virtualization of disk-like abstractions called block storage devices.

- File systems are virtualized by moving them into separate computers that act as file servers, or by aggregating them into a single, larger file system. Applications use file access protocols to read and write file data stored by file servers. CIFS and NFS are the two dominant file access protocols.
- The two main benefits of file server-based file system virtualization are access to remotely stored files and the sharing of data files among multiple clients running different operating systems on different types of computers.
- Advanced distributed file system virtualization technology adds scaling and a shorter I/O path to the list of advantages. Though not yet mature in the market, this technology shows promise as high-performance managed storage for many heterogeneous application servers.

PART 1

TECHNOLOGY

We live in a society exquisitely dependent on science and technology, in which hardly anyone knows anything about science and technology.

—Carl Sagan

CHAPTER 2

A discovery is said to be an accident meeting a prepared mind.

—ALBERT SZENT-GYORGYI

Disk Virtualization

In this chapter . . .

- How data is organized on magnetic disks
- How virtualization is used to simplify the interface between disks and computers
- Why virtualization of a single disk's storage makes sense

The buzz surrounding storage virtualization today is all around the virtualization of block storage devices—using RAID systems, storage network appliances, or server-based volume managers to create and manage disk-like virtual devices. But storage virtualization is not a new concept. It was first introduced by the disk drive industry segment in the mid-1980s, in the form of an abstract model for disk drives expressed in the SCSI standard. This chapter discusses the what and why of virtualization of the storage capacity inside an individual disk drive.

WHY VIRTUALIZE A DISK?

Of the technologies used for persistent data storage, the most prevalent by far is the rotating magnetic disk. Magnetic disks have several properties that make them the preferred solution for storing persistent data:

▼ **FIGURE 2–1** *The Result of Disk Drive Virtualization*

- ***Low cost:*** Today, magnetic disk storage costs less than half a penny per megabyte. This is less than a fiftieth of the cost of dynamic random access memory.
- ***Random access:*** Data stored on magnetic disks can be accessed in arbitrary order with approximately equal access time. This allows programs to execute and process files in an order determined by business needs rather than by data access technology.
- ***Reliability and stability:*** Magnetic disk drives are among the most reliable electromechanical devices in the world. Vendors routinely specify mean time between failures of up to a million hours (~114 years). Data stored on disks is typically stable for the lifetime of the disk (4–5 years).
- ***Universality:*** Over the course of the last 15 years, disk interface technology has standardized, allowing most disk drives to be used with most computer systems. This *virtualization* of the storage within a disk drive has created a competitive market that fosters a cycle of improving products and decreasing prices.

Virtualized I/O interfaces allow disk technology to evolve *without significant implications for clients.* A disk drive might be implemented using radically different technology from its predecessors, but if it responds to I/O commands, transfers data, and reports errors in the same way, support implications are minor, making market introduction easy. The virtualized I/O interface concept is embodied in standards such as SCSI, ATA, and Fibre Channel Protocol (FCP). Disk drives that use these interfaces are easily supportable when they are introduced, enabling applications to immediately exploit the technology benefits they deliver.

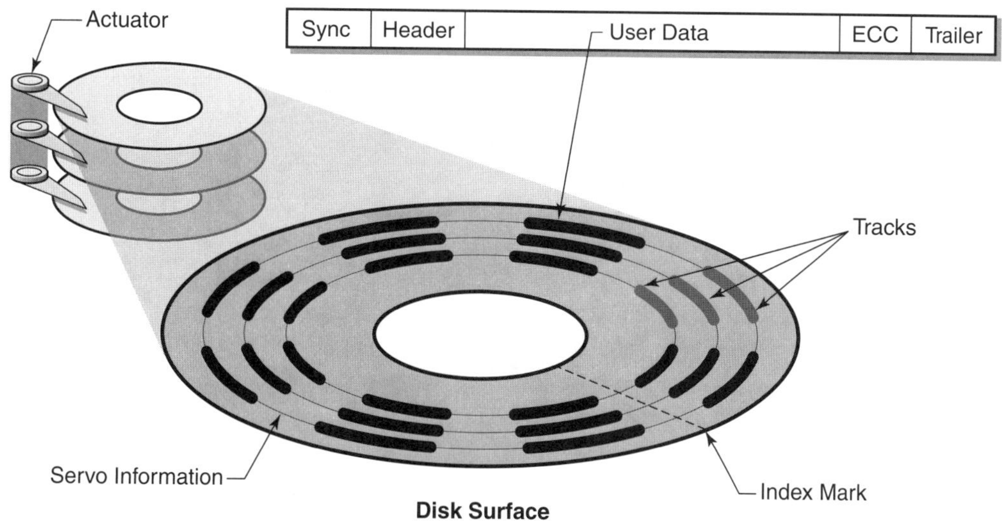

▼ **FIGURE 2–2** *Magnetic Disk Data Layout*

DISK DRIVE DATA LAYOUT

Today, data stored on disk drives is organized in fixed-length blocks arranged in nominally concentric circular **tracks,** as Figure 2–2 illustrates. Sensors (heads) to read and write data are mounted on **actuators** that move them from track to track.

On each track, data is stored in blocks of fixed size (usually 512 bytes). Each disk block is completely self-contained, and includes its own error correction code (ECC). The space between adjacent blocks is occupied by **servo patterns** that help read/write heads stay centered. An index mark identifies the start of each track.

Figure 2–2 illustrates one surface of one disk. On disk drives with two or more recording surfaces, the tracks at a given nominal radius comprise a **cylinder.**

The disk drive illustrated in Figure 2–2 has the same number of blocks on each track. The storage capacity of a drive containing such disks is given by:

$$\begin{aligned} \textit{Disk capacity (bytes)} = \; & \textit{number of blocks per track} \\ & \times \textit{ number of tracks} \\ & \times \textit{ number of heads (data surfaces)} \\ & \times \textit{ number of bytes per block} \end{aligned}$$

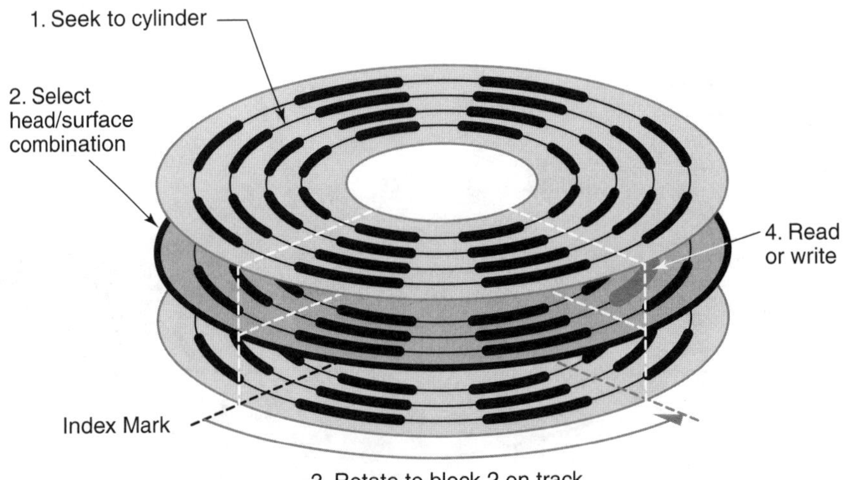

▼ **FIGURE 2–3** *Locating Data on a Disk*

A block of data stored in a drive with this data layout can be located ("*addressed*") by specifying cylinder, head (recording surface), and relative block numbers, as Figure 2–3 illustrates. This is called cylinder, head, sector, or *C-H-S,* addressing.

Figure 2–3 indicates the three primitive operations required to locate ("address") a block of data on a multisurface disk drive:

- ***Seeking*** moves the actuator to position the recording heads approximately over the track on which the target data is located.
- ***Selection*** connects the electrical output of the head that will read or write data to the drive's I/O channel. This head also senses servo signals from the track and uses them to center itself.
- ***Rotation*** of the disk stack brings the data block to be transferred directly under the head, at which time the read or write channel is enabled for data transfer.

DISK VIRTUALIZATION: LOGICAL BLOCK ADDRESSING

C-H-S addressing is inconvenient for operating system disk drivers, file systems, and database managers that access disk storage directly because it requires that they be aware of disk drive **geometry.** To locate data using

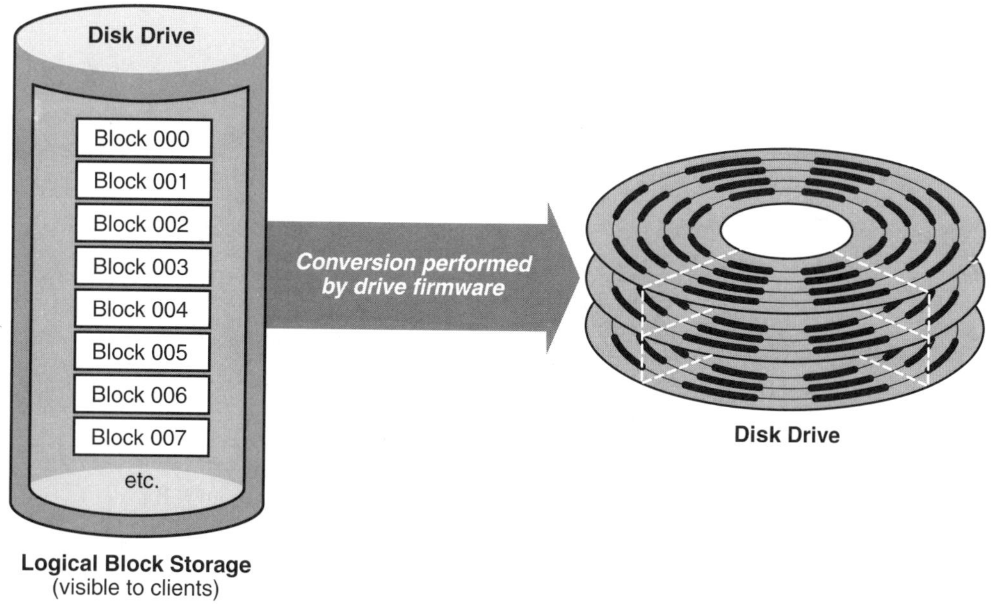

▼ **FIGURE 2–4** *The Logical Block Disk Data Addressing Model*

C-H-S addressing, a program must use the (unique) number of cylinders, disk surfaces, and blocks per track for each drive it deals with. Though this was formerly done, today's drives are *virtualized.* Rather than exposing their geometry, they present the *logical block* model as illustrated in Figure 2–4.[1]

With logical block addressing, disk blocks are numbered in a logical sequence. To read or write a stream of data, a client specifies a starting logical block address (LBA). Disk drive firmware converts between logical block addresses and their C-H-S equivalents, as Figure 2–5 illustrates.

Zoned Data Recording

Each block on the outermost track of the disk platter illustrated in Figure 2–3 occupies considerably more length than the corresponding block on the innermost track, even though both contain the same amount of

1. By an industry convention of long standing, as well as in standards documents, the blocks of storage capacity made available by a disk drive are called logical blocks, even though they are identified and located by virtualization techniques.

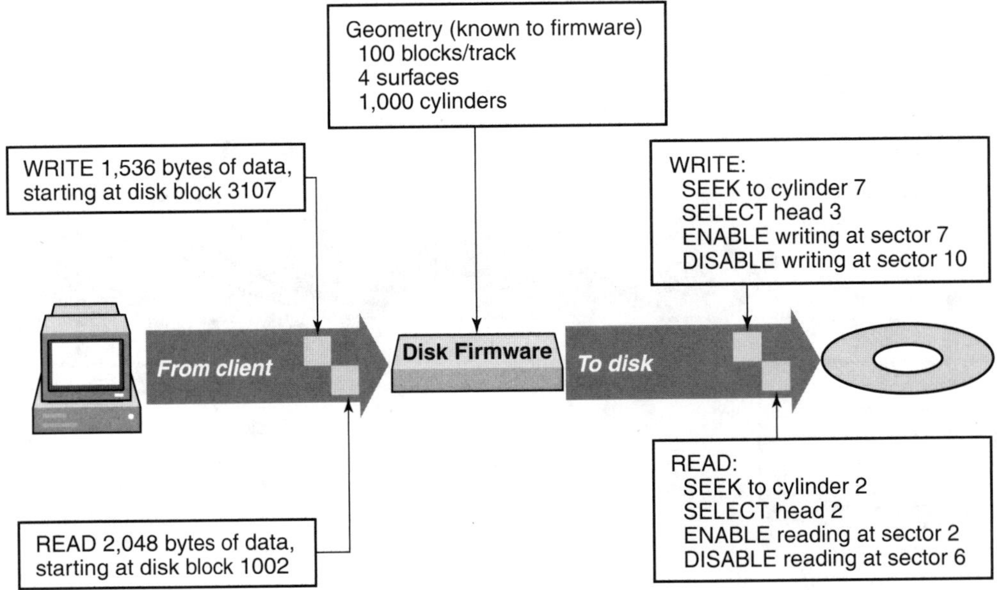

▼ **FIGURE 2–5** *Conversion between Logical Block and C-H-S Addressing*

data. During the early 1990s, disk drive engineers began to develop drives whose outer tracks contained more blocks than their inner ones. This technique, called **zoned data recording (ZDR),** increased storage capacity for any given head and media technology by as much as 50%. The cylinders of a ZDR disk drive are grouped into **zones,** each of which holds a different number of data blocks. Figure 2–6 illustrates a disk surface from a ZDR drive with two zones.

Each track in the inner zone of Figure 2–6 contains 8 blocks, while each track in the outer zone contains 16. Capacity is 50% higher than that of the disk illustrated in Figure 2–3, with negligible incremental cost.[2] Because it reduces raw storage cost, zone data recording has essentially become ubiquitous. Because it makes disk geometry so much more complex, zoned data recording makes the virtualization achieved by logical block addressing even more desirable.

2. Figure 2–6 uses unrealistically low numbers of blocks for illustrative clarity. Typical ZDR disks have 20 or more zones, with between 100 and 200 blocks per track. For 3.5" diameter disks, outermost zone tracks usually hold about twice as many blocks as those in the innermost one.

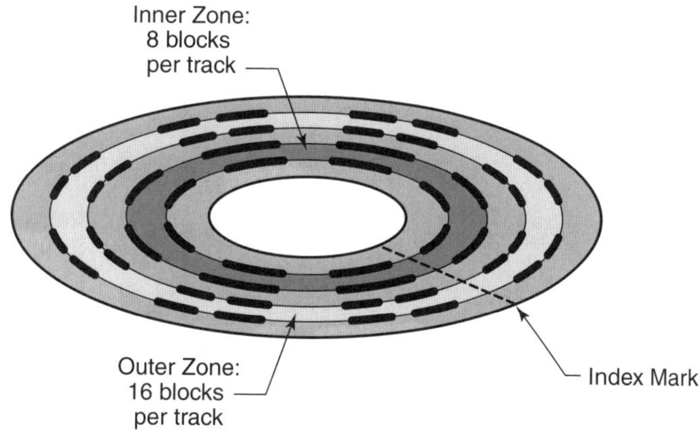

▼ **FIGURE 2–6** *One Platter of a Disk Using Zoned Data Recording*

Disk Media Defects

At high data densities, minuscule material defects can make part of a disk surface unusable. Blocks that overlap these surface areas are usually *defective,* and attempts to read or write data in them fail. Drive firmware deals with defective blocks by reserving a small percentage of media capacity to be substituted for them. Persistent tables within the drive relate the addresses of defective blocks to their substitutes. Virtualization firmware makes the drive appear to be defect free. Figure 2–7 illustrates such a table, often called a *revectoring* table, and the **revectoring** of a client-specified block number that converts to a defective block into the C-H-S address of its substitute.

Like address conversion, revectoring is device technology-specific, and is best performed by drive firmware. Disk drives hide these aspects of their internal architecture and present their clients with virtual images of defect-free block storage devices.

Viewed from a client, a disk drive is a block-addressable storage device with consecutively numbered blocks. Within the drive, block addresses specified by clients are treated as *logical,* and are translated into physical (C-H-S) media locations before data is transferred. The virtual block addresses used to communicate with clients have come to be known as **logical block addresses,** or **LBA**s.

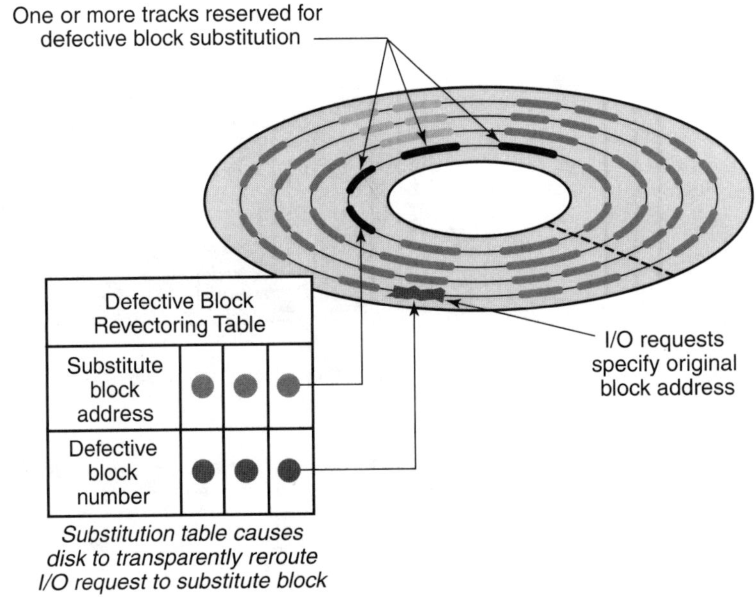

▼ **FIGURE 2–7** *Defective Block Substitution*

Intelligent Disks

Improvements in integrated circuit density and speed have made it feasible to put an intelligent controller in every disk drive, making the drive in effect a complete system as the block diagram in Figure 2–8 illustrates.

An important implication of the disk drive architecture illustrated in Figure 2–8 is the *abstraction* of the external interface. Clients do not communicate directly with disk drive data channels. Instead, they communicate with the virtualizing interface labeled "Client Interface" in Figure 2–8. The disk drive itself transforms I/O commands sent to this interface. Among its activities, this processor:

- ***Transforms*** client-specified logical block addresses into C-H-S addresses and revectors as necessary
- ***Converts*** client commands into seek, select, and I/O channel enable and disable operations, which it executes
- ***Manages*** data transfer to or from clients using internal buffers

All of this activity is transparent to clients, which use virtualized read and write commands that specify logical block addresses.

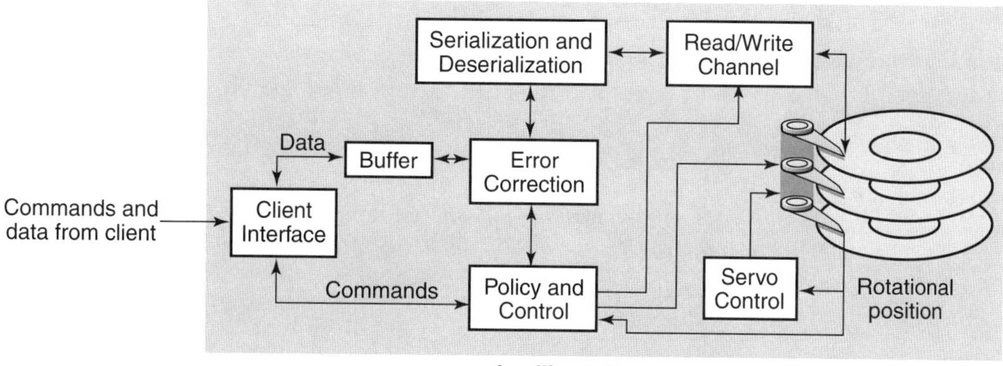

▼ **FIGURE 2–8** *Block Diagram of an Intelligent Disk Drive*

CHAPTER SUMMARY

- Magnetic disk drives are the universal choice for storing online computer data.
- Disk drives store data in fixed-length blocks, usually of 512 bytes.
- Each disk drive model has a unique *geometry,* or data layout, which must be known in order to access data. Geometry includes both cylinder-track-sector organization and reserved space for defective media, head positioning, and block identification.
- Disk drives contain internal processors that virtualize their storage by abstracting their geometry, and presenting clients with a flat logical block address (LBA) space interface like that shown in Figure 2–1. As a result, all disk drives "look alike" (approximately) to clients, and it is easy for operating systems to support new disk models, even if their implementation technology differs radically from that of previous ones.
- Among the important functions that disk drive virtualization hides from clients are media defect handling and zoned data recording. The former increases manufacturing yields, lowering disk drive cost; the latter increases the storage capacity of a disk drive at a given data density, with the same effect.

CHAPTER 3

Challenges are what make life interesting; overcoming them is what makes life meaningful.

—JOSHUA J. MARINE

RAID: Performance and Availability in Virtual Block Storage

In this chapter . . .

- RAID: the underlying technology of virtualization
- What RAID is and where it came from
- The two fundamental techniques of RAID

In one sense, block storage device virtualization is neither new nor complicated. Any control software that virtualizes a set of block storage devices[1] invariably uses *RAID* techniques to enhance the properties of online disk storage. This chapter discusses the basics of RAID technology.

RESILIENT VIRTUAL STORAGE WITH RAID

RAID technology has become pervasive in data centers. Today, essentially all enterprise storage systems incorporate some form of RAID to enhance

1. This chapter and the ones that follow use the term *block storage device* to denote disk drives and virtual block storage devices collectively.

their I/O performance, data availability, and manageability. *Server-based* RAID provides similar benefits, sometimes combining capacity from two or more storage systems to further increase capacity or to enhance I/O performance or availability. System architects and administrators responsible for application storage strategies are faced with RAID implementation choices, to be sure, but they almost always have access to RAID, usually in multiple forms, to meet I/O performance and data resiliency needs.

RAID: What's in a Name?

RAID is an acronym for ***redundant array of independent disks:***

- ***Redundant*** means that part of the devices' storage capacity is used to store **check data.** Check data is information about user data that is redundant in the sense that it can be used to recover it if the device that contains it becomes unusable.
- ***Array*** simply refers to the set of devices managed by control software that presents their net capacity as one or more **virtual block storage devices.** Server-based control software (typically called a **volume manager** or **logical volume manager**) runs in an application server. In disk systems (commonly called **RAID systems**), control software runs in specialized processors within the systems.
- ***Independent*** means that the devices are capable of functioning (and failing) separately from each other. RAID is a family of techniques for advantageously combining ordinary storage devices under common management.[2]
- ***Disks*** are the disk drives or other block storage devices whose storage capacity is virtualized.

RAID techniques can be implemented anywhere in the I/O path where there is processing capacity. Figure 3–1 illustrates RAID system, application server, and network-based arrays of disk drives virtualized using RAID techniques.

---

2. When the acronym RAID was introduced in 1988, it stood for redundant array of inexpensive disks. By the time the technology gained wide commercial acceptance, the single large expensive disks ("SLEDs") to which RAID was originally compared had disappeared from the market, and the cost comparison was no longer applicable. Common industry usage has replaced "inexpensive" with "independent."

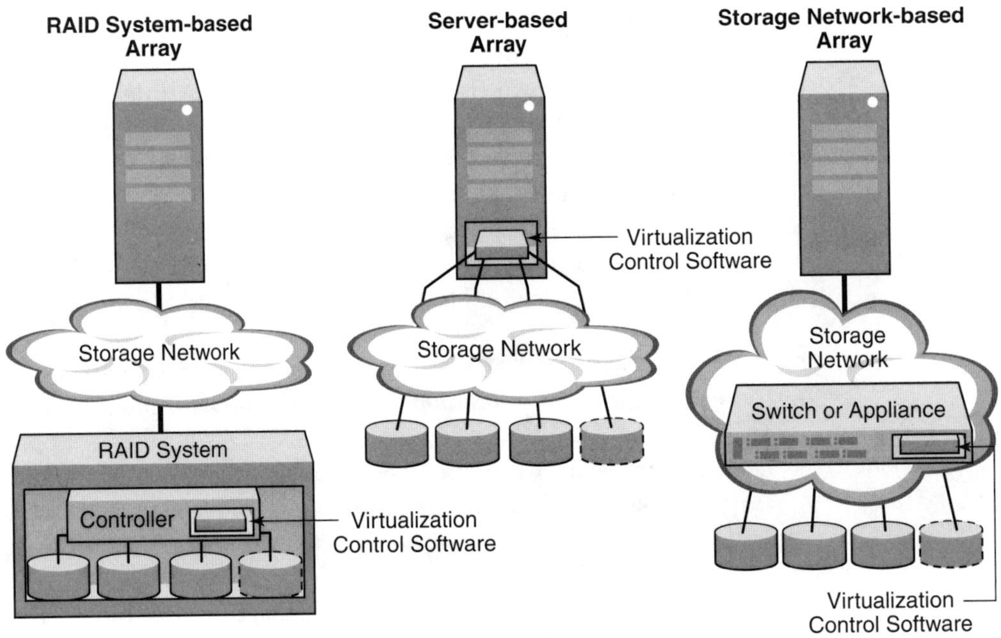

▼ **FIGURE 3–1** *Server, Storage Network, and Disk System-Based RAID Arrays*

The terms *disk array* and *RAID array* are sometimes used to refer to a collection of physical disk drives mounted in a single cabinet and connected to the same I/O buses or storage network segment. This book refers to such a collection as a *RAID system,* or, occasionally, *disk system.* The term *array* is used to refer to a collection of block storage devices managed as a unit by control software.

A BRIEF HISTORY OF RAID

In 1988, researchers at the University of California at Berkeley published a landmark paper entitled "A Case for Redundant Arrays of Inexpensive Disks (RAID)."[3] The paper described research demonstrating that arrays

3. http://www-2.cs.cmu.edu/~garth/RAIDpaper/Patterson88.pdf

of low-cost disk drives made for personal computers could be effective substitutes for the larger, high-performance drives that were used in data centers at the time. The paper described five different disk array models, called *RAID Levels,* in terms of:

- mechanisms for using redundant *check data* stored on the drives to recover unreadable user data, and
- algorithms for converting exported user data addresses and check data blocks to the logical block addresses of the disk drives.

The first RAID Level described in the paper was **mirroring,** already in commercial use at the time. The remaining four RAID Levels were essentially proposals for more cost-effective types of arrays. RAID Levels 2 and 3 required special-purpose hardware. Although examples of both were built, the special-purpose hardware made them economically unattractive, and neither is commercially available today. RAID Levels 4 and 5 used the same data recovery mechanism, **user data parity,** with slightly different user and check data block address translation algorithms.

RAID Today

Of the five RAID Levels described in "A Case for Redundant Arrays of Inexpensive Disks (RAID)," three are of commercial significance today:

- ***RAID Level 1,*** or *mirroring.* The mirroring technique consists of making two or more identical copies of each block of user data on separate devices. Mirroring provides high data availability at the cost of an "extra" storage device (and the adapter port, enclosure space, cabling, power, and cooling capacity to support it) to hold check data for every device holding user data. Most mirrored virtual devices deliver somewhat higher read performance than equivalent unmirrored devices, and only slightly lower write performance. This book uses the term *mirrored virtual device* (and the related terms *mirror* and *mirroring*) in preference to the less common term *RAID Level 1.*

VERITAS RAID Levels

Server-based VERITAS block virtualization control software supports the most important RAID levels—RAID 0 (striping, as well as concatenation), RAID 1 (mirroring), RAID 5 (parity RAID), as well as the layered RAID levels, striped mirrors (sometimes called RAID 1+0) and mirrored stripes (sometimes called RAID 0+1).

VERITAS™ Volume Manager RAID layouts can be changed online without disrupting user data access, making it easy to adapt to changing application requirements without information service downtime.

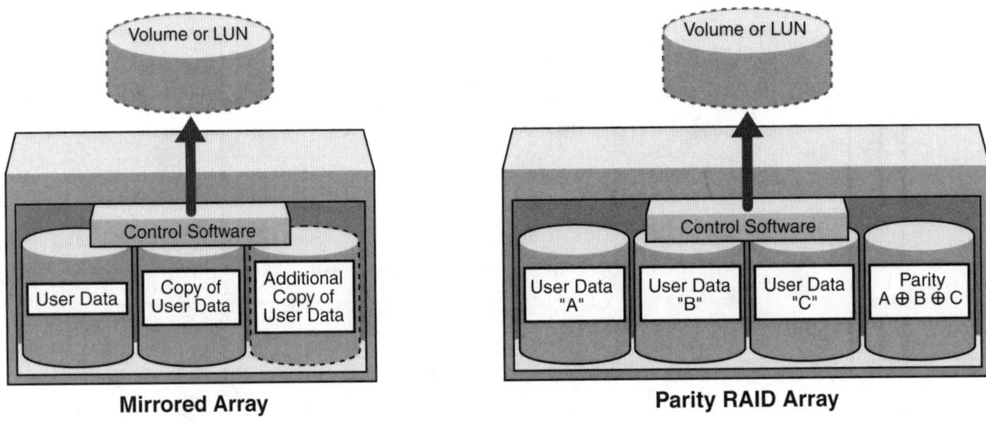

▼ **FIGURE 3–2** *Check Data in Mirrored and Parity RAID Arrays*

- ***RAID Levels 4 and 5*** (collectively called **parity RAID** in this book) both interleave check data (in the form of bit-by-bit parity of positionally corresponding blocks) with user data throughout the array. At times, a parity RAID array's storage devices operate independently, allowing multiple small application I/O requests to execute simultaneously. At other times, they operate in concert, executing one large I/O request on behalf of one application.

  Parity RAID is suitable for applications whose I/O consists principally of read requests. Many transaction processing, file and database serving, and data analysis applications are in this category. Particularly in server-based implementations, parity RAID is not well suited for write-intensive applications such as data entry or scientific and engineering data collection.

In addition to these, the term *RAID Level 0* has come into common use to denote arrays in which user data block addresses are *striped* across several devices (as described in Chapter 4), but in which there is no check data. Striped arrays provide excellent I/O performance in almost all circumstances, but do not protect against the loss of unreadable user data. Other forms of RAID are described in Appendix B.

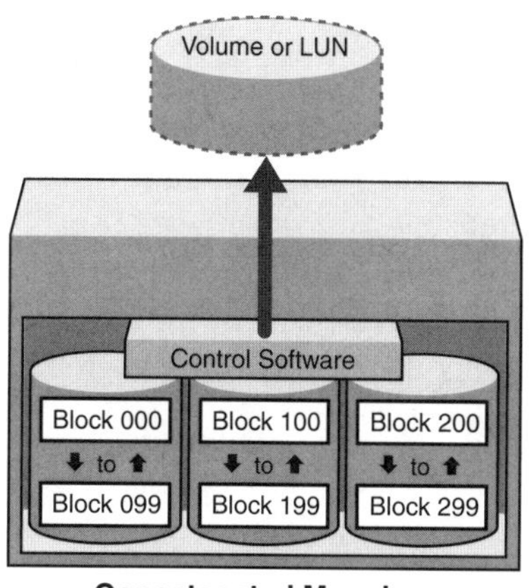

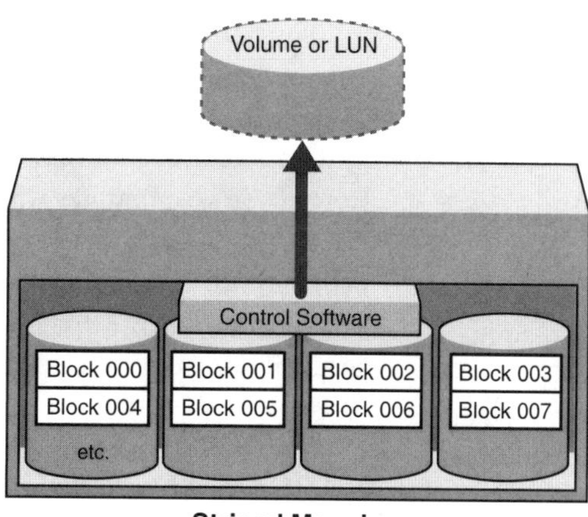

▼ **FIGURE 3–3** *Concatenated and Striped Data Block Address Conversion*

THE TWO FUNDAMENTAL RAID-BASED VIRTUALIZATION CONCEPTS

All types of RAID have two distinguishing features:

- ***They provide failure tolerance through data redundancy.*** RAID arrays hold redundant information about user data in the form of *check data.* Check data enhances user data availability by enabling recovery of user data blocks that have become unreadable. For example, mirrored virtual disks use one or more complete copies of user data as check data; parity RAID virtual disks use a parity function computed on several positionally corresponding user data blocks as described later in this chapter. Figure 3–2 illustrates mirrored and parity RAID check data, and Chapter 4 discusses check data in more detail.
- ***They convert virtual device block addresses to physical storage device block addresses.*** The most common forms of conversion used in RAID arrays are concatenation and striping, the latter of which enhances I/O performance by balancing most I/O loads across some or all of an array's storage devices. Whether mirrored or parity RAID, block storage virtualizers typically stripe data across devices in a regular geometric pattern, or offset user data block addresses by some fixed amount, or a combination of the two. Figure 3–3 illustrates

concatenated and striped block address conversion, and Chapter 7 discusses block address translation in more detail.

Data redundancy and block address conversion are both done by control software, sometimes with assistance from specialized hardware (e.g., for fast parity computation or low-overhead data movement). The two are independent, however. Either can be (and indeed, occasionally is) implemented without the other. Most disk arrays combine the two to deliver high data availability *and* optimum I/O performance.

Virtual Devices and LUNs

RAID is a collection of techniques for enhancing block storage I/O performance and data availability. The other piece of block storage virtualization is the presentation of the enhanced storage to servers for use by data managers and applications. An array of cooperatively managed disks is typically presented as one or more virtual devices on which file systems can be formatted and user data files or databases stored. Virtual devices presented by RAID systems are frequently referred to as *LUNs* (Logical UNits), a term adapted from the SCSI[4] nomenclature for addressing I/O devices. A virtualized disk array may be presented as a single LUN, or its usable capacity may be subdivided by the virtualization control software and presented as multiple LUNs. LUNs differ from the *partitions* that are commonly encountered in Windows[5] and UNIX storage systems. LUNs are virtual block storage devices to which I/O commands sent to bus or network addresses are directed. Operating system partitions are subdivisions of the capacity of a single disk or LUN. All of the partitions (e.g., **/dev/hda0, /dev/hda1, . . .**) of a single physical or virtual device (e.g., **/dev/hda**) are addressed by the same LUN when I/O commands are issued.

Storage Management Trends?

Today's storage industry trend is a holistic end-to-end management of storage from application via the network to the storage layer. Systems have become so complex that it is no longer adequate to manage objects in one layer separately from the others. This requires unified knowledge of the entire path from physical storage devices through their logical representations within the application server (as partitions or device paths), up to logical database and business application objects. This unified picture of storage and data is at the core of VERITAS' future strategy. A comprehensive picture of all aspects of storage and data that enables active storage management by applications with quality of service guarantees and accurate accounting for storage consumers.

4. Small Computer System Interface—a set of standard protocols that governs interactions between application servers and block storage devices.
5. Windows is a registered trademark of Microsoft Corporation.

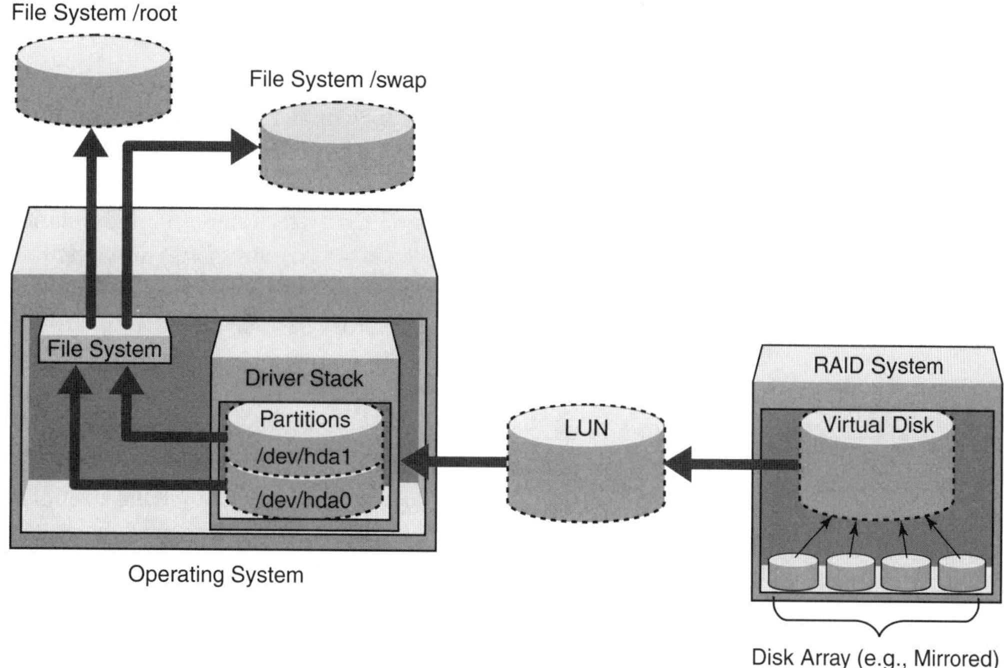

▼ **FIGURE 3–4** *Virtual Disks, LUNs, and Partitions*

Figure 3–4 illustrates a disk array implemented by a RAID system's controller using four physical disks. The disks are aggregated into a single virtual disk, which the RAID system presents to its external interfaces as a LUN. The LUN is seen by a server's operating system driver stack, which organizes it into two partitions, each of which is formatted with a file system. In this case, the file system issues block I/O commands addressed to partitions to the driver stack. The driver stack recognizes that both partitions consist of storage capacity on the same LUN, and readdresses the I/O commands to it. The RAID system fields the I/O commands, and issues corresponding commands to the physical disks that comprise the array presented as the LUN to which the application server's I/O commands are addressed.

CHAPTER SUMMARY

- RAID is an acronym for redundant array of independent disks.
- An academic paper published in the late 1980s enumerated five dif-

ferent models for RAID arrays, called *RAID Levels,* of which three are in broad commercial use today.

- *Mirroring,* or maintaining two or more identical copies of data on separate devices, is the technique known as RAID Level 1. This book uses the term *mirroring* and related terms in preference to RAID Level 1.
- RAID Levels 4 and 5 use the same parity technique for redundancy. This book uses the term *parity RAID* to denote them collectively.
- The term *RAID Level 0,* or *RAID 0,* is applied to arrays in which user data block addresses are striped across several disk drives without redundancy. The term is technically inappropriate due to the lack of redundancy in such arrays, but has become pervasive in the literature and in common usage.
- The two fundamental concepts in the virtualization of block storage are failure protection through data redundancy and virtual-to-logical block address translation. Both of these are implemented by control software, sometimes with special-purpose hardware assistance.

CHAPTER 4

A common mistake that people make when trying to design something completely foolproof is to underestimate the ingenuity of complete fools.

—Douglas Noel Adams

Failure Tolerance in Virtual Block Storage

In this chapter . . .

- How block storage is made failure tolerant
- The two most common disk failure tolerance techniques: parity and mirroring
- Failure tolerance differences between parity and mirroring

The word *redundant* in the acronym RAID refers to the use of part of an array's raw storage capacity to store some form of redundant data. This chapter describes the properties of the two predominant forms of redundancy in virtual block storage.

MIRRORING FOR FAILURE TOLERANCE

Mirroring is so-called because the user data stored in each underlying device block is identical to that stored in corresponding blocks on other devices. A mirrored array's control software writes application data to each mirror[1] in the array.

1. The term "mirror" is used as a convenient shorthand for a set of devices containing one complete copy of user data. A mirrored array with two copies of user data has two mirrors, and so forth.

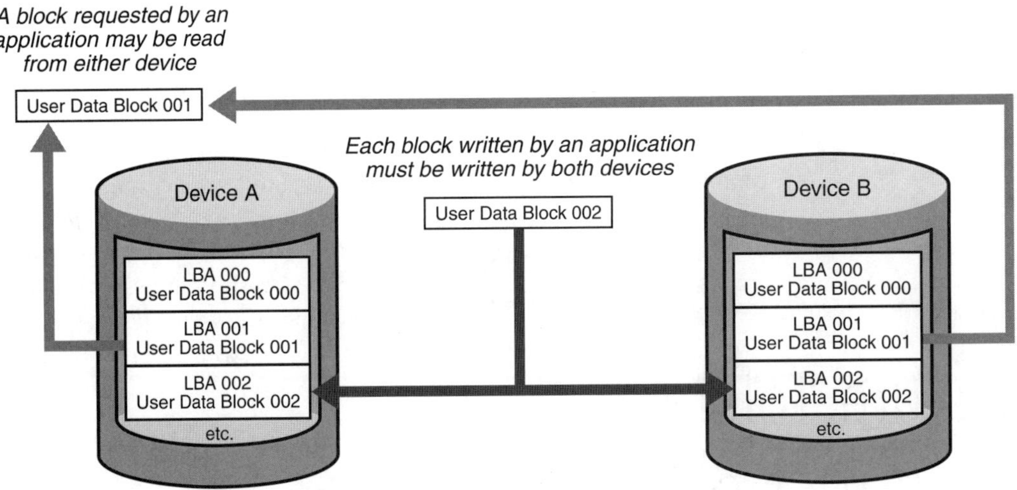

▼ **FIGURE 4–1** *The Basic Mirroring Principle*

In a mirrored array, as Figure 4–1 illustrates, redundancy is easy to understand—a second copy of data stored on a separate device leaves it accessible if either of the devices fails. Each block in a mirrored array *is* the check data for the corresponding blocks of user data on the array's other mirrors. To satisfy an application read request, control software reads from one of the mirrors. Various algorithms are used to optimize read and write performance (e.g., choosing the mirror with the shortest I/O queue to satisfy application read requests).

Mirrored arrays have higher hardware cost than parity RAID; every gigabyte of usable storage requires the purchase, housing, powering, cooling, and connection of two, three, or more gigabytes of physical storage. As noted earlier, however, the decreasing cost of physical storage capacity and the increasing importance of online data to enterprise operations are combining to make mirrored storage practical for more and more critical online data requirements.

Splitting Mirrors for Point-in-Time Data Snapshots

A mirrored array may contain two, three, or more complete copies of user data. While relatively costly in hardware terms, arrays of three mirrors can reduce overall information services costs by enabling backup or data mining using snapshots of user data without disrupting application processing.

N-Way Mirrors and Snapshots

With sufficient storage capacity, creating multimirror mirrors is easy. The VERITAS™ Storage Foundation–Volume Manager enables administrators to create 32-way mirrored volumes. Keeping several mirrors identical, especially after failures or off-host procedures, can be tricky. The VERITAS™ Storage Foundation Volume Manager has three ways to resynchronize volumes, as well as an enhanced option called VERITAS™ FastResync (part of the VERITAS™ Copy Service Option product).

Full resynchronization is used when a mirror is added to a volume or when a device containing a mirror is replaced. While necessary, if nothing is known about the added mirror's contents, full resynchronization is resource and time-consuming.

Read-writeback synchronization can be used when a system crash leaves a mirrored volume in an indeterminate state. With this procedure, volumes can be mounted and used immediately, but mirror identity is not guaranteed until every volume block has been read and written back.

Read-write synchronization can be combined with *dirty region logging*. The VERITAS™ Storage Foundation–Volume Manager uses a dirty region log to keep track of block address regions that are not synchronized due to partially completed writes. Only these block address regions need be resynchronized after a system crash.

A mirror (a single complete copy of user data) can be *split* from a mirrored array, and used independently by applications or backup. User data on a split mirror is effectively "frozen" at the instant of splitting; no changes are made to user data after the split appears on the split mirror, which is called a **snapshot.** Split mirror snapshots are especially useful for making consistent "point-in-time" backups of application data while applications continue to run and update data on the main array.

To create a split mirror snapshot, an administrator typically starts by pausing the applications using the array momentarily, allowing transactions to complete and any cached data to be flushed. When all data on the array's devices is up-to-date and consistent, one mirror is logically disconnected from it:

- The disconnected mirror can be mounted as an independent device and the data on it used for backup or data mining. Because no further updates are made to the split mirror, a snapshot, or point-in-time image, of application data is backed up or mined, even though applications may be updating data on the main array.
- As soon as the mirror has been split (usually a few seconds), application access to data on the main array can be re-enabled. Updates to data on the main array do not affect backup or mining done on the split mirror snapshot. Using a split mirror snapshot for backup or mining therefore greatly reduces the impact of backup on application performance.

Figure 4–2 illustrates the use of a split mirror snapshot for backup while an application continues to execute.

When a split mirror has served its purpose, it must be rejoined to the main array from which it was split, so that it is available when next

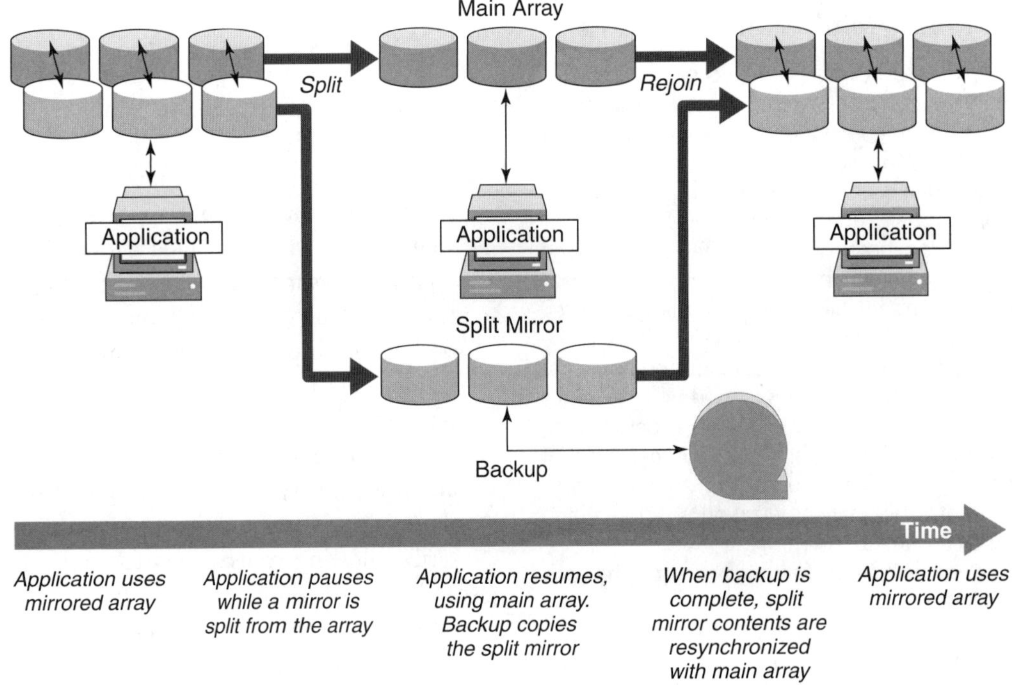
Main Array
Split
Rejoin
Application
Application
Application
Split Mirror
Backup
Time
Application uses mirrored array
Application pauses while a mirror is split from the array
Application resumes, using main array. Backup copies the split mirror
When backup is complete, split mirror contents are resynchronized with main array
Application uses mirrored array

▼ **FIGURE 4–2** *Using a Split Mirror for Backup while Application Executes*

required. The rejoined mirror must be **resynchronized** by copying main array data updated during the split to it. Some control software copies the entire contents of the main array to the rejoined mirror. More sophisticated implementations perform **fast mirror resynchronization** by keeping a log of data changes to the main array during the split, and copying only changed data to the rejoined mirror. Figure 4–2 also illustrates the rejoining of a split mirror to its array.

Multidevice Mirrored Arrays

A mirrored array contains two or more complete copies of some body of user data. A mirror may be contained on a single physical device, or spread across several devices. There are two basic techniques for combining multiple storage devices into a single mirror—*concatenation* and *striping*. With concatenation, illustrated on the left of Figure 4–3, each mirror combines the blocks of several storage devices into a single virtual block

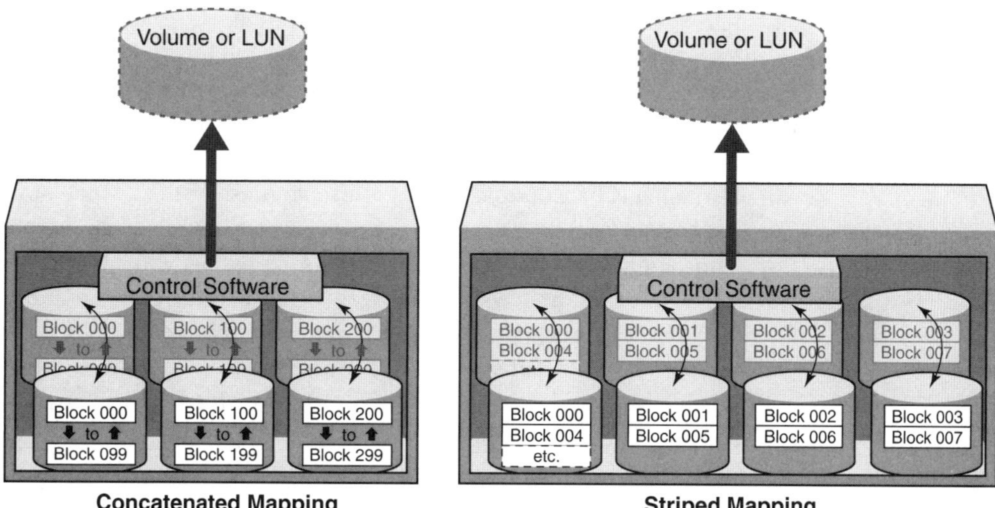

▼ **FIGURE 4–3** *Concatenated and Striped Data Block Address Translation*

address space simply by numbering them consecutively and presenting the resulting single virtual block address space to clients. The spaces are then mirrored with each other.

Striping, illustrated on the right of Figure 4–3, distributes virtual block addresses across the storage devices comprising each mirror. This tends to balance I/O across physical resources for most applications. Chapter 7 discusses the performance characteristics of virtual block address striping.

Either of these techniques enables the creation of arbitrarily large mirrored virtual storage devices. Virtual storage device capacity is not bounded by the capacity of available physical devices.

VERITAS™ Copy Service Option

As part of its Copy Service Option technology, VERITAS offers a sophisticated high-performance fast mirror resynchronization (VERITAS™ FastResync) technology. When FastResync is enabled on a mirrored volume, the VERITAS™ Storage Foundation–Volume Manager uses a Data Change Map to track all updates. During resynchronization, only blocks indicated in the Data Change Map need be resynchronized. Data Change Maps are usually stored on separate volumes associated with the mirrored volumes they map, so that maps survive failures and system reboots.

Multiway Mirrored Arrays

In the example of Figure 4–2, main array storage is not redundant (and therefore data is not protected against device failures) while the mirror is split for backup. Three-mirror arrays eliminate this risk. With three mirrors, application data remains protected against all single device failures (and most dual device failures) for the duration of the split. As the cost of disk drives falls, and the business importance of online data increases, three- and even four-mirror arrays are becoming increasingly popular.

If an array contains four mirrors, two can be split at the same time for simultaneous backup and mining on separate snapshots, while applications continue to process data on the still-protected main array. Another important application for four-mirror arrays is possible with storage networks that can read and write data over distances of several kilometers (Chapter 17). With such a network, data can be redundant at both of two widely separated data centers, with two mirrors at each. With this (admittedly costly) configuration, up-to-date data is available for disaster recovery at either center. With two mirrors at each site, storage device failure at either center is survivable. As the importance of disaster recovery in information technology planning increases, storage architects are discovering the value of mirroring data over distance to protect against both local faults and major disasters.

Like any availability measure, two- and three-mirror arrays come at a cost. The cost is not only financial—"extra" storage devices and supporting hardware—but also in application I/O performance. Application write requests to a mirrored array complete when the last (slowest) of the mirrors has been written. The lengthening in I/O response time is slight, but the heavier load on I/O channels and storage networks must also be considered. For write-intensive applications, I/O channels and storage networks saturate at lower application I/O levels with multicopy mirrored storage than with nonmirrored storage.

PARITY RAID REDUNDANCY

RAID Levels 4 and 5 rely on another type of redundancy—*parity.* Parity RAID reduces the hardware cost of protection (by requiring fewer "extra" storage devices), but protects against fewer types of failures. Instead of a complete copy of data, each parity RAID check data block contains the parity of contents of a *group* of other data blocks. Parity allows the contents of any single data block in the group to be computed ("regenerated"), as long as the check data and the contents of the rest of the group's blocks are available. Figure 4–4 illustrates the principle of parity RAID. In the figure, Devices A and B contain user data. Each block of Device C holds check data computed from the corresponding blocks on Devices A and B.

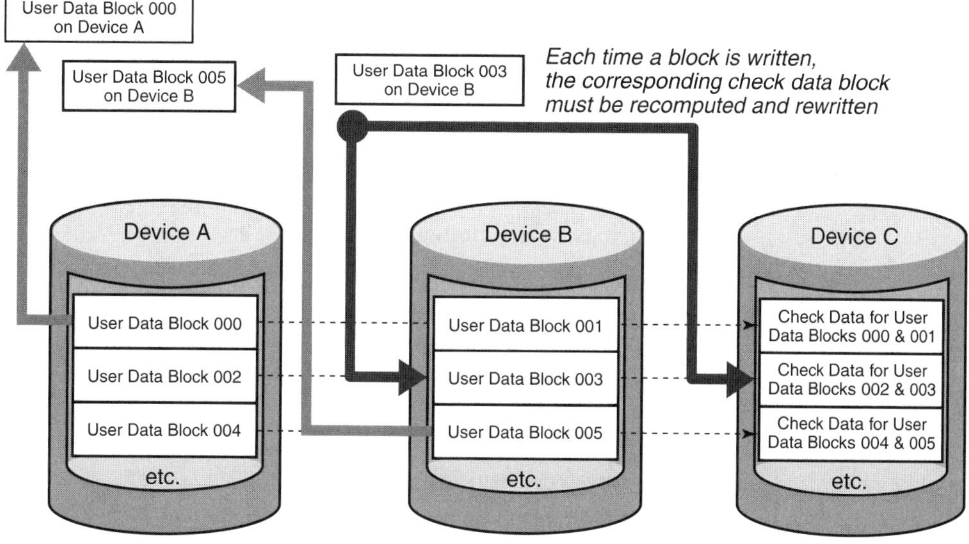

▼ **FIGURE 4–4** *Parity RAID Principle*

- If Device A fails, any block of data on it can be regenerated by performing a computation using the corresponding blocks from Devices B and C.
- If Device B fails, any block of data from it can be regenerated by performing a computation using the corresponding blocks from Devices A and C.
- If Device C fails, protection against additional failures is lost; but all user data remains accessible.

From a data protection standpoint, RAID Levels 4 and 5 are identical. They differ in the location of their parity check data. In a RAID Level 4 array, one device is completely occupied by check data, whereas in a RAID Level 5 array, the check data is distributed across some or all of the devices. Chapter 7 describes check data location in parity RAID arrays and its effect on I/O performance.

The Hardware Cost of Parity RAID

The hardware overhead cost of data protection in the parity RAID array illustrated in Figure 4–4 is lower than that of the mirrored array of

Figure 4–1—one "extra" storage device (and support hardware) for every *two* devices of usable storage capacity, compared to one or more extra devices per user data device with mirroring.

Parity check data is computed as a bit-by-bit *exclusive OR*[2] **XOR**) of the contents of all corresponding data blocks in an array. In the example of Figure 4–4, two devices hold user data, so the first parity block holds the **XOR** of the contents of the first blocks of the two data devices, and so forth. Obviously, all devices in a parity RAID array must have the same number of blocks. Some server-based volume managers allow devices of different capacities to be combined in a parity RAID array. When this is done, the array's capacity is determined by the device with the smallest capacity.

With parity check data, it is possible to configure arrays with any number of data devices using only one parity disk. The array illustrated in Figure 4–4 has a storage overhead of 50% (1.5 megabytes of physical storage are required for each megabyte of usable storage). Larger parity RAID arrays with lower storage overhead can be configured. For example, a parity RAID array with eleven devices provides ten devices of usable storage, and has a storage overhead of 10%.

It is common to refer to a parity RAID array by the number of devices full of data it can store, plus the parity device. For example, a parity RAID array with four devices is called a "three plus one" array because its usable data capacity is three devices. Figure 4–5 illustrates some of the more popular parity RAID array sizes encountered in practice.

LIMITATIONS OF PARITY RAID ARRAYS

In addition to protecting against only one device failure, a parity RAID array does not contain a complete redundant copy of user data, and so cannot be split for snapshot backup or data analysis as mirrored arrays can. The "1 in N" property poses other limitations as well, most of which are related to the number of devices in an array.

Because the capacity of a single check data device protects an arbitrarily large number of data devices, the optimal strategy for configuring parity RAID arrays would seem to be to designate one device for check

2. *Exclusive OR* (**XOR**) is a 1-bit function of two bits whose value is 1 if the two bits differ and 0 if they do not. The **XOR** of two bit strings of equal length is a third string whose values are the **XOR**s of corresponding bits in the two strings.

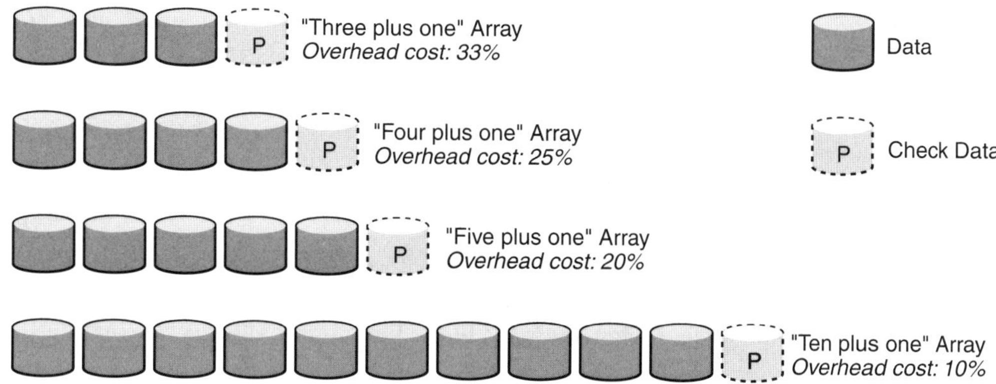

▼ **FIGURE 4–5** *Some Popular Parity RAID Array Sizes*

data and add user data devices as more capacity is required. There are limitations to large parity RAID arrays, however:

- ***Limited protection:*** Parity protects an array's devices against failure of any *one* of them. If a second device fails, data is lost.[3] A three-device parity RAID array "fails" (loses data) if two drives in a population of three fail simultaneously. A six-device array fails if two devices in a population of six fail simultaneously. The more devices in an array, the more likely it is that two failures will overlap in time and cause the entire array to fail.
- ***Exposure to loss:*** When a parity RAID array fails, *all* data stored in it is inaccessible, not just data from the failed devices. Thus, the larger an array, the more serious the consequences of failure are likely to be. Smaller arrays reduce the probability of array failure, and mitigate the consequences when a failure does occur.
- ***Window of exposure:*** When a device fails and is replaced, the replacement drive's contents must be **synchronized** so that check data is consistent with data blocks throughout the array. Synchronization requires reading all blocks on all devices and computing user or check data for the replacement device from their contents. Arrays with more devices take longer to resynchronize, increasing the interval during which the array could fail due to loss of a second device.

3. Depending on the nature of the failure, data may not be destroyed, but only inaccessible.

- ***Intrinsic write performance:*** Large parity RAID arrays have poor write performance. Application writes to a parity RAID array require carefully serialized sequences of reads and writes on at least two devices, as well as a write to a persistent[4] log. The larger an array, the more likely an application's writes are to be serialized with other I/O operations.

Economics and experience have led most RAID system designers to optimize their systems for RAID arrays containing four to six devices. Some designs allow users to choose the number of devices in each array; vendors of these also tend to recommend arrays of four to six devices.

Parity RAID Check Data

Parity RAID check data is conceptually simple. A bit-by-bit exclusive OR (**XOR**) of all corresponding user data blocks in an array is computed and written to the corresponding block of the check data disk. Using the **XOR** function has two advantages:

- ***Computational simplicity:*** The function lends itself to hardware assist, which reduces computational overhead, but it is also suitable for software implementation in smaller systems or where capital cost is a primary consideration.
- ***Symmetry:*** Check data computation is identical to user data regeneration. Whether a user data update requires a check data update, or a failed disk requires data regeneration, the same logic performs the computation, again leading to simpler, more robust implementations.

Figure 4–6 illustrates the computation of parity check data for a three-device array, and shows Block 0 on each of a parity RAID array's three storage devices. The blocks on Devices A and B contain user data. Block 0 on Device P contains the bit-by-bit **XOR** of the user data on Devices A and B.

If the check data on Device P is updated every time user data on Devices A or B changes, it can be used to regenerate unreadable user data from either Device A or B. Figure 4–7 illustrates user data regeneration.

4. In data storage and I/O contexts, the term *persistent* is used to describe objects such as logs that retain their state without electrical power. In practice, RAID array logs are usually stored on separate devices or in nonvolatile memory.

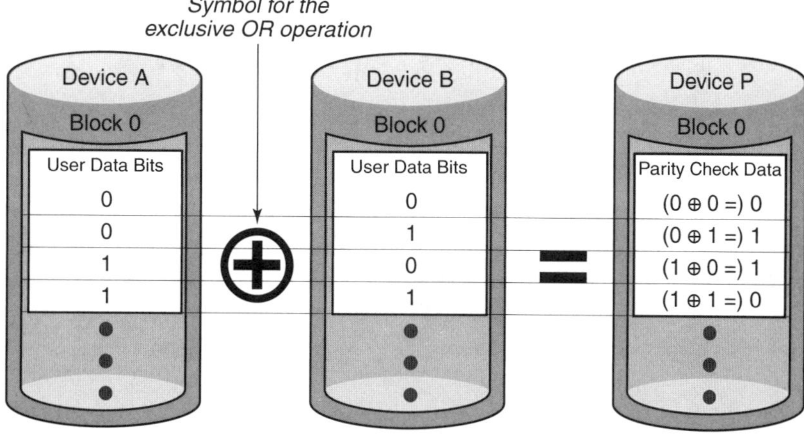

▼ **FIGURE 4–6** *XOR Parity in a Three-Device Array*

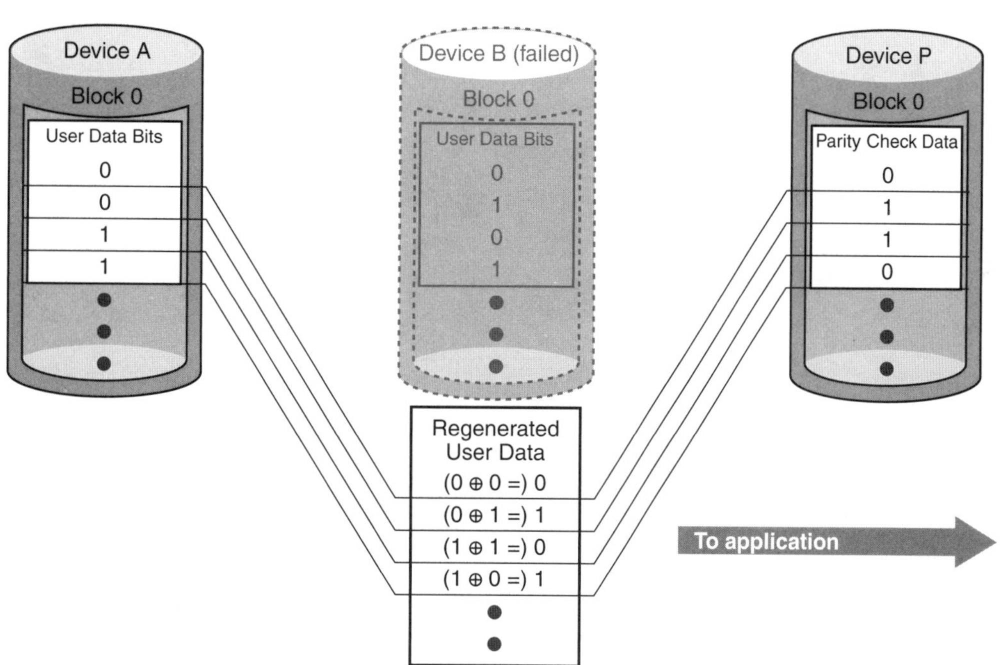

▼ **FIGURE 4–7** *Using XOR Parity to Regenerate User Data*

Check Data Computation

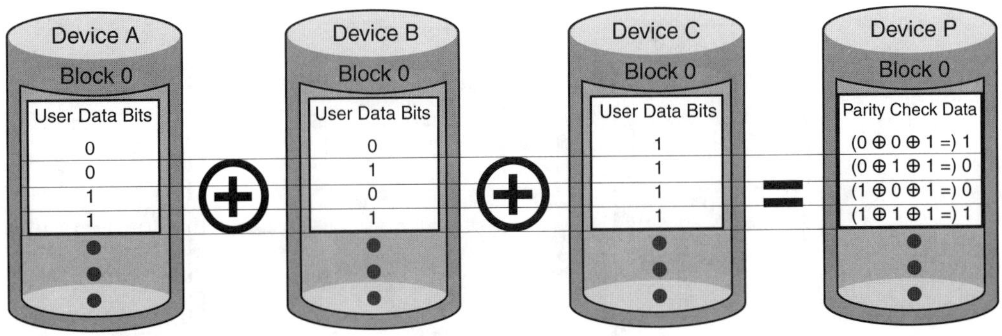

User Data Regeneration

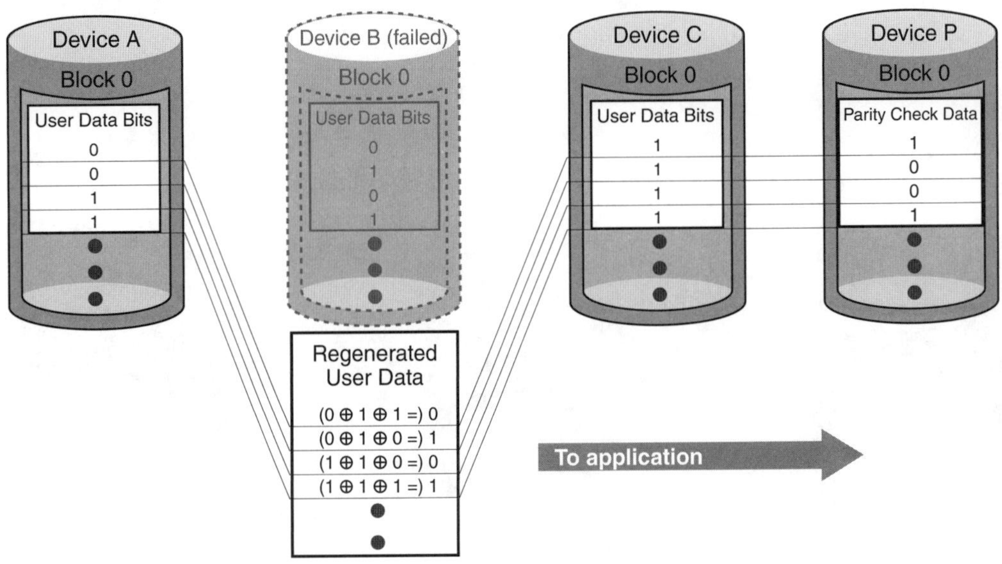

▼ **FIGURE 4–8** *User Data Regeneration in a Four-Device Parity RAID Array*

In Figure 4–7, Device B has failed. If an application requests the data that had been stored in Block 0 of Device B, the array's control software reads Block 0 from both Device A and Device P, computes the bit-by-bit **XOR** of the two, and delivers the result to the application. Delivery may be a little slower than if Disk B had been available, but otherwise the failure is transparent to the application.

The **XOR** computation is a binary addition with carries ignored. A result bit is zero if an even number of the bits from which it is computed are 1s, and 1 if the computation includes an odd number of 1s. This function can be used to compute one block of check data for any number of user data blocks. Figure 4–8 illustrates an **XOR** check data computation in a four-disk array, as well as its use to regenerate user data after a disk failure. This principle extends to any number of devices. Thus, parity RAID arrays of any size can be configured, subject only to the considerations enumerated earlier.

CHAPTER SUMMARY

- Most virtualized disk arrays include redundancy in some form. The two most common forms of redundancy are mirroring and parity RAID.
- A mirrored array contains two or more complete copies of user data, each called a mirror. A mirror may consist of a single device, or it may consist of several concatenated devices or devices with block addresses striped across them.
- Mirrors may be split from an array for data mining or backup. Arrays with three or more mirrors remain protected against disk failure during a split.
- A split mirror must be resynchronized after it is used. Advanced virtualization techniques log changes to a main array during a split, and perform fast mirror resynchronization by copying only changed data when a split mirror is rejoined to its array.
- Parity RAID carries a lower hardware overhead cost than mirroring, but protects against fewer failure modes.
- Parity for corresponding blocks of user data on each of an array's devices is computed by taking the **XOR** of the blocks' contents.
- Parity RAID arrays can consist of any number of devices, with a constant overhead of a single one of them. Practical considerations usually limit the number of devices in a parity RAID array to five or six.
- A parity RAID array can survive one device failure, no matter how many devices comprise the array.
- Parity RAID arrays have no functionality comparable to splitting mirrors to create snapshots of data for backup or analysis.

CHAPTER 5

> *Imagine if every Thursday your shoes exploded if you tied them the usual way. This happens to us all the time with computers, and nobody thinks of complaining.*
>
> —Jeff Raskin

Virtual Storage Availability

In this chapter . . .

- Recovery times and recovery points
- What contributes to storage system unavailability
- An example of the differences between ordinary and highly available storage

The purpose of a virtual storage system is to make data available to applications and users. Data availability is something of a commodity; more (higher) availability can usually be purchased at additional cost. A virtual storage system should be configured to provide "enough" availability. How much is "enough" is determined by a combination of the system's importance to the enterprise, by its duty cycle, and by the types of threats to which it is likely to be subjected. For example, in a system used during an 8-hour workday to generate routine reports, nightly backup and tape vaulting might well provide sufficient availability guarantees. In contrast, a Web retailer's order-taking system probably justifies continuous data replication and even a proactive disaster recovery plan. Similarly, a system whose operators and administrators are not highly skilled is likely to experience more human-induced errors than a system administered by highly experienced staff or a "lights out" system.

Availability is not an on or off condition. Data may be partially available to applications (e.g., a storage device failure might incapacitate some but not all tables of a database), or it might be available at less than full performance (e.g., if a RAID system's cache module fails, application I/O performance is diminished because all data must be read from and written to disks).

Data availability might also suffer because of heightened risk, with no impact on performance at all. For example, if one mirror of a two-mirror array fails, performance for a write-intensive application might actually improve slightly (because only half as much write bandwidth is being used), but the data written is at risk if there is a second storage device failure.

COMPONENTS OF DATA AVAILABILITY

The data availability provided by a storage system can be increased by minimizing the amount of data lost when a failure occurs, by shortening recovery time, or by a combination of the two. To analyze the effect of various data availability measures, it is helpful to understand how data becomes and remains unavailable.

Recovery Time Objectives

Figure 5–1 represents a storage system outage. The instant of failure is labeled T_1. The system is "down" until T_2, when service is restored. The interval between T_1 and T_2 is called the **recovery time,** and its duration is determined largely by the recovery technology. Storage systems should be configured to reliably meet required **recovery time objectives (RTOs),** or expectations of the time required to repair failures and restore service. Different storage system configurations imply different RTOs:

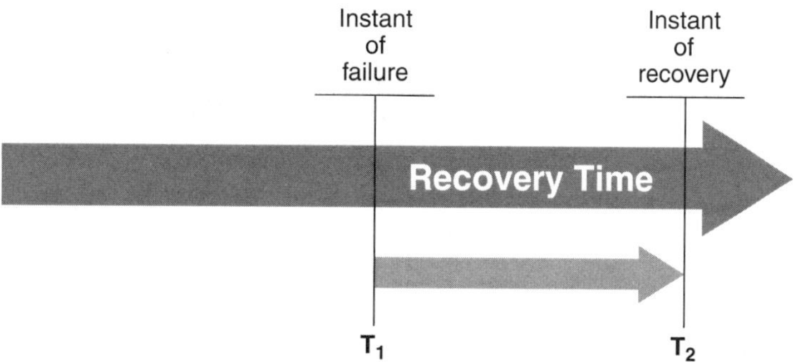

▼ **FIGURE 5–1** *Storage System Outage and Recovery Time*

- ***Restore from backup (hours):*** If a storage device protected only by backup tapes fails, a substitute device must be allocated (and possibly installed), tapes must be located and mounted, and data restored from them to the substitute device. Depending on the amount of data to be recovered and the availability of substitute hardware, recovery time can extend to hours or even days.
- ***Remote data replication (minutes):*** If a replicated virtual device fails, its replica can be used to resume application processing. Before a replica can be used, however, file system and database integrity must be verified. Recovery times are typically measured in minutes, partly due to human interaction. Asynchronous replicas may further complicate recovery because the replica may be out of date by a few writes, which must be recovered in some way or deliberately ignored.
- ***Mirroring (seconds or less):*** With mirrored storage, recovery from a disk failure is effectively instantaneous, because a mirror takes over the function of the failed disk. Other types of failures may imply longer recovery times (e.g., failure of the only host bus adapter that connects two mirrored storage devices).

Thus, with some technologies and some types of failures, nearly instantaneous recovery time objectives can be met. For others, recovery inherently takes much longer.

Recovery Points

Failures have a second, potentially more significant effect on information services: unrecoverable loss of data that represents business actions taken prior to the failure. For example, data restored from a backup is no more current than the time of the backup. Online updates representing sales made, bills collected, orders shipped, and so forth, that occurred after the backup are lost, and must be reconstructed by other means.[1] The time to which a recovery technique recovers data is called a **recovery point,** and is represented by T_0 in Figure 5–2. The interval between T_0 and T_2 is sometimes called **data currency,** because it describes how out-of-date data is after recovery, both because recovered data is older than T_1 and because any business state changes in the interval between T_1 and T_2 are not reflected in the recovered data.

1. Alternatively, the business may consciously accept the loss and resume operations leaving a gap in its records. This is often the most reasonable approach for low-value manufacturing, software development, and scientific inquiry. For others, notably high-value financial applications, this is not a tenable solution.

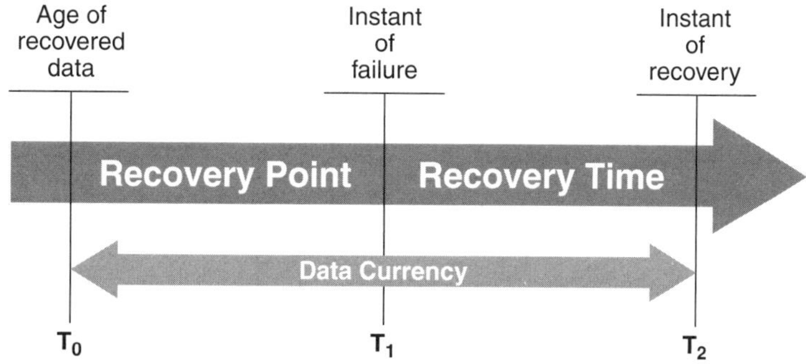

▼ **FIGURE 5–2** *Data Recovery Point*

As Figure 5–2 illustrates, data loss extends both forward and back in time from the point of failure. Some technologies result in recovery points very close to the instant of failure (little or no data lost), while others recover significantly aged data:

- ***Restore from backup (days):*** Data restored from backup tapes represents the state of business at the time the backup was made. This may be hours or even days prior to the time of failure.
- ***Asynchronous replication (minutes):*** Data in flight at the instant of failure is lost. For severe failures that permanently destroy the source data center, data queued for replication may also be unrecoverable. Partially complete transactions may have to be "backed out" of the replica used for recovery, by playing back a database log, for example. As a result, a recovered replica typically represents a business state a few minutes prior to the failure.
- ***Mirroring (essentially instantaneous):*** When a mirror fails, the recovery point is the instant of failure. A surviving mirror assumes the function of the failed one, and no data is lost.

Virtual storage systems should be configured to meet recovery time and recovery point objectives that are appropriate for the applications they support. Table 5–1 suggests appropriate values for some common enterprise applications.

Other Contributors to Availability

Two other factors affect data availability. The first is the **degraded operation interval (DOI)** between functional recovery and restoration of full protection against further failures. For example, the recovery point for a

▼ **TABLE 5–1** *Typical RPOs and RTOs for Common Enterprise Applications*

Application	Recovery Point Objective	Recovery Time Objective
file service	seconds	hours
application development	hours	hours
Web server	days	seconds
E-commerce	seconds	seconds
human resource database	seconds	hours

mirror failure is instantaneous. The DOI, however, lasts until the failed device has been replaced and data has been resynchronized. During the DOI, I/O performance may suffer (in this example, because resynchronization I/O contends with application I/O, or because the mirror is not available to partly satisfy a heavy read load). From an availability standpoint, the risk is heightened as well; a second device failure during the DOI might result in major permanent data loss.

If a disaster incapacitates an entire data center, causing information services to fail over to a recovery site and use a data replica, the DOI lasts until a replacement data center can be secured and provisioned. On the other hand, if a recovery site is pre-provisioned with equipment equivalent to that of the primary data center, there may be no application performance degradation or local failure susceptibility during the DOI (there is, of course, heightened risk of a second disaster with no recovery site).

Degraded operation intervals are of concern because of reduced application performance, but more importantly because permanent data loss may result if additional failures occur during them. In Figure 5–3, the DOI runs from T_2, when the system is returned to service after the outage, until T_3, when the failed component has been replaced.

The final contributor to outage time is the interval between T_3 and T_4 in Figure 5–3, called **restorative downtime.** Restorative downtime is outage time that must be scheduled to restore full component redundancy, for example, to replace a spare disk drive that has been automatically deployed because of a data disk failure. Similarly, if a data center is destroyed, planned downtime may be required to transfer information services from the recovery site after a new data center has been built and provisioned.

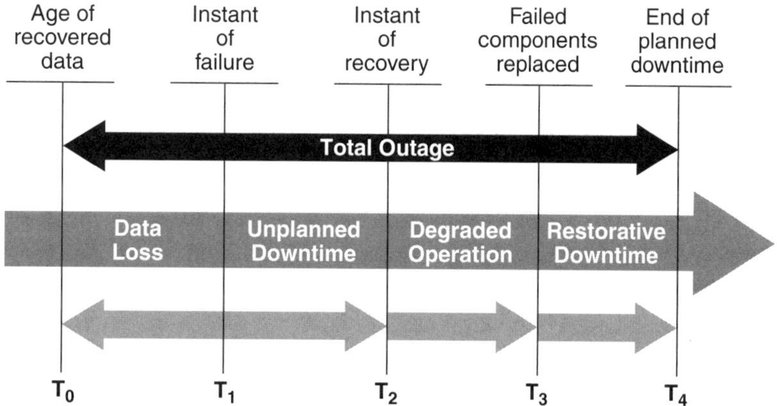

▼ **FIGURE 5–3** *The Completed Outage Timeline*

Like degraded operation, restorative downtime may not cause data and information services to become completely unavailable. For example, most RAID systems allow for "hot swapping" of failed disks. When a failed disk is replaced, the replacement disk's contents must be synchronized with those of the other devices in the redundant array. Whether an array is mirrored or uses parity RAID, synchronization is I/O intensive, and is likely to degrade application performance noticeably.

Local stocking of common spare parts can minimize both DOIs and restorative downtime. Local stocking allows failed NICs, HBAs, cables, and disk drives to be replaced in minutes rather than days, particularly if components can be hot-swapped, and if enterprise staff are trained to perform service operations.

What Kind of Downtime When?

Not all failures result in all four of these outage types. For example:

- A system with *no* highly available storage only incurs data loss and unplanned downtime. All component replacement occurs as part of the unplanned downtime interval, and when recovery is complete, operation is not degraded.
- Some data availability techniques completely eliminate one or more of the outage intervals for certain failures. For example, if a mirrored disk array has a pre-designated "hot spare," a disk failure causes a spare drive to be co-opted to replace the failed one. There is no data loss or unplanned downtime, but operation is degraded (through

reduced performance and increased risk) until the failed drive is replaced and resynchronized. If the disk enclosure supports "hot swapping," planned downtime is not required either.

- Outages due to application software or operating system crashes may cause data loss, as well as unplanned downtime for rebooting or restarting. There are no components to replace, however, so there is no DOI or planned downtime interval. Once the recovery time (T_2) is reached, recovery is complete and the system returns to full service.
- Most disaster recovery strategies migrate information services to recovery sites. DOIs in this case may be very long, lasting either until the original data center returns to service, or until a new data center is acquired and provisioned. If the original or new data center is to become the primary one, moving services to it may result in planned downtime.

EXAMPLES

Two examples will illustrate how different storage system designs affect the four components of outage time:

- Failure of a single disk drive
- A disaster that destroys an entire data center

In each example, the effects of failure on both an "ordinary" system (one with no highly available components) and on a highly available system are discussed.

Single Disk Failure

When an unprotected disk drive fails, the data it contains is irretrievably lost. For such a system, restoring a backup is the only data recovery mechanism. A highly available system, on the other hand, typically uses mirrored disk storage with hot-swappable drives and a policy of automatic sparing. Table 5–2 lists expected durations of the four outage components for these two systems due to a disk drive failure.

In the ordinary system (middle column of Table 5–2):

- The recovery point is the time of the last backup. All data updates between then and the time of the disk failure are lost, and must be recreated by other means.

▼ **TABLE 5–2** *Outage Times Resulting from Disk Drive Failure*

	Ordinary System	Highly Available System
Recovery Point (T_0–T_1)	**Hours—days** Data updates made since the most recent backup are lost	**Immediate** Storage is mirrored, so no data is lost
Recovery Time (T_1–T_2)	**Minutes—days** Service is unavailable until a replacement disk drive is installed and a backup is restored	**None** Since storage is mirrored, information service continues to operate
Degraded Operation (T_2–T_3)	**None** Component replacement time is included in recovery time	**Minutes—days** System runs without hot spare until a replacement spare is installed
Planned Downtime (T_3–T_4)	**None** Data restoration time is included in recovery time	**None** Failed disk drive can be hot swapped while system is operating

- Recovery time varies depending on the state of preparedness (e.g., are replacement disk drives in stock?), but a lower bound is the time it takes to replace the failed disk, restore data from a backup, restart applications, and do whatever it takes to recreate the lost data updates from the T_0–T_1 interval.
- When the failed disk is replaced, this system has a full complement of hardware, so there is no degraded operation period. However, the enterprise may have to operate without the lost data forever. In this sense, the degraded operation period might be regarded as permanent.
- Similarly, no planned downtime is required in this scenario, because once the disk has been replaced and data has been restored (both during the recovery time period), the system is physically complete. "Restoring data," however, may include recovering permanently lost data by reacquiring it manually.

This system is not poorly managed; indeed, the opposite is probably true. It is simply not designed to tolerate or recover from disk failures. For low-value applications, for example, Web-based opinion surveys, this may be appropriate. High availability is expensive, and may not be cost-justified. For mission-critical services, however, this level of availability is definitely *not* appropriate. The highly available system in this example has mirrored disk storage and dedicated spare drives. When a disk drive fails, the storage system automatically allocates a spare and begins to synchronize its contents with those of surviving mirrors. For this system (described in the third column of Table 5–2):

- No data is lost; data remains accessible as long as at least one mirror survives.
- There is no recovery time; applications continue to run with full access to data.
- There is a degraded operation interval, but the "degradation" is minor—one less spare disk drive is available for recovery from additional failures. The DOI lasts until a spare disk is installed (typically replacing the failed one).
- No planned downtime is required because the failed drive can be replaced "hot" while the system is operating.

There is always a cost associated with failure tolerance and recoverability—in this case, the "extra" disk drives for mirroring and sparing, as well as the more expensive packaging typically associated with highly available storage systems. In addition, the virtualization software that sequences and controls the recovery operations is often an extra-cost component.

Data Center Destruction

Table 5–3 describes the outage consequences of a disaster that incapacitates an entire data center. The data center is assumed to be incapacitated for long enough that information services must be migrated to a recovery site. The highly available system is assumed to replicate its critical data to a recovery site, and to have clustering technology capable of automating application failover to the recovery site.

For the ordinary system (middle column of Table 5–3), a data center must be arranged for, and backup tapes transported there and restored. For this system:

- The recovery point is the time of the last available backup (the newest backup tapes may have been destroyed in the disaster). All data modifications between then and the time of the disaster are lost, and must be recreated by other means.

▼ **TABLE 5–3** *Outage Times Resulting from a Data Center Disaster*

	Ordinary System	Highly Available System
Recovery Point (T_0–T_1)	**Hours—days** Data updates made since the most recent backup are lost	**Seconds** Critical online storage is replicated to the recovery site, so little data is lost
Recovery Time (T_1–T_2)	**Hours—weeks** Services are unavailable until data is restored and applications restarted at a replacement data center	**Minutes—hours** With automated remote failover and replicated data, applications automatically restart at the recovery site
Degraded Operations (T_2–T_3)	**None** Included in recovery time	**Days—weeks** Services run as usual, but with no (or one fewer) spare data center
Planned Downtime (T_3–T_4)	**Hours—days** Required to switch services back to original data center or to a new one	**Hours—days** Required to switch services back to original data center or to a new one

- Recovery time is the time required to arrange for recovery facilities, restore data from a backup, restart applications, and reconnect clients.
- If the recovery data center is fully provisioned, there is no degraded operation interval, but the enterprise must recreate data updates made between the time of the disaster and the recovery point. This may degrade the information services from a business standpoint, possibly forever.
- When the destroyed data center is again serviceable, or a permanent alternate has been arranged, planned downtime is usually required to transfer services from the recovery site to a permanent home. This downtime is averted if the recovery center becomes the permanent data center.

By contrast, a highly available data center prepared to recover from this type of disaster has its critical data replicated to a recovery site provisioned with computing equipment adequate for running critical services. Application failover is automatic, so applications at the recovery site restart quickly with minimal human intervention, using up-to-date replicated data. For this system, the components of outage time (third column of Table 5–3) are:

- The recovery point is at or within a few seconds of the instant of disaster, depending on whether data updates were in transit. (Information service recovery strategies must account for the possibility that a few updates may be permanently lost, and either "live without" or employ transactional techniques to recover to a business-consistent state.)
- Recovery time is the time required to validate or restore the integrity of data replicas at the recovery site, restart applications, and reconnect to clients. Depending largely on the state of the data replicas, recovery time can be as short as a few minutes or as much as several hours.
- The degraded operation interval lasts until the primary data center is again in service. If the recovery site is adequately provisioned, service levels can be met, but survivability is diminished. In some instances (for example, with server-based replication, which does not require identical devices for source and replicated data), there also may be reduced performance or increased susceptibility to failure while replicated data is in use. The DOI in this case may last from a few days (e.g., power grid failure) to many weeks (e.g., hurricane or flood).
- In disasters of this type, there is usually planned downtime as applications are migrated from the recovery site back to the primary data center or to a replacement. Staggering the migration of different applications can mitigate the impact of planned downtime. There is no planned downtime if the recovery site becomes the permanent primary data center.

Disaster Recovery Technologies

A complete range of storage management technologies is required to completely protect a data center from disaster. Based on the RPO and RTO for a business, multiple storage management services are required. VERITAS is unique in that the company provides a full set of information technology disaster recovery capabilities for all major open server and storage platforms. Backup managers like VERITAS Backup Exec™ and NetBackup™ with Remote Vaulting form the last line of defense for enterprise information services. To shorten recovery times, the company offers data replication in several forms such as VERITAS Volume Replicator™ and VERITAS Storage Replicator™. To fully automate failover to remote data centers, the VERITAS Availability Manager™ integrates data replication with clustering technology that reduces dependency on (often unavailable) storage administrators and application experts, and guarantees the shortest possible recovery times. The VERITAS Availability Manager™ can be integrated with VERITAS replication as well as with hardware-based replicators.

As with the preceding example, the ordinary system is not poorly configured or managed; it is simply not prepared to recover from a major disaster. The system is designed for resumption of information services after a disaster, but not for *rapid* resumption. For some services, this strategy may be appropriate—many passive information services do not require rapid resumption after a disaster. For others, such as financial services, being online is critical to success (and indeed, survival), and the cost of deploying and managing rapid recovery technologies is unavoidable.

As these examples illustrate, increasing cost and operational complexity can reduce outage time. In general, shorter outage times come at substantial cost. In designing data availability strategies, storage architects make decisions that affect each of the segments of outage time. The importance of each segment, and therefore the justifiable investment, is determined by the value of the data, the type of threat against which protection is required, and the recovery time and recovery point objectives.

CHAPTER SUMMARY

- Storage architecture may be defined as assessing availability and performance requirements and configuring components, interconnects, virtualization techniques, and operating procedures that meet them.
- Availability is a function of cost. Cost can be reduced if lower performance and reduced function are acceptable under adverse conditions.
- As many as four different outage times can result from failures or disasters.
- Recovery time is the time between the instant of failure and the restoration of an information service.
- The recovery point is the "age" of recovered data when a service resumes.
- The degraded operation interval is the interval during which performance is reduced or risk is increased as a result of the failure or disaster.
- Planned downtime is time required to restore full information service performance and availability by replacing and reconfiguring failed components and facilities.
- Storage architects must configure online storage for each application's data to meet required objectives for each of the four contributors to outage time. These objectives are typically specified in service level agreements between information service providers and users.

CHAPTER 6

Science is the knowledge of consequences, and dependence of one fact upon another.

—THOMAS HOBBES

Making Virtual Storage Systems Highly Available

In this chapter . . .

- Necessities for storage system high availability
- How good are mirroring and RAID at protecting data?
- Failures that mirroring and RAID don't protect against

The cost of making storage systems highly available is determined by two factors: the failures against which protection is afforded and the performance required, both under normal circumstances and during a failure.

For example, if a server-based volume manager manages a mirrored array of two storage devices connected to a single HBA, an HBA failure is equivalent to array failure. Connecting each device via a separate HBA adds cost, but protects against HBA failure. Moreover, because each device is accessed on a separate I/O path, performance improves. If an HBA fails in this configuration, data remains accessible, but performance is reduced, because only one storage device and I/O path are engaged in executing application I/O requests.

MAKING VIRTUAL STORAGE HIGHLY AVAILABLE

Storage systems are typically made highly available through the use of redundant components. Highly available storage systems typically include redundant I/O paths, mirrored storage devices, multiple network connections, and so forth. A few components (e.g., backplanes and cabinets) are not normally duplicated because the probability that they will fail is extremely low.

Redundant components configured for automatic replacement minimize virtual storage downtime. Virtual storage is made highly available by identifying the components most likely to fail and configuring multiples of them so that one can take over if another fails. For example, RAID systems include redundant disk drives, internal data paths, power and cooling components, and external interfaces. Servers (and therefore volume managers) are generally made highly available through the use of clustering software that organizes them into mutually protective groups. Storage networks are made highly available by configuring two identical unconnected networks and connecting them to the same servers and storage devices.

Active and Passive Redundant Components

Storage system components configured for redundancy may be *active* (used during normal operation) or *passive* (present but not used during normal operation). Passive redundant components do nothing productive unless the components they protect actually fail. Passive redundancy is expensive, so highly available systems are often configured with active redundant components.

Active redundant components effectively reduce the cost of high availability because they contribute to a system's performance when everything is working properly. Highly available storage systems typically include many active redundant components that operate alongside the components they protect.

- Mirrored storage devices share I/O load.
- I/O is balanced across two storage network paths to storage devices.
- Cluster volume managers enable server-based virtual devices to be accessed by multiple servers.

Clearly, there is an advantage to active redundant components—assets are used during the great majority of the time during which things are running normally. But, as elsewhere in information technology, there are trade-offs. Users quickly learn to count on the performance delivered by active redundant components and paths. When an active redundant component fails, performance degrades. If the degradation is unacceptable, the reduced cost of active redundant components may be unaffordable.

Hot Spares and Relocation/Hot Relocation

Storage redundancy technologies such as mirroring and RAID are essential to data availability. But even though redundant elements keep data available if a disk or path fails, what about the next failure? And what about the performance degradation caused by the missing element? The VERITAS™ Volume Manager provides *hot relocation* capabilities to minimize the window of risk when a failure does occur. Hot relocation automatically replaces failed mirrors with spare storage, restoring redundancy and no special layout or designation of the spare pool is required. Redundant data on surviving disks may be relocated if necessary, and the failed data are reconstructed, all without system administrator intervention. Hot relocation treats some or all of the free storage pool as a source of space to create new mirrors when a disk fails.

After a failed disk is replaced, data can be relocated to it in its original location in the storage configuration by administrative action.

Making Redundant Components Work

Highly available storage systems monitor their components and automatically redirect workload when a failure necessitates it. Examples of redirection include:

- Storage virtualizers monitor mirrored devices and redirect I/O requests when a device fails.
- I/O path management software detects failed interconnects and reroutes traffic to alternate paths.
- Cluster failover software monitors cluster volume managers and restarts their master instances on alternate servers if they fail.
- Storage networks, switches, and routers monitor each other and automatically route traffic when paths fail.

Redundant components enable high availability, but sophisticated control software throughout a distributed system is required to make the components effective.

Minimizing the Cost of Highly Available Storage

The cost of highly available storage can be minimized if an enterprise can accept:

- ***Protection against a smaller set of failures:*** So-called "*N+1*" redundancy (e.g., parity RAID) uses fewer components than full redundancy, but protects against only one failure in a set of *N* components.
- ***Reduced system performance under adverse conditions:*** Configuring active redundant components to increase performance under normal

circumstances reduces cost. This strategy uses assets effectively, but performance is necessarily reduced when a component fails. For example, application read requests can be balanced across mirrored storage devices. If a device fails, less balancing occurs, and peak performance diminishes accordingly.

There is another cost of highly available systems that is more challenging to minimize—people. Storage system administration is increasingly automated, but people remain critical to high availability. Virtual storage must be configured and provisioned, and decisions must be made in response to unplanned events. Even the most automated highly available storage system requires an administrator to direct recovery from unanticipated combinations of faults.

Highly available virtual storage requires all three—redundant components, supporting software, and skilled people—to administer it and react to unanticipated situations. These skills themselves must be redundant, so that, for example, a disaster that prevents a data center operations staff from reaching the recovery site doesn't leave an enterprise unable to access its data.

VIRTUAL STORAGE AND DATA AVAILABILITY

RAID and mirroring technology protect against destruction of data and loss of access to data due to storage device failure or failure of all I/O paths to a device. When a disk drive in a mirrored or RAID array fails, the array is said to be *degraded.* Failure of a second drive before the first is replaced and resynchronized can result in loss of access and usually also permanent data loss.

RAID does not prevent data loss; it just improves the odds against it. It is legitimate to ask how good RAID is in protecting against disk drive failures, as well as how important disk failures are in the overall scheme of storage availability.

Disk drive reliability is usually expressed as a **mean time between failures (MTBF),** measured in device operating hours. MTBF is not the average time between two successive failures of a single device, but rather the expected number of device operating hours between two failures in a large population of identical devices.

Typical disk drive MTBF values are in the range of 500,000 hours. This means that in a population of, say 1,000 drives operating under identical circumstances, a failure is to be expected every 500 hours (about every three weeks). In a population of 100 operating drives, a failure can be expected every 5,000 hours (about every 7 months).

Mirroring and Availability

One hundred disk drives can be configured as 50 mirrored pairs. With a 500,000-hour MTBF, about every seven months, one mirror of one mirrored pair can be expected to fail. Data is still available from the surviving mirror. The question for storage architects is, "While that drive is out of service, what events could make data unavailable, and how likely are those events?"

The answer to the first question is simple. If the surviving mirror of a pair fails before the first failed mirror is replaced and resynchronized, data will become unavailable. To answer the second question, Figure 6–1 presents an analysis of this scenario, which while not mathematically rigorous, provides an intuitive understanding of why mirroring technology is valued so highly by storage architects.

From a pool of 100 identical disk drives (with a 500,000-hour MTBF) configured as 50 mirrored pairs, in any 5,000-hour window a failure is to be expected. While a failed drive is out of service, failure of its mirror would result in data loss. The failed drive's mirror is one specific disk, the population for the next stage of analysis.

One more piece of data is required to answer the question—the **mean time to repair** the failed drive **(MTTR).** In order to restore protection against further failures, not only must the failed drive be replaced with a working one, but the contents of the replacement drive must be synchronized with the surviving mirror. If drive replacement and resynchronization takes, for example, five hours, the question then becomes: "what is the expectation that in a population of one disk, a failure will occur in a five-hour period?" The rough answer is that with 1/100th of the population and 1/1,000th of the time period in which one failure is expected, the chance of the second failure is 1/100,000th as great as the first drive failure.

Two conclusions may be drawn from this analysis:

- Mirroring does not eliminate the possibility of data loss due to disk failure, but does reduce the odds of it greatly.
- Mirroring is not a substitute for good data center management practices. For example, reducing mean repair time from 5 hours to 20 minutes would reduce the chance of data loss to one in a million; increasing it to 50 hours would increase it to one in ten thousand.

This analysis can be extended to cover three-mirror arrays, which have a vanishingly small probability of data loss due solely to disk failure.

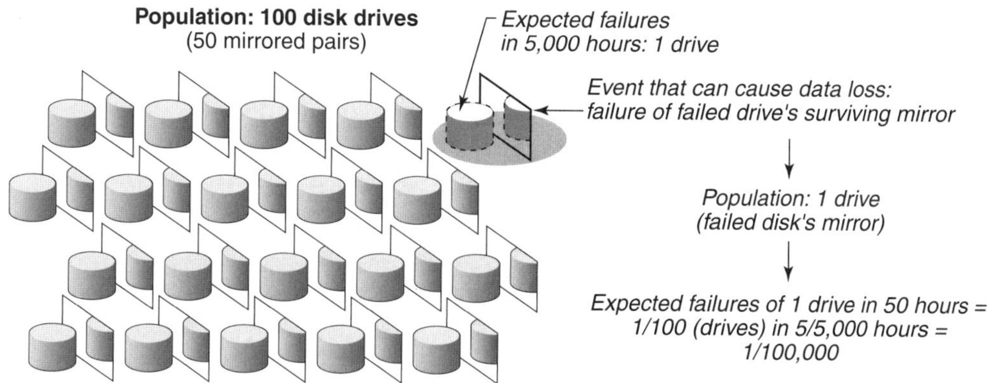

▼ **FIGURE 6–1** *Mirroring and Failure Rates*

Parity RAID and Availability

If the same 100 disk drives are arranged in 20 five-drive parity RAID arrays, one drive failure in every seven-month window is still to be expected. When the failure occurs, data remains available from the four surviving disk drives. Again, the question for storage architects is what events could cause data loss, and how likely are they? If any surviving disk drive in a degraded parity RAID array fails before the first failed drive is replaced and resynchronized, data will be lost.

Figure 6–2 illustrates this scenario. Once a parity RAID array is degraded, failure of any of its remaining disk drives results in data loss. The question is therefore "What is the expectation that in a population of four disk drives, a failure will occur in a given 5-hour period?" With 1/25th of the full population and 1/1,000th of the time period in which one failure is expected, the chance of the second failure is one in 25,000. For many applications, this level of protection is adequate. For others, the importance of continuous data availability makes two- or even three-copy mirroring a preferred solution.

Storage architects deal with questions like this as they configure storage systems for application use. They balance protection cost ("extra" devices and supporting hardware) against the cost of downtime, and configure accordingly. This simple analysis concentrates on disk drive failures; when designing virtual storage for data centers, architects must consider I/O paths (storage networks), host bus adapters, and other components as well.

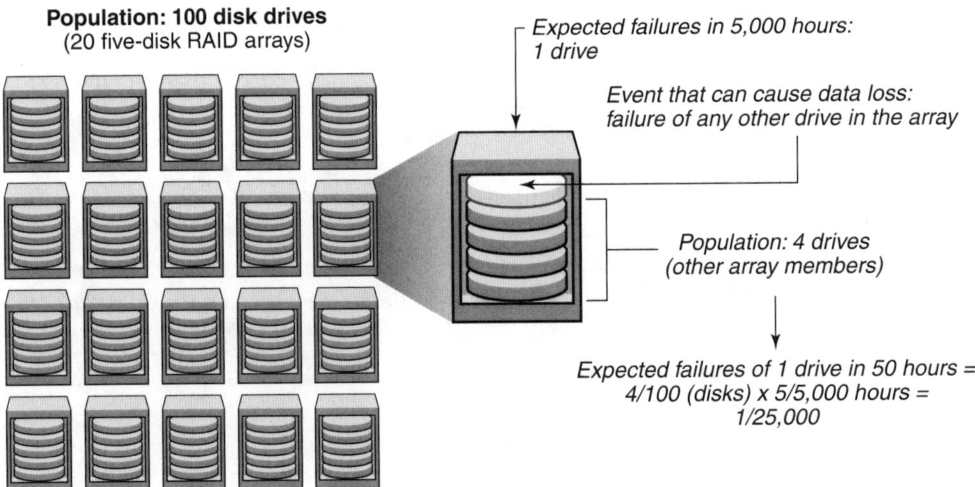

▼ **FIGURE 6–2** *Parity RAID and Failure Rates*

WHAT MIRRORING AND RAID DON'T DO

Mirroring and RAID reduce the probability of online data loss significantly. Odds of one in 25,000 aren't bad. But the foregoing discussion focuses entirely on disk drive failures. Failure of other storage system components can cause data loss as well:

- ***Network cables, I/O adapters, and interface ASICs:*** These collectively form a **path** to a storage device. Failure of one may block communication with several devices. If storage is configured so that only one device in an array is connected to any given path, path failure is survivable. If not, path failure results in unavailable data (but probably not *lost* data unless there are accompanying device failures).
- ***Power and cooling systems:*** A failed power supply causes all the devices it powers to "fail." Fan failure eventually destroys devices by overheating. Power supplies and fans are usually configured in redundant pairs, each powering or cooling several disk drives, and sized so that one can adequately power or cool the drives if its companion should fail.
- ***External RAID controllers and appliances:*** Failure of the RAID controller or storage appliance through which several storage devices are accessed makes the devices inaccessible, and is generally regarded as

unacceptable design. RAID systems and storage appliances should be configured in pairs that connect to the same storage devices and application servers. When everything is functioning normally, I/O load is shared. When one fails, its partner takes control of all devices and executes all I/O requests.

- ***Embedded RAID controllers:*** From a storage access standpoint, failure of an embedded RAID controller is equivalent to failure of the computer in which it is embedded. Some vendors have improved on this situation by devising controllers that interact with operating systems to fail over disk drives from a failed embedded controller to a second controller embedded in a different server.
- ***Application servers:*** Except in the case of server-based volume managers, a server failure is not precisely a failure of the I/O system. Increasingly, however, business requires that applications resume quickly after a server failure. This need has given rise to **clusters** of servers that "backstop" each other, with a designated alternate taking over a failed server's work. Server **failover** has slightly different impact on different types of storage systems. Volume managers and embedded RAID controllers must take control of a failed server's storage devices, verify array consistency, and present arrays as virtual devices to applications in the alternate server. External RAID systems and storage appliances must present the failed server's LUNs to the alternate server, typically on different I/O paths. Server failure does not affect the internal consistency of these arrays, although consistency of file systems or databases on them must be verified.

In addition to these storage system component-related factors, there are two additional, possibly more important, potential causes of data loss—human error and application fault. Mirrored and RAID arrays store blocks of binary data reliably, regardless of its meaning. It is sometimes ironically observed that a RAID array stores incorrect data just as reliably as it stores correct data. Mirroring and RAID do not protect against data corruption due to human errors or application faults. A combination of high-integrity data managers (e.g., logging file systems and database managers) and regular backup with professional media management offer the only realistic protection against these causes of data loss.

As users have become more sophisticated, they have learned that protection against storage device and other component failures is necessary, but not sufficient for high data availability. The entire I/O system, as well as servers and applications, must be protected against both physical and logical failures. Mirroring and RAID are building blocks for highly available data access, but not the entire solution.

CHAPTER SUMMARY

- In online virtual storage, mirroring and RAID are the primary mechanisms for protecting against storage device failures.
- Mirroring offers significantly better device failure protection than RAID (in addition to advanced functionality such as splitting for backup and analysis).
- Besides mirroring and RAID, a highly available storage system requires other hardware features, including redundant power and cooling, hot swapping of failed components, and redundant I/O paths between storage and clients.
- Mirrored and RAID arrays require careful configuration so as not to introduce single points of failure. For example, the devices comprising a single array should all be connected to separate I/O buses or storage network paths.
- Even with thorough storage system design for high availability, protection against human errors and application faults is required, usually in the form of backups or point-in-time snapshots of data.

CHAPTER 7

Science is the knowledge of many, orderly and methodically digested and arranged, so as to become attainable by one.

—JOHN FREDERICK WILLIAM HERSCHEL

Locating User Data on Virtual Block Storage

In this chapter . . .

- Concatenated and striped data block address translation
- Partitioning to subdivide large virtual devices
- How striping affects application I/O performance

Every block of data "stored" on a virtual storage device must ultimately be stored at some logical block[1] on a (virtualized) disk drive. Virtualization control software must rapidly and reliably convert between virtual device block addresses specified in client I/O requests and logical block addresses it uses to issue commands to the storage devices it is virtualizing. This conversion is sometimes referred to as the **mapping** of virtual device block addresses to logical block addresses.

There are basically two block address conversion techniques: table lookups and algorithms. Storage virtualization implementations typically use both for different purposes.

Table lookups have the advantage of allowing completely arbitrary conversions, and are therefore very flexible. Any object, A, can be made

1. Chapter 2 explains why the blocks of a physical disk in which data is stored are called logical blocks.

to correspond to any other object, B, by placing some signature that uniquely identifies B in the table entry where control software will look to find B's address. Block storage virtualizers commonly use table lookups to indicate which devices are members of an array, and which virtual device addresses are being used to present an array's virtual storage to clients. The tables used for this purpose are typically held in the virtualizer's cache for rapid access, and also stored on the virtualized devices themselves for persistence.

While table lookup is a very flexible address conversion technique, it is necessarily either time-consuming or unreliable for large address spaces, such as are encountered in translating a large device's virtual block addresses to logical equivalents. Either the lookup tables must be stored persistently, or they may be eradicated if the system holding them crashes. Neither of these options is particularly attractive for converting virtual block addresses to logical ones. Control software converts block addresses for every client I/O request, so conversion must be rapid. Because virtual-to-logical address conversion is the only means of determining which client data is stored where on which devices, destruction of lookup tables would mean that data could not be located.

So table lookup schemes for converting virtual device block addresses to logical block addresses are generally unattractive. Instead, algorithms are employed that allow logical block addresses to be computed from a virtual block address and some seldom-changing parameters of the array (which may be determined from a table lookup). Two basic algorithms are used for converting virtual addresses to logical ones: concatenation (and partitioning) and block address striping. The sections that follow discuss these techniques.[2]

LARGER VIRTUAL DEVICES: CONCATENATION

The simplest way to combine storage devices for increased net capacity is to concatenate their logical block address spaces into one larger virtual device address space, as Figure 7–1 illustrates.

2. Table lookup schemes for mapping virtual storage addresses to physical storage locations have been used, notably in StorageTek's *Iceberg* technology, still possibly the most technically sophisticated implementation of RAID system virtual storage ever delivered. Today, however, algorithmic mapping schemes are used universally for block address mapping.

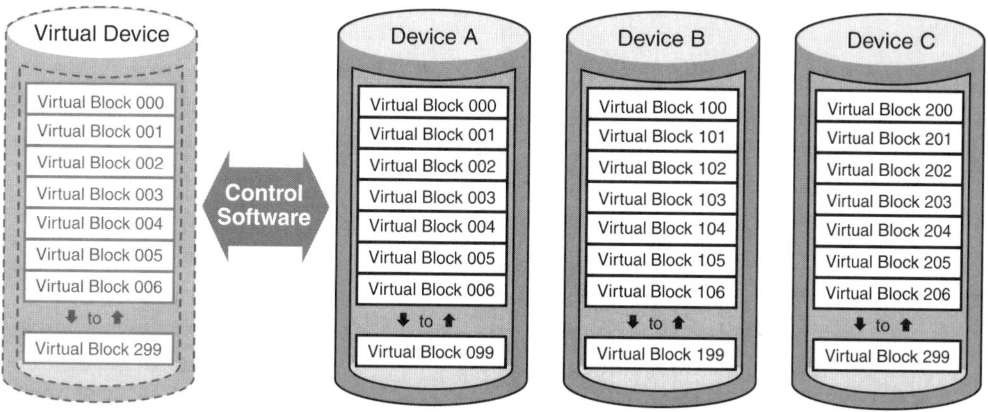

▼ **FIGURE 7–1** *Array with Concatenated Block Address Spaces*

Each of the three devices illustrated in Figure 7–1 has 100 logical blocks, numbered from 000 to 099.[3] The resulting array has 300 virtual blocks, numbered from 000 to 299. The first 100 virtual blocks correspond to the 100 logical blocks of Device A; the second 100 to the 100 logical blocks of Device B, and the third 100 to the 100 logical blocks of Device C.

Described in algorithmic terms,

```
if (virtual_block_number < 100)
then {
    logical_block_number = virtual_block_number;
    device = A;
    }
else if (virtual_block_number < 200)
then {
    logical_block_number = virtual_block_number - 100;
    device = B;
    }
else if (virtual_block_number < 300)
then {
    logical_block_number = virtual_block_number - 200;
    device = C;
}
else invalid_block();
```

3. As usual, artificially small disk capacities are used in the examples for ease of comprehension.

The device result from this algorithm is the device (network or bus address) to which the virtualizer addresses its I/O commands. The **logical_block_number** result is the starting block number to be specified in those commands. This algorithm can clearly be evaluated in a small number of steps. The long-lived array parameters it requires are the device identifiers, the number of logical blocks on each, and the order in which the devices appear in the array.

Characteristics of Concatenation

Concatenation can enlarge the capacity of a virtual device to beyond that of the largest storage device available. There is no intrinsic limit to the number of devices that can be concatenated into an array, nor is there any intrinsic requirement for all devices in a concatenated array to have the same capacity, although implementations and operating environments may impose limits on either or both. One commonly encountered limit is in the ability of an operating system or file system to address the number of blocks in a very large virtual storage device. Systems with "32-bit" roots may be limited to addressing virtual devices with 2^{32} blocks (4,294,967,296 blocks, or 2,199,023,255,552 bytes—about two terabytes) or fewer. Even if a storage system supports larger virtual devices, there may be no way for such an operating system to address blocks with higher addresses.

It is easy to add capacity to a concatenated array by adding devices. A new device's capacity is appended to the end of the virtual device's block address space. Blocks need not be rearranged when capacity is added to a concatenated array, but clients (operating systems, file systems, and database managers) must somehow become aware of the enlargement, and must be capable of dealing with the increased capacity. With RAID system and network-based arrays, administrative action is typically required to cause an operating system to **rescan** its devices to make it aware of increased capacity. Further administrative action is usually required to cause file systems to adjust to expanded device capacity. Some file systems and server-based volume managers are integrated with each other so that a single administrative command causes device expansion to be recognized and the file system to adjust to it.

Capacity Change Awareness

Most users implement both the VERITAS™ Volume Manager and the VERITAS File System™, delivered together as the VERITAS™ Storage Foundation. Because of the close integration between the two, file system awareness of volume expansion is automatic and instantaneous. Applications are immediately able to use expanded file system capacity. The same is true if a volume's capacity is reduced, for example, to deploy storage capacity for other purposes. The VERITAS File System™ shrinks as well, without application disruption. Without this feature, a file system capacity reduction would require manual administration in offline mode, resulting in downtime.

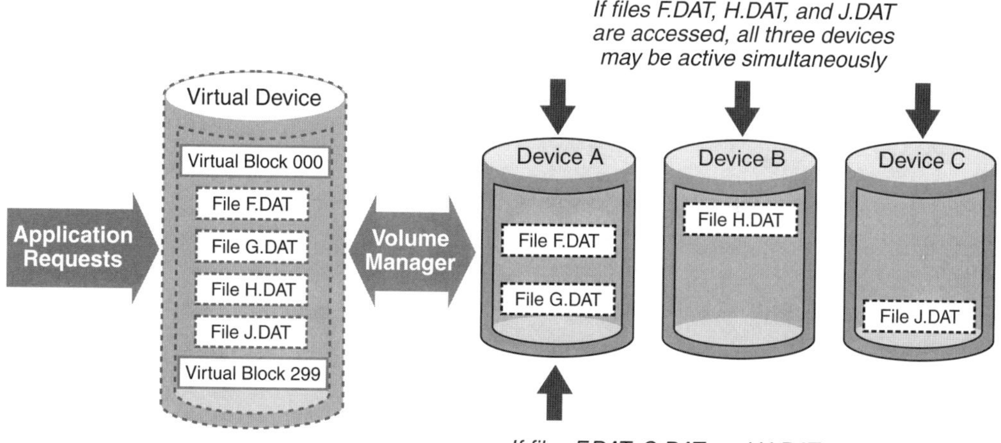

▼ **FIGURE 7–2** *Simultaneous File Access on a Concatenated Virtual Device*

I/O Performance of Concatenated Arrays

A concatenated array may provide a measure of I/O load balancing, although this is largely fortuitous and difficult to predict. Figure 7–2 illustrates how an array of concatenated devices might balance I/O load under some circumstances. It also shows a virtual device containing a file system with four files allocated. The files are stored in virtual blocks that convert to blocks on Devices A, B, and C.

If applications access the four files concurrently, I/O load is somewhat balanced across the three devices. Device A satisfies requests for data in files F.DAT and G.DAT. Device B satisfies requests for H.DAT, and Device C satisfies requests for J.DAT. By contrast, if several applications were to make concurrent access requests for one of the files, or for files F.DAT and G.DAT only, only one of the devices would be active. The other two would be idle, because no data stored on them is being requested. Whether the I/O load on a concatenated array actually balances across its devices depends on whether applications make concurrent requests to files whose data blocks are stored on separate devices, a factor essentially impossible for an administrator to control.

From a practical standpoint, any load balancing produced by a concatenated array is fortuitous. It is wise not to plan on systematic I/O performance enhancement from this type of array. Concatenated block address

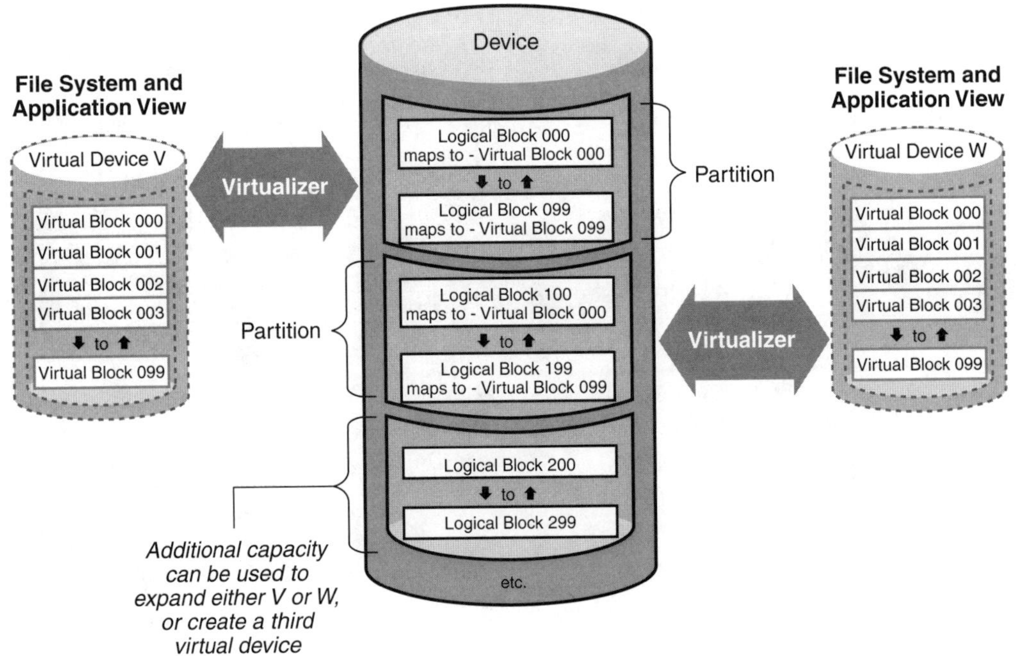

▼ **FIGURE 7–3** *Partitioning*

translation is most suitable for combining odd segments of otherwise unused storage capacity for easier management and for arrays whose capacity must be able to expand rapidly with no impact on applications.

SMALLER VIRTUAL DEVICES: PARTITIONING

Just as virtualizers can concatenate storage devices into larger virtual ones, they can **partition** the capacity of large devices or arrays into smaller virtual devices for technical feasibility or administrative convenience. Partitioning may be thought of as the opposite of concatenation. A single device's storage capacity is subdivided into smaller virtual devices. Figure 7–3 represents a storage device (or array) with two partitions occupying parts of its capacity, as well as additional capacity as yet unallocated to a virtual device.

Each storage network or RAID system-based virtual device created by partitioning has a unique I/O bus or storage network address on which it

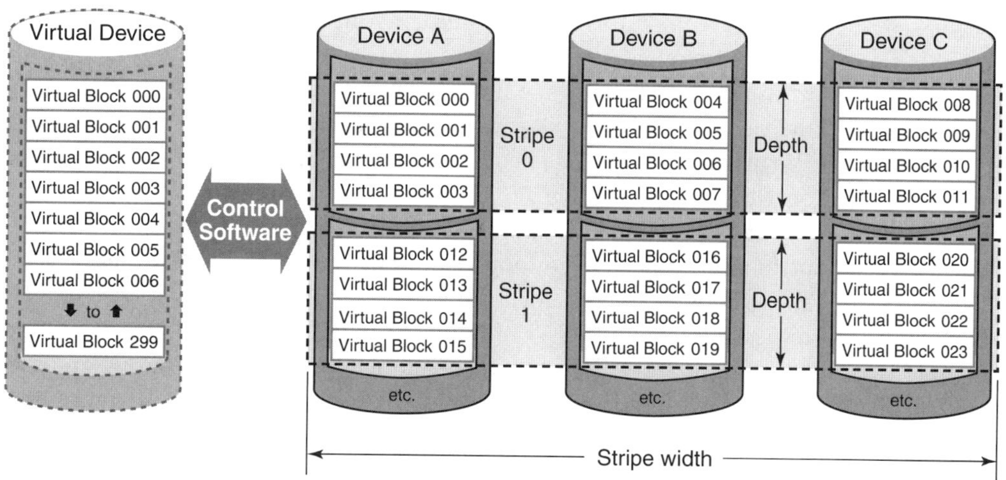

▼ **FIGURE 7–4** *A Disk Array with Striped Block Addressing*

receives I/O commands. Server-based volume managers can also *partition* the arrays that they create. In this case, the volume manager converts between the virtual device name and an I/O bus or storage network address and starting block number for the partition.

UNIX and Windows operating systems without volume managers also employ storage device partitioning to subdivide the capacity of storage devices for the purpose of creating multiple file systems. In this case, the operating system itself converts partition block addresses used by file systems and applications into storage device addresses and issues I/O commands to the underlying storage device.

BLOCK ADDRESS STRIPING

The most frequently used technique to convert virtual device block addresses to LBA counterparts is to *stripe* them across an array's devices in a repeating pattern. Figure 7–4 illustrates block address striping in a three-device array.[4]

4. Figure 7–4 illustrates unrealistically small devices in order to demonstrate the principle without making the drawing unnecessarily complex. A 72-gigabyte disk drive contains about 144 million blocks; a virtual device representing an array of three 72-gigabyte drives would have 432 million blocks of storage capacity.

Figure 7–4 illustrates a 300-block virtual device made up of 100 blocks of storage capacity from each of three devices. The striping control software translates the first four virtual block addresses to Device A, the next four to Device B, and the next four to Device C. The fourth group (Virtual Blocks 12–15) is converted to the second group of four blocks on Device A, the fifth group to Device B, and so forth.

In the example of Figure 7–4, virtual blocks are divided into groups of four, and successive groups are located on successive devices. Successive groups of virtual blocks located at corresponding locations on their respective devices (for example, Virtual Blocks 000–003, 004–007, and 008–011) are called a **stripe.** The number of blocks in a group (four in the example) is called the array's **stripe depth.**[5] The stripe depth multiplied by the number of devices in the array (the **stripe width**) is called the **stripe size.** The stripe size of the array depicted in Figure 7–4 is twelve blocks.

With this address conversion algorithm, it is easy to translate any virtual disk block number to a logical block on a device. The first step is to determine the stripe in which the block resides by dividing the virtual block number by the array's stripe size (12 in the example). The quotient is the number of the stripe containing the block (with stripe 0 containing the lowest numbered virtual blocks); the remainder is the block's relative location within the stripe.

The next step is to divide this remainder by the array's stripe depth. The quotient represents the disk on which the block is located (0 = Device A, 1 = Device B, and 2 = Device C in the example); the remainder is the block number within the stripe.

The final step is to multiply the stripe number by the stripe depth, and add the product to the relative block number. The result is a logical block number to be used as a starting address in commands to the disk containing the data.

For example, if an application makes a request to read or write virtual block 18, as illustrated in Figure 7–5, the first computation is:

$$\text{Stripe number} = \text{quotient}[18/12] = 1$$

$$\text{Block number within stripe} = \text{remainder}[18/12] = 6$$

5. In practice, stripe depths are typically between 150 and 300 blocks.

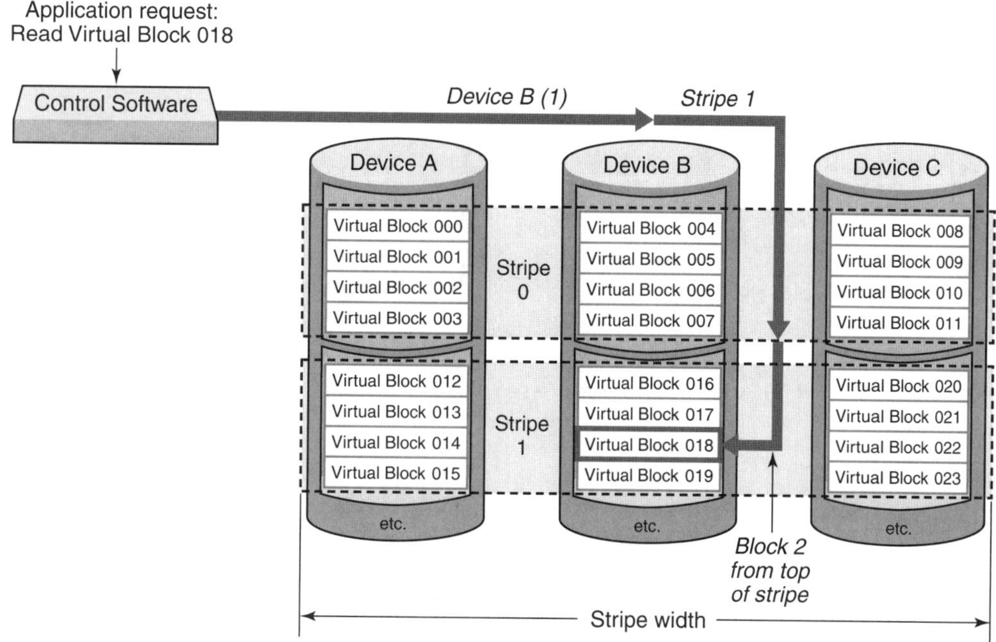

▼ **FIGURE 7–5** *Locating Data Blocks in a Striped Array*

Next:

$$\text{Device} = \text{quotient}[6/4] = 1 \text{ (i.e., Disk B)}$$

$$\text{Block within stripe} = \text{remainder}[6/4] = 2$$

Thus, the array's control software must access block 2 in stripe 1 on Device B. In an I/O command, such as a SCSI **Command Data Block (CDB),** which requires logical block addresses, control software would address its I/O request to:

$$\begin{aligned}\text{LBA} &= \text{stripe number} \times \text{stripe depth} + \text{block within stripe}\\ &= 1 \times 4 + 2 = 6\end{aligned}$$

Thus, when presented with an application request to read or write virtual disk block 18 in this array, control software would address a read request to block 6 of Device B. Any virtual block address can be converted using this algorithm.

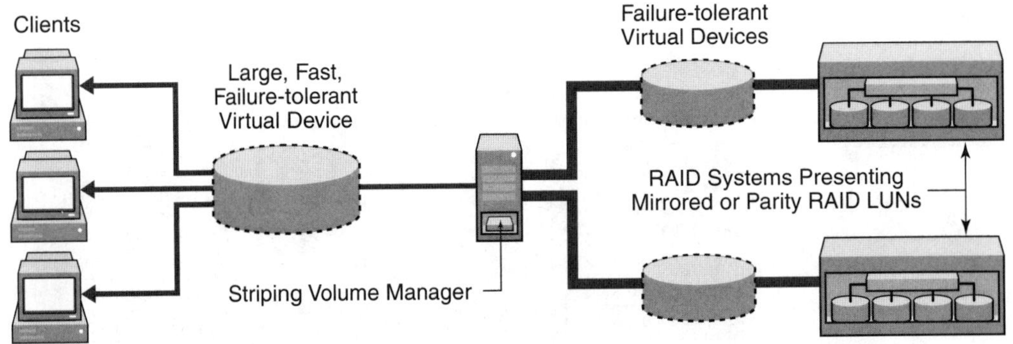

▼ **FIGURE 7–6** *Server-Based Striping of RAID System-Based Arrays*

APPLICATIONS FOR ARRAYS WITH STRIPED BLOCK ADDRESSING

Figure 7–4 does not represent a RAID array, because there is no redundant check data. All of the devices' logical blocks correspond to virtual blocks in which user data can be stored. Such an array is called a *striped*, or *RAID Level 0* array, although strictly speaking, the RAID designation is inappropriate.

Striped arrays have a higher probability of failure than individual devices (when any device fails, all data in the array becomes inaccessible), but are nonetheless appropriate for data of low permanent value, or data that can be easily reconstructed.

Server- or storage network-based striping is useful for aggregating the capacity and performance of LUNs presented by RAID system-based mirrored or parity RAID arrays. Figure 7–6 illustrates this and the use of striping to aggregate failure-tolerant LUNs presented by RAID systems into a single larger virtual device. The *large, fast, failure-tolerant virtual device* presented to clients is easier to manage, and will generally outperform the two *failure-tolerant virtual devices* presented individually due to load balancing. Server- or network-based mirroring can similarly enhance RAID system availability.

BLOCK ADDRESS STRIPING AND PARITY RAID

Although it enhances I/O performance, striped block addressing also increases both the probability of data loss and the impact of device fail-

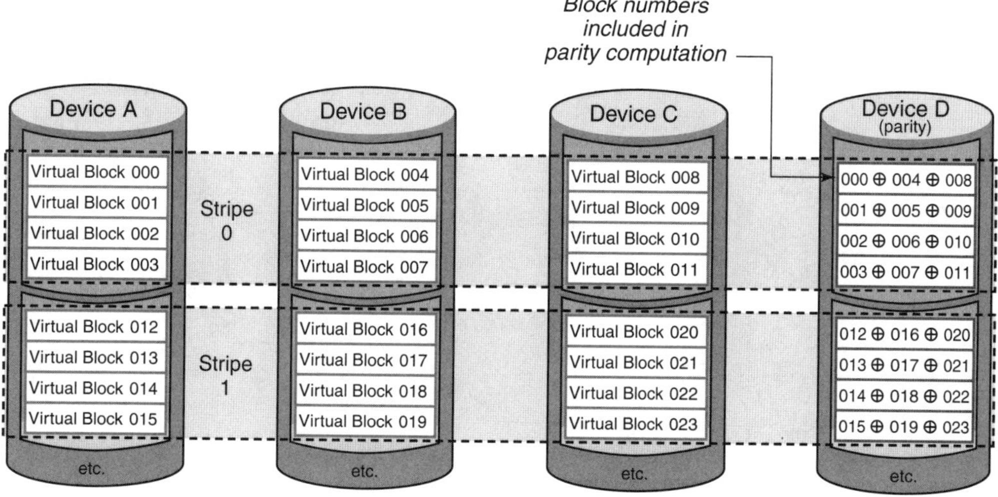

▼ **FIGURE 7–7** *Block Address Striping with a Parity RAID Device (RAID Level 3 or 4)*

ure. If a device in a striped array fails, there is no reasonable way to recover *any* of the data in the array. Therefore, when striping is used to improve performance, it is crucial to protect it against device failure. Block address striping and RAID redundancy are a natural match for each other. Figure 7–7 illustrates a striped array augmented with a "parity device" for redundancy. This is the check data layout that defined RAID Levels 3 and 4 in "A Case for Redundant Arrays of Inexpensive Disks."

Device D in Figure 7–7 holds no user data. Each of its blocks stores **XOR** parity of the corresponding blocks on the array's other three devices. Thus, Block 000 of Device D contains the bit-by-bit **XOR** of the contents of Virtual Blocks 000, 004, and 008, and so forth. As noted in Chapter 4, no matter how many devices a parity RAID array includes, the capacity of one device is sufficient for parity check data. Hardware overhead cost decreases with larger numbers of devices, but so does the level of protection. Arrays such as that depicted in Figure 7–7 provide RAID data protection levels and the I/O performance benefits of striping . . . almost.

The Parity Device Bottleneck

One important goal of block address striping is I/O load balancing. Even with a perfectly balanced I/O load of overlapping writes to the array depicted in Figure 7–7, there is a natural bottleneck. Each application

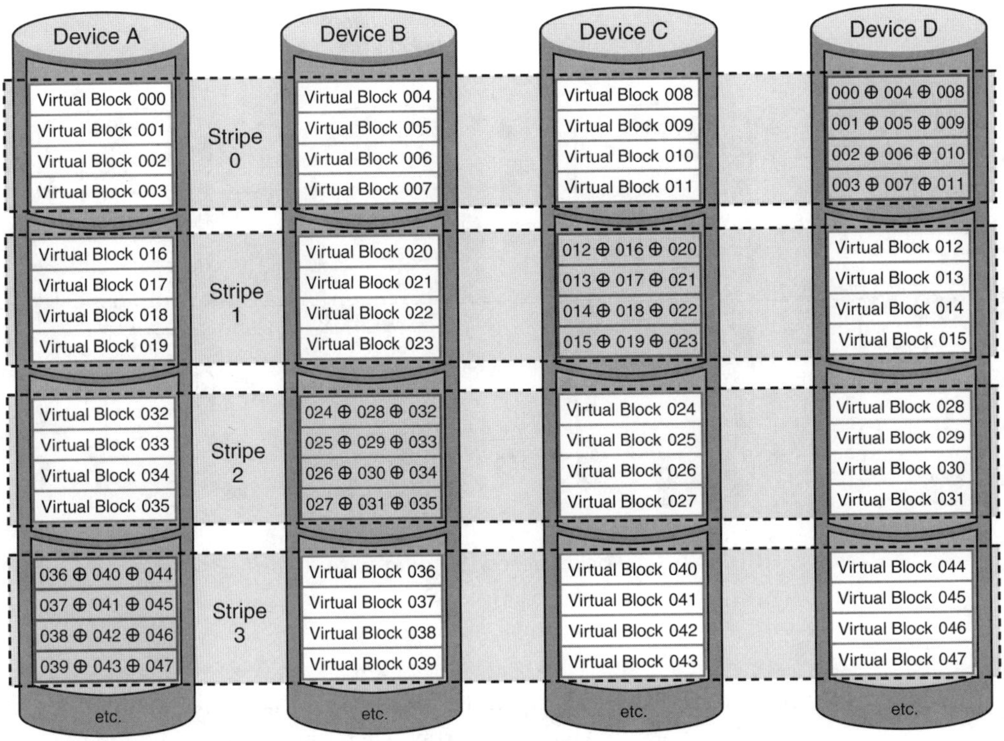

▼ **FIGURE 7–8** *Block Address Striping with Interleaved Parity (RAID Level 5)*

write request results in a series of device reads and writes to update parity. In particular, every application write requires that block(s) on Device D (the "parity device") be overwritten, making it a write performance limitation. Application writes cannot be executed at a rate any greater than about half the average speed with which the parity device can satisfy I/O requests.

This bottleneck was discerned by early RAID researchers, who devised a means of balancing parity I/O load across an entire array by interleaving parity with striped user data, distributing both across all devices. Figure 7–8 illustrates a striped array with interleaved parity.

The concept of parity interleaving is simple. Parity blocks for the first stripe are stored on the array's "rightmost" device. Parity blocks for the second stripe are stored on the device to its left, and so forth. In the example of Figure 7–8, the parity blocks for Stripe 4 (not shown) would be located on Device D, those for Stripe 5 on Device C, and so forth.

Distributing parity across all of an array's devices balances the "overhead" I/O that results from parity updates. Parity updates must occur, but they are not directed to a single device. In the best case, an array with interleaved parity can execute random application write requests at about one-fourth the combined capacity of all the devices in the array.

With or without a cache to mask the effect of writing, interleaved parity improves array performance, so most arrays today use this technique. The combination of interleaved parity check data and user data block address striping was called RAID Level 5 in "A Case for Redundant Arrays of Inexpensive Disks." The "5" does not refer to the number of devices in the array as is sometimes thought. RAID Level 5 arrays with as few as three and as many as 10 devices are routinely implemented. Typically, however, RAID Level 5 arrays are configured with between four and ten devices, as illustrated in Figure 4-5.

CHAPTER SUMMARY

- The conversion between virtual disk block addresses and logical block addresses to which I/O commands can be addressed is sometimes called *mapping*.
- There are two basic types of block address conversion: table lookup and algorithmic. Block storage device virtualization typically uses table lookup for infrequently changing data such as array membership. Algorithms are used to convert between virtual device and logical block addresses.
- Concatenation, partitioning, and striping are the three block address conversion algorithms used most often in block storage device virtualization.
- The main advantage of concatenation is administrative convenience. Its load balancing properties are highly application and file system layout dependent.
- Partitioning is primarily useful for subdividing large logical units, such as LUNs presented by RAID systems, into more convenient administrative units.
- Striping is the most prevalent form of address conversion used in block virtualization because it tends to balance I/O load across I/O resources.
- Server- and network-based striping done by volume managers or appliances, respectively, can aggregate the capacity and performance

of failure-tolerant (e.g., mirrored or parity RAID) LUNs presented by RAID systems.

- Parity RAID data protection is usually combined with block address striping. In a parity RAID array, the capacity of one device is required to hold parity check data, no matter how many devices the array includes.
- To mitigate the parity RAID write bottleneck, parity is usually distributed across an array's devices. Distributing parity does not eliminate parity RAID small write overhead, but it does mitigate the bottleneck of a single parity device. The combination of striped data and distributed parity is called RAID Level 5.

CHAPTER 8

It is not the strongest of the species that survives, nor the most intelligent; it is the one that is most adaptable to change.

—CHARLES ROBERT DARWIN

Performance of Virtual Block Storage

In this chapter . . .

- The two types of I/O-intensive applications
- Data block striping and its impact on I/O performance
- How mirroring and parity interact with data block striping

Virtual block storage devices have the same essential properties as the physical devices[1] of which they are made up. They store data persistently in fixed-length blocks that are individually addressable; they can overwrite the data in any block any number of times; and so forth. They improve upon physical device properties, for example by aggregating the capacity of multiple devices to simplify management. Probably the two most important improvements are in data availability and I/O performance. Virtual storage devices improve data availability by protecting against component failures. This protection adds "overhead" I/O and computation to the execution of application requests, which alters virtual device performance (relative to physical device performance) in ways that can impact applications significantly. This chapter describes the effect of block address striping and mirroring, as well as parity RAID, on virtual device I/O performance.

1. As in other chapters, the term *physical device* refers collectively to disk drives and LUNs presented by RAID systems.

APPLICATION I/O PERFORMANCE CHARACTERISTICS

Block address striping improves I/O performance for most I/O-intensive applications.[2] To understand why, it is helpful to recognize that nearly all I/O-intensive applications fall into one of two broad categories:

- ***I/O request intensive:*** These applications typically process transactions, making large numbers of I/O requests for relatively small amounts of randomly addressed data. They usually consist of several concurrent execution threads, so many of their I/O requests are made without waiting for previous requests to complete, and are thus available to the I/O system for concurrent processing.
- ***Data transfer intensive:*** These applications read and write long sequential streams of data. Scientific, engineering, graphics, video, and other multimedia applications typically have this characteristic. These applications typically process one file at a time. Their I/O requests usually specify large amounts of data, and are often issued ahead of time ("double buffered") to minimize idle time.

BLOCK ADDRESS STRIPING AND I/O PERFORMANCE

Striping block addresses across an array of devices, as described in Chapter 7, improves the performance of both I/O request-intensive and data transfer-intensive applications for different reasons. Most virtualizers support user adjustment of array stripe depth. If an application's I/O characteristics are highly predictable, stripe depth adjustment can be used to "tune" an array to perform optimally with one type of I/O load or the other.

Block Address Striping and I/O Request-Intensive Applications

The performance of I/O request-intensive applications is often limited by how fast storage devices can execute I/O requests. A typical disk drive takes about 10 milliseconds to seek, rotate, and transfer data for a single small request (around 4 kilobytes). The upper limit on the rate at which a drive can execute randomly addressed small requests is therefore about

2. An *I/O-intensive* application is one whose performance is primarily determined by the speed at which its I/O requests are executed.

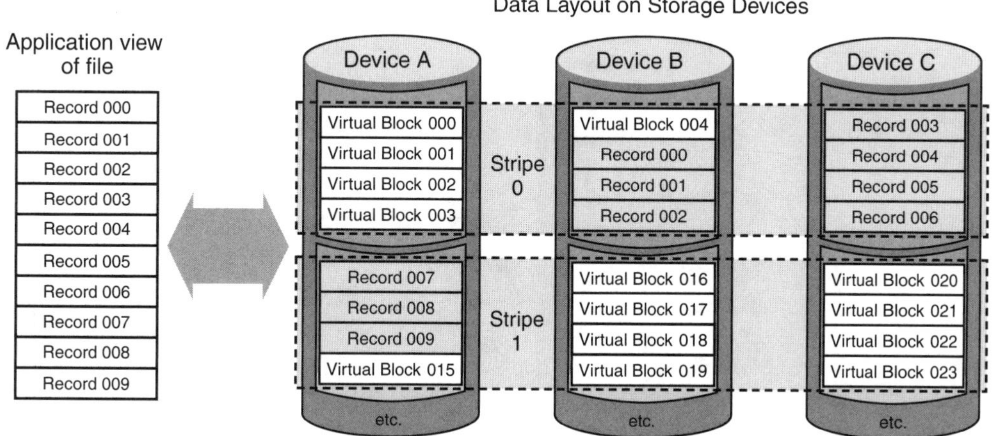

▼ **FIGURE 8–1** *Effect of Block Address Striping on File Location*

100 per second (*1,000 milliseconds per second ÷ 10 milliseconds per request = 100 requests per second*). Many enterprise applications require substantially more than this.

In principle, an application's maximum I/O request execution capability should be increased by breaking its data into several files and storing each on a separate device. This technique would multiply the maximum I/O request processing capability available to the application by the number of devices used. In practice, however, there are some limitations to this scheme:

- ▼ It is awkward to implement, inflexible to use, and difficult to maintain.
- ▼ Application I/O requests do not necessarily distribute evenly across the devices.

So while data is sometimes divided into multiple carefully positioned files, particularly with large applications, it is not a guaranteed path to better I/O performance.

Block address striping, on the other hand, *does* tend to balance application I/O load uniformly across storage devices, eliminating the need to split data into multiple files. An application that uses a striped array "sees" one large device. Physically, however, data is spread across the array's devices, as Figure 8–1 suggests.

Figure 8–1 shows a ten-block file stored on a three-device striped array with a stripe depth of four blocks. Virtual storage allocated to the

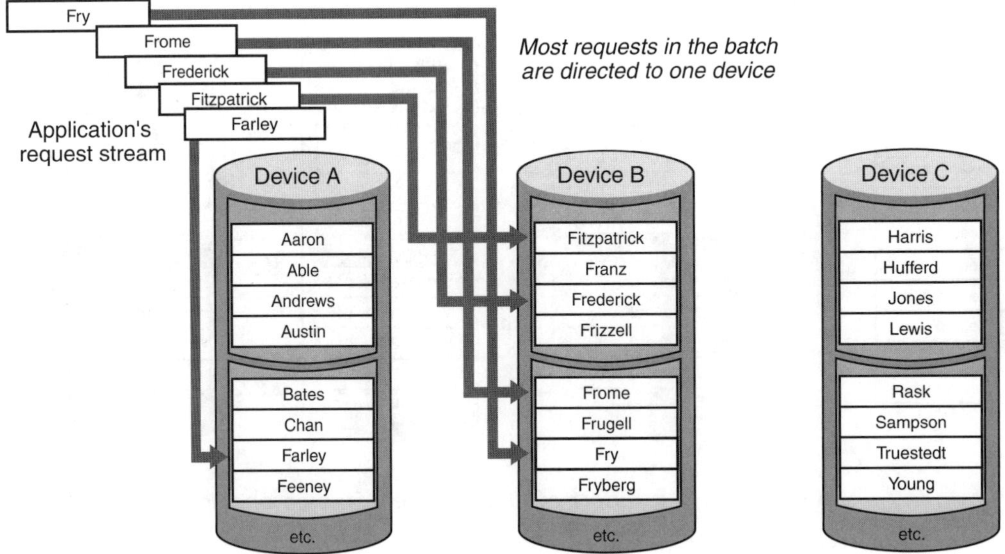

▼ **FIGURE 8–2** *Nonuniform I/O Request Distribution in a Concatenated Array*

file starts at Virtual Block 5, which is located on Device B. To applications and file systems, the file appears to be stored in consecutive storage device blocks. In fact, however, the file's records are spread across the array's three devices.

If an application were to access the records in this file with a uniform random distribution of record numbers (as is common in transaction processing), about 30% of the requests would be executed by Device A, 30% by Device B, and 40% by Device C. The larger a file, the more evenly the blocks it occupies are distributed across the devices comprising a striped array.

Uniformly distributed requests for records in files that are large compared to individual storage device capacity tend to distribute uniformly across the devices of both concatenated and striped arrays. When request distribution is *not* uniform, however, as for example when a batch process updates records in alphabetical order, I/O load imbalance can result in concatenated arrays, as Figure 8–2 suggests.

In Figure 8–2, most accesses to records beginning with the letter F are directed to Device B, since it holds most of that part of the file. Devices

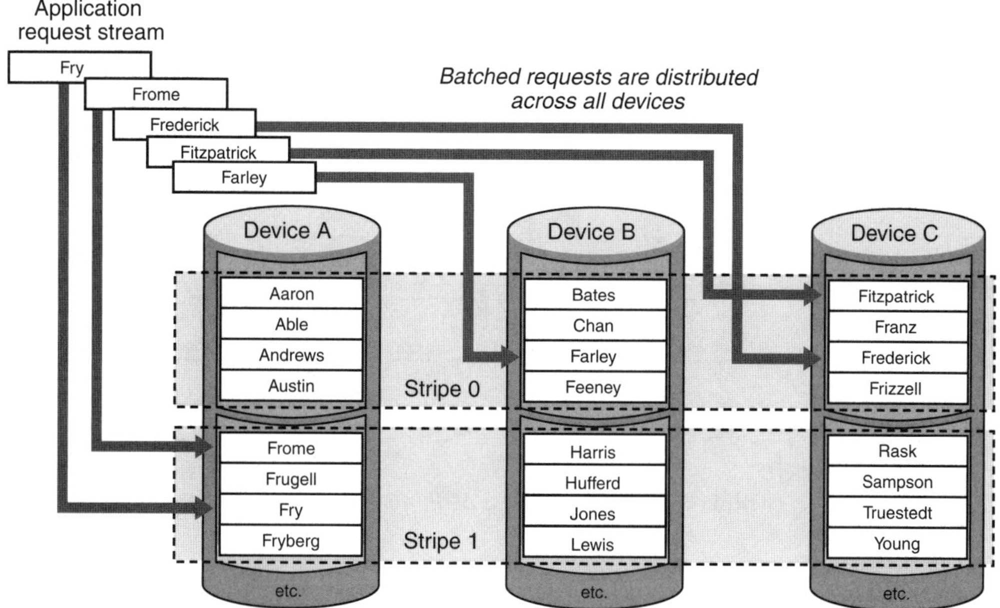

▼ **FIGURE 8–3** *Effect of Block Address Striping on I/O Request Distribution*

A and C remain nearly idle. Chapter 7 describes how a similar phenomenon can occur with small files. A small file is likely to be entirely contained on a single device in a concatenated array (Figure 7–2), so other devices would remain idle, no matter how frequently the small file were accessed.

By contrast, in arrays with striped block addressing, even nonuniformly distributed random access patterns tend to distribute I/O load across all devices, as Figure 8–3 suggests. Even when application I/O patterns change, I/O request loads tend to remain balanced across the devices that comprise an array.

Block address striping does not reduce execution time for any single I/O request; instead, it improves **average response time** for a large number of requests by reducing the average time a request must wait for others to complete before it can be executed. Striping only improves application performance if at least some I/O requests overlap with each other in time. This differs from the way in which striping improves the performance of data transfer-intensive applications.

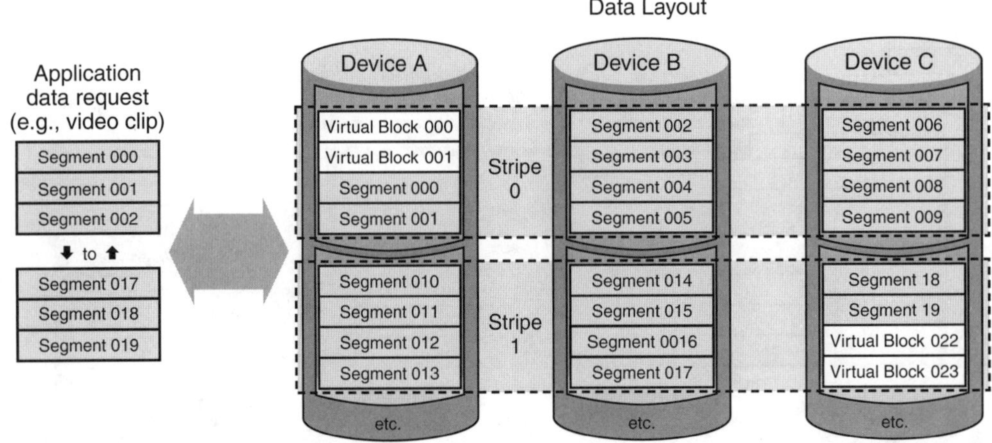

▼ **FIGURE 8–4** *Block Address Striping and Data Transfer-Intensive Applications*

Block Address Striping and Data Transfer-Intensive Applications

A data transfer-intensive application's I/O goal is to move a large amount of data as quickly as possible. These applications usually process sequentially accessed files that occupy thousands of consecutively numbered blocks.

If a data transfer-intensive application's data is stored on one device, application I/O performance is limited by the speed with which the device can read or write a large continuous data stream. Today's high-performance disk drives typically transfer data at an average of 25–40 megabytes/second. (RAID systems and I/O interfaces like ATA and SCSI are capable of higher speeds, but a single disk drive can only deliver or absorb data as fast as disk media can rotate past a head.)

If a data transfer-intensive application uses a striped array, however, multiple devices cooperate to transfer data faster. Figure 8–4 illustrates a data transfer-intensive application's use of a striped array as well as a request to read a large file consisting of 20 consecutive *segments.*[3] (Segments have no intrinsic meaning to applications; they are artificial subdivisions of the file for buffer management purposes.) When an

3. For simplicity, the segments are shown as disk blocks. In practice, they would be much larger, as would both disk capacity and stripe depth. Again, artificially small parameters are used to keep diagrams simple.

application reads or writes this file, it reads or writes the entire file, and the faster the transfer, the better. In the extreme, an application might make one I/O request to the virtual device for the entire file. The array's control software would translate such a request into:

1. A request to Device A for Segments 000 and 001
2. A request to Device B for Segments 002 through 005
3. A request to Device C for Segments 006 through 009
4. A request to Device A for Segments 010 through 013
5. A request to Device B for Segments 014 through 017
6. A request to Device C for Segments 018 and 019

Because the first three requests are addressed to different devices, they can execute simultaneously. This reduces data transfer time compared to a transfer from a single device. The control software can make the fourth request as soon as the first completes, the fifth as soon as the second completes, and the sixth as soon as the third completes.[4] Overall data transfer time would be about the time to transfer the eight segments from Device B, just a little over a third of the data transfer time for the entire file from one device.

Summarizing the Effect of Block Address Striping on I/O Performance

Figure 8–5 is a qualitative comparison of the I/O performance of a striped array with that of a single device. The faded icon at the center of the graph represents the baseline performance of a single device. The other two icons represent estimated striped array performance relative to that.

Figure 8–5 has two dimensions because there are two important ways to measure application I/O performance. One is *throughput,* or the amount of work accomplished per unit time. Throughput can be measured in requests per second or in bytes per second. The other important measure of I/O performance is average execution time for an individual request (not including time spent waiting to be executed).

The icon labeled "Small random reads and writes" in Figure 8–5 suggests that for I/O request-intensive applications, block address striping improves throughput relative to a single device, but does not change average request execution time. Throughput improves because striping tends

4. Features of many operating systems and I/O hardware called *scatter reading* and *gather writing* (described in Appendix C), further reduce the number of these operations to three.

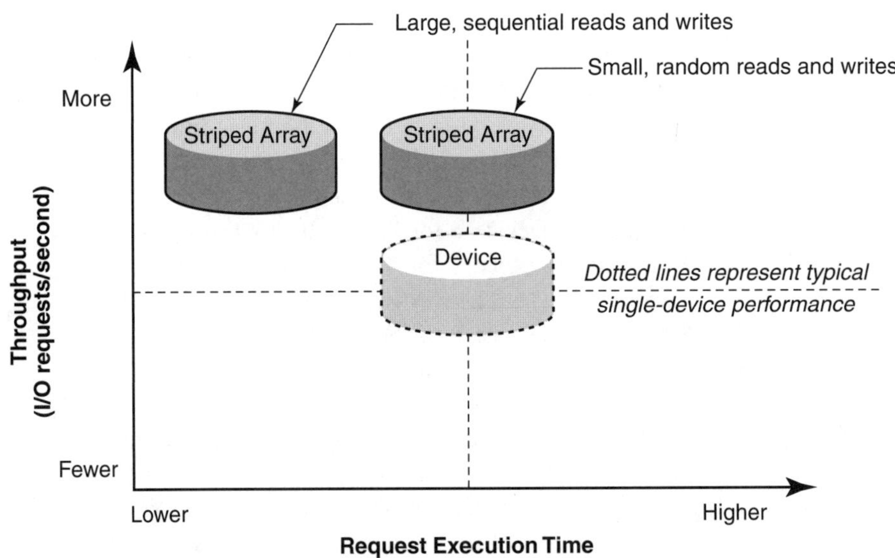

▼ **FIGURE 8–5** *Relative Performance of Striped Virtual Devices*

to balance the I/O requests across the devices, keeping several of them "busy" concurrently. Request execution time does not change because a single device executes most requests in both cases.

Even though request execution time does not change, time spent waiting for previous requests to complete is less with a striped array than with a single device. Users are likely to perceive that requests execute faster, simply because they start executing sooner after they are issued. Of course, if there is nothing to wait for, a request to a striped array completes in about the same time as a similar request to a single device. As a striped array gets busier, its performance relative to a single device appears to improve, up to the point at which it *saturates* (all of its devices are working at full capacity).

I/O loads of large sequential requests also perform better with striped arrays. In this case, both throughput and request execution time improve relative to those of a single device, as the icon labeled "Large sequential reads and writes" in Figure 8–5 suggests. Individual request execution time is lower because data transfer (which accounts for most of it) is done concurrently by some or all of the array's devices. Throughput is greater because each request executes in less time, so a continuous stream of requests completes faster. In other words, more work gets done per unit time.

PARITY RAID AND I/O PERFORMANCE

Writing Data to a RAID Array

RAID data protection "works" because parity blocks always represent the **XOR** of the data blocks to which they correspond, as Figure 4–7 and Figure 4–8 (Chapter 4) illustrate. Each time an application writes data to a virtual block, the parity that protects that block becomes invalid, and must be updated. For example, if an application writes Virtual Block 012 in the array illustrated in Figure 8–6 (below), the contents of the corresponding parity block on Device D must be changed from

(old) Block 012 contents ⊕ Block 016 contents ⊕ Block 020 contents

to

(new) Block 012 contents ⊕ Block 016 contents ⊕ Block 020 contents

In other words, when an application writes Virtual Block 012, the parity RAID control software must:

- Read the contents of Virtual Block 016 into an internal buffer
- Read the contents of Virtual Block 020 into an internal buffer
- Compute the **XOR** of Virtual Blocks 016 and 020
- Compute the **XOR** of the above result with the (new) contents for Virtual Block 012
- Make a log entry, either in nonvolatile memory or on a disk, indicating that data is being updated
- Write the new contents of Virtual Block 012 to Device A
- Write the new parity check data to Device D
- Make a further log entry, indicating that the update is complete[5]

Figure 8–6 illustrates the reads and writes to devices in the array illustrated in Figure 7–7 that are required by a single application write request to the virtual device.

An Important Optimization for Small Writes

A useful property of the **XOR** function is that adding the same number to an **XOR** sum twice produces the same result as not adding it at all. This

---

5. A small performance optimization can be achieved by doing this log write "lazily," as the consequences of it not getting done are small.

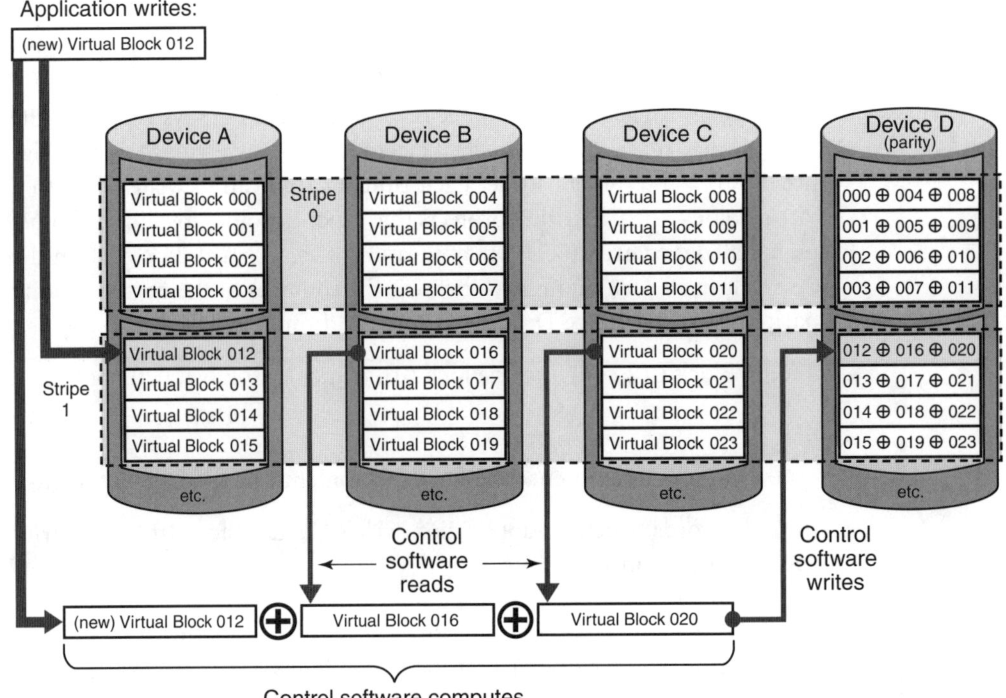

▼ **FIGURE 8–6** *Parity RAID Write Algorithm*

can be seen by observing that the **XOR** of a binary number with itself is zero. This property can be used to simplify RAID parity updates.

$$\text{(old) Block 012 contents} \oplus \text{(old) parity}$$

is equivalent to:

$$\text{(old) Block 012 contents} \oplus$$
$$[\text{(old) Block 012 contents} \oplus \text{Block 016 contents} \oplus \text{Block 020 contents}]$$

But the **XOR** operation is associative, meaning that the order in which a series of **XOR** operations is performed is immaterial (i.e., $[A \oplus B] \oplus C$ produces the same result as $A \oplus [B \oplus C]$). Therefore, this expression can be rearranged as:

$$[\text{(old) Block 012 contents} \oplus \text{(old) Block 012 contents}] \oplus$$
$$\text{Block 016 contents} \oplus \text{Block 020 contents}$$

which is equal to:

$$\text{Block 016 contents} \oplus \text{Block 020 contents.}$$

In other words, the **XOR** of the data to be replaced with its corresponding parity is equal to the **XOR** of the other corresponding user data blocks in the array. This is true no matter how many devices a parity RAID array contains.

This property suggests an alternate technique for updating parity:

- Read the data block to be replaced
- Read the corresponding parity block
- Compute the **XOR** of the two

These steps eliminate the "old" data's contribution to the parity, but leave all other blocks' contributions intact. Computing the **XOR** of this result with the "new" data written by the application gives the correct parity for the new data. Expressed symbolically, updated parity for the above example would be computed as:

$$\text{(new)parity} = \text{(old)parity} \oplus \text{(old)Block 012 contents} \oplus \text{(new)Block 012 contents}$$

Using this technique, it is never necessary to access more than two devices (the device to which application data is to be written and the one containing its parity) to execute a single-block application write to a virtual device. The sequence of steps for updating Block 012 (Figure 8–7) would be:

- Read Virtual Block 012 contents into an internal buffer
- Read the corresponding parity block on Device D into an internal buffer
- Compute the **XOR** of the two
- Compute the **XOR** of the above result with the (new) Virtual Block 012 contents
- Make a log entry, either in nonvolatile memory or on a disk, indicating that data is being updated[6]
- Write the new contents of Virtual Block 012 to Disk A
- Write the new parity check data to Device D
- Make a log entry indicating that the update is complete

The number of read, write, and computation steps using this algorithm is identical to that in the preceding example. For arrays with five or more devices, however, this algorithm is preferable, because it never

6. Log entries are not shown in the figures. They record which blocks of data are being modified, and can greatly shorten the time required to validate a RAID array's data integrity after a crash of the control software.

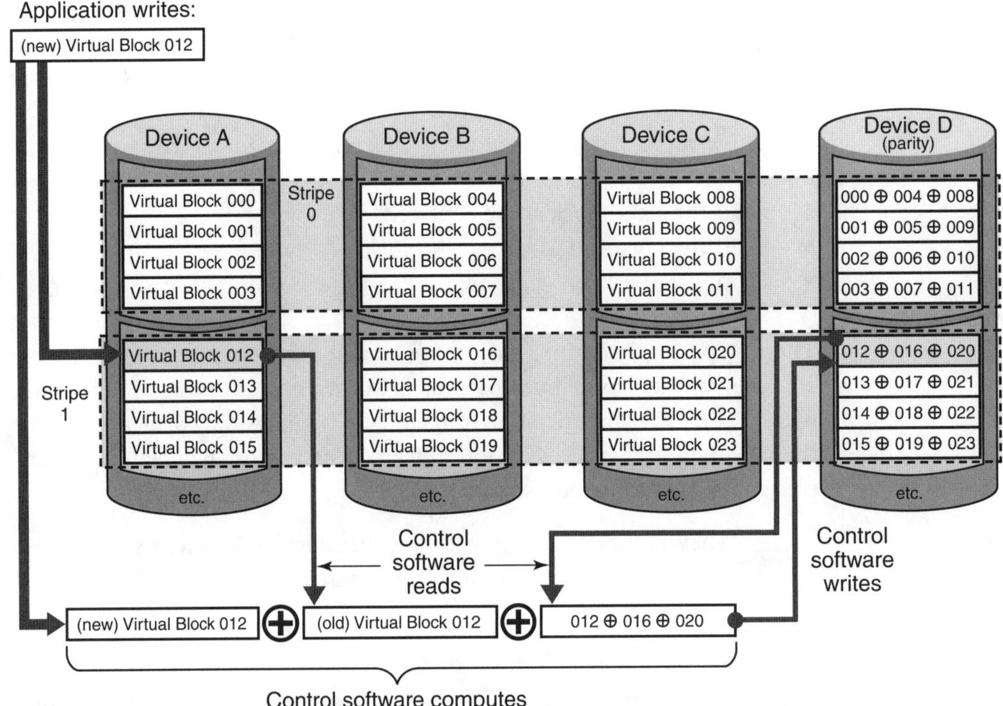

▼ **FIGURE 8–7** *Optimized Parity RAID Write Algorithm*

requires accessing more than two devices, whereas the preceding algorithm would require that all devices containing user data unmodified by the application's write be read. Parity RAID control software therefore uses this algorithm wherever possible.[7]

An Important Optimization for Large Writes

Very large application write requests may overwrite all of the data in a stripe. In Figure 8–7, for example, an application request to write Virtual Blocks 12–23 would cause all user data in Stripe 1 to be overwritten.

7. These examples deal with the case of an application write of a single block, which always maps to one device in a parity RAID array. The same algorithms are valid for application writes of any number of consecutive blocks that map to a single device. More complicated scenarios arise when an application write maps to blocks on two or more devices.

When an entire stripe is overwritten, the new stripe's parity can be computed entirely from the data supplied with the application's request. There is no need to read "old" data or parity as there is with writes that modify only part of a stripe. Once new parity has been computed, the entire stripe, both data and parity, can be written at once. This speeds things up, because the large data transfer is partitioned and written concurrently to multiple devices, as with the striped array in the example of Figure 8–4.

Even with these optimizations, the "extra" computation and I/O consumed by parity RAID update algorithms take time and consume resources. Many storage users considered early RAID systems unusable because of this "write penalty." In today's RAID systems, the write penalty is largely hidden from applications through the use of nonvolatile cache memory.[8] In either case, with applications that do a lot of writing it is still possible to distinguish between the performance of a disk or striped array and the performance of a parity RAID array.

Summary of Parity RAID I/O Performance

Figure 8–8 summarizes the performance of a parity RAID array relative to that of a single device. As with Figure 8–7, this summary reflects only disk and control software operations, and does not include the effect of write-back cache, hardware-assisted **XOR** computations, or other performance optimizations.

As Figure 8–8 suggests, parity RAID typically executes both large sequential and small random read requests at higher throughput than a single device. This is due to the load balancing that results from striping data across devices as shown in the example of Figure 8–4. When writing to a parity RAID array, however, there is simply more work to be done. A parity RAID array therefore takes longer to complete an application request than does a single device. For writes that encompass entire stripes of data, this penalty can be mitigated by precomputing parity. For small writes, however, an entire set of operations equivalent to those required to update Block 012 in the example of Figure 8–7 must be performed, resulting in significantly more I/O (4 times) and computation than is necessary to simply write data to a disk.

---

8. Nonvolatile memory is not usually available to server-based virtualizers, so it is more difficult for them to hide the write penalty. For this reason (among others) a combination of mirroring and striping is generally preferable with server-based virtualization.

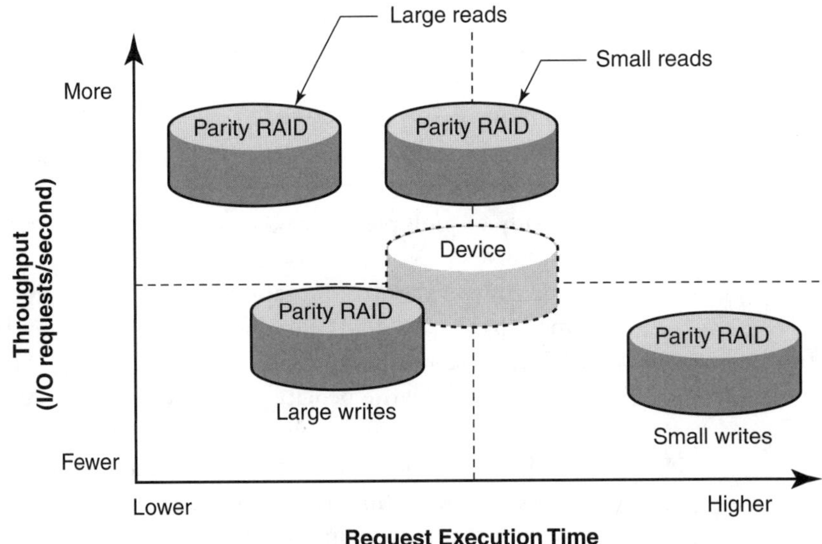

▼ **FIGURE 8–8** *Relative Performance of Parity RAID Arrays*

STRIPING WITH MIRRORING

Block address striping can be combined with mirrored data protection to create very large virtual devices, as Figure 8–9 illustrates. In the example of Figure 8–9, Devices A, B, and C effectively form a striped array, as do Devices D, E, and F. The array's control software chooses a device to satisfy each client read request, and mirrors all application writes to both striped arrays. Combining striping and mirroring has several advantages:

- Virtual devices of very large capacity can be created. The only inherent limitation on the capacity of a virtual device of this type is the operating system's or I/O bus's ability to address the number of virtual blocks it contains.
- I/O performance is high for both I/O request-intensive and data transfer-intensive applications due to striping. In addition, there is the opportunity for virtualization control software to make a "least busy" choice for each read request.
- The "write penalty" (extra I/O required to keep check data synchronized with user data—in this case, writing a second copy concurrently with the first) is much lower for mirrored arrays than for parity RAID ones.
- Data availability is very good. Striped and mirrored arrays can tolerate more than one disk failure in some circumstances.

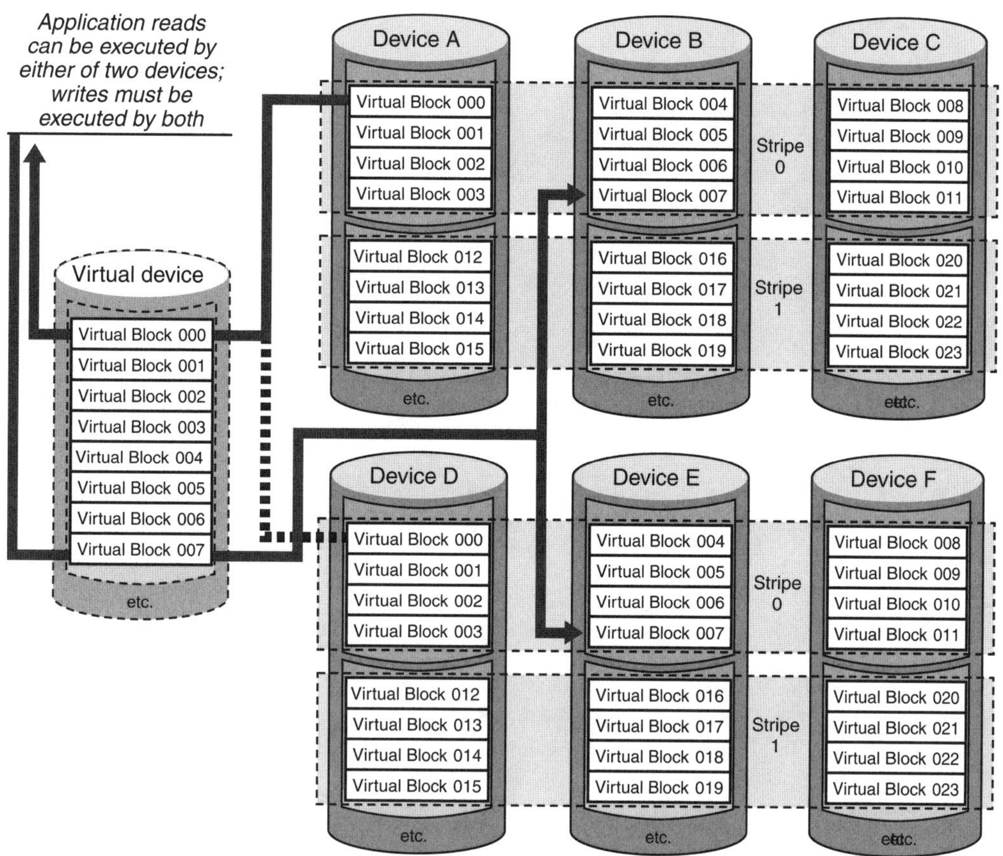

▼ **FIGURE 8–9** *Block Address Striping Combined with Mirroring*

- Because it is not computationally intensive, the combination of striping and mirroring is very well suited to server-based implementations.
- Arrays with three or more mirrors enable a mirror to be split for backup or data analysis without impacting application performance or online data protection.

About the only drawback to arrays of striped and mirrored devices is hardware component cost—the primary factor that originally motivated parity RAID. Users must purchase, enclose, power, cool, and operate two or three times as much storage as their business data requires. In the days of ten dollar per megabyte disk storage, keeping two or three copies of data online was prohibitively expensive. Today, with high-performance server disk prices in the neighborhood of a penny per megabyte (includ-

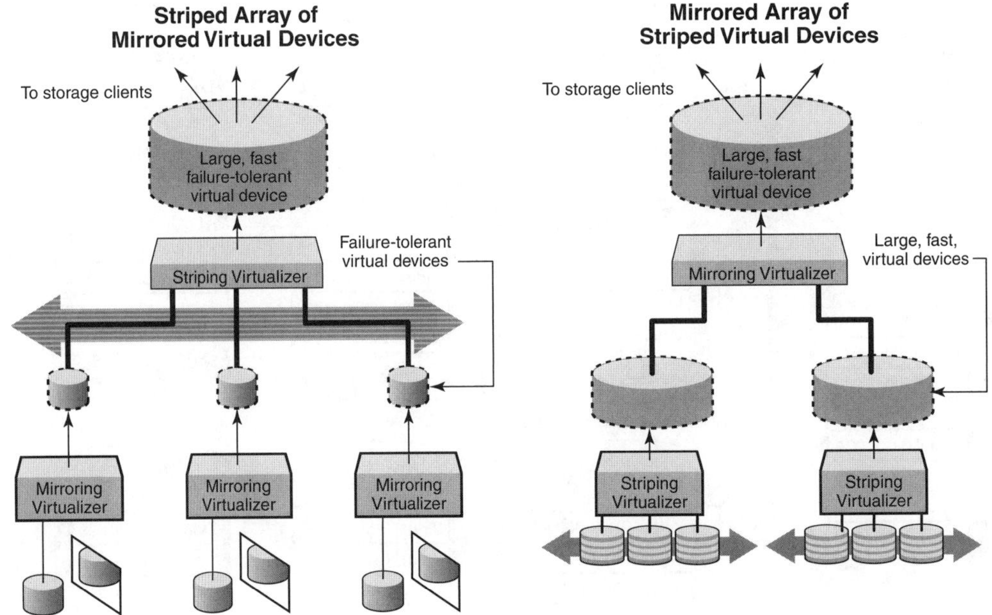

▼ **FIGURE 8–10** *Block Address Striping Combined with Mirroring*

ing housing, power, and cooling), and RAID system prices not much higher, striped and mirrored storage is very attractive for much of enterprise online data.

Striped Mirrors or Mirrored Stripes?

Combining block address striping with mirrored data protection is common, particularly when virtualizers at multiple levels are employed. For example, it is fairly common practice to use a server-based volume manager to stripe block addresses across mirrored LUNs presented by a RAID system. Server-based mirroring of RAID system-based striped LUNs is also possible. In general, a storage architect can:

- Mirror the storage capacity of two striped arrays, as illustrated on the right side of Figure 8–10
- Stripe virtual block addresses across a collection of mirrored arrays, as illustrated on the left side of Figure 8–10

The inherent performance characteristics of these two alternatives are essentially equivalent. The failure tolerance story is different, however. The virtualizer that mirrors the two striped arrays on the right of Figure 8–10 has no visibility inside either. Nor do the striping virtualizers "know" that the virtual devices they present are to be mirrored. If a device fails, a striping virtualizer has no choice but to declare its entire array inaccessible, incapacitating all of its devices. Thus, a single device failure reduces a mirrored pair of striped arrays by half of its devices. A failure of any of the surviving devices results in array failure.

This contrasts with a virtualizer that stripes data across several virtual devices, each of which is a mirrored LUN, as the left side of Figure 8–10 illustrates. Again, neither layer of virtualization is aware of the other. If a mirror fails, only that device is lost. All of the other mirrored LUNs remain mirrored, providing the availability and performance enhancements of mirroring. Any device failure except that of the failed one's surviving mirror can be tolerated without failure of the array.

It is clear, therefore, that whenever the opportunity exists, striping block addresses across several mirrored arrays is superior to mirroring the block address spaces of two striped virtual devices.

CHAPTER SUMMARY

- I/O-intensive applications are typically either I/O request intensive or data transfer intensive, but not both.
- Striped block addressing benefits I/O request-intensive applications by its tendency to balance concurrent I/O requests across physical I/O resources.
- Striped block addressing benefits data transfer-intensive applications by splitting up long data transfers into parts, which it executes concurrently.
- Parity RAID has an inherent small write overhead, which can be mitigated (but not eliminated) by proper algorithm choice.
- Large writes to parity RAID arrays can be made to perform well by precomputing parity and writing full stripes to the array's devices.
- Striping is often combined with mirroring to increase capacity (as well as I/O performance for applications with I/O loads dominated by read requests).
- When there is a choice, as with hybrid arrays implemented, for example, by a combination of server-based volume management and RAID system control software, it is preferable to mirror raw storage and stripe data across the mirrored virtual disks rather than the reverse.

PART 2

IMPLEMENTATIONS

Once a new technology rolls over you, if you're not part of the steamroller, you're part of the road.

—STEWART BRAND

CHAPTER 9

Facts do not cease to exist because they are ignored.

—Aldous Leonard Huxley

Conventional Block Storage Virtualization

In this chapter . . .

- Where in the I/O path block virtualization can be implemented
- Virtualization in the RAID system
- Virtualization in the application server (volume managers)

The technology descriptions in Part 1 demonstrate that:

- Virtualizing block storage can both improve the quality of service delivered to enterprise information service users and reduce the cost of providing those services through better asset utilization and reduced management expense.
- Block storage virtualization consists of block address conversion and data protection techniques that have been used in volume managers and RAID systems for over a decade. Both RAID systems and volume managers are block storage virtualizers that can be used alone or in combination.
- Storage networks extend the scope of block storage virtualization beyond the server or RAID system to the data center and beyond.

Each of the three possible locations for implementing virtualization—server (volume manager), RAID system, and appliance in the storage network—has unique characteristics and limitations. Indeed, the best solutions are often constructed by combining multiple virtualizers to "stack" their benefits.

BLOCK STORAGE VIRTUALIZATION IMPLEMENTATIONS

Although they are sometimes hardware assisted, the two fundamental virtualization processes, failure protection by redundant check data and the conversion of virtual block addresses to storage device logical block addresses (LBAs), are essentially software techniques. Virtualization control software can execute in:

- ***Embedded RAID systems:*** Virtualization control software for these devices executes in processors on disk controller modules that connect to servers' internal I/O buses (e.g., PCI). It typically manages disk drives connected to one or more private Fibre Channel, SCSI, or ATA channels.
- ***External "bridge" RAID systems:*** These devices' virtualization control software executes in processors external to the server(s) the RAID system supports, and connected to them only by Fibre Channel or SCSI buses. External RAID systems typically form a bridge between their host buses and other Fibre Channel or SCSI buses that connect to disk drives. Most external RAID systems can connect to multiple servers, and most are capable of connecting to more disk drives than typical embedded RAID systems.
- ***Servers:*** Server-based virtualization control software executes in the application server to which it presents virtual devices. It is typically part of an operating system or sold as a **volume manager.** A volume manager can virtualize any storage devices supported by the operating system in which it runs.
- ***Storage network appliances:*** Storage network-based virtualization control software executes appliances or storage network switches, in some cases assisted by server-based companion components. **Out-of-band** virtualization control software functions are distributed between a **metadata management appliance** and the application servers that use the virtual storage. **In-band** virtualization control software runs in cooperating storage network switches or appliances.

The question of which type of virtualization is "right" for any given situation is already complex, and becoming more so as storage network virtualization technology matures. In most instances, the optimal solution is virtualization at multiple levels, taking advantage of the unique capabilities of each.

Virtualization within a RAID System

With RAID system-based virtualization, one or more dedicated processors within the RAID system execute the virtualization algorithms. Because they are designed specifically for one function—virtualizing the disk storage connected to them—RAID systems often include specialized hardware assists, such as inline **XOR** computation engines and nonvolatile cache memory, that enable them to perform certain tasks much faster than other virtualizers. Particularly in its external or bridge form, RAID system-based virtualization has unique advantages:

- One RAID system can present virtual storage devices (LUNs) to multiple server platforms of different types
- Provides better parity RAID write performance (if equipped with hardware assists for the purpose)
- Can cache more aggressively than other forms of virtualization (if equipped with nonvolatile cache), again leading to higher performance
- Is operating system independent[1] (at least in external RAID system configurations) and is therefore most likely to be redeployable with other platforms
- Does not impact application performance, because block address conversion and data protection algorithms execute on RAID system processors

RAID system-based virtualization is discussed further later in this chapter.

"Lite" Virtualization for Windows

Many Windows administrators are unaware they are using storage virtualization in their Windows 2000 systems. The Windows Logical Disk Manager (LDM), included as part of the Windows 2000 operating system, is actually a server-based virtualizer. The LDM is, in fact, a "lite" version of the VERITAS™ Volume Manager for Windows. The fully featured VERITAS Volume Manager for Windows extends and enhances the capabilites of LDM. Volumes created with LDM are fully upward compatible with the VERITAS Volume Manager.

1. Approximately. It is still prudent to seek statements of mutual support from both RAID system vendors and operating system platform vendors, especially when advanced RAID system features like virtual disk expansion or snapshots are to be used.

Virtualization by Server-Based Volume Managers

As a general rule, server-based volume manager virtualization:

- Has the lowest hardware entry cost and incremental cost, because it has no special hardware requirements
- Offers the highest growth potential, because both disk drives and large LUNs presented by RAID systems can be virtualized, as Figure 7–6 illustrates
- Performs better when run on higher performance servers, because server processors execute the block address conversion and data protection algorithms, or with higher performance storage devices
- Can provide very high resiliency when coupled with RAID systems and clustering software for high overall system availability

Server-based volume management is discussed in more detail later in this chapter.

The VERITAS™ Volume Manager

Many enterprise computer users associate the generic term *volume manager* with VERITAS. In fact, VERITAS developed its widely used control software for UNIX storage management more than 10 years ago, and continues to provide valuable functionality enhancements with each new release. The VERITAS™ Volume Manager and VERITAS™ File System together comprise the VERITAS™ Foundation Suite, whose availability has recently been extended to the LINUX and AIX platforms, thus realizing the VERITAS Adaptive Software Architecture vision to deliver the same storage management software capabilities for all five major PC operating systems (Solaris, Windows, HP-UX, AIX, and LINUX).

Not only does the VERITAS Foundation Suite virtualize block storage, it also includes advanced storage management features such as heterogeneous dynamic multipathing (DMP), hot sparing and relocation, N-way mirroring, FlashSnap, and FastResync, all discussed in earlier inserts.

Virtualization by Storage Network Appliances

In-band storage network virtualization is performed by "appliances" that connect storage devices to application servers. These appliances play a role very similar to that of RAID system controllers. They are usually interconnected in clusters for greater scaling and resiliency. In-band virtualizers offer the following advantages.

- ***Broad applicability:*** Like RAID systems, in-band virtualizers present virtual block storage devices to application servers. Because block storage device behavior has long been standardized (by SCSI and Fibre Channel standards), most computing platforms support most types of network virtualized block storage.
- ***Consolidated storage management:*** With a large, robust appliance cluster, the storage for an entire data center can be virtualized and presented from a single management point.

- ***High security:*** In-band appliances have extensive capabilities for restricting connections (authentication) and traffic (authorization) so that administrative policies can be set and adhered to.

Out-of-band storage network virtualization is also performed by appliances, sometimes called metadata management appliances, in cooperation with application server software components. Out-of-band virtualizers can be thought of as lightweight volume managers that share access to a single base of virtualization metadata (e.g., which devices are part of which arrays, which metadata structures are locked for updating, and so forth). Out-of-band virtualizers have shorter I/O paths than in-band ones, and because they are inherently distributed, they normally scale better as well.

The following sections describe RAID system and server-based implementation in more detail. Chapter 10 discusses storage network-based virtualization techniques. Table A–1 (Appendix A) summarizes the characteristics of different forms of virtualization on one page.

RAID SYSTEM VIRTUALIZATION

Although RAID systems have many auxiliary functions, such as power and temperature management, their principal role is virtualization, performed by intelligent controllers that manage the flow of commands and data between servers and disk drives. Figure 9–1 represents the essential elements of a RAID system that presents virtual storage to an application server, or **storage client.**

A typical RAID system contains a processor (the **policy processor** in Figure 9–1) that converts between virtual block addresses on LUNs and LBAs on disk drives. For example:

- If the array presents a mirrored LUN, policy processor control software schedules a write to each mirrored drive for each application write to the LUN. For each read from the LUN, control software selects a drive and reads data from it.
- If the array presents a striped LUN, control software uses the address conversion algorithms described in Chapter 7 to determine the disk drive and block addresses to which application I/O requests to the LUN should be directed.

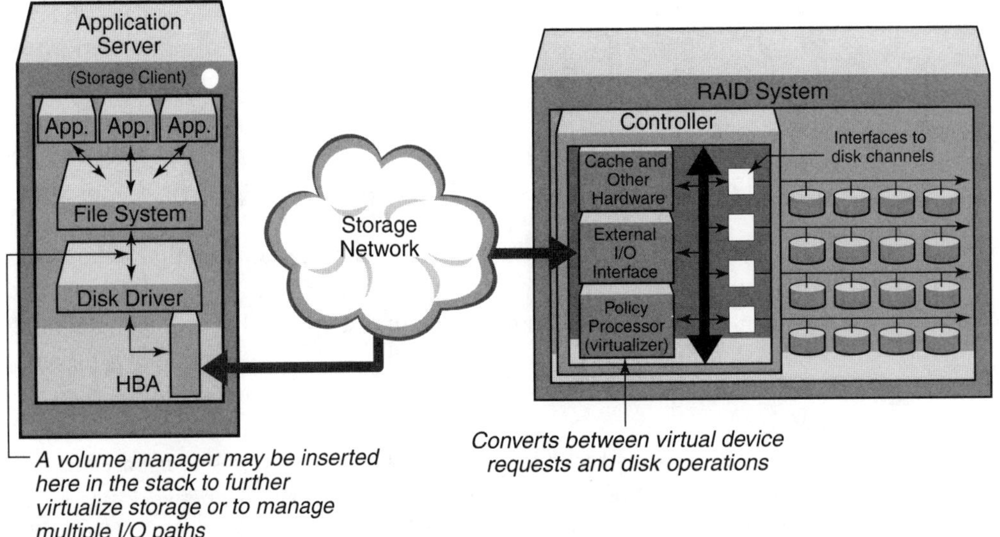

▼ **FIGURE 9–1** *RAID System Virtualization Detail*

RAID system-based virtualizers have been available in the market since the early 1990s. With over a decade of field operation, they are among the most mature forms of virtualization available today.

Figure 9–2 illustrates RAID system-based virtualization in a multi-server data center. The RAID system's policy processor virtualizes groups of disk drives, and presents LUNs to application servers. The leftmost RAID system in Figure 9–2 illustrates a key advantage of RAID system virtualization—a single RAID system can present LUNs to two or more servers, thus enabling consolidation of storage into a single location for improved manageability.

The rightmost RAID system represented in the figure also illustrates a key property of RAID system virtualization—the ability for two or more application servers to access a single LUN. This capability enhances **failover clusters** (Chapter 11), which improve application availability. Redundant virtual storage that protects against device failures provides recoverable storage for recoverable clustered servers.

Advantages of RAID System-Based Virtualization

As a mature form of storage virtualization, RAID systems offer important advantages:

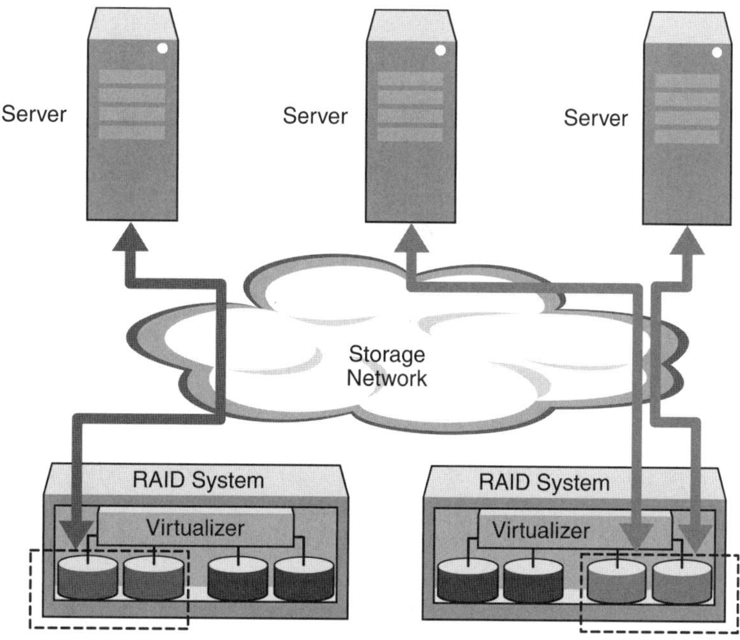

▼ **FIGURE 9–2** *Storage System-Based Block Storage Virtualization*

- ***Storage consolidation:*** Enterprise RAID systems incorporate upwards of 100 disk drives in a single enclosure under common control. With today's disk drive capacities, these systems can store 10 terabytes of data or more. Consolidating storage is advantageous for large data centers, as it reduces floor space, power, cooling, physical security, and asset management requirements. Viewed another way, storage consolidation enables a data center to provide a consistent high-quality physical environment for its storage and to track its storage assets.
- ***Universal applicability:*** One by-product of disk virtualization (Chapter 2) is that all disk drives respond to the same SCSI or FCP[2] commands in the same way. This simplifies operating system disk driver software, and also provides a template for LUN behavior. LUNs respond to SCSI or FCP commands as though they were disk drives, and therefore operating systems can typically support them with little or no effort. This has been a primary reason for the ready acceptance of RAID systems.

2. Fibre Channel Protocol, the command protocol used by disk drives with Fibre Channel interfaces, is discussed further in Chapter 17.

- ***Better performance:*** RAID systems are highly optimized for reliable block storage device virtualization. Their control software is specifically tuned for maximum performance of the algorithms described in Chapter 7 and Chapter 8. Many contain special-purpose hardware to optimize repetitive operations such as parity check data computation, redundant cache writing, and internal copying of data.
- ***Better storage utilization:*** Consolidating a large number of disk drives in a RAID system that can allocate storage capacity very flexibly improves storage utilization. LUNs of almost any desired capacity can be created. More importantly, it is possible to redeploy storage capacity, taking drives from an array that has more than it needs and reallocating them to other arrays within the RAID system that have additional capacity needs.
- ***Better security:*** Finally, consolidating disk drives in a RAID system improves storage asset security. Not only is one large RAID system enclosure easier to secure physically than many small ones, but most RAID system management interfaces support administrator-controlled **LUN masking,** restricting which servers may access which LUNs. LUN masking prevents "rogue" or failed servers from erroneously overwriting data that belongs to other servers.

In sum, these advantages constitute a powerful value proposition that has made the RAID system a staple in large and small data centers over the last decade.

Limitations of RAID System Virtualization

As successful as they have been, RAID systems by themselves do not enable enterprise-wide management of online storage of all types. The major limitation in reaching this goal is limited management scope. A RAID system's policy processor controls the disk drives connected to it, and no others. With the exception of remote data replication (described in Chapter 12), RAID systems have few facilities for coordinating with other like systems, and none at all for coordinating with RAID systems of other types. Thus, while vendors provide tools for managing multiple RAID systems, these tools typically treat each system as a separate case, and are not able to coordinate storage management across them.

Moreover, because RAID system management tools are often developed by RAID system vendors, most can only manage the developing vendor's systems, creating either vendor lock-in or a need for users to develop skills in managing multiple types of storage, either of which tends to increase storage cost of ownership.

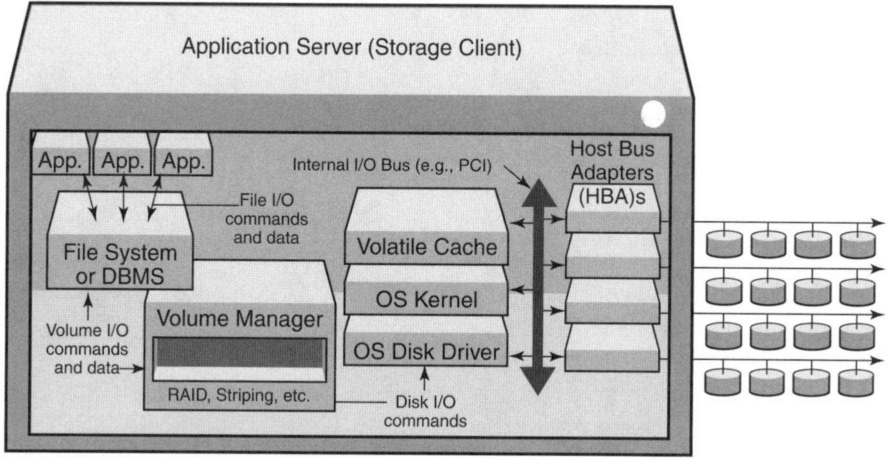

▼ **FIGURE 9–3** *Server-Based Virtualization*

SERVER-BASED VIRTUALIZATION

Volume managers are another mature form of block storage virtualization. Volume manager virtualization control software runs on an application server in the **I/O software stack,** as Figure 9–3 illustrates.

Figure 9–3 represents an application server with disk drives connected directly to it through four host bus adapters. Each drive is presented individually to the OS Disk Driver. Without a volume manager, the disk driver would allow file systems and database managers to make I/O requests to individual drives.

In the example, a volume manager sits logically between the disk driver and the file system. The volume manager takes control of all storage devices to be virtualized, organizes them into arrays of the required type, and presents them as virtual devices for use by the file system or database manager.

Because RAID system LUNs respond to SCSI or FCP commands, volume managers can also virtualize them, as Figure 9–4 illustrates. In the figure, the RAID system presents a parity RAID array as a LUN with about 266 gigabytes of storage capacity (because it is an eight-disk-drive parity RAID array, the virtual disk has a capacity equal to that of seven 38-gigabyte disk drives). This virtual disk might be too large for any one application, or it may be desirable to subdivide it for other purposes, such as controlling the amount of storage consumed by different organizations or applications.

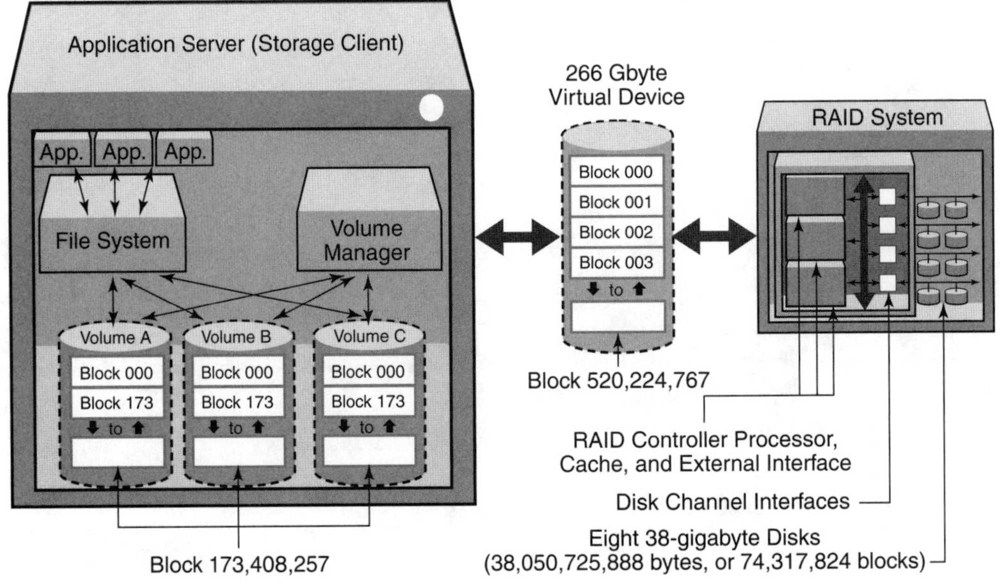

▼ **FIGURE 9–4** *Using a Volume Manager to Subdivide a Large Virtual Device*

The Volume Manager partitions the 266-gigabyte LUN into three smaller virtual devices of about 88 gigabytes each, and presents them to the File System. The File System treats these virtual disks as it would treat disk drives; it is unaware of their virtual nature.[3] The Volume Manager intercepts File System I/O requests, converts the virtual block addresses in them to device LBAs, and converts the requests into SCSI or FCP commands to the 266-gigabyte LUN.

Multilevel storage virtualization, in this case volume manager-based virtualization of RAID system LUNs, has several applications. The more important ones are:

- ***Capacity aggregation:*** A volume manager can aggregate the capacity of two or more of the largest LUNs that a RAID system can present into a single virtual device by concatenating them or striping data across them.

3. This is true for purely disk drive-like I/O functions. Certain advanced functions, such as volume expansion and RAID system-based data replication, require volume manager awareness of virtual device characteristics.

- ***RAID system aggregation:*** A volume manager can mirror data between LUNs from two RAID systems, so that even complete RAID system failure leaves data available to applications.
- ***Multiple I/O paths:*** A volume manager can access storage devices on multiple "paths" (I/O bus or network addresses). This capability complements a RAID system's ability to present a LUN on any of several storage network addresses. When access to a RAID system's LUN switches from one path to another, a volume manager that supports dynamic multipath access can make the switch transparent to file systems and applications.
- ***Device capacity expansion:*** An advanced feature of most virtualizers is their ability to expand and contract virtual device storage capacity. This is useful for meeting unplanned requirements to increase application storage capacity, but is only of value if application servers can recognize that a virtual storage device has changed in size. Volume managers detect changes in virtual device capacity, and report them to file systems and database managers, which modify their data structures to reflect the additional or diminished capacity.
- ***Transparent migration:*** Volume managers are able to copy virtual device contents from one set of devices to another *while the virtual devices are in use by applications.* Virtual device *migration* is useful when storage hardware is upgraded, when applications outgrow their servers or storage facilities, and when there is early indication of a failing device.
- ***Long-distance replication:*** Chapter 12 discusses replication of data across distances too great for mirroring to be practical. In essence, network latency and reliability require more elaborate techniques than mirroring when data is copied over long distances in (almost) real time. Volume managers implement these techniques, using enterprise networks to transport data, and enabling replication between storage devices of unlike types.

Volume managers increase the flexibility of block storage virtualization by enabling diverse storage devices to be virtualized and by combining LUNs presented by different RAID systems. Figure 9–5 illustrates the use of volume managers in a data center with multiple application servers and RAID systems.

In Figure 9–5, the leftmost server's volume manager imports a LUN presented by the leftmost RAID system. The middle server's volume manager virtualizes two LUNs, each presented by a different RAID system. The rightmost server's volume manager virtualizes two disk drives that are directly connected to the storage network into a single virtual device.

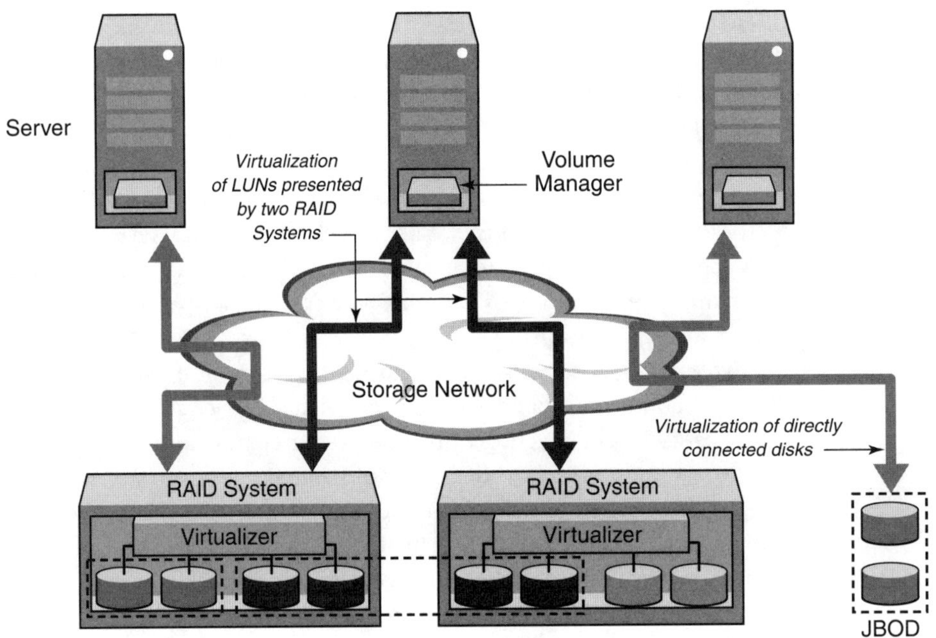

▼ **FIGURE 9–5** *Server-Based Block Storage Virtualization (Volume Management)*

Advantages of Server-Based Volume Managers

Server-based volume managers offer a similar, but not identical, value proposition to that of RAID system-based virtualizers. Their advantages include:

- ***Configuration flexibility:*** Volume managers generally support configurations that use different types of storage devices in fairly flexible ways. For example, most can be configured to mirror between LUNs of different types, or between LUNs and disk drives. This flexibility is particularly useful for getting the most out of **legacy** (pre-existing) storage resources of different types.
- ***Availability:*** By making it possible to configure virtual devices from LUNs presented by two or more RAID systems, volume managers increase failure tolerance beyond that offered by a single RAID system (which is already quite high). Additionally, if they support **dynamic multipathing** (the ability to recognize and use two or more access paths to a device), volume managers protect against data loss due to access path failures. Finally, most are able to migrate virtual

device contents to alternate locations while applications are using the devices, enabling online storage reconfiguration.

- ***Performance:*** Volume managers' ability to process I/O requests scales with the resources available to them. For example, faster servers make volume managers run faster as well. More devices and more adapters increase bandwidth and I/O request handling ability. Volume managers can aggregate the performance of LUNs from two or more RAID systems (including parity RAID LUNs), thus providing higher overall performance than any single RAID system.
- ***Utilization:*** Volume manager flexibility is arguably greater than that of RAID systems, because they manage storage resources more globally than a RAID system can. Volume managers' ability to intermix diverse storage device types makes storage resource deployment very flexible. As storage capacity is replenished, older devices can be combined with newer ones, or recombined among themselves in alternative ways to meet growing requirements.
- ***Security:*** Volume managers are subject to security provided by RAID system **LUN masking.** Additionally, as an operating system component, a volume manager is administered by a (presumably trusted) system administrator.
- ***Close relationship to data managers:*** Though this advantage is not inherent, in practice, volume managers tend to be more closely integrated with file systems and database managers than other forms of virtualization. Close

Dynamic Multipathing

Dynamc Multipathing (DMP) is a very powerful feature of the VERITAS™ Volume Manager. DMP is a virtual path technology that improves availability and I/O throughput of storage devices. If there are multiple paths between a server and a storage device, DMP automatically discovers available multiple paths and combines them into a single virtual path and balances I/O traffic across them for greater I/O throughput. Similarly, path failure does not interrupt application access to data, because DMP automatically switches the entire I/O load to remaining paths.

Several RAID systems are delivered with proprietary server-based path failover software. Not only is such software RAID system-specific; it is usually an extra-cost option. Both of these considerations are important for large heterogeneous storage environments. The VERITAS™ Volume Manager's heterogeneous Dynamic Multipathing feature can reduce requirements for such failover software significantly, as well as simplifying management for better total cost of ownership. Although the VERITAS Volume Manager eliminates the need for RAID system-specific failover tools, DMP can co-exist with most such tools.

Migrating Data to New Storage Devices

The VERITAS Volume Manager makes migration of data from older storage devices to newer ones very easy. After a new storage system is installed (either SAN-attached or direct-attached using the SCSI interface), mirrors of the volumes stored on the old devices can be created on the new devices using full synchronization to make the volume contents identical. When synchronization is complete, the original mirror is detached, and the devices it occupies redeployed or decommissioned.

VERITAS Enterprise Administrator

Because it supports volume managers on all of the major UNIX platforms and Windows, the VERITAS™ Enterprise Administrator is able to concentrate much of the administration of server-based virtual storage in a single location. Based on an object-oriented logical bus design, the VERITAS Enterprise Administrator is able to manage physical disks, LUNs, and virtual volumes for an entire data center from a single console. The administrator simplifies data center-wide administration of server-based virtual storage. VERITAS Enterprise Administrator allows management of different hosts on different platforms, from a single console, with a common look and feel regardless of what product or platform it is deployed with.

integration enables advanced functions, such as hourly online backups using copy-on-write snapshots (Chapter 14) and detection and deployment of expanded virtual disk capacity, that are not as readily available with other forms of virtualization.

Limitations of Server-Based Volume Managers

Server-based volume managers do not automatically enable data center-wide storage management (although as with RAID system-based virtualizers, most vendors offer tools that enable management of all server-based volume managers in a network from a single server. Although volume managers manage disk drives and LUNs presented by several RAID systems, they do not coordinate storage for multiple servers. If LUNs presented by a single RAID system must be allocated to two different servers, this fact must be known to administrators; volume managers provide no inherent cooperation between, or indeed, awareness of, other servers in the data center.

Virtual Volumes for Clusters

The VERITAS™ Cluster Volume Manager makes complete server-based virtualization capabilities available to clusters of servers. With the VERITAS Cluster Volume Manager, server-based virtual volumes can be imported on all of the servers in a VERITAS cluster simultaneously. Cluster volumes can be used directly (for example, by a shared data parallel database manager such as Oracle Real Application Cluster). When coupled with the VERITAS™ Cluster File System delivered as part of the VERITAS™ Storage Foundation Cluster File System HA, they enable the simultaneous mounting of file systems on all of a cluster's servers.

The second major limitation of server-based volume management is that the technique can only be used with platforms for which volume manager software exists. This contrasts with RAID system virtualization, which presents LUNs that use SCSI or FCP command protocols supported by all server operating system platforms.

Server-based volume management has some tactical limitations as well. For example, since they typically do not have special-purpose hardware available to them for parity computation, their parity RAID performance is usually noticeably lower than that of RAID systems.

The chapter that follows describes storage network-based virtualizers that combine the advantages of server-based and RAID system ones.

CHAPTER SUMMARY

- Storage networks suggest the possibility of applying block virtualization techniques across the data center to simplify online storage management.
- Block storage device virtualization can be implemented in servers, in embedded or external RAID systems, or in storage network infrastructure components.
- RAID systems present LUNs that are indistinguishable from disk drives, from a device driver software standpoint.
- RAID system LUNs typically provide high I/O performance, especially for parity RAID, because of specially optimized hardware and software components within the RAID system. The primary limitations of RAID system-based block virtualization are limited management scope and lack of interoperability with other types of devices.
- Server-based virtualization software goes under the name of *volume manager.* Volume managers are flexible, in that they can virtualize either disk drives or LUNs presented by multiple RAID systems for a server.
- It is often useful to configure server-based virtualization in conjunction with RAID system virtualization. For example, a volume manager can partition very large LUNs for application convenience, or aggregate smaller LUNs into a large virtual device for increased capacity, performance, or availability.
- Volume managers increase the scope of storage management, in that they consolidate management of a server's storage, no matter how many devices provide it. Coordination among volume managers is not generally the case, however, so data center-wide storage management is by agreement among system administrators.

CHAPTER 10

The significant problems we face cannot be solved at the same level of thinking we were at when we created them.

—ALBERT EINSTEIN

Block Storage Virtualization in Storage Networks

In this chapter . . .

- Block storage virtualization in the network
- In-band storage network virtualization
- Out-of-band storage network virtualization

Volume managers and, to a lesser extent, RAID system virtualizers are *server-centric,* in that the tactics for managing them tend to be motivated by the requirements of individual servers rather than by a data center-wide storage virtualization strategy. It is also possible to implement storage virtualization in the network, increasing the scope of management to span entire data centers. This chapter describes network infrastructure components that virtualize block storage.

SERVER-CENTRIC STORAGE VIRTUALIZATION

With RAID systems and volume managers, different servers' virtual storage needs are coordinated by informal cooperation among system administrators, using "management by spreadsheet" techniques. Figure 10–1 suggests an important consequence of this style of online storage management.

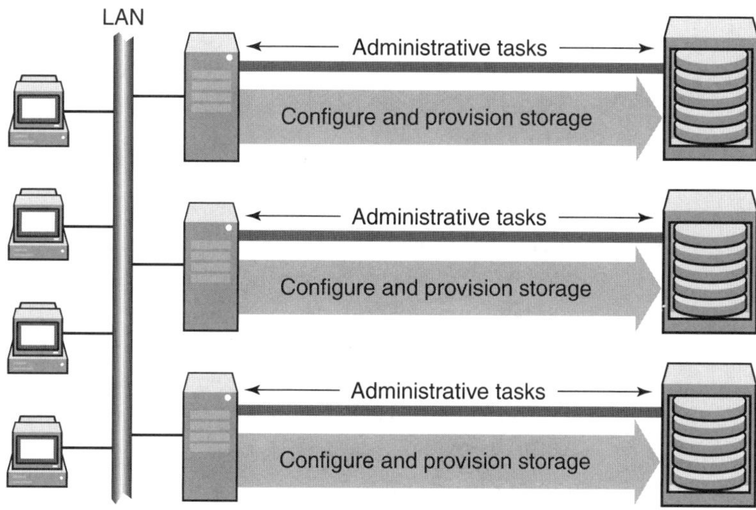

▼ **FIGURE 10–1** *Server-Centric Virtualization*

Figure 10–1 shows three servers in a data center, each managed by an administrator who is responsible for the server, the applications that run on it, the clients that use it, and the storage connected to it. For each application, an administrator negotiates storage capacity, performance, and availability requirements with an application manager. System administrators may also have to negotiate with their counterparts if the data center shares a RAID system's storage among multiple servers. In any case, each server's administrator performs the actions required to make the agreed-upon storage available to applications that run on that server. These consist of:

- ***Configuration:*** Creation of arrays with the required capacity, performance, and availability properties
- ***Provisioning:*** Allocation of virtual devices from the configured arrays to the servers that require them

When storage is managed in this way (on a per-server basis), administrative cost grows at least linearly with the number of servers in a data center. Each additional server requires a negotiation between an application manager and a system administrator with storage skills, followed by additional negotiations among system administrators, to coordinate storage resource use. Arguably, cost may grow faster than linearly, because the larger the number of servers, the more potential interactions between them and storage devices that must be tracked and managed.

STORAGE NETWORKS AND MANAGEMENT COST

In data centers whose primary storage interconnect is parallel SCSI, not much can be done about this source of management cost. The parallel SCSI bus is really designed to connect a single computer ("initiator") to several storage devices (15 or fewer). Two initiators may be connected to the same bus in an **availability cluster** configuration, but beyond that, the characteristics of the parallel SCSI bus protocol lead to unpredictable I/O performance. Each server's storage devices are connected directly to it, and must be managed in that way.

Connecting storage devices and servers to a common network, as illustrated in Figure 10–2, changes the equation significantly. Three key characteristics of storage networks can potentially reduce management cost by enabling data center-wide management and virtualization of online storage:

- ***Complete interconnection:*** Perhaps the most fundamental property of storage networks is that they interconnect all of a data center's storage devices to all of its servers. The ability of a particular server to communicate with a particular storage device may be restricted by administrative policy, but from a physical connectivity standpoint, storage networks make it possible for any server to transfer data to and from any storage device.
- ***Heterogeneous servers and storage devices:*** The storage network technologies available today, Fibre Channel and the variants of TCP/IP for storage access, are standards-based. They have been (and continue to be) developed by consortia in which membership is open to any companies and individuals wishing to participate. Storage network standards are freely available to anyone wishing to develop hardware or software components that implement them. As a result, it is possible to interconnect server I/O bus adapters and storage devices from a variety of vendors in a single storage network. From a storage management standpoint, this means that networked storage devices of different types can be logically combined to meet the needs of any of an enterprise's computing platforms.
- ***Infrastructure intelligence:*** Unlike the parallel SCSI I/O bus, whose intelligence is entirely contained in its end points (server I/O bus adapters), storage network infrastructure components (switches, hubs, routers, and extenders) all have processing capability of one kind or another. Intelligence in the infrastructure suggests the possibility of moving some storage management functions from end points (servers and storage devices) into the network itself. With full

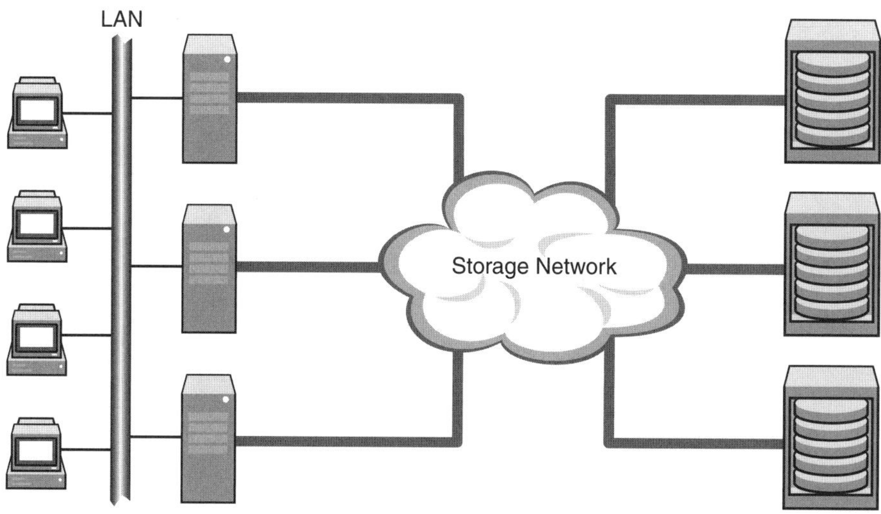

▼ **FIGURE 10–2** *Storage Connected to a Network*

interconnectivity, it should be possible for storage infrastructure components to manage storage for an entire data center and provision it to servers as application requirements dictate.

These characteristics have motivated developers to explore the possibility of using the storage network infrastructure to manage storage, and in particular to virtualize it for presentation, on a data center-wide basis. Two basic approaches have resulted from these explorations, which have come to be known by the names **in-band** and **out-of-band** storage network virtualization, respectively.

In-Band and Out-of-Band Virtualization

To understand the differences between these two types of storage network-based virtualization, it is helpful to analyze the functional components required to virtualize block storage. Figure 10–3 illustrates the essential components.

As Figure 10–3 suggests, file system and database manager I/O requests made to virtual devices must be converted to operations on disk drives or LUNs and executed. A single application request may be converted to one (e.g., a read request to a mirrored virtual device), two (e.g., a write request to a mirrored virtual device), or more (e.g., a write request

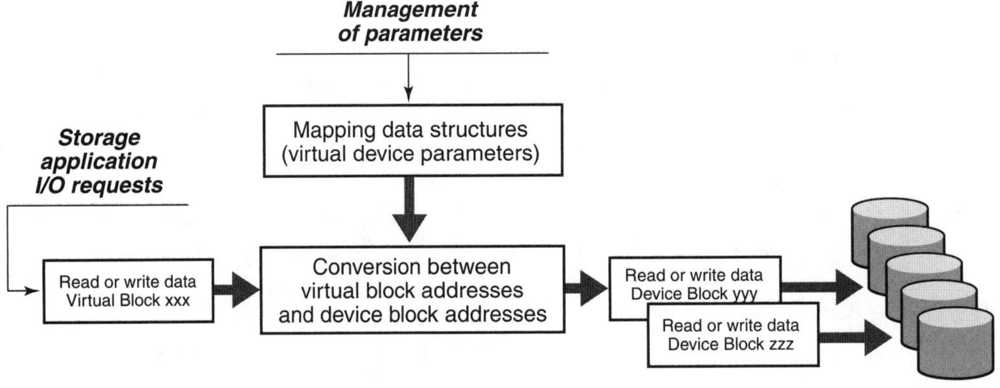

▼ **FIGURE 10–3** *Key Components of Block Storage Virtualization*

to a parity RAID virtual device) operations on an array's devices. This conversion is required for every application I/O request, no matter which type of virtualization is used or where it is implemented.

As Chapter 3 describes, disk array block address conversion is performed by a combination of table lookups and parameter-driven algorithms. Table lookups are typically used to locate infrequently changing array parameters, such as the names, network addresses, and ordering of the devices that make up an array, as well as block address conversion parameters like starting addresses and stripe depth. Algorithms such as those described in Chapter 7 use these parameters to convert read and write requests to virtual devices and block addresses into read and write operations addressed to physical device block addresses.

Both of these block address conversion algorithms require parameters. For example, determining array membership requires storage device names; striped block address conversion requires stripe depth and starting block addresses. Whenever an array's parameters change, as, for example, when a device is added to the array, this change must be communicated to the control software that is converting block addresses for each application I/O request. Thus, the parameters of a disk array must be:

- Used to translate block addresses during I/O request operation
- Stored and managed, so that capabilities such as online expansion of a virtual device or movement of all or part of the storage capacity can be accommodated

In storage virtualization contexts, the terms *in-band* and *out-of-band* refer to the location at which virtualization parameters are persistently stored and managed. If the entity (volume manager or network virtualization control software) that performs I/O request block conversion also manages virtualization parameters, the virtualization is said to be *in-band.* If virtualization parameters are managed by a separate entity that communicates changes to inline control software, virtualization is said to be *out-of-band.*

IN-BAND STORAGE NETWORK VIRTUALIZATION

According to the definition in the preceding section, virtualization is in-band if the entity that performs block address conversion for I/O operations also manages block address conversion parameters. RAID systems and volume managers both fulfill this condition. In practice, however, the term *in-band virtualizer* usually denotes a separate device within the storage network.

Devices that perform in-band virtualization are known by various names. The terms **SAN appliance, virtualization engine,** and **virtualization appliance** have all been used. Whatever the terminology, an in-band SAN virtualizer is an intelligent device optimized to move large amounts of data at high levels of performance. Figure 10–4 illustrates the important components of an in-band virtualizer, and their architectural relationship to the rest of a distributed computing system.

In Figure 10–4, the in-band virtualization appliance at the center of the diagram is a conventional server. Conventional operating system drivers control its I/O bus adapters. These adapters connect to disk drives (or, more likely, to LUNs presented by RAID systems) over a storage network.

Other I/O bus adapters, capable of being I/O command targets, are used to connect to another storage network, providing access to application servers. The drivers for these adapters are customized to behave like storage devices from the perspective of application servers.

ServPoint SAN Appliance Software

VERITAS software has been used as the basis for in-band network block virtualization appliances. Based on the VERITAS Cluster Server and Cluster Volume Manager, appliance software would transform a Solaris or Linux server into a decidated block virtualization appliance.

With this appliance software, scalability, performance, and connectivity requirements would determine the hardware platform choice. The Cluster Volume Manager would be used to create virtual volumes from physical disks and LUNs, and present the volumes to application servers as parallel SCSI or Fibre Channel LUNs.

These appliances would be manged through adapted versions of the VERITAS Cluster Server and Volume Manager user interfaces, minimizing incremental training requirements for users familiar with the latter products.

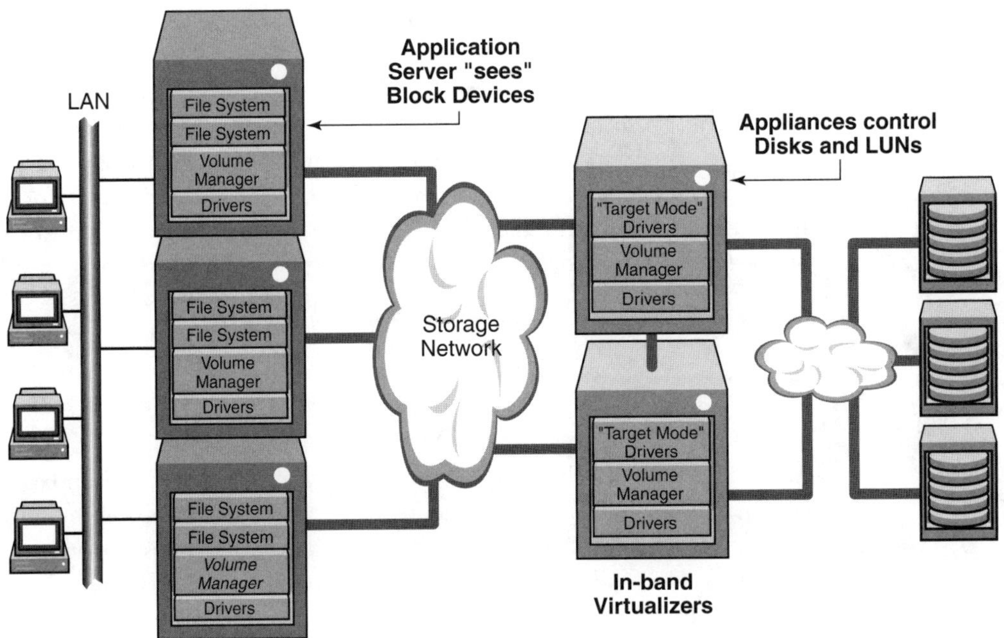

▼ **FIGURE 10–4** *An In-Band Storage Network Virtualizer*

Within the virtualization appliance, software whose function is identical to that of a server-based volume manager (labeled "Volume Manager" in Figure 10–4) virtualizes the storage devices controlled by the appliance. The virtualized storage is presented to application servers as LUNs, just as if the appliance were a RAID system.

As Figure 10–4 suggests, a system that includes an in-band virtualization appliance can grow by the addition of either more storage capacity or more servers, and these two dimensions are independent of each other.

Figure 10–4 illustrates two interconnected in-band virtualization appliances, both of which are connected to the same storage devices and the same clients. As Chapter 11 discusses, these are the two requirements for a cluster. Most in-band virtualizers available today can be clustered in some form, either with adapted application clustering technology or with purpose-built technology. Clustering enables an in-band virtualizer to scale beyond the capabilities of a single appliance, and in addition, improves system robustness by protecting against the failure of the virtualizer itself.

Figure 10–5 shows another view of in-band virtualization, emphasizing the virtualizer's relationship with other system components. As with server-based volume managers, in-band virtualizers can virtualize

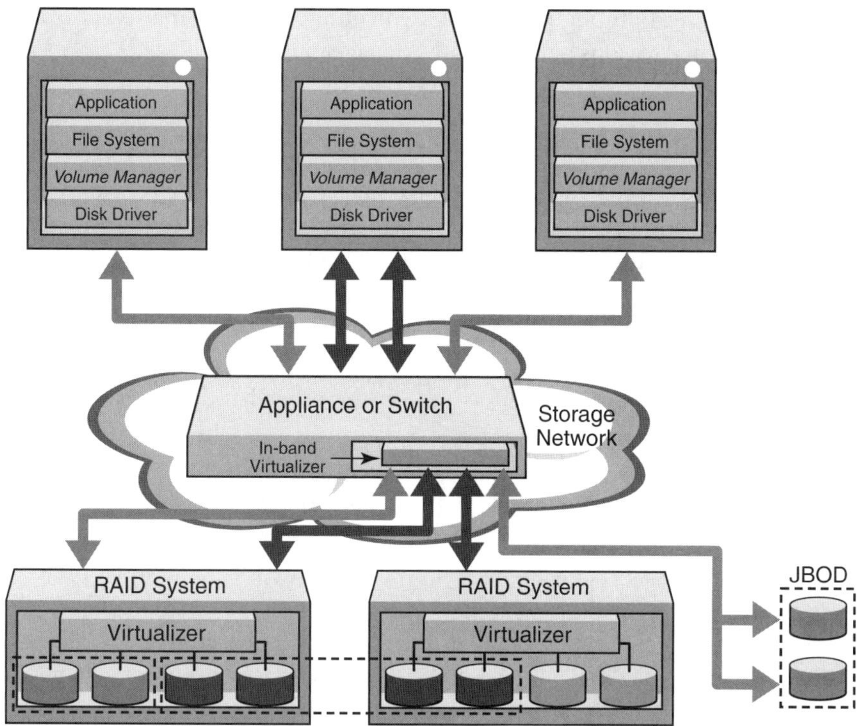

▼ **FIGURE 10–5** *In-Band Storage Network-Based Block Virtualization*

any type of storage.[1] As the figure also suggests, storage capacity from multiple devices can be part of the same array. Finally, the figure suggests that an array organized by an in-band virtualizer can be partitioned and its capacity presented to application servers as multiple virtual devices.

The key point illustrated by Figure 10–5, however, is that the scope of in-band network storage virtualization may be as much as the entire data center. Any storage devices connected to the storage network can be virtualized and presented to any servers in the data center, the latter because there is no software component, or "footprint" required in the

1. The ability of a volume manager or in-band virtualizer to manage "any" type of storage is grounded in the assumption that all disk drives implement SCSI and FCP protocols identically. Since a volume manager uses operating system drivers to access storage, any online storage supported by the operating system should be virtualizable. In actual fact, volume manager and in-band virtualizer vendors believe strongly in product qualification, and provide lists of supported storage devices.

server (although a server-based volume manager may still be desirable for other reasons, such as path management).

In-Band Virtualization and Storage Networks

Figure 10–4 and Figure 10–5 suggest slightly different options for connecting an in-band storage virtualization appliance to a storage network. Figure 10–4 illustrates one "back-end" storage network used to connect the appliance(s) to storage devices, and another used to connect the appliance(s) to application servers. Figure 10–5, on the other hand, suggests a single storage network to which all application servers, storage devices, and in-band virtualizers are connected.

While the latter configuration is possible, the former is to be preferred under most circumstances. One limitation of appliance-based in-band virtualization is that every I/O request, whether a read or a write, results in data moving at least twice through the virtualizer—once when it is received from the originating application server (for writes) or storage device (for reads), and again when it is delivered to storage devices (for writes) or to an application server (for reads). If the entire data center operates on a single storage network, then storage network loading during periods of peak activity is twice what application I/O throughput requirements would suggest.

VERITAS Powered™

The roots of VERITAS' technology are in storage management software that runs in application servers. As storage networks become more prevalent in and vital to enterprise data centers, network-centric storage management, including network-based virtualization, becomes a must. Network-based virtualization can be provided either by conventional servers running special-purpose software or by similar software running in the switches that comprise the storage network. The VERITAS Powered™ initiative is aimed at making the company's virtualization, high-availability, and data protection capabilities available in the storage network infrastructure products of its Powered™ partners. The goal of the VERITAS Powered™ program is to combine the cost-performance advantages inherent in custom switching technology with the functional richness of VERITAS storage management software.

Careful storage network design can localize traffic in a storage network like that shown in Figure 10–5, and so minimize interference between virtualizer-storage device traffic and virtualizer-application server traffic. Careful designs must be carefully maintained, however, and a carefully tuned storage network can have its balance upset by the addition or removal of a device in the wrong place. If, on the other hand, the storage network is designed along the lines suggested by Figure 10–4 (effectively, separate networks for servers and storage devices), the possibility that application server traffic will interfere with back-end storage traffic is far smaller than with the other approach.

Storage Network Infrastructure and In-Band Virtualization

In-band virtualization is typically implemented by customizing conventional server and operating system platforms. Such servers are usually configured with maximum numbers of I/O bus adapters and large memories for caching data on its way between application servers and storage devices. A glance at Figure 10–4, however, shows that the in-band virtualizer adds a step in the path between an application server and its storage devices—the virtualizer is an "extra" system element that limits performance and availability. To overcome this, developers are embedding virtualization capability directly in the switches and directors that make up storage network fabrics. In addition to reducing the "box count" in a data center, with the attendant reduction in I/O path length, storage network switches are also highly optimized for data movement, and so should provide superior performance. There are technology challenges to be overcome, however, such as configuring adequate processing power and cache, and developing clustering technology to enable multiple switches to cooperate as a highly available distributed virtualizer. Nonetheless, the potential benefits are attractive. Virtualizing storage network infrastructure components are expected to become available in the relatively near future.

Developments in Switch Virtualization

As this book goes to press, switch-based block storage virtualization seems to be a very promising technology. The combination of switching and storage virtualization technologies was originally pursued by start-up companies. More recently, major storage network infrastructure suppliers appear to be positioning themselves to enter the emerging market for virtualizing storage network switches. In 2001, VERITAS partner Cisco acquired Andiamo, a developer of smart switches. In November 2002, Brocade Networks acquired Rhapsody, also a participant in the VERITAS Powered™ initiative. Introduction of virtualizing storage network infrastructures from both of these major suppliers is expected during 2003.

Advantages of In-Band Virtualization

As with every aspect of information processing technology, in-band virtualization has inherent benefits and limitations. In some ways, it combines benefits of server-based volume managers and RAID systems. For example, like volume managers, in-band virtualizers use operating system I/O drivers to access storage devices. Operating systems tend to support a relatively wide range of physical and virtual storage devices compared to RAID systems, so in-band virtualizers can perform their services for many types of storage. On the other hand, an advantage of RAID systems is that they present LUNs with disk-like behavior, so there is no requirement for specialized software in the application server as with the volume manager approach.[2] This is true as well with in-band virtualizers, thus extending virtualization services to a broader range of server platforms than is typically the case with volume managers.

One powerful advantage of in-band virtualization is security. In-band virtualizers include functionality equivalent to storage network zoning and RAID system LUN masking (see Chapter 17). Administrative operations on an in-band virtualizer make it possible to control which application servers communicate with which storage devices. It is even possible for an in-band virtualizer to force a server or storage device to authenticate itself. This becomes increasingly important as the scope of storage networks grows and larger and more diverse fabric topologies become common.

In-Band Appliances as "Storage Firewalls"

A firewall completely controls every logical connection that passes through it. Because all managed data flows through it, an in-band SAN appliance makes an ideal security control center or *storage access firewall.* An in-band SAN appliance permits no I/O to volumes from servers without appropriate access rights.

An in-band SAN appliance volume typically has an Access Control List (ACL) of permissions for all eligible servers. This type of security is similar to RAID system LUN masking, but applies to all volumes created and presented by an appliance, no matter what their underlying physical storage. With an in-band SAN appliance, JBOD storage and LUNs can both be organized into failure-tolerant volumes and presented securely to clients.

Limitations of In-Band Virtualization

Similarly, in-band virtualization technology has some intrinsic limitations. Some of these are perceptual, grounded in computer system users' natural reluctance to embrace new and different concepts for mission-critical functions such as storage and data access. Others are real, and are addressed by other technologies. In the category of perception are:

- ***Complexity:*** Figure 10–4 and Figure 10–5 both illustrate approaches to storage virtualization that add components to the data center. In addition to the application servers, switches, directors, routers, and storage devices, another component, the in-band virtualizer, is introduced. The perception is "more interconnections, more boxes to manage." Though this is true, it sidesteps the question of where the

2. There may be other reasons, such as combining storage presented by two virtualizers, partitioning a large virtual disk drive, or dynamic multipathing, for using an application server-based volume manager in conjunction with an in-band virtualizer, but nothing inherent in the virtualization technique requires doing so.

Server and Network Virtualization

Will network-based block storage virtualization replace the server-based variety? From today's vantage point, the answer is emphatically no; the two promise to work synergistically together much as server-based and RAID system-based virtualization work well together in today's data centers. Network-based virtualization has the advantage of potentially supporting any type of server and storage, while server-based virtualization is more application-aware (for example, it is closer to file systems and database managers). Server-based virtualization additionally enables path failover and load-balancing from the server's point of view, which is difficult for a network-based virtualizer.

complexity in managing online storage comes from. In a large data center, it is very likely to result from the number of uncoordinated points at which virtualization must be understood and managed. For example, each RAID system must be configured, and each volume manager must be configured to properly utilize the virtual storage presented by the RAID systems. By centralizing more of this function in a single location, the in-band virtualizer actually tends to simplify the management of virtualization, even though it is indeed an additional "box."

- ***Robustness:*** Similarly, Figure 10–5 suggests that an in-band virtualizer might limit a data center's failure tolerance. A failure of the virtualizer would block access to all storage by any servers, shutting down the entire operation. Developers of in-band virtualizers realized this early, and have generally compensated by enabling two or more of their devices to be configured as virtualization clusters, with multiple paths to both storage devices and application servers.

On the other hand, there are some genuine limitations inherent in in-band virtualization. These include:

- ***Scaling:*** Although very powerful servers can be employed as in-band virtualizers, doing so is probably not cost effective. Moreover, however large it is, a virtualizer necessarily has a maximum connectivity and a maximum data throughput. When one of these limits is reached, another network is required. Thus, while a cluster of cooperating in-band virtualizers may support quite a large storage network, it is possible to reach a point from which expansion is only possible by subdividing storage into two disjoint networks.
- ***I/O path length:*** In-band virtualizers implemented using conventional servers work by receiving data into their memories and forwarding it to its destination. This introduces an additional **store and forward** switching point in the I/O path (others include disk drive RAID systems, and HBA buffers). No matter how optimized the implementation, storing and forwarding data takes longer than continuous

transmission, so the I/O path between application and storage is inherently longer with an in-band virtualizer than without it. This penalty can be mitigated somewhat on the average by cache in the virtualizer, but for cache "misses," the I/O path is longer when storage is virtualized in band.

- ***Component cost:*** In addition to the (not inconsiderable) virtualization appliance itself, in-band virtualization effectively requires two storage networks—one connecting servers to the virtualizer and one connecting the virtualizer to storage devices. With careful configuration, these can be the same physical network, but additional network ports are required to connect the in-band virtualization appliance to both servers and storage devices. Because the cost of storage network ports is relatively high (compared to that of messaging network ports), incremental port requirements should be considered when determining an in-band storage virtualization strategy.

To reduce or eliminate these two inherent limitations of in-band virtualization, developers hit upon the other primary technique used to virtualize storage from within the network—**out-of-band virtualization.**

OUT-OF-BAND STORAGE NETWORK VIRTUALIZATION

With in-band virtualization, the essential factor that lengthens the application I/O path is that data is stored in and forwarded from virtualizer buffers on its path between storage device and server. An in-band virtualizer's processor translates virtual and device block addresses for each I/O request, as Figure 10–3 illustrates. The same processor manages the persistent data structures that hold virtualization parameters—structures that describe array membership, virtualization algorithms, stripe depth, starting block numbers, and so forth.

The out-of-band virtualization approach separates these two functions—block address translation during I/O request execution and persistent storage and management of virtualization parameters. With out-of-band virtualization, block address translation is done by volume manager-like virtualization software components that run in the client application servers. Virtualization parameter management is centralized in a single location, called the "Metadata Manager" in Figure 10–6, which illustrates out-of-band storage network-based virtualization. A metadata

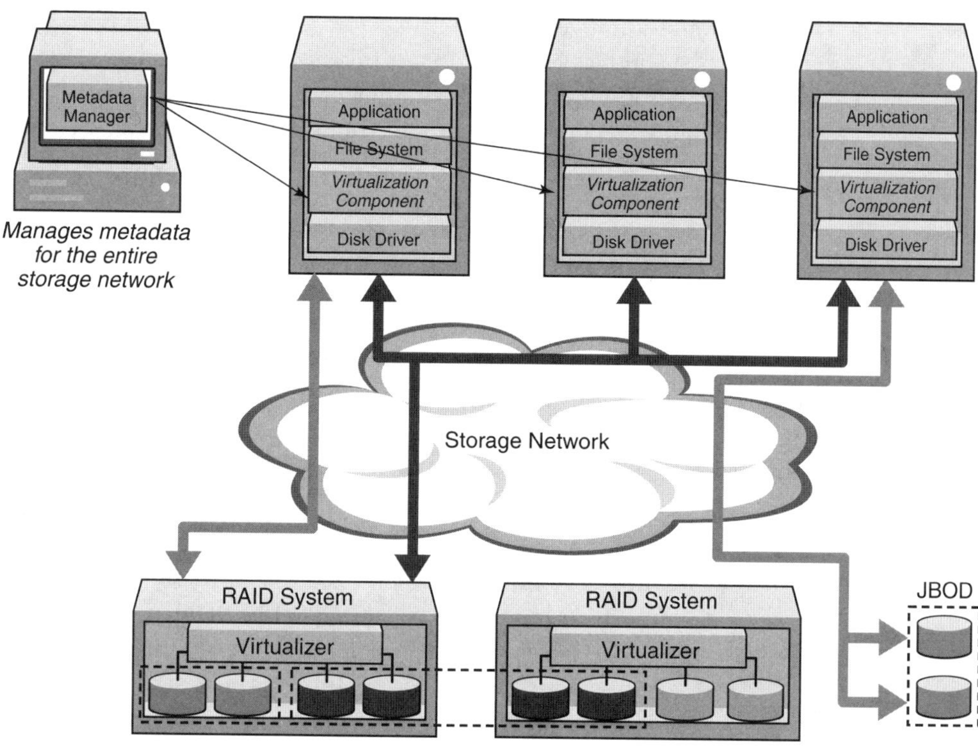

▼ **FIGURE 10–6** *Out-of-Band Storage Network-Based Block Virtualization*

manager may be a separate server dedicated to the task (and part of a cluster for availability), or it may be a function performed by one of the application servers participating in virtualization. In either case, some form of clustering is obviously required so that the metadata manager (and therefore the virtualization components' access to virtualization parameters) could survive application server crashes.

The blocks labeled "*Virtualization Component*" in Figure 10–6 translate the virtual block addresses in file system I/O requests to storage devices' LBAs and issue read and write commands to the devices. The virtualization components obtain the parameters that drive their translation algorithms from the central metadata manager, shown as running in a separate computer in the figure. The metadata manager might also be a software component that runs in an application server.

Administrative operations such as creation and deletion of virtual devices, addition of capacity, addition or removal of mirrors from mirrored arrays, movement of virtual storage segments from one physical device to another, and so forth, are initiated by the metadata manager. The virtualization components running in application servers may be involved in the execution of these operations either actively (for example, copying data to a newly added mirror) or passively (for example, blocking I/O to virtual devices momentarily so that metadata changes can be recorded persistently), but all such operations are completely controlled by the metadata manager.

Advantages of Out-of-Band Virtualization

Like their appliance-based in-band counterparts, out-of-band virtualizers can utilize any type of storage device supported by the server and operating system platforms on which they run. Unlike in-band virtualizers, however, out-of-band virtualizers have a *client footprint*—they can only virtualize storage on behalf of those client platforms for which a cooperating software component exists. Thus, out-of-band virtualizers are less broadly applicable than in-band ones.

From Figure 10–6 it can be seen that with an out-of-band virtualizer, the I/O path between storage device and application server is direct; out-of-band virtualization adds no store-and-forward points to the I/O path. Changes in virtual device parameters involve the metadata manager, but these are infrequent and generally have minimal effect on application I/O performance. Application I/O requests are translated by the local virtualization component and sent directly to the devices that will satisfy them.

As Figure 10–6 suggests, out-of-band virtualization has no inherent bottleneck analogous to that of the in-band virtualizer. With out-of-band virtualization, it is possible to distribute application I/O loads across physical resources, adding more storage devices and storage network bandwidth as requirements dictate and budgets allow.

Finally, out-of-band virtualization does not require any additional storage network ports beyond those that would be required to connect servers and storage devices to the network without virtualization. This represents a saving compared with appliance-based in-band virtualization.

VERITAS and Out-of-Band Virtualization

In keeping with its philosophy that different data center requirements demand different storage virtualization strategies, VERITAS has announced plans to develop network-based out-of-band virtualization to augment its server-based and in-band network-based offerings. On delivery of this program, VERITAS will be in the unique position of offering any combination of server-based and network-based virtualization, both in-band and out-of-band. The primary advantage of out-of-band network-based virtualization is scaling in very large enterprise storage networks.

Limitations of Out-of-Band Virtualization

Perhaps the most significant limitation of out-of-band virtualization is that the technology is even less familiar to storage and application architects than that of in-band virtualization. While the potential benefits—data center-wide coordinated management of storage resources with no inherent bottlenecks except those imposed by the storage network itself—are significant, the apparent risks are great as well. One apparent risk lies in the maturity of the technology. Because out-of-band virtualization requires a server component, only those server platforms for which such components exist can participate in out-of-band storage virtualization. Because the technology is young and products are new, platform coverage tends to be incomplete. An adopter of out-of-band virtualization may be faced with limitations in the server platforms supported and therefore be forced to adopt multiple storage management schemes for a data center.

A second risk in out-of-band virtualization is the robustness of the metadata manager. Though failure of the metadata manager would not disrupt application servers' ability to access their storage, it would make any changes in storage configuration or order management operations impossible. As with in-band technology, developers have turned to clustering technology to make metadata managers robust.

Another risk in out-of-band virtualization is that no standards exist for communication with distributed virtualization components. Each developer creates unique, proprietary protocols for communicating metadata changes between the metadata manager and the virtualization components running in application servers. Thus, to adopt out-of-band virtualization is to commit to a single vendor's product line, at least until standards for out-of-band virtualization emerge.

But perhaps the largest risk in out-of-band virtualization lies in the insecurity of today's storage access protocols (compared to those of messaging networks). Storage access protocols (parallel SCSI and Fibre Channel Protocol) are rooted in a concept of computer system architecture in which storage devices are peripheral to a single computer. An important consequence of this is an underlying assumption that if a master (e.g., a SCSI initiator) can communicate with a slave (e.g., a SCSI target), the slave should execute whatever commands it receives from the master. This assumption clearly does not hold in a network environment where multiple masters are the rule rather than the exception. With Fibre Channel, the risk is mitigated somewhat by the necessity for devices to "log in" to the network, and to establish connections before intercommunicating.

This level of security is inadequate for out-of-band virtualization, however. For example, it does not prevent an application server with a legitimate right to access a certain range of block addresses on a storage device from accessing blocks outside that range, to which it has no access rights. As long as all virtualization components and the application servers on which they run are trustworthy and perform flawlessly, there is no problem. If, however, a virtualization component (or indeed, *any* software component in the I/O path) contains a bug, data belonging to other completely unrelated servers can be corrupted, unbeknownst to its owner. Because an in-band virtualizer does all data routing between the devices it virtualizes and the application servers it serves, this problem does not exist in the in-band environment. With out-of-band virtualization, however, this risk is inherent with Fibre Channel Protocol. Because it layers on TCP/IP, the iSCSI storage network protocol that is beginning to appear in the market promises to improve this situation somewhat.

CHAPTER SUMMARY

- Neither RAID systems nor server-based volume managers lend themselves to expanding the scope of online storage management to entire data centers. Thus, the cost of managing online storage using these techniques tends to grow as the number of servers in a data center grows.
- The connectivity, heterogeneity, and infrastructure intelligence of storage networks make it possible to contemplate managing and virtualizing online storage from within the network itself. Two basic techniques, called *in-band* and *out-of-band* virtualization, respectively, have arisen to do this.
- Virtualization has two main components—translation between virtual device and data block addresses and those of physical storage devices, and management of virtualization parameters such as device addresses, block ranges, stripe depths, and so forth.
- With in-band virtualization, there is a single virtualizer, or point of control, through which both application I/O requests and virtualization parameter management pass. In-band virtualization is typically performed by dedicated servers called appliances.
- In-band virtualization is broadly applicable and secure, but may represent a performance or availability choke point. Vendors have mitigated this possibility by incorporating cluster technology into virtualizers, providing failure tolerance and a degree of scaling.

- With out-of-band virtualization, a metadata manager manages virtualization parameters for multiple virtualizer instances that run in application servers for which storage is being virtualized.
- Out-of-band virtualization has both a shorter I/O path and better inherent scaling than in-band virtualization, but may have security risks with current storage network protocols.

CHAPTER 11

A distributed system is one in which the failure of a computer you didn't even know existed can render your own computer unusable.

—LESLIE LAMPORT

Storage Virtualization in Shared Data Clusters

In this chapter . . .

- Cluster technology, features, and benefits
- Shared nothing and shared data clusters
- Virtual block storage in a cluster environment

Chapter 10 describes out-of-band storage network-based virtualization, a technique in which one control point manages data structures used by many virtualizers to convert application I/O requests to virtual storage devices into device addresses and LBAs for execution. This chapter discusses a similar form of out-of-band virtualization in which one server-based volume manager instance manages virtualization data structures for an entire *cluster* of servers. This approach increases the scope of virtualization from a single server to several cooperating servers, and more importantly, enables file systems and database managers to share data among several servers.

CLUSTERING, STORAGE, AND DATA

Clustering is a software technology that coordinates the operation of interconnected servers to improve application availability, scaling, and manageability. Clustering technology is used to create **clusters** consisting of several interconnected servers (sometimes called "nodes") that have access to the same storage devices and are accessible by the same clients. The actions of clustered servers are coordinated by instances of cluster manager software running in each server. Cluster manager instances intercommunicate to:

- ***Present*** the same view of cluster state to all servers at all times
- ***Monitor*** server, application, and other resource state so that failures are detected and applications are restarted as necessary
- ***Balance*** application workload equitably among a cluster's servers
- ***Synchronize*** access to storage devices so that different servers' concurrent I/O requests do not interfere with each other and corrupt data

Clusters are most effective when all servers can access any application data. While two servers connected to storage by parallel SCSI buses can form a cluster, network storage, as illustrated in Figure 11–1, enables much more flexible configurations.[1]

Clustering Benefits

Clustering enhances application availability, scaling, and manageability. The technology is attractive to users because it solves some significant data center problems:

- ***Server failure:*** If a server or application crashes, another server can take control of ("**fail over**") its resources and resume service to clients.
- ***Unplanned application growth:*** If application requirements exceed server capacity, additional servers can be added, and the workload repartitioned.
- ***Network failure:*** If client communication paths fail, clients can access information services on other servers on alternate paths.

1. In Figure 11–1, the private disks are not accessible by all servers in the cluster. In practice, clustered servers often use private disks to store operating system and application images and other local administrative data.

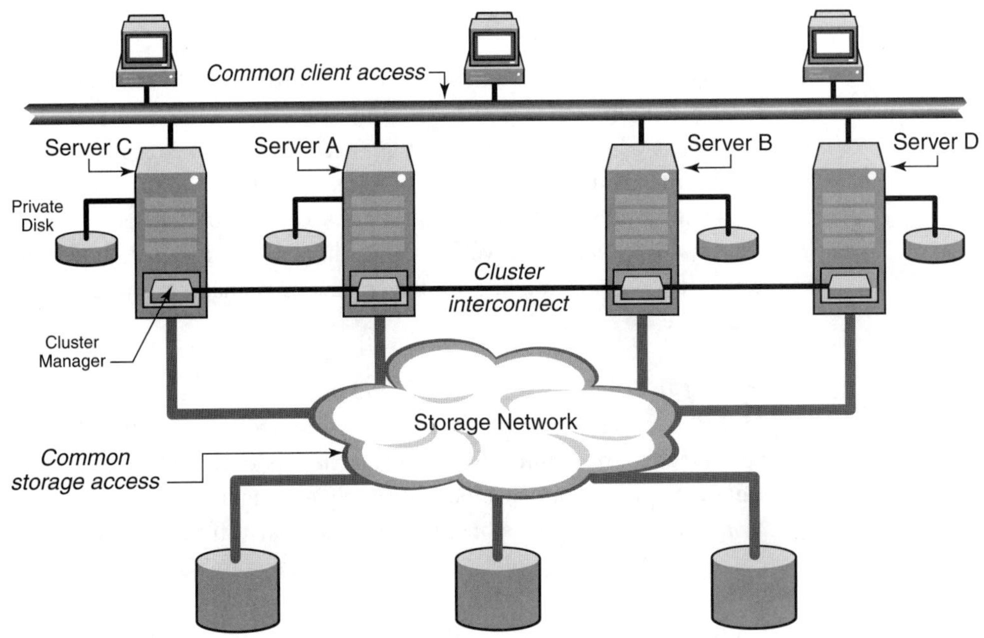

▼ **FIGURE 11–1** *Basic Architectural Features of Clusters*

- ***Disaster recovery:*** If an entire computer room is incapacitated, clustered servers elsewhere in a campus can restart applications.
- ***Management cost:*** The servers in a cluster are interchangeable. This maximizes administrative flexibility (applications can run anywhere in the cluster) and enlarges the administrative scope of control.

Clustering improves application availability by making it possible for applications to restart on alternate servers after a primary server failure. Of course, if an alternate server is already in use, failing an application over to it increases the load on it, and presumably affects the performance of both applications. Configuring a cluster is thus an exercise in balancing cost ("extra" computing resources) against availability (the ability to restart an application and the performance at which it will run in the event that its primary server fails).

Clusters and Virtual Storage

Clustering makes a set of servers more available, scalable, and manageable. Ideally, online storage for clusters should have similar properties.

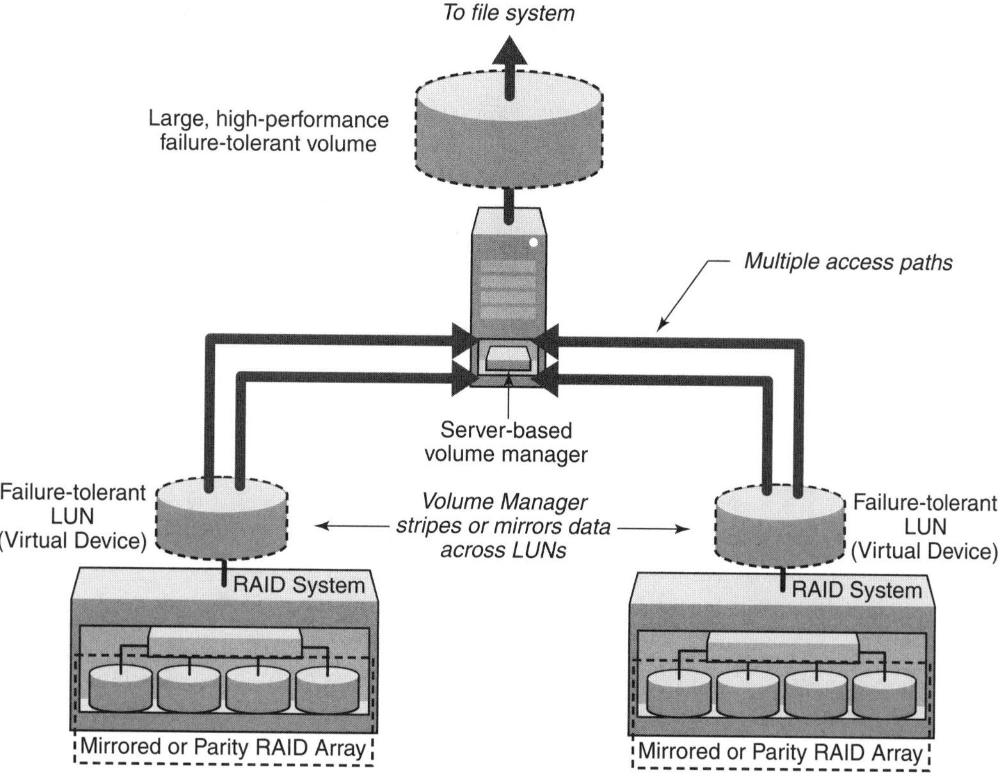

▼ **FIGURE 11–2** *Volume Manager Virtualization of RAID System LUNs*

RAID systems are a good match for clusters because they are designed for high capacity and multiple client connections. RAID systems are resilient; they can survive disk drive, power supply, cooling device, storage network interface, and other failures without losing data or interrupting I/O service. Most are capable of storage, cache, and client interface expansion, and include tools that allow several systems to be managed from one location.

RAID system and storage network appliance storage virtualization are transparent to the servers in a cluster. As Figure 11–2 illustrates, server-based volume managers complement RAID systems, both because they can combine LUNs for greater availability and I/O performance, and because they can coordinate access to LUNs and disks over multiple access paths. Server-based volume management is not transparent to clustered servers, however, because volume managers run in the servers.

Data Access Models for Clusters

Clustered servers must coordinate with each other when executing I/O requests to common storage devices, so as not to corrupt data. There are two basic cluster storage access models:

- ***Shared nothing:*** In a **shared nothing cluster,** each storage device is "owned" (accessed) exclusively by one server at a time, with ownership enforced by the cluster manager. Ownership of a storage device may pass from one server to another, but a server must relinquish device ownership before another can claim it. In a shared nothing cluster, applications running on different servers may not access the same file system or database partition concurrently.

- ***Shared data:*** In a **shared data cluster** (so called because it enables applications to share data), all servers can access the common storage devices at the same time. In the simplest of such clusters, servers share access to storage devices on which they create private virtual devices, with exclusive access enforced by the volume manager. More sophisticated shared data clusters allow concurrent access to files and databases from all servers.

VERITAS Cluster Server

The VERITAS™ Cluster Server (VCS) is available for the Solaris, HP-UX, AIX, Linux, and Microsoft Windows operating systems. VCS uses a shared nothing architecture, and supports clusters of up to 32 servers. All servers in a VCS cluster must run the same operating system, but hardware configurations need not be identical.

During a VCS failover, the server that "owns" a volume releases it for importation by other servers. Which of a VCS cluster's servers receives a failover is determined by VCS's flexible administrative policies. Applications that normally run on one server can be configured to fail over to several other servers in the cluster. The VCS Traffic Director option provides active workload management by directing incoming client traffic to specific servers based on administratively defined loading criteria. The combination of these capabilities means that VCS provides both high-availability and optimal application performance within a cluster environment.

Shared Nothing Clusters

Today, the dominant use of shared nothing clusters is application availability enhancement. If an application or its server fails, a **failover server** takes control of the application's storage devices and other resources and restarts it. Figure 11–3 illustrates a two-server shared nothing cluster. As the figure suggests, each server controls its own storage devices, even though both servers are connected to all devices.

Shared nothing clusters also allow applications that require only read access to shared data to outgrow a single server. Many Web service applications fall into this category. Multiple instances of such applications can run on clustered servers,

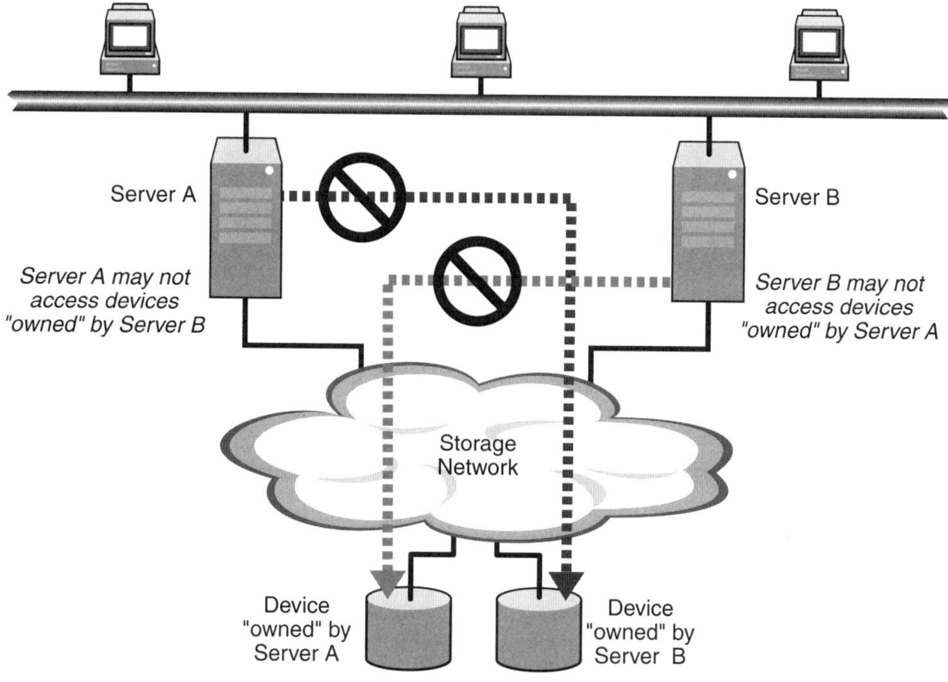

▼ **FIGURE 11–3** *Shared Nothing Cluster Model*

each accessing a separate copy of data, with client requests routed to particular servers by load-balancing software.

Some database managers use shared nothing clustering techniques to improve database scaling. These managers, which include Sybase and DB2, partition a database among several servers, and use a central dispatcher to direct each client request to the server that manages the data it references.

Shared Data Clusters

Shared data clusters, as the name implies, enable servers to share concurrent access to data. Like shared nothing clusters, they improve application availability. In addition, they support data sharing file systems and **parallel database managers** that enable applications running on different servers to read and write files and databases at the same time. Because all applications in a shared data cluster access the same copy of data, all have instant access to all updates. Figure 11–4 illustrates a two-server shared data cluster model.

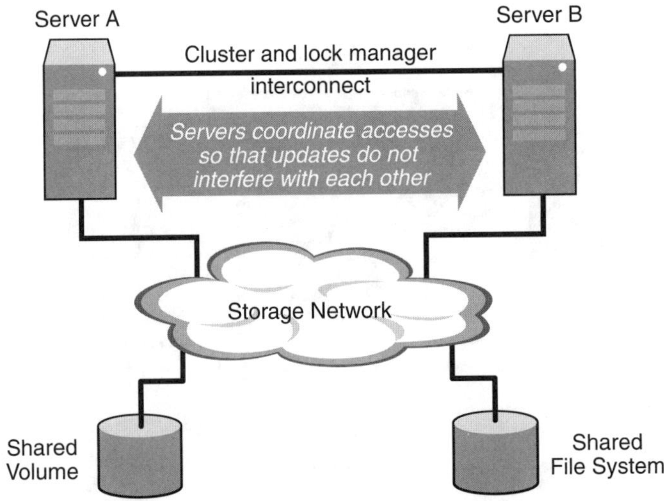

▼ **FIGURE 11–4** *Shared Data Cluster Model*

Shared data clusters are applicable to a broader range of applications than shared nothing ones. Sharing data, however, requires coordination of I/O requests so that writes from different servers do not interfere with each other. Server-based storage virtualizers for shared data clusters must be **cluster-aware.**

STORAGE VIRTUALIZATION FOR SHARED DATA CLUSTERS

Server-based volume managers are useful components of an overall storage virtualization strategy, along with RAID system and network-based virtualization. Volume manager designs are generally predicated upon a single point of control for each virtual device. During a virtual device state change (for example, when a disk fails or when a virtual device is expanded or contracted), the control point temporarily blocks application I/O requests while virtualization metadata is updated, so that every request is executed against a consistent virtual device. The single point of control approach works in shared nothing clusters, where each virtual device is managed and used by a single server. In the shared nothing cluster model illustrated in Figure 11–3, if an application or server fails, the cluster manager transfers ownership of the devices containing its data to the server on which it will restart.

Cluster Volume Managers

The conventional volume manager single point of control model does not support cluster-wide sharing of virtual storage. Cluster-aware volume management is required for consistent virtualization of online storage for all servers in a cluster. In addition to conventional volume management functions, a cluster volume manager:

- Enables simultaneous access to virtual devices from multiple servers
- Provides consistent virtual device naming across the cluster
- Shows a consistent view of virtual device state throughout the cluster
- Allows virtual device administration from any server in the cluster
- Keeps virtual devices accessible by surviving servers after server failures
- Enables applications to fail over without requiring virtual device failover

Cluster volume managers are effectively out-of-band network storage virtualizers (Chapter 10). All servers in a shared data cluster use the same virtualization metadata to translate application I/O requests to storage device operations. Metadata is managed by one server, which distributes it to the others. Being server based, cluster volume managers are flexible; most can combine different types of storage, for example, mirroring LUNs with disk drives. With cluster volume managers, the I/O path is short, as with ordinary volume managers and out-of-band network virtualizers.

From an architectural standpoint, cluster volume managers are typically cluster applications themselves. Most support only homogeneous servers in one cluster. In this they differ from out-of-band virtualizers, which support heterogeneous servers that may not be cooperating with each other in other ways.

VERITAS™ Storage Foundation Cluster File System

The VERITAS™ Storage Foundation Cluster File System is the company's shared data cluster manager. SANPoint Foundation Suite/HA includes a Cluster Volume Manager for common access to volumes by multiple servers, a Cluster File System for high-integrity shared file access, and the VERITAS™ Cluster Server for application failover and load balancing. The Cluster Volume Manager makes server-based virtual block storage devices available to all servers in a cluster simultaneously, thus reducing storage capacity and management costs by enabling consolidation.

The VERITAS™ Storage Foundation Cluster File System enables the creation of file systems of up to 32 terabytes of capacity, large enough even for the most demanding databases and file-based applications.

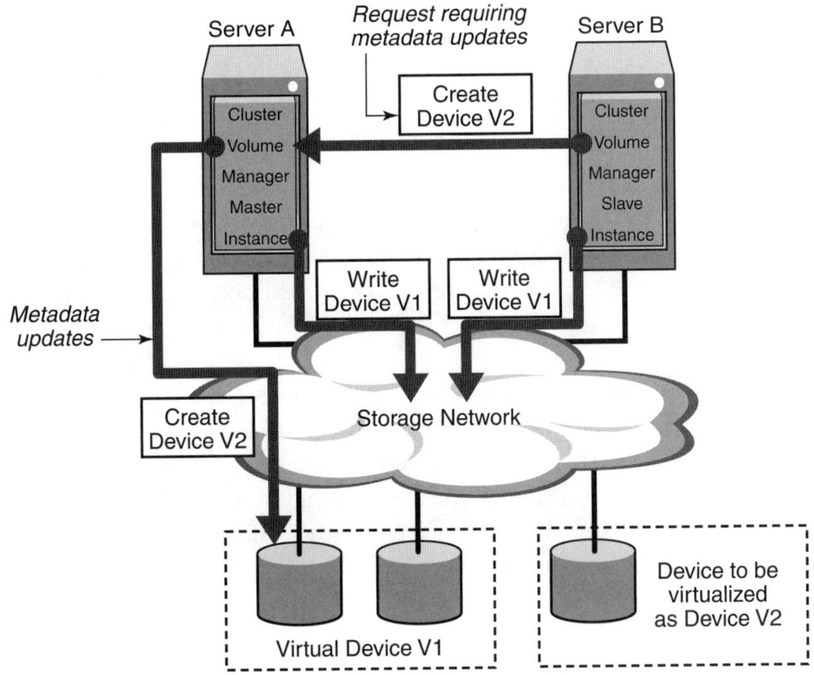

▼ **FIGURE 11–5** *Master-Slave Cluster Volume Manager Operation*

Cluster Volume Manager Architectural Concepts

When clustered servers start up, one server initially *forms* the cluster, becoming a temporary master with which other servers coordinate. Similarly, one instance of a cluster volume manager must be the first to recognize and take control of shareable disks during startup. Once a cluster volume manager is running, control of virtual devices may be *centralized* in one instance using a master-slave model, or *distributed* throughout the cluster. With the master-slave model, one volume manager instance makes all metadata changes (e.g., to create new virtual devices, resize virtual devices, remove mirrors from mirrored virtual devices, and so forth). With distributed control, any volume manager instance in the cluster may update virtual device metadata. Both models block all servers' access to virtual devices during critical changes so that state changes take effect simultaneously throughout the cluster.

With the master-slave architecture, a single **master** server manages all virtualization metadata. Other servers are **slaves** to it with respect to meta-

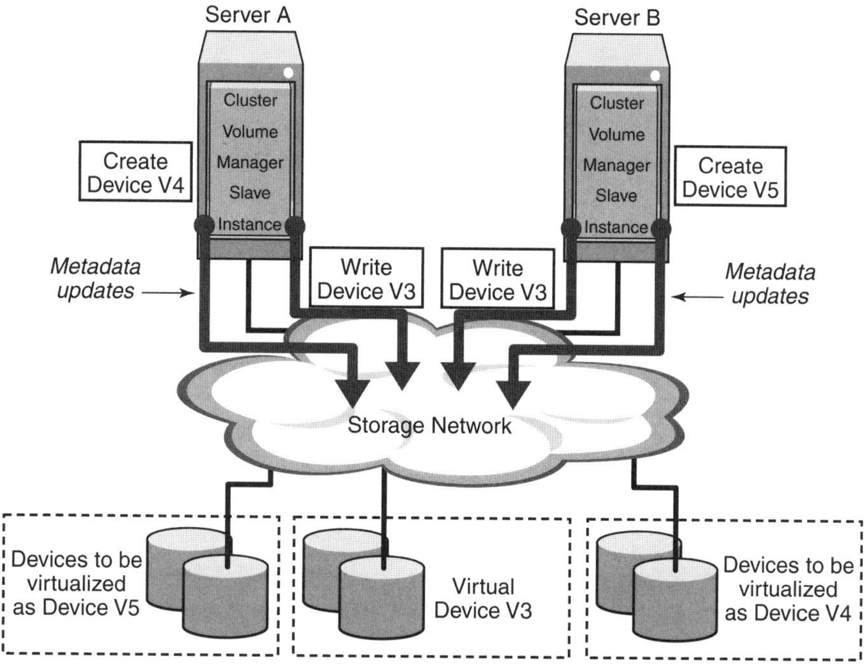

▼ **FIGURE 11–6** *Distributed Cluster Volume Manager Operation*

> **SANPoint Foundation Architecture**
>
> The VERITAS SANPoint Foundation uses a dynamic master-slave architecture. A designated master server manages each cluster volume group and file system. Master servers do not require any extra or special hardware. Should a master server fail, SANPoint Foundation Suite/HA automatically fails its volume groups and file systems over to another server in the cluster. Using a form of out-of-band storage virtualization technology, master servers execute all volume and file system metadata updates. All other servers in the SANPoint Foundation Suite/HA cluster access data directly. SANPoint Foundation Suite/HA dynamic master-slave architecture means low inter-server locking traffic for better performance and less complex (and therefore more robust) implementations.

data updates. Volume manager instances read and write data directly from the servers on which they are running, as Figure 11–5 indicates. Only the master server updates metadata, however. To update metadata (e.g., for an application running on Server B to create virtual device V2), a slave server makes a request to the master, which creates the device. This design guarantees metadata consistency because only one server ever modifies it.

In contrast, Figure 11–6 illustrates distributed cluster volume manager operation. As with the master-slave architecture, all servers satisfy application read and write requests by accessing storage devices directly.

Unlike the master-slave architecture, however, metadata updates, such as those that create virtual devices V4 and V5, are performed directly by the servers on which they are requested. With this architecture, there *is* no master volume manager instance. To update metadata, a volume manager instance blocks all access to critical data structures before manipulating them. The distributed volume manager architecture balances metadata update processing across a cluster's servers at the expense of increased implementation complexity and lock message traffic.

Cluster Volume Access

Like conventional volume managers, cluster volume managers present virtual devices with block storage device semantics for use by file systems and database managers. Like the block storage devices they emulate, virtual devices execute block I/O requests indiscriminately, without regard for applications' rights to access the data in the blocks. Without some form of coordination at the data manager level, updates could interfere with each other, or one server's read executed during another's write could return inconsistent "in-flight" data. In single-server systems, the file system or database manager controls all access to each virtual device. In a cluster, however, it is possible for multiple servers to read and write overlapping block ranges at the same time. Cluster volume managers also do not guarantee that different servers' I/O requests will not interfere with each other. Cluster-aware file systems and database managers must provide such guarantees. Their mechanisms for doing this are discussed in Chapter 15 and Chapter 16, which describe how cluster file systems and parallel database managers, respectively, maintain integrity when several instances are updating the same data.

Very Fast Cluster Failover

VERITAS™ Storage Foundation Cluster File System includes the VERITAS™ Cluster Server, and indeed, both Cluster Volume Manager and Cluster File System masters are implemented as VCS application service groups.

But failover is only required if the server running the volume manager or file system master fails. If other servers or applications fail, volumes and file systems continue to be available. The result is much faster application recovery time, because volumes need not be imported, nor must file systems be integrity checked and remounted. In many cases, application restart time can be shortened further if an alternate copy of the application is already loaded and ready to run on the failover server.

Cluster Volume Managers and Server Crashes

A server running a volume manager might crash while writes to virtual devices are partially complete, leaving device contents in an inconsistent state. For example, with a mirrored virtual device, some mirrors might have been updated and others not. Restoring virtual device consistency after a crash is a well-understood storage virtualization problem with known solutions. For example, one simple solution for mirrored devices is to designate one mirror as a master, and copy its entire contents to the device's other mirrors after a crash. This technique is time-consuming, and therefore limits data and application availability, so more sophisticated techniques are usually adopted.

A more elegant solution would be for a volume manager to log the virtual device block address ranges affected by an update before updating, as well as the completion of each update. During crash recovery, the volume manager would repair data in only those block address ranges indicated as possibly at risk in the log. Because only a small fraction of a virtual device's blocks are likely to be at risk at any instant, recovery time would be short—seconds rather than the tens of minutes are more typical for large virtual devices.

Whatever technique is used to restore virtual device consistency after a crash, there must clearly be a single control point for each virtual device during repair. For this reason, one cluster volume manager instance must control each virtual device until content consistency has been restored.

If the server running a cluster volume manager master fails, virtualization metadata may also be at risk. Surviving servers must elect a new master, which must block application I/O while it checks virtual device integrity. When the check is complete, I/O is unblocked, and application processing resumes. To an application, I/O requests stall momentarily during the integrity check, but otherwise the transition is transparent. Because slave servers do not update virtualization metadata, slave server failure does not require metadata repair. Recovery from slave server failure is therefore typically faster than recovery from master server failure.

CHAPTER SUMMARY

- A cluster is a collection of servers whose operations are coordinated by *cluster server* software. Clusters improve application availability, scaling, and manageability.
- Clusters may implement either *shared nothing* or *shared data* storage access models. In a shared nothing cluster, each storage device is controlled by one of the cluster's servers. In a shared data cluster, the servers cooperate to coordinate simultaneous I/O requests to storage devices.

- Cluster volume managers are software components that perform coordinated server-based storage virtualization for entire clusters. A cluster volume manager presents a consistent view of virtual devices to all of the cluster's servers at all times.
- Cluster volume managers may use either distributed control or master-slave architecture to update metadata.
- Cluster-wide virtual devices are used by parallel database managers and by cluster file systems. These data managers enable distributed applications running on multiple servers in a cluster to share access to databases and files.

CHAPTER 12

The foresight that awaits
Is the same Genius that creates.

—RALPH WALDO EMERSON

Data Replication

In this chapter . . .

- Differences between block storage replication and mirroring
- What data objects can be replicated and how to choose among them
- Where block storage replication can be implemented

It is often desirable to maintain identical physical copies of a master set of data at two or more widely separated locations. Examples include:

- ***Publication and consolidation:*** Distribution, or *publication,* of data from a central data center to remote locations is a common distributed data processing strategy. Examples of publication include regional Web sites and catalogs maintained by global enterprises. Similarly, some enterprises require periodic consolidation of data accumulated at field offices to a central data center, where it is "rolled up" into enterprise management information. In this case, data from many sources is replicated to a single target location.
- ***Off-host processing:*** It is often necessary to process a snapshot of data without impacting applications that are using the live data. The most common example is backup. Business considerations often make it impractical to stop or even impede application execution for any appreciable period. Even if snapshots are used, backup or analysis overhead can lead to unacceptable application performance. If

data is replicated to another server, however, that server can back up or analyze data with no impact on live application performance.

- ***Disaster recovery:*** Perhaps the most important use of data replication is to maintain copies of vital data at remote locations for quick recovery from disasters that incapacitate entire data centers and make high-availability mechanisms ineffective.

When distances between data source and target are short, split mirrors can meet these requirements. Often, however, the geographic separation between source and target precludes mirroring. In these cases, data replication is often a viable alternative.

GETTING DATA TO REMOTE LOCATIONS

From a storage management standpoint, the aforementioned requirements have two important characteristics: (1) data must be copied from one source to one or more target locations; (2) data replicas at target locations are not used while the copy is occurring. Publication and off-host processing usually require snapshots, while disaster recovery benefits from the most up-to-date data image possible, but both applications make use of data after copying has finished or been interrupted.

Data Replication and Mirroring

Data replication technology has evolved to meet these needs. The technology differs from mirroring in that it takes three important factors into account:

- ***Latency:*** The time to communicate between an application server and the location at which data is replicated may be significant. Increasing application response time by the wait for remote writes to complete may be unacceptable.
- ***Communication reliability:*** Communications between an application server and a replication site may fail occasionally. Brief outages should be transparent to applications; intrusive recovery procedures should only be required for lengthy outages (tens of hours).
- ***Source to target:*** Unlike mirroring technology, in which all mirrors are regarded as equal, replication has a definite source and definite targets.

These factors lead to data replication designs that differ considerably from mirroring, which superficially delivers similar results, at least over short distances.

Alternatives to Data Replication

Replication is not the only way to solve these data management problems. Publication, consolidation, and off-host processing can also be done by transporting backup tapes or with network file copies. Disaster protection can sometimes be achieved by mirroring across extended storage networks. Each of these techniques has drawbacks, however:

- ***Backup*** requires tape drives and media at target sites as well as media transportation and manipulation. The time required to transport and restore a backup is time during which applications at the recovery site are either unavailable or working from out-of-date data.
- ***Network file copies*** must be made from quiescent data. Even if file copying is automated by scripting, this means relatively long periods of application outage.
- ***Mirroring*** is useful over short distances. Remote mirrors are always current and there is no delay until remote data can be recovered and used. When the distance between mirrors makes transmission time significant, however, the increase in application response time is usually unacceptable.

Moreover, mirroring and network file copying both require completely reliable networks. External communications are more prone to varying latencies and brief outages than the short interconnections within a data center. Neither mirroring nor network file copying are designed to recover rapidly from network outages.

FORMS OF REPLICATION

The term data replication is used to denote several technology variants, distinguished primarily by the data objects they replicate. Technology exists for replicating:

- ***Database updates,*** regardless of the file or virtual device containers in which the source and target databases reside

- ***File updates*** within a file system, including both data and metadata such as ownership, access permissions, and time stamps, used to manage the files
- ***Updates to virtual block storage device contents,*** regardless of the file system or database structures stored on the devices

Each of these forms of replication has different properties, at least partly because the replicated objects themselves have different properties. Although the primary focus of this book is on virtual block storage device replication, the following sections describe the three different forms.

Database Replication

Some database managers are able to replicate data between database instances managed by different servers. There are different ways to replicate updates to databases, but all incorporate the concept of replicating complete database transactions. Figure 12–1 illustrates database replication.

Database managers have considerably more contextual information about data than volume managers and file systems, in particular, about transactional relationships among updates. For example, a transaction that transfers money from one bank account to another typically includes two key data updates—one to the debited account's balance and one to the credited account's balance. Application designs typically assume that either both updates will be reflected in a database, or neither will (e.g., because of some failure from which the database has recovered).

From a block storage device standpoint, the two key updates in this transaction cannot be associated with each other. Even from a file system standpoint, the updates may be to different files in different file systems, and therefore not easily correlated. A database manager, on the other hand, *can* relate the corresponding updates, because they occur in the context of the same transaction, so database replication can replicate them atomically (as a unit). Two additional advantages of database replication are:

- ***Delayed replication:*** Most database managers can be directed to hold updates in a queue, and delay application to the database replica for a period of time (or alternatively, to apply updates at specific times). As long as the errors are discovered in time, this feature is useful for recovering from data corruption due to application or data entry errors.
- ***Concise expression:*** A database manager can replicate entire bundles of related updates, or it can send a transaction description (e.g., a SQL

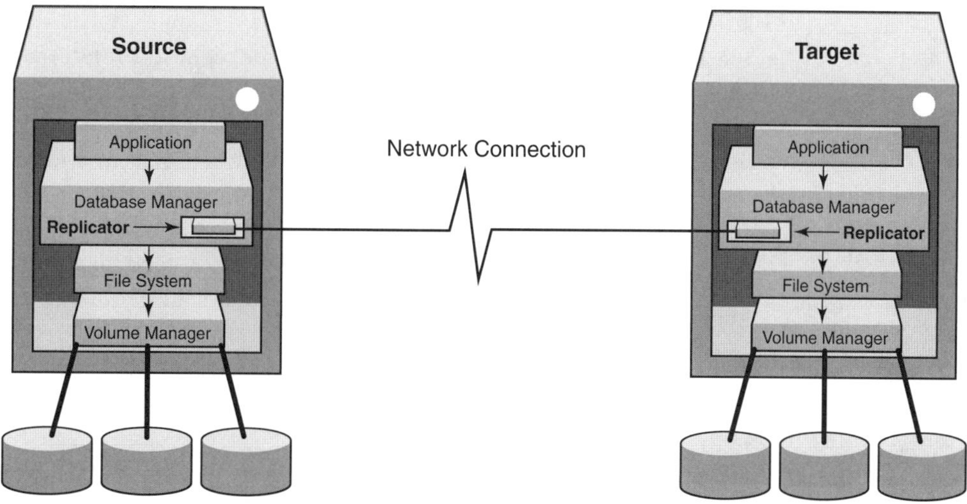

▼ **FIGURE 12–1** *Database Replication*

procedure) to be executed by the database manager at the replica site. A trivial example is a "raise all prices by 5%" transaction, which can be expressed in a few hundred bytes of SQL, but which causes every price record in a database to be read and overwritten with an updated price. Clearly, sending the procedure and executing it at the replica site consumes much less network bandwidth.

- ***Selectivity:*** With database replication, it is possible to replicate only selected tables or row ranges of records. This capability can be used, for example, to distribute centrally maintained data to several remote locations, each of which requires only a subset of the data.

Offsetting these advantages are complexity (the intimate knowledge of database structure needed to configure and manage it requires the skill and knowledge of a database administrator) and some functional limitations of database replication. For example, most database managers are incapable of replicating changes in database structure. If a field is added to a table, replication must be completely reconfigured, reinitialized, and restarted.

Database replication is also limited in that it replicates *only* data that is part of a database. Replication of logs, control files, and other data outside the database must be accomplished by other means and managed separately.

File Replication

Figure 12–2 illustrates file replication. The source replicator intercepts file I/O requests before they reach the file system. Because the replicator is file-aware, replication can be selective—it can be limited to specified sets of files. This is useful for applications whose data is stored in a fixed set of directories—the directories can be specified as replication objects, and thereafter, any files added to them are automatically replicated. Some file replicators are able to replicate different file sets to different target locations. This is useful for publication and consolidation applications.

VERITAS File Replication

The VERITAS data replication product family includes file system replicators for both UNIX (VERITAS™ File Replicator) and Windows (VERITAS™ Storage Replicator) products.

The VERITAS File Replicator enables UNIX servers to share access to file systems over local or wide area networks. For performance reasons all reads occur from the local file system, but the writes are distributed to all server nodes sharing the file system. The VERITAS File Replicator does not require the VERITAS™ Volume Manager or File System, but it integrates seamlessly if these components are present.

The VERITAS™ Storage Replicator (VSR) provides similar capabilities for Windows operating systems. VSR capabilities include one: many replication, periodic or continuous replication, and directed replication of specific file sets to specific targets.

Like database replicators, file replicators typically queue replica writes in a persistent log. The source replicator sends requests and data from the log to target replicators at network speed; the targets write data to file systems at target locations. Thus, it is possible for replicated files to lag behind the files they are replicating. File replicators can usually be configured to limit the number of updates by which they will "fall behind" before blocking further updates at the source.

File systems that hold replicated files can be used during replication. As Figure 12–2 suggests, replicated data is written through the target file system, which coordinates all file writes. File access permissions, locking, and simultaneous access rules are all in effect. From the target file system's point of view, the file replicator is just another application. Since file systems control all accesses to file data, including those of target replicators, replicated files can be read by applications as long as they are not being written or extended by the replicator.

File replication does not require that source and target file systems (or storage devices, for that matter) be identical. For example, files can be replicated to target directories with different names. This property is useful for data consolidation. Each source location can replicate identically named files to a central file system at the target location. The central file system writes the replicated data from each source in a separate directory; thus, there is no naming conflict.

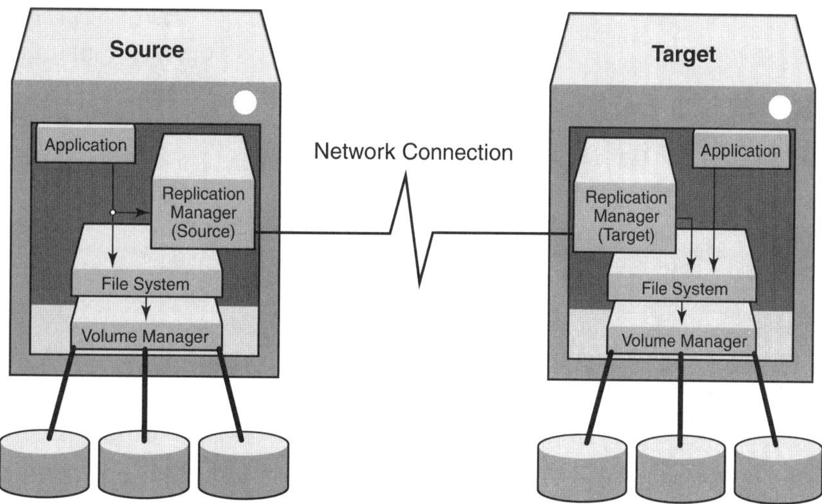

▼ **FIGURE 12–2** *File Replication*

Virtual Block Storage Device Replication

A virtual device replicator replicates updates to data on a set of **source devices** to a set of **target devices** of equivalent capacities, preserving the order of updates to ensure that target virtual device contents are recoverable at any point in time.

Like any block storage facility, virtual device replicators have no information about the meaning and interrelationship of I/O requests. They cannot determine the state in which any given update leaves a device. For example, the metadata updates that create a file must be atomic (i.e., either all must occur, or none may occur), even though each one entails several block updates. No information about the interrelationship of these updates (or about their *lack* of interrelationship with others) is available to a virtual device replicator. The replicator cannot determine whether file creation is complete or in progress. For this reason, applications cannot access a data replica while replication is occurring. This characteristic of virtual device replication makes it most suitable for two general classes of application:

- ***Data reuse:*** Software testing, backup, and data analysis ("mining") all require access to snapshots of application data. These can be created by replicating the virtual devices containing it, pausing the application, and stopping replication.

VERITAS™ Volume Replicator

The VERITAS™ Volume Replicator (VVR) is implemented as a data service of the Volume Manager virtualizer. VVR is a storage device-independent replicator—it will replicate volume contents from any type of storage to any type of storage.

VVR extends the Volume Manager paradigm to geographically mirrored data. Its close relationship to the VERITAS™ Volume Manager makes it easy to incorporate volume replication into a Volume Manager environment—"If you know VERITAS Volume Manager, you know the VERITAS Volume Replicator." Administrators may choose synchronous replication (for greatest data currency) or asynchronous replication (for minimal impact on application performance), and still be assured of 100% data consistency due to VVR's write order fidelity in both modes.

Because it is based on the VERITAS Volume Manager, VVR automatically supports all types of storage supported by the Volume Manager.

- ***Disaster recovery:*** Groups of virtual devices containing critical application data can be replicated to a disaster recovery location. If a disaster destroys the primary data center, the integrity of the replica can be restored through conventional means and applications restarted at the recovery site with (nearly) up-to-date data.

In both of these applications, data at the target location is used by applications *after* replication stops, rather than while it is occurring.

A server-based virtual device replicator "taps in" to the I/O request stream above the volume manager, as Figure 12–3 illustrates. The source replicator sends an equivalent of each write request to one or more target replicators, and passes the request on for local execution. In most implementations, the replicator logs requests persistently, and transmits them at network speed. This decouples replication from application execution, and makes application performance nearly independent of network speed, replication target performance, and the number of replicas. Most server-based replicators can be configured to limit how far behind replication is permitted to fall, usually in terms of number of updates.

In spite of the fact that data on replicated virtual devices cannot be used during replication, the technology is often preferred over others for two reasons:

- ***Low overhead:*** Because a block replication context is relatively simple, processing overhead and message traffic between source and target are predictable—each application write corresponds to a write and an acknowledgment for each target. In contrast, overheads due to file or database replication can depend on both the nature of update operations and on current load at target locations.

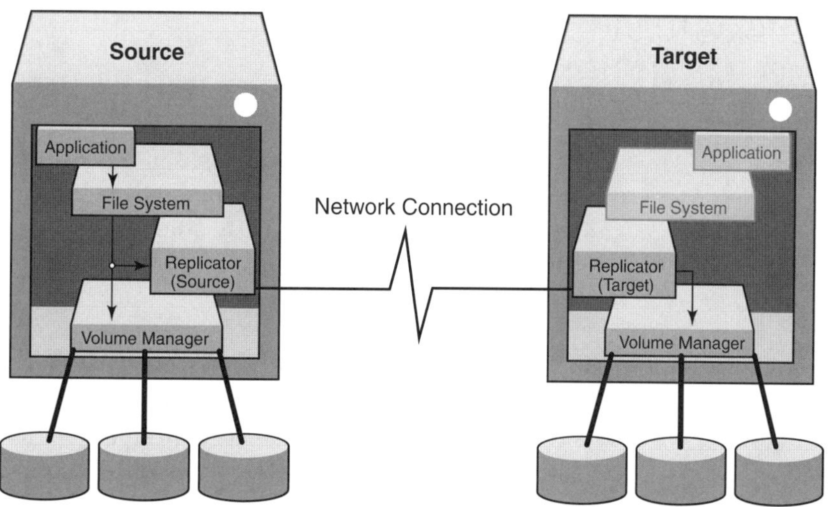

▼ **FIGURE 12–3** *Server-Based Block Storage Device Replication*

Replication on TCP/IP Networks

The VERITAS™ Volume Replicator (VVR) supports up to 32 concurrent replication targets in either synchronous or asynchronous mode, or in a mixture of the two. VVR minimizes replication network traffic because once replication is initially synchronized, only changed volume blocks are transmitted.

Because it uses the TCP/IP network, VVR can share bandwidth with other user traffic on a WAN, minimizing overall network infrastructure cost. Because VVR is storage independent, it is possible to replicate between different types of storage devices supplied by different vendors; only volume capacity must be identical between source and target. This allows disaster recovery sites to be equipped with lower cost storage, and minimizes total cost of ownership compared to hardware-based solutions that require identical storage devices at both sites.

The VERITAS Volume Replicator can be integrated with and managed by the VERITAS™ Availability Manager to completely automate site failover, resulting in shorter recovery times in case of data center disasters.

▼ ***Universal applicability:*** Virtual block storage device replication replicates *all* data stored on a group of virtual devices, no matter what file system or database manages it. This is particularly important for database applications that store ancillary information in files outside the database. Virtual device replication captures all modifications to databases, files, file system metadata, and other application data structures.

Virtual device replication is generally the preferred technique for disaster recovery. Because *all* virtual device contents are replicated, administrators need not remember to explicitly specify that newly created objects should be replicated. Therefore, a group of replicated virtual devices is certain to contain any data needed for recovery.

BLOCK STORAGE REPLICATION IMPLEMENTATION ALTERNATIVES

Like block storage virtualization, to which it is closely related, virtual device replication can be implemented in servers, in RAID systems, and in storage network infrastructure components (switches and appliances). Each of these implementations has unique properties that are discussed in the sections that follow.

Server-Based Replication

Figure 12–4 illustrates the key properties of server-based replication. As the figure suggests, a server-based **replicator** software component intercepts application write requests to replicated virtual devices, and sends them with their data to target locations, where a complementary replicator writes them to persistent storage. The advantages of server-based replication are:

- ***Storage independence:*** With server-based replication, storage devices at the source and target locations may be different. This allows, for example, re-purposed or lower-cost storage devices to be employed at target locations.
- ***Enterprise network sharing:*** While dedicated network connections may be configured for performance, server-based replication is TCP/IP based, and can therefore share network facilities with other traffic. This can reduce both the expense and the complexity of managing replication.

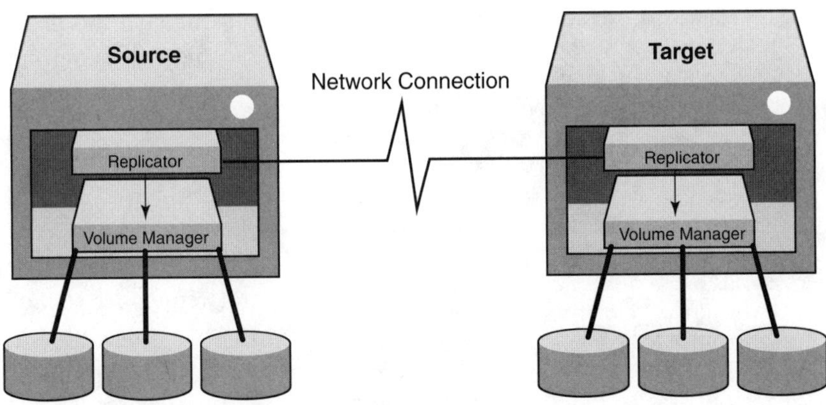

▼ **FIGURE 12–4** *Server-Based Replication*

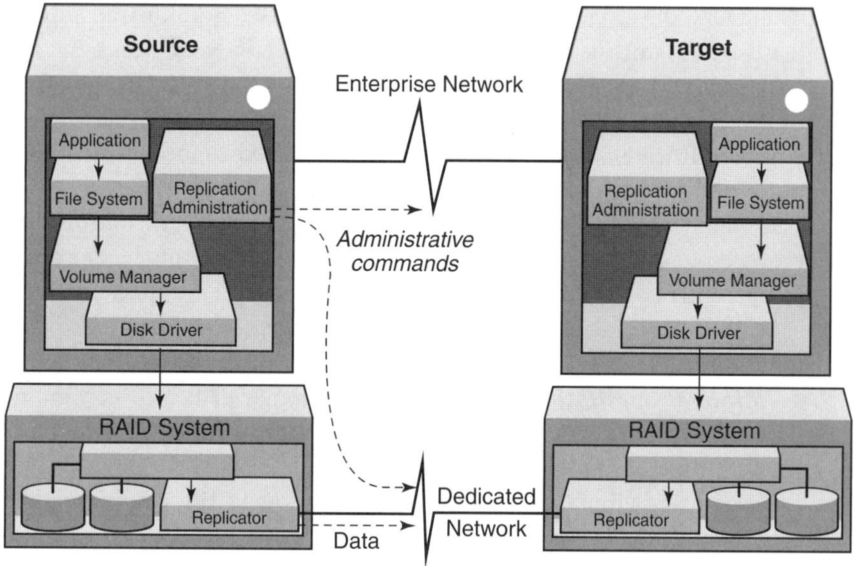

▼ **FIGURE 12–5** *RAID System-Based Virtual Device Replication*

Today's server-based replication technology generally requires that source and target platforms be of the same type. They can replicate data between storage devices of different types, but only if the devices are connected to servers of the same type.

RAID System Replication

Like server-based replicators, RAID system replicators have no information about the meaning of data in the virtual device blocks they replicate, so virtual devices are the only objects that can be replicated by RAID systems. Figure 12–5 illustrates virtual device replication between a pair of RAID systems.

As Figure 12–5 suggests, the source RAID system itself sends write requests made to virtual devices to a companion RAID system at the target location, where they are written to virtual devices of equivalent capacity. Some RAID systems are able to replicate between different types of virtual devices, for example, from a mirrored device to a simple or striped one, but with today's technology, source and target RAID systems must be of the same type.

The data copying phase of RAID system replication is transparent to both source and target servers. Starting, stopping, and adjusting parameters, however, typically requires server-based administrative tools that issue commands to the RAID systems, either *in-band* (using the I/O path) or *out-of-band* (e.g., using an auxiliary communications channel connected to an Ethernet port on the RAID system).

Some RAID system replicators require dedicated connections between source and target. These systems replicate data with no application overhead. The application server starts and stops replication and controls data recovery, but during replication, application writes at the source are copied transparently to target LUNs with minimal impact on application performance. The principal advantages of RAID system-based replication are:

- ***Minimal application server resource:*** Though dedicated communications can be costly, minimal application impact is an offsetting factor. Some RAID systems support replication over TCP/IP networks (e.g., using Fibre Channel Protocol over IP, or FCIP), eliminating the expense of a dedicated replication network.
- ***Application server platform independence:*** A single enterprise RAID system at the source can replicate data for multiple server platforms of different architectures to one or more target locations.[1]

RAID system-based replication typically requires that both source and target RAID systems be of the same model. Thus, a RAID system can replicate data for different server types, but only between storage devices of the same type.

Network Appliance-Based Replication

VERITAS ServPoint NAS Appliance Software is designed to run on Solaris and Linux servers, turning them into highly functional file server appliances. The Solaris and Linux execution environments make it easy to extend appliance functionality with advanced features like mirroring, RAID, point-in-time copy, and clustering. In addition, the VERITAS Volume Replicator can be used with a ServPoint NAS-based appliance, expanding its role to that of a highly available resilient multi-data center storage solution.

Storage Network Replication

Replication can also be implemented in virtualization appliances that are part of the storage network. One such configuration is illustrated in Figure 12–6. In the figure, a replicator running in an in-band virtualization appliance intercepts application write requests addressed to virtual devices and transmits them with their data to a remote appliance, which writes them to corresponding virtual devices that it instantiates.

1. Of course, the replicated data's format must be compatible with each target platform that will process it.

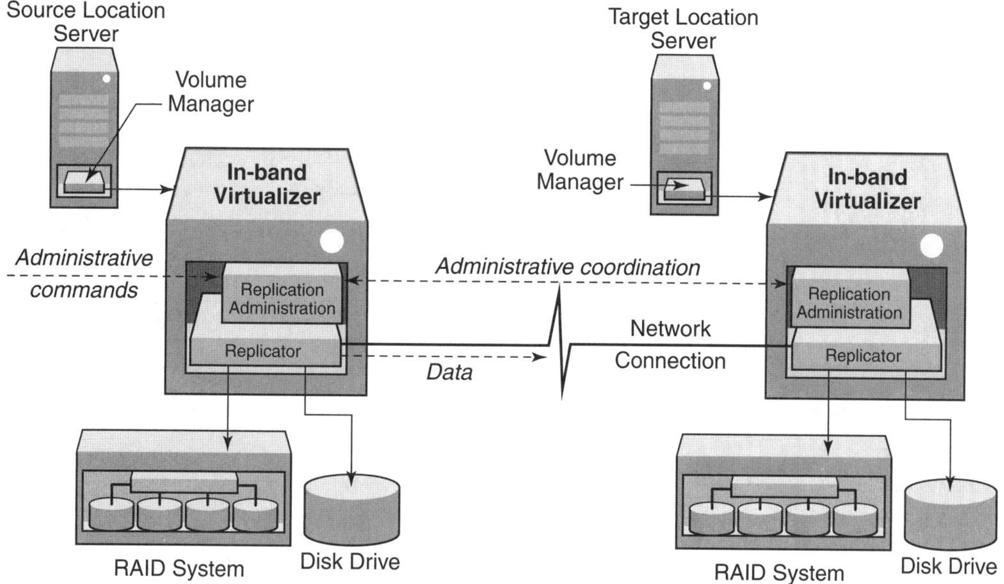

▼ **FIGURE 12–6** *Replication by an In-Band Storage Network Appliance*

Out-of-band storage network appliances represent a more complex case. Figure 12–7 illustrates one replication configuration in an out-of-band network virtualization environment. In the figure, out-of-band virtualization appliances at source and target locations cooperate to replicate data from one to the other.

In the scenario illustrated in Figure 12–7, the appliance that runs the virtualization metadata manager also runs a replication component. This replication component has access to the metadata manager's virtualization metadata, so it is able to replicate the block contents of virtual devices to a companion replicator at a remote location. The replication component must communicate closely with the server-based virtualization components that run in application servers when out-of-band network replication is in use, so that it becomes aware of updates to replicated virtual devices immediately as they are written by application servers. In this configuration, replication can be administered from any point in the network at which replication components run, including both application servers and the metadata manager appliance itself.

Like RAID systems, block virtualization appliances, whether in-band or out-of-band, have no file system or database awareness, so they are limited to replicating virtual block storage devices. The advantages of storage network appliance-based replication are:

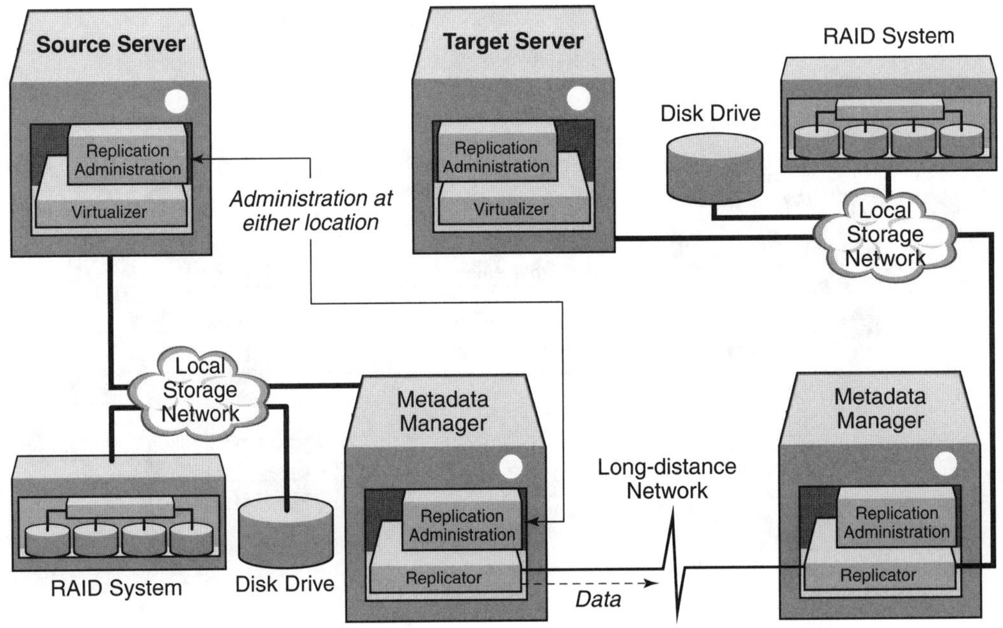

▼ **FIGURE 12–7** *Replication by an Out-of-Band Storage Network Appliance*

- ***Network flexibility:*** Storage network appliance-based replication can use either the enterprise network or a storage network. Load permitting, it is often possible to share the network connections used for replication with other network traffic, minimizing implementation cost and management complexity.
- ***Storage and server independence:*** As with server-based replication, source and target storage devices may be different. As with RAID system-based replication, storage device contents can be replicated for multiple server platforms of different architectures.

Storage network appliances can replicate data between storage devices of different types on behalf of servers of different types.[2] In this sense, it would seem to represent a kind of functional ideal. With both in-band and out-of-band virtualization appliance replication, however, scaling is a con-

2. Although as with RAID system-based replication, target platforms that will mount and use device replicas must use data formats compatible with those of the replication source devices.

cern. The most likely limitation of a replicating storage network appliance is its ability to replicate the amount of data apt to be required by critical enterprise applications in a timely fashion. This limitation, of course, can be overcome through the use of multiple replicating appliances, which sacrifices the single central point of management to some extent.

USING REPLICATED DATA FOR DISASTER RECOVERY

Recovering After a Disaster

Replicating block storage device contents places up-to-date (or nearly up-to-date) data at a disaster recovery site, but it doesn't necessarily guarantee that the devices containing the data are in a fit state to be used when a disaster interrupts processing at the main data center. The problem arises because disasters can occur at awkward times—during a file system metadata update or a database manager cache flush, for example.

Before virtual device replicas can be used, the file systems on them must be mounted and restored to a consistent state, databases must be recovered by database manager recovery tools, and any other application-specific crash recovery actions must be taken. Thus, the process of restarting information services at a recovery site after a disaster is similar to that of restarting services after a crash at the main data center, provided that updates are replicated in the same order as they are applied at the main data center. The **write order fidelity** property of replication is discussed in Chapter 13.

Bidirectional Replication

Any replicated data set has one source and one or more targets. A server or appliance can be the source for one replicated data set and the target for others. Two replicators acting as sources for some replicated data sets and targets for others can protect against disasters in either of the two locations. Figure 12–8 illustrates the use of replication to protect two locations against disaster at either of them.

In Figure 12–8, Location L is the source for Application A, which processes data on virtual devices controlled at Location L. The source replicator running at Location L replicates data to a target at Location M. Similarly, Application B normally runs at Location M, processing data on virtual devices controlled by that location. Application B's data is replicated to a target at Location L.

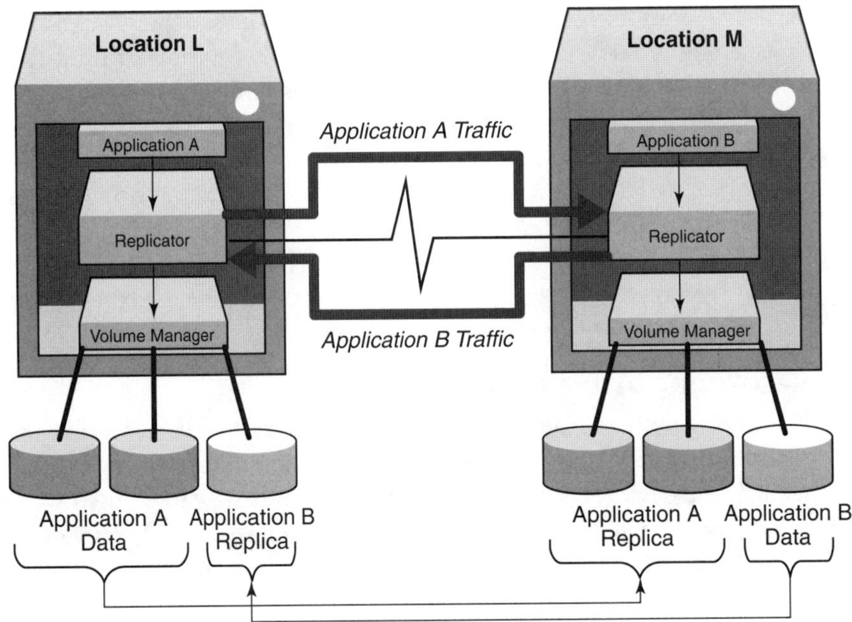

▼ **FIGURE 12–8** *Bidirectional Data Replication*

If a disaster incapacitates either location, the surviving one can run both applications, because up-to-date data for both is available to it. Of course, both servers must be configured with sufficient resources to run both applications at acceptable performance levels. Bidirectional replication uses resources more effectively than **active-passive** recovery scenarios in which recovery servers remain idle until a disaster requires that they be activated. When bidirectional replication is used, care must be exercised to synchronize the server configurations at both locations so that each location can actually run the other's applications. Configuration considerations include memory, local storage, client access, software licenses, patch levels, and client access.

CHAPTER SUMMARY

- Data can be replicated in real time between widely separated computer systems for purposes of publication and consolidation, for off-host processing, or for disaster recovery.

- Data replication differs from mirroring in that source and target roles are clearly distinguished, and have different access latencies and reliabilities.
- Virtual device contents, files in file systems, and databases can all be replicated. Each form of replication has unique characteristics that suit it best to particular applications. In particular, virtual device replication is the best choice for disaster recovery because it replicates *all* of an application's data objects.
- Virtual block storage device replication can be implemented in servers, in RAID systems, and in storage network appliances. File and database replication can only be implemented in servers (including file servers) because only they have information about the meaning of data stored in virtual device blocks.

CHAPTER 13

They always say time changes things, but you actually have to change them yourself.

—ANDY WARHOL

Characteristics of Virtual Device Replication

In this chapter . . .

- The impact of replication on application I/O performance
- Problems that arise during replication and how to solve them
- How to get replication started

To minimize impact on application performance, most virtual block storage device replication implementations allow replication to lag source updates to data by a bounded amount of time or number of I/O requests. This chapter discusses the effects of replication on application performance and the implications for recovering online data from an out-of-date replica.

VIRTUAL STORAGE DEVICE REPLICATION AND APPLICATION PERFORMANCE

Database and even file replication updates may be deliberately delayed to increase network efficiency, or for protection against data corruption. Virtual block storage device replication updates should normally be applied as quickly as possible, because with no semantic information about the updates available, there is nothing to be gained by delaying them. Updates to virtual block storage devices may be replicated:

- ***Synchronously,*** with write request completion not signaled to applications until updates have been transmitted and written to persistent storage at the replication target location[1]
- ***Asynchronously,*** with write request completion signaled to applications as soon as updates have been logged on persistent storage at the source. Asynchronous replication minimizes impact on application performance.

Figure 13–1 summarizes the factors that affect the timing of virtual block storage device replication. Each application write must be processed and data written, causing the application thread that made the request to stall for a few milliseconds.[2] Application designers base designs on this behavior. An application interaction with a user might result in 100 I/O requests and deliver response time of a second or two. An interaction that results in thousands of I/O requests must be designed so the response of tens of seconds is perceived as reasonable (e.g., with user-visible progress indicators). The time required to complete a local I/O request is indicated as T_1 in Figure 13–1.

The replicator intercepts each I/O request, adding a negligible amount of processing time. The time to transmit write requests and their data is indicated as T_2 in Figure 13–1. The time to write data persistently to the replica is indicated as T_3 in Figure 13–1. Finally, the success of the replica write must be acknowledged in a message to the source, whose transmission time is shown as T_4 in Figure 13–1.

Synchronous Replication

Breaking down a replicated write into these parts clarifies the difference between synchronous and asynchronous replication. Because writing to local devices and network transmission are independent, T_1 can overlap with any of T_2, T_3, and T_4. Transmission to the target site, writing to the

1. Because this chapter is disaster recovery-oriented, the descriptions of block virtual device replication are presented in terms of a single target. Most implementations, however, support multiple replication targets, and all descriptions of behavior in this chapter would remain valid with multiple targets.
2. This simple analysis ignores the speed-up effect of nonvolatile write-back cache found in some RAID systems.

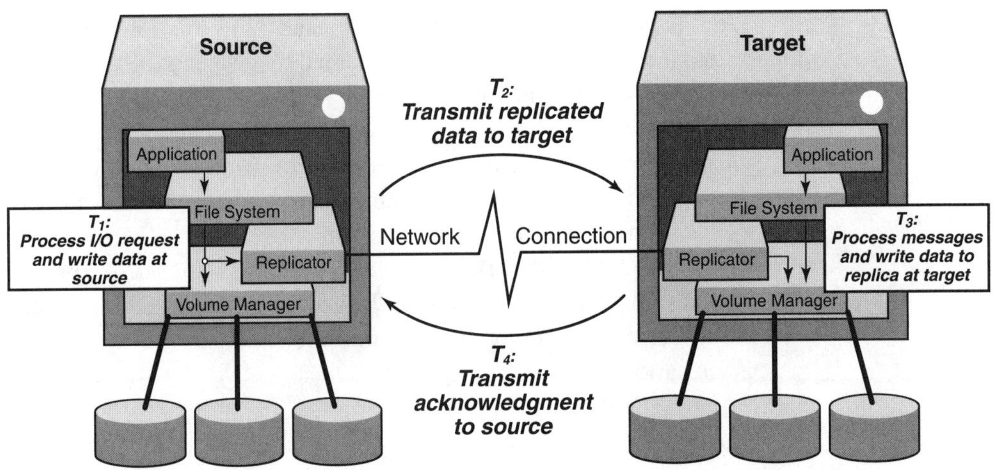

▼ **FIGURE 13–1** *Virtual Block Storage Device Replication Timing*

replica, and signaling success of the write to the source are necessarily sequential (no one of them can begin until the previous one is complete), so intervals T_2, T_3, and T_4 are also sequential. The time line in Figure 13–2 illustrates this.

As Figure 13–2 suggests, writing data to persistent storage at the source can be concurrent with transmission to target locations. Data cannot be written at the target, however, until it has arrived there (i.e., until transmission is complete). Similarly, the target's acknowledgment message must follow writing; otherwise it is meaningless.

With synchronous replication, the application's I/O request is not considered complete until writing to persistent storage at the target is complete and has been acknowledged. The net effect of replication is that applications' write requests take longer to execute—by as much as 100% (assuming approximately equal I/O performance at source and target). For update-intensive applications, this can increase user response time to unacceptable levels. For example, with an application interaction that makes 50 block updates, and storage devices that execute write requests in 10 milliseconds, synchronous replication could increase response time by half a second on an unloaded network. If transmission of updates is delayed by other network activity, T_2 is further elongated by queuing, and application response time could increase even more.

For some uses of replication, such as database logs, synchronization of source and target data may be critical. For these, replication must be synchronous, with a time line similar to that illustrated in Figure 13–2. For most data, however, a more aggressive approach can be adopted to

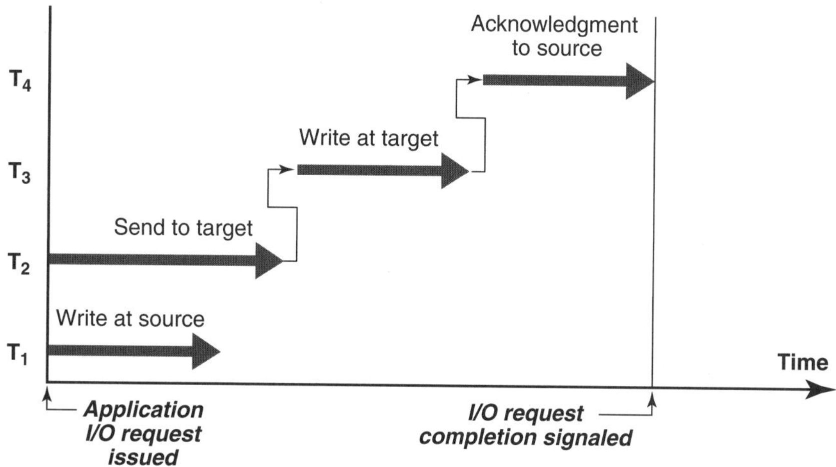

▼ **FIGURE 13–2** *Synchronous Replication Time Line*

maintain good application response. These approaches basically make some or all of T_2, T_3, and T_4 concurrent with each other.

Synchronous-Asynchronous Switching

Most VERITAS™ Volume Replicator (VVR) implementations are configured to switch automatically between synchronous and asynchronous replication modes. Under normal circumstances, when sufficient network bandwidth is available, synchronous mode keeps target site volume contents up to date. If a temporary network outage occurs, VVR automatically changes to asynchronous replication mode, and uses a storage replication log (SRL) to minimize functional and performance impact on applications.

VVR also supports a fast resynchronization using a delta logging mechanism. If replication is interrupted for a long enough period for the SRL to fill, VVR can log modified block regions without maintaining write order fidelity. When communications are restored, modified blocks can be copied to targets, and then replication with write order fidelity can resume without the need for full initial synchronization.

Asynchronous Replication

There are two common techniques for asynchronous replication:

- Acknowledging receipt of data at the target without waiting for it to be stored persistently.
- Signaling application I/O request completion without waiting for data to be sent to the target location.

Figure 13–3 illustrates a data replication time line using the first of these techniques. The target sends its acknowledgment as soon as it receives an application update and its data (without waiting for the data to be written to persistent storage). The meaning of the acknowledgment changes from “data received and stored” to “data received.”

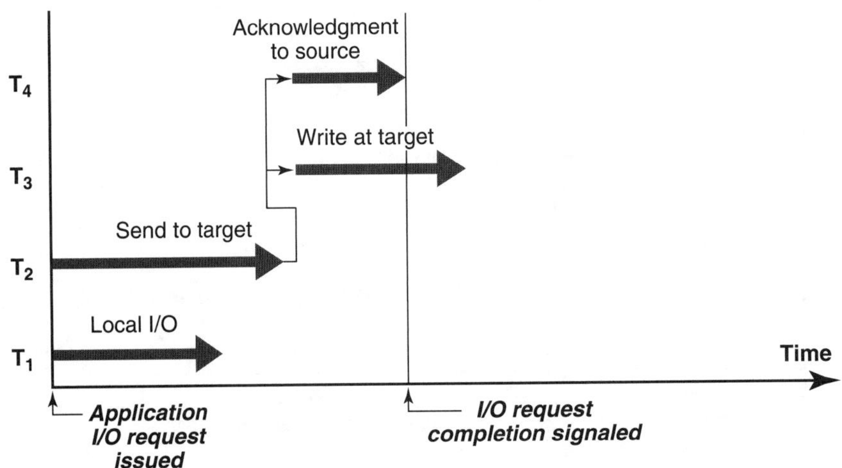

▼ **FIGURE 13–3** *Asynchronous Replication Time Line*

Although it shortens application write request execution time, this technique changes the semantics of replication in one rare scenario. If a target fails (recoverably) and an unrecoverable disaster occurs at the source almost simultaneously, replicated data that has been acknowledged but not yet stored persistently can be lost. The chances of simultaneous source site disaster and target system failure are so remote that users are generally willing to accept that risk to gain the resulting improvement in response time. By acknowledging data immediately, a target effectively eliminates its I/O time (presumably comparable to T_1), from application response time.

The second technique for improving replication performance decouples *all* target activity from application response time. Figure 13–4 illustrates this technique.

In Figure 13–4, another step has been added to replication—data is queued at the source and sent to the target *asynchronously* with application execution. Instead of transmitting updates and waiting for target acknowledgment before signaling completion to applications, the source replicator queues updates locally and signals I/O completion to the application immediately. Updates are transmitted to the target as network bandwidth and other resources permit. With this strategy, each I/O request's contribution to application response time is reduced to T_1', essentially the same as if data were not being replicated.

This technique introduces a risk: If the source replicator fails while data is queued for replication, the queued data could be lost. To mitigate

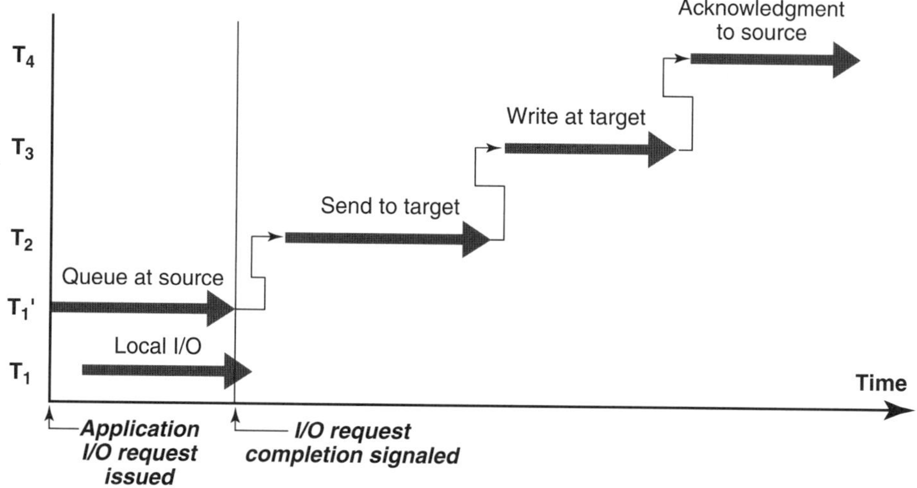

▼ **FIGURE 13–4** *Time Line for Asynchronous Transmission*

this risk, updates are queued on persistent storage at the source. The source replicator adds an entry to its queue for each application write and removes entries when the writes they represent have been transmitted and all targets have acknowledged receiving them. Because the queue is persistent, it survives local system failures, and replication can resume from the point of interruption after recovery from a source, target, or network failure.

Asynchronous replication makes momentary network and processing overloads transparent to applications. Applications continue executing as soon as their writes are queued by the local replicator, whether or not resources are overloaded. If network bandwidth or processing time is not immediately available, the queue may grow, but application execution continues. Asynchronous replication is a virtual necessity with very long distances or complex networks with significant transmission latency.

FAILURES, DISASTERS, AND DATA INTEGRITY

One important difference between replication and mirroring is that replication is designed to cope with less-than-fully-reliable target connections. Mirroring implementations typically treat connection failure as tantamount to device failure. Resuming replication after a connection outage is repaired is a major complexity in replication designs that is not present with mirroring.

Connection Outages

Persistent logging enables asynchronous replication to resume after brief connection outages. When a connection between source and target fails, the source replicator continues to queue application writes. The queue grows, because it cannot be discharged to targets. As long as the connection recovers before the queue fills to overflowing, replication can "catch up." There is risk of lost data if an unrecoverable disaster occurs at the source location while a connection is down—all updates that have not been sent to the recovery target are lost. The only alternative, however, is to stop applications whenever the recovery location is unreachable. Some replicators support this option.

Replication queues are typically designed to streamline I/O and minimize impact on application performance. They typically consist of consecutive ranges of disk blocks that cannot be expanded without stopping replication. Such queues can fill if a network or target outage persists for too long. Replicators have two basic ways of handling queue overflow:

- ***Application I/O throttling:*** This technique forestalls overflow. When a queue reaches some "high water mark," the replicator delays further application I/O requests by a small amount. Applications run more slowly, providing time in which to repair the outage and drain the queue. For very long outages that fill the queue completely despite throttling, replicators typically offer a choice between blocking application execution and abandoning replication.
- ***Fallback techniques:*** A replication queue can fill during a network or target outage because neither the number of application writes nor the amount of data that can be written is bounded. If, instead of recording write operations in order, a replicator simply tracks *which* virtual device blocks are updated, the required space is both bounded and small. For example, each megabyte of virtual device capacity could be represented by a bit in a bitmap. A replicator whose queue overflows can switch to setting bits in this bitmap each time data is modified. When target access is restored, modified megabytes can be sent to it to resynchronize the replica with source virtual device contents.

Some replicators use this fallback mode to survive indefinite network outages without impeding source application execution. Fallback mode differs from asynchronous replication in that it does not capture application write order. When communications are restored following an outage, all data modified during the outage must be replicated atomically. But since the amount of data modified during an outage is usually much less than full device capacity, recovery time is short compared to a full copy.

Write Order Fidelity and Causality

For recoverability, it is essential that the order of replication target writes be the same as the order of source writes. An example may clarify this. Suppose a demand deposit application processes three checks deposited to the same account in succession. The application reads the record containing the account current balance, adds the amount of the check it is processing, and rewrites the record.

Each addition to the balance requires a read and a write of data at the same file address. The data written contains the updated current balance, but no information about the prior balance or the amount that was added.

Each record written by the application has a larger balance than the previous one. If a replicator writes records out of order, however, a lesser balance from an earlier update may overwrite a greater balance from a later update, with no indication of error. The effect of an update is obliterated, even though all writes have been replicated.

The solution to this problem, and the key to recoverability of a replica, is the preservation of write order across all the virtual devices in a replica. If write order is not preserved, it is impossible to guarantee restoration to a consistent state because recovery mechanisms (file system check and database recovery utilities) are based on assumptions about the order in which file systems and database managers write data and metadata. Out-of-order replication could result in a replica state that does not reflect a previous source virtual device state.

Write order fidelity must extend across all virtual devices used by an application, as Figure 13–5 suggests. In this example, Server A runs an application that stores data on virtual devices V_x and V_y. Writes to the two devices arrive and are executed in the indicated order, and are queued for replication to equivalent devices connected to Server B. Writes to replica devices V_x and V_y at Server B must be performed in the same order as the corresponding writes to devices V_x and V_y at the source.

Virtual device replicas cannot be used during replication. To use a target replica, replication must be stopped, the replica devices mounted, and file systems and databases recovered using database log playback and file system verification techniques. If a recovery mechanism can restore file

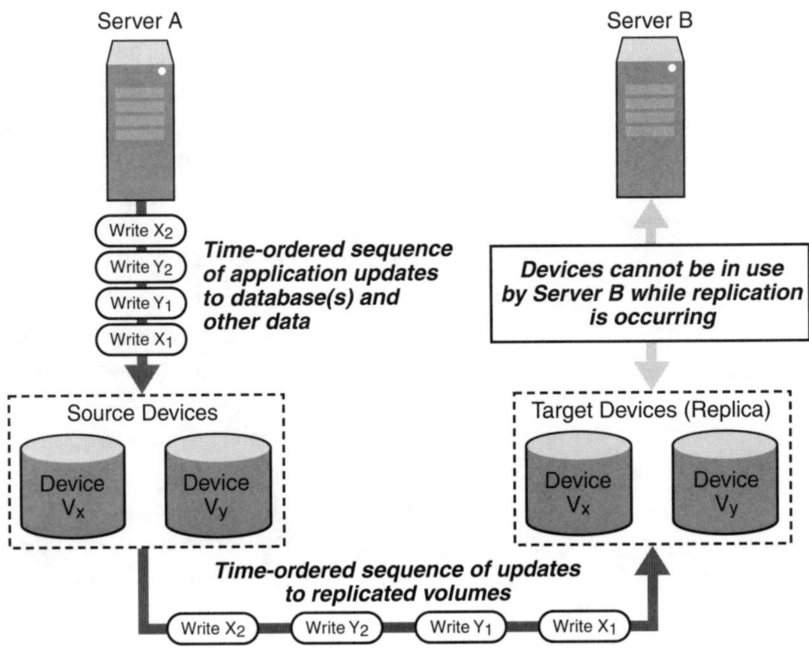

▼ **FIGURE 13–5** *Maintaining Virtual Device Write Order*

system or database consistency from a given state, the same mechanism can make a replica consistent from that state.

Executing target write requests in the same order in which they are executed at the source makes recovery from a replica possible. A related technique called **causality** also produces this behavior while allowing slightly more parallel I/O. Figure 13–6 illustrates causality.

Causality is based on the observation that there is no guarantee of the order in which two concurrent write requests will complete. Applications must therefore be designed to perform correctly regardless of the order in which overlapping write requests execute. If applications are indifferent to the execution order of a set of writes, a replicator may be indifferent as well. A replicator that uses causality to control write ordering provides the same degree of concurrency in target writes as the source when applications initially write the data. It produces only replica device states that are possible states for the source devices, whether or not they actually occurred. Because every state in which a replica can be left *might* have occurred at the source, it must be recoverable by file system checkers and database manager recovery utilities.

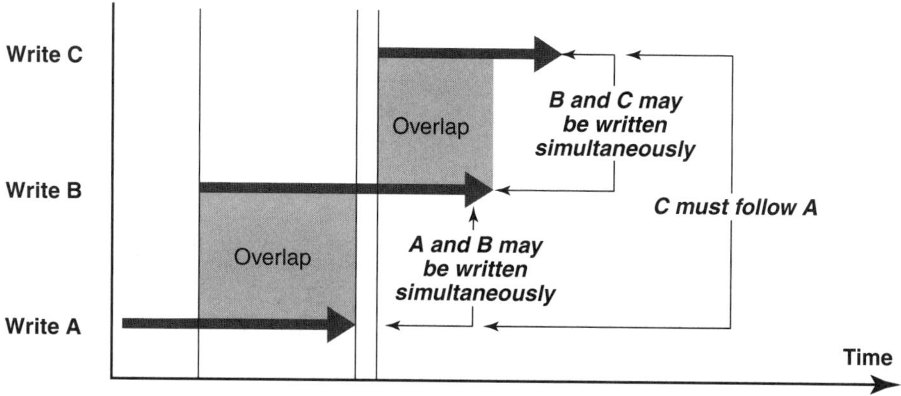

▼ **FIGURE 13–6** *Replication I/O Time Line Illustrating Causality*

GETTING VIRTUAL DEVICE REPLICATION STARTED

Before replication begins, source and target data objects must be identical. Making the two identical is called *initial synchronization*. Where large amounts of data are replicated—hundreds or thousands of gigabytes—initial synchronization is a significant problem. The steady-state data update rate may be low—a few tens of kilobytes per second—but a large amount of data must be copied from source to target to get started.

Some virtual device replicators start with a bulk network data copy. Some accept an administrator's assertion that source and target virtual device contents are identical without verification.[3] The latter capability allows copies of source device images (on tape, for example) to be restored to target devices of identical capacity. Image copies are crucial, because contents of source and target blocks with identical block numbers must be identical for virtual device replication to succeed.[4]

When all locations' device contents are identical, replication can be started by administrative action. Figure 13–7 illustrates the steps in initial synchronization.

Both of these initial synchronization methods share a significant drawback: They require that data remain unmodified by applications during initial synchronization. This may well be unacceptable, particularly in

3. Checksum comparison techniques over fairly large block ranges can be used to verify that source and target device contents are in fact identical.
4. File-oriented backup and restore would not guarantee this property.

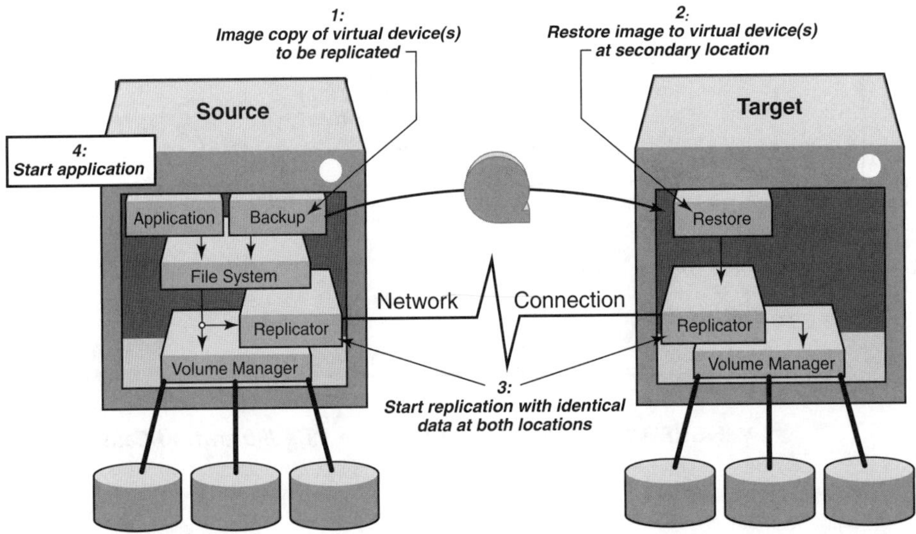

▼ **FIGURE 13–7** *Initial Synchronization for Virtual Device Replication*

cases where replication is used to create periodic snapshots of continuously active operational data.

To relieve this limitation, some replicators allow replication to be started administratively at a specified time (e.g., when source device image backups complete) with connections blocked, as though they had failed. The replication queue fills as applications write data. When target devices are ready (e.g., images have been restored), connections are unblocked and queue contents are sent to the target and written. This minimizes application downtime for initial synchronization.

Another initial synchronization technique implemented by some replicators is automatic synchronization by copying complete source device contents to target devices block by block, without preserving write ordering. Applications may update source devices during autosynchronization. When copying is complete, regions updated during copying are recopied. When source and target device contents are identical, normal (write-ordered) replication begins.

Log Overflow and Resynchronization

Brief target or communication outages are usually not fatal to asynchronous replication. As long as the source queue does not overflow, replica-

Sizing Replication Resources

When VERITAS™ Volume Replicator is used for asynchronous replication, the size of the storage replication log (SRL) must be adequate. Sizing an SRL requires planning, detailed knowledge of the network infrastructure, and an understanding of data update rates based on the business applications.

VERITAS strongly recommends that users engage knowledgeable consultants for the initial installations of the VERITAS Volume Replicator. The VERITAS Consulting organization has developed a useful tool to measure the rate at which volume data changes. This measurement should be run against live volumes that are candidates for replication for at least two weeks. By analyzing data captured by this tool, along with network bandwidth and loading, VERITAS consultants are able to estimate the required storage replication log size. The time invested in this analysis and planning is recovered in shorter implementation time and reduced downstream maintenance.

tion resumes when all resources are again available and the queue eventually drains. If a lengthy outage fills the queue, however, further application I/O would make replicas useless. The only choices are to stop applications or stop replication. If replication is stopped, source and target device contents would have to be completely resynchronized before it could restart, a procedure equivalent to initial synchronization.

Some virtual device replicators switch to a mode in which they keep track of source device block changes after a queue fills (for example, using a bitmap with a bit for each block region), but not their order or the content of the changes. After the outage, only changed blocks need be copied to resynchronize. This reduces resynchronization time significantly, especially if changes during the outage are confined to a few blocks.

Tracking changed blocks speeds up recovery after outages of arbitrary duration, but true replication with write order fidelity does not resume until resynchronization is complete. A bitmap denotes *which* blocks have changed, but gives no information about the order in which changes occurred. Thus, all blocks modified during an outage must be copied atomically; only then can write-ordered replication resume.

Periodic Replication for Point-in-Time Copy Creation

When the purpose of replication is disaster recovery, data is replicated continuously until a disaster occurs, at which time the replica is repaired and becomes the "real" application data. If data is replicated to create a snapshot for remote backup or analysis, replication can stop at any appropriate time after source and target are synchronized. For example, field office sales data might be replicated to a central backup server at the end of each business day. Initial synchronization could start at any time during the day, and continue until close of business. At the end of the day, replication would be stopped, and the replica backed up by the target server. Compared to conventional network file copying, this technique allows backup to begin earlier, since little if any data remains to be copied after the close of business.

As with any technique that uses snapshots, replication must be stopped at a point when the replica is consistent from an application standpoint. Typically, this means that applications and databases must pause (to drain transactions in progress) and file systems must be unmounted (to flush their caches). When replicas are consistent, replication can be stopped, and applications can resume using nonreplicated data. Resynchronization is required after a stopped replica snapshot has been backed up.

Because most replicators support simultaneous replication to multiple targets, multiple snapshots—for, say, backup and data mining—can be created simultaneously. In the preceding example, sales data might be replicated to two targets. At the end of each day, one replica could be analyzed while the other is backed up. This technique is especially useful in Windows environments, where low server cost motivates information processing strategies that use more single-purpose servers rather than fewer multipurpose ones.

CHAPTER SUMMARY

- Data replication may be synchronous or asynchronous. Asynchronous replication decouples application performance from replication overhead.
- Asynchronous replication introduces a risk that unsent updates could be lost in the event of an unrecoverable source-side disaster.
- For data integrity, replicated data must be written with *write order fidelity* (in the same order at source and target). Sophisticated replicators use the principle of causality to increase parallelism while preserving write order fidelity.
- Before replication can start, source and target data must be identical. Initial synchronization may be achieved by network copying or by restoring an image backup.
- Initial synchronization time can be shortened by starting replication with communications blocked as soon as an image copy of source data exists. When the image has been restored at the target location, communications are unblocked and replication commences by draining the built-up queue of updates.

- If replication is stopped for any reason, and the source log overflows, resynchronization is required. Resynchronization can be treated as initial synchronization, or if the replicator tracks changes made during the outage, can be speeded up by copying only blocks whose contents changed during the outage.

PART 3

APPLICATIONS

Science is facts. Just as houses are made of stones, so is science made of facts. But a pile of stones is not a house and a collection of facts is not necessarily science.

—JULES HENRI POINCARE

CHAPTER 14

Never underestimate the bandwidth of a station wagon full of tapes hurtling down a highway.

—ANDREW S. TANENBAUM

Backup and Virtual Block Storage

In this chapter . . .

- Today's top backup issues
- Using virtual storage to minimize backup impact on applications
- Other techniques for minimizing backup windows

Backup is a fact of information services life. No enterprise can ignore it, but it consumes a large and increasing share of data center resources in the form of capital equipment, I/O bandwidth, and management. Effective use of virtual storage can significantly reduce the impact of backup on online information services.

CONTEMPORARY BACKUP ISSUES

Client-server backup (Figure 14–1) is ubiquitous in large enterprises. The defining feature of client-server backup architecture is that a few **backup servers** run backup jobs for many application servers. **Backup client** software running in application servers uses the enterprise network to send data to be backed up to the backup servers.

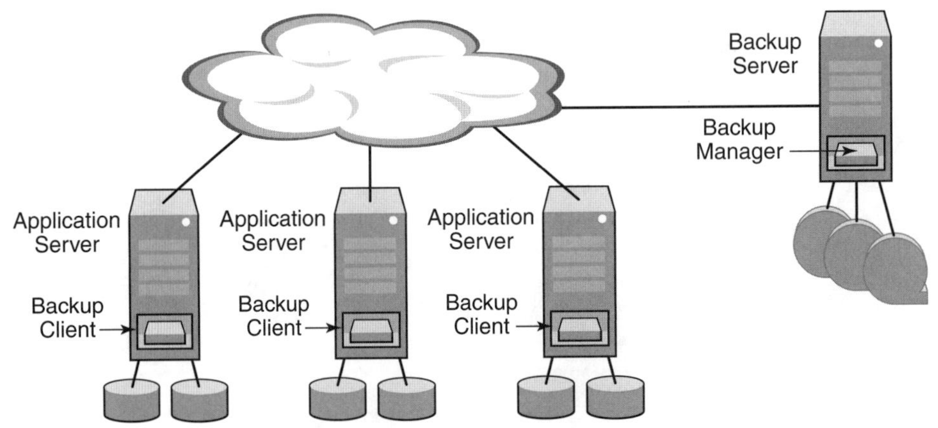

▼ **FIGURE 14–1** *Client-Server Backup*

Compared to backing up each server and application with local resources, client-server backup consolidates tape drive and media library resources, improving data and physical asset control. It reduces the cost and improves the quality of backup management by centralizing scheduling and media management. Finally, it reduces hardware needs (compared to backing up at every application server). Even with the advantages of client-server backup architecture, however, backup continues to have significant impact on data center operations for several reasons:

- ***Backup windows:*** Increasingly, enterprises are finding it necessary to operate their information services continuously—24 hours a day, seven days a week. To be usable for recovery, a backup must generally represent a point-in-time snapshot of data. But stopping information services to establish a backup window in which data remains static while it is backed up may be impractical.

VERITAS™ FlashSnap

Today, most snapshot technology is delivered in proprietary products that support only specific RAID systems or server operating systems.

VERITAS™ FlashSnap may be the most open (and therefore cost-effective) snapshot technology available today. FlashSnap is a license-key upgrade option to the VERITAS™ Volume Manager, File System, Foundation Suite and ServPoint Appliance. It supports all major server platforms, disk storage products, and RAID systems with a common "look and feel" for administrative simplicity.

FlashSnap can create either split mirror snapshots for off-host backup and data analysis or copy-on-write storage checkpoints for rapid recovery from data corruption. The technology is closely integrated with all major VERITAS storage management capabilities for seamless data protection and disaster recovery solutions.

Bare Metal Restore

Restoring data from a backup doesn't just mean restoring user data. If a server crashes, for example, due to a system disk failure, the entire system disk has to be rebuilt from scratch, including operating system, applications, patches, scripts, control files, and so forth. In case of a data center disaster, old systems must be restored and restarted on completely new servers.

Even when basic operating and application environments have been recreated, the backup manager that created user data backups must be reinstalled in order to restore user data to its original locations. All of this must be accomplished flawlessly under the pressure of recovering information services from a disaster, with the most experienced storage administrators possibly unavailable.

VERITAS Bare™ Metal Restore (BMR) automates this entire process for VERITAS NetBackup users. By minimizing manual intervention, BMR speeds up server restores and allows a large number of servers to be restored from scratch by a small number of administrators. By guiding administrators through a simple restore startup process, BMR minimizes the requirement for skills and experience. The result is faster, more reliable restores, even if the most experienced people aren't available to perform them.

- ***Impact on application performance:*** Database managers have developed techniques for shortening and even eliminating backup windows. These techniques basically capture application changes to data during the backup in a log, and play the log back against the restored backup copy. Though these techniques do shorten backup windows, they tend to impact application performance significantly, because they access the same data that applications are processing. Backup and applications contend for both I/O and processing resources.
- ***Restore times:*** Restoring data from backups is almost always done under pressure. Rapid restore is paramount; resource consumption is not an issue. Backup priorities are just the opposite—*minimize impact on applications.* This motivates techniques such as incremental backup, that get the job done quickly with minimal impact, but organize data in ways that are less-than-optimal for rapid restore.[1]
- ***Tape drive resource utilization:*** Although client-server backup reduces tape drive requirements and improves utilization, imbalances can still exist. One backup server may have idle tape drives, while another queues up jobs because its drives are all busy. Tape drive sharing, made possible by connecting tape drives to a storage network, and the virtualization of tape drives by special-purpose network devices improve utilization in data centers with multiple backup servers.

1. *Synthetic backup*, discussed later in this chapter, helps to minimize restore times.

BACKUP WINDOWS AND BLOCK STORAGE VIRTUALIZATION

There are two basic techniques for creating backups from which data can be restored to a consistent state:

- Copying data while it is changing and capturing information about the changes in a log that can later be used to make restored data consistent. This technique is generally available only for databases, and is discussed further in Chapter 16.
- Copying snapshots, or **frozen images** of data, created at points in time when the data is known to be consistent from an application point of view.

Perhaps the biggest impact of virtual block storage on backup is its ability to create point-in-time snapshots of virtual device contents. Snapshots enable major reductions in backup window size. Instead of being out of service while a (possibly very large) data set is copied, an application need only pause until its data is made consistent and a snapshot is established, then it can resume execution.[2]

RAID systems, network-based virtualization appliances, and volume managers are all capable of creating snapshots of virtual block storage device contents on command. The challenge for backup managers is to issue those commands at a time when data stored on the devices is consistent from an application standpoint—when debits match credits, billing records match shipping orders, and so forth.

Most backup managers are capable of creating snapshots of data being used by applications and making backup copies from them. For such a **hot backup** to be consistent, a backup manager or administrator must have at least rudimentary control over applications using the data so it can stop them from accessing it momentarily while it creates a snapshot. Some applications provide **application programming interfaces** (APIs) that suspend their activity momentarily. Today, these APIs are application-

Simple, Consistent Snapshots

Unmounting a file system in order to flush its cache prior to making a snapshot requires administrative action. To simplify this task, VERITAS integrates automatic synchronization functionality in its FlashSnap backup manager option to automatically write all data from file system buffers to persistent storage. Administrators need not be concerned with the details of making a consistent snapshot of data; FlashSnap does it automatically.

2. Of course, the ideal backup window would be no information service interruption whatsoever. This is possible with some databases, as Chapter 16 explains, but in general, can only be approached with file-based applications.

specific, and custom backup manager components called **agents** are required to utilize them.

Consistent Data for Backups

One obvious way to make data consistent before creating a snapshot for backup is to shut down the applications using it. For any commercial application, orderly shutdown causes all work in progress to be completed or abandoned, and all data to be stored persistently. If the file system managing an application's data uses a cache, its contents must also be flushed to persistent storage. Most file system caches can be flushed by administrative command, and unmounting a file system always results in a cache flush. Thus, in order to establish a snapshot of application data that is known to be consistent, an administrator must:

- Shut down applications using the data, or at least pause them in such a way that no work is in progress
- Flush data manager caches, so that what applications "think" is stored persistently has actually been written to virtual devices, and is not held in file system cache
- Create the snapshot by administrative command

Once a snapshot has been created, file systems can be remounted (if necessary) and applications can resume or restart.

Although this procedure does interrupt information services, interruption is typically brief (tens of seconds to a few minutes) compared to backup time (tens of minutes to hours) and, more importantly, is independent of the size of the data set to be backed up. Figure 14–2 compares backup windows with and without the use of snapshots.

As Figure 14–2 suggests, a backup that uses a snapshot of live data can shorten application unavailability time dramatically compared to a **cold backup** that requires applications to be stopped for its duration. The window is reduced from the time required to copy all data to the time required to pause or stop applications and initiate a snapshot. Backup managers can use either **split mirror** or **copy-on-write snapshots,** but the backup characteristics of the two approaches differ.

Backup Using Split Mirror Snapshots

A split mirror snapshot (described in Chapter 4) is made by separating a mirror from its virtual device. The backup server imports the split mirror's devices as a new **snapshot virtual device,** and mounts the file

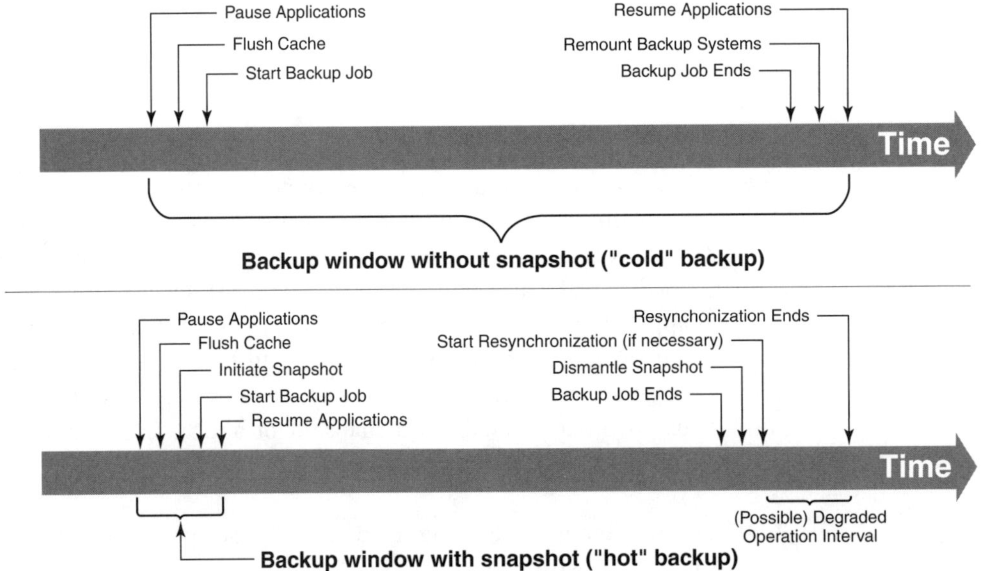

▼ **FIGURE 14–2** *Backup Windows with and without Snapshots*

system it contains.[3] Files on the snapshot virtual device can be backed up, while applications continue to process "live" data on the original virtual device.

A split mirror snapshot contains a complete copy of data on the virtual device from which it is split. From the instant of splitting, the snapshot is independent of its parent device. Split mirror snapshots have two unique advantages:

- ***Off-host backup:*** If the devices that comprise a split mirror are connected to a storage network, they can be transferred to a separate server for backup. The backup server reads source data from the split mirror and writes it to tape media, without using any application resources, so application performance is not affected (if storage network bandwidth is adequate).
- ***Device failure protection:*** The devices that comprise a split mirror are different from those that remain part of the original virtual

3. If a mirror is split from its virtual device when the file system on it is not internally consistent, the split mirror's copy of the file system must be validated before use. File system caches should be flushed before mirrors are split from the virtual devices they occupy.

VERITAS FlashSnap Technology

VERITAS FlashSnap technology makes off-host backups easy because it automates the creation and management of split mirror snapshots. For volumes with fast resynchronization enabled, FlashSnap causes a persistent Data Change Map to be created. The Data Change Map holds a persistent record of which volume blocks are updated after snapshot creation. It is used for rapid resynchronization of a snapshot after a backup has been made from it.

FlashSnap moves snapshots into separate Volume Manager disk groups that can be imported by backup servers and backed up with no performance impact on applications, which continue to execute using data in the original volume group.

After backup, snapshots could simply be deleted, but most administrators rejoin snapshots to their original Volume Manager disk groups. FlashSnap resynchronizes the snapshots with their original volumes (using fast resynchronization if it is enabled) so that another snapshot can be made and split from its volume when it is time for the next backup.

device. If the parent virtual device should fail, the snapshot represents a complete (albeit out-of-date), rapidly accessible data image from which recovery can be quickly initiated.

Backup is a perpetual process. Once the data on a split mirror has been backed up, the devices that comprise the mirror must be rejoined to their parent virtual device, and their contents **resynchronized** with those of the parent, so that the mirror can be split for the next backup. There are two basic techniques for split mirror resynchronization.

- ***Full content copy:*** The complete contents of the parent virtual device are copied to the newly rejoined mirror.
- ***Fast resynchronization:*** If a virtualizer logs all changes to a mirrored virtual device from the moment at which a mirror is split for read-only use until the moment at which it is rejoined, the rejoined split mirror can be resynchronized by copying only changed blocks from its parent. (This technique obviously requires that the split mirror's contents not be modified while it is split.) It is typical for only a small percentage of the data in a large data set to change during a backup; fast resynchronization typically completes much more quickly and with much lower resource utilization than a full content copy.

Though fast resynchronization of split mirror snapshots causes less resource contention than a full content copy, both do contend with applications for I/O resources during resynchronization. A good practice when using split mirrors is to choose rejoin times that will have minimal effect on application performance.

The other important consideration with split mirror snapshots for backup is capital cost. Each mirror requires as much physical storage as its parent virtual device. A terabyte mirrored virtual device requires two terabytes of physical storage (devices, enclosures, power and cooling, interconnects, and floor space); a three-copy mirror requires three terabytes, and so forth. Though the decreasing cost of storage makes this less of a barrier, it is nonetheless a factor when choosing a snapshot backup strategy.

With a storage network and some careful system management procedures, a multi-application data center whose backup schedules can be staggered can minimize cost by passing storage devices from application to application, successively mirroring each one's data, splitting the mirror, and making a backup. This technique requires full content copy for resynchronization, and is therefore most applicable with applications that have predictable periods of low activity.

"Virtual Backup" to Disk

The VERITAS File System uses an enhanced version of copy-on-write snapshots called *storage checkpoints.* Storage checkpoints are sequences of persistent copy-on-write snapshots that are linked to each other by administrative policy. Using a graphical interface, a storage administrator can configure the number of storage checkpoints to be kept and the schedule on which they should be made.

For example, a storage checkpoint of a database's container files might be scheduled every 3 or 4 hours during a business day. In essence, each storage checkpoint is a virtual backup of the database. If the database becomes logically corrupted, it can be restored to any point in time for which there is a storage checkpoint, a much faster procedure than restoring from backup tapes. After the database is restored, redo logs must be reapplied to restore the database to a point in time just prior to the corruption. Since the storage checkpoint is taken within a few hours of the corruption event, less log playback is required, further speeding the recovery.

Storage checkpoints do not replace frequent tape backup—the latter is still required for recovery from online storage device failure, for example. But the technology does provide superior protection against corruption, particularly by shortening recovery times.

Backup Using Copy-on-Write Snapshots

Copy-on-write snapshots can also be used as source data for point-in-time backups. The essence of copy-on-write snapshots is that they preserve the prior contents of any data block updated after snapshot initiation. Figure 14–3 illustrates one implementation of the copy-on-write snapshot concept.

As Figure 14–3 suggests, this copy-on-write snapshot consists of a list of blocks whose contents have changed since snapshot initiation and a private data area containing the blocks' contents prior to the change.

A virtualizer that supports copy-on-write snapshots includes logic to make them available as separate read-only **snapshot virtual devices.**[4] A backup manager can request blocks of data from a snapshot virtual device. Blocks unmodified since snapshot initiation are read from their original locations. Modified blocks' prior contents are retrieved from the snapshot's

4. Historically. copy-on-write snapshots have been implemented as part of file systems, although this is not inherently necessary.

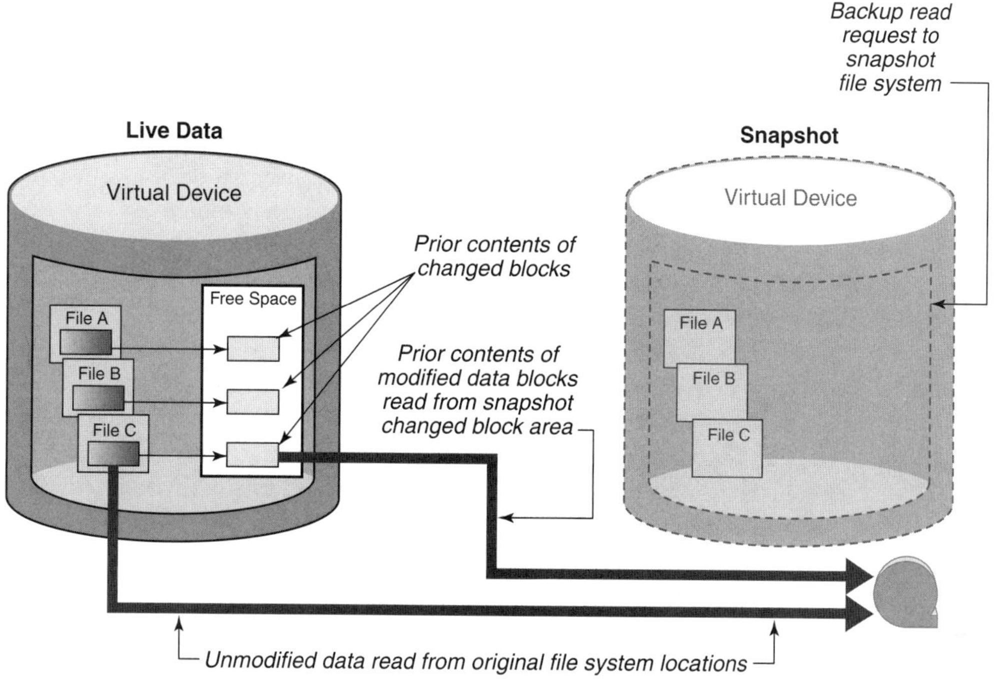

▼ **FIGURE 14–3** *Copy-on-Write Snapshot*

changed block area. The net effect is that backup (and other applications that access the snapshot) sees the image of data as it stood at the instant of snapshot initiation.

Copy-on-write snapshots are attractive for two reasons:

- ***They consume less physical storage than split mirror snapshots.*** Aside from the data structures that describe it, the storage required by a copy-on-write snapshot is determined by the rate of unique block changes to its parent virtual device rather than by the parent's size. Since it is typical that small fractions of large data sets change during backups, the copy-on-write technique can enable an administrator to keep several snapshots online, as a kind of disk-based backup that protects against application data corruption and human error.
- ***They impose no resynchronization overhead.*** When a copy-on-write snapshot has served its purpose, the storage space it occupies is simply returned to whatever free space pool it came from (a file system's free space pool or unallocated space managed by a block storage virtualizer). There is no resource contention comparable to that resulting from split mirror snapshot resynchronization.

Copy-on-write snapshots have unique limitations as well. The most obvious is that backup and applications necessarily contend for the same physical I/O resources. Paradoxically, the less change to a virtual device for which snapshots are in effect, the more contention will exist, because applications and backup contend for the same data images. Prior contents of modified blocks can be kept on different storage devices, but backup and applications access the same unmodified data blocks.

Another effect of copy-on-write snapshots is that application updates to live data take longer when a copy-on-write snapshot is in effect. Using the technique suggested by Figure 14–3, for example, the first application update of a block after snapshot initiation requires that the block's prior contents be read and rewritten to a changed block area. (Once a block has changed and its prior image has been saved, the snapshot imposes no further incremental overhead.) The more unique data blocks an application updates while copy-on-write snapshots are in effect, the longer its average write times will be.

Because backup of a copy-on write snapshot and application live data access contend for the same unmodified data blocks, moving backup "off-host" is only possible with a cluster file system (Chapter 11). Even then, only application server processing contention is eliminated, not I/O resource contention (although cache contention between applications and backup is eliminated). Not all cluster volume managers and file systems support snapshot capability.

Copy-on-write snapshots do not protect against data loss if their parent virtual devices are destroyed or become inaccessible. Locating a file system and its copy-on-write snapshots on failure-tolerant virtual devices may provide this protection. Unlike a split mirror snapshot, a copy-on-write snapshot is no longer useful if its parent is destroyed.

Snapshots and Replication

Copy-on-write snapshots can be combined with virtual device replication to provide both disaster protection and protection against data corruption in one package, as Figure 14–4 illustrates, with an information service operating on live data through a file system. The file system supports multiple copy-on-write snapshots for rapid recovery from data corruption or human error.

The virtual device containing the file system and its snapshots is replicated (Chapter 12) to a device of equivalent capacity at a remote location. As long as the replicator maintains write order fidelity of the replicated device, both the file system's live data and the snapshots are available at

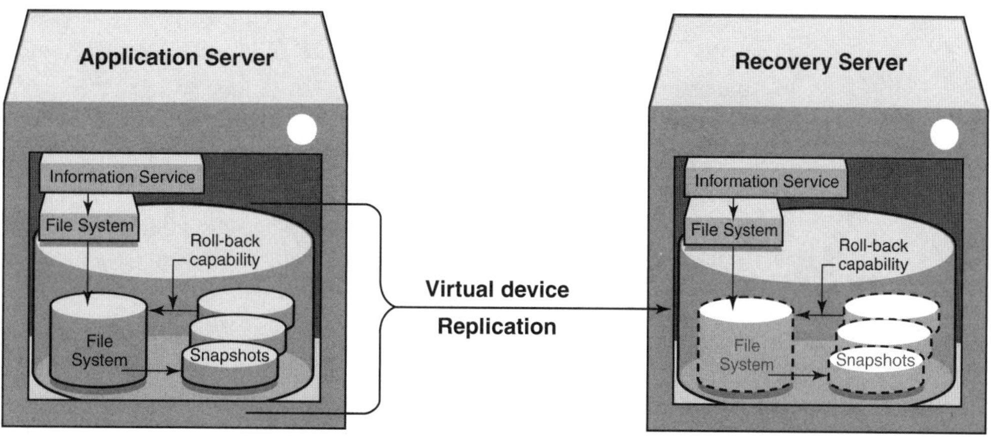

▼ **FIGURE 14–4** *Combining Copy-on-Write Snapshots with Replication*

the recovery site. If a disaster destroys the main data center, information services can be restarted at the recovery location, using any available snapshot as the recovery point.

OTHER TECHNIQUES FOR MINIMIZING BACKUP WINDOWS

Another important technique for minimizing the impact of backup on application operations is **incremental backup**—backing up only files that have changed since a previous backup that is still available. Backup managers scan file metadata to locate files that have been modified since the previous backup, and copy only those files.

Restoring a file system from incremental backups requires restoration of a full backup to establish a baseline, followed by in-order restoration of all newer incremental backups. Incremental backups usually increase media manipulation. Administrators often adopt one of two procedures to minimize media handling during restore:

- ***Hybrid full and incremental backup strategy:*** Most data centers that use incremental backup actually perform periodic full backups with more frequent incremental backups between them. For example, weekly full backup with daily incremental backup is one popular schedule. This technique limits media handling—a worst-case restore would require mounting media for the full backup and six incremental ones.

- ***Synthetic full backup:*** Some backup managers are able to combine incremental backups with the full backup on which they are based, resulting in a new full backup whose effective date is the date of the newest incremental one. With this technique, one could theoretically make one full backup and forever thereafter run only incremental ones.

Incremental backup is not directly related to block storage virtualization (although it is quite reasonable to make incremental backups from virtual device snapshots), but the copy-on-write snapshot concept can be adapted to solve a backup problem unique to databases. A typical database stores its data tables in a small number of large **container files.** A few updates to the database can result in changes to most or all of those files. Since file-based incremental backup copies any modified file, an incremental backup of database container files is often tantamount to a full backup, even though only a few blocks may have changed. By tracking the changes to blocks in a file system, copy-on-write snapshot technology provides the basis for detecting which blocks in a set of database container files have changed. Chapter 16 discusses the use of copy-on-write technology for **block-level incremental backup** of databases.

The VERITAS Shared Storage Option

The VERITAS Shared Storage Option (SSO), available with both NetBackup and Backup Exec, is a server-based tape drive virtualizer. With SSO, NetBackup *media servers* (backup servers) with SAN-attached tape drives are configured with logical tape drive names. These logical names map to a common pool of physical tape drives.

The mapping from logical to physical objects typical of virtualization is found here. When a media server requests access to a logical tape drive by name, the SSO virtualizer assigns the best suited available physical drive and blocks access to the drive from other servers. SSO reduces tape drive capital cost and increases utilization by enabling media servers to share common pools of like drives. In addition, tape drive pooling increases backup system resiliency because any drive in a pool can be assigned to meet any backup requirement. Backups need not fail because a specific tape drive is down.

TAPE DRIVE VIRTUALIZATION

Though not the main topic of this book, another form of storage virtualization has become very important to backup—**tape drive virtualization.** Tape drives are virtualized for cost and availability reasons. Tape drives suitable for enterprise backup duty are expensive by themselves, and even more expensive when combined with robotic media libraries that may accommodate thousands of media.

Most of the time, most application servers are *not* running backups. Therefore, a tape drive connected directly to an

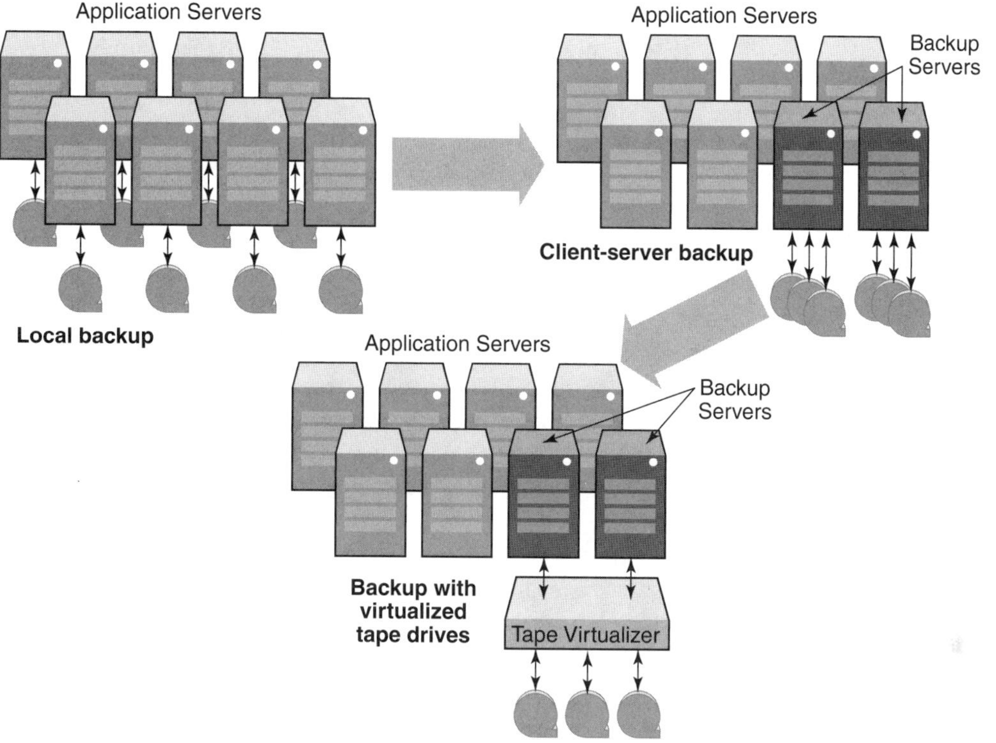

▼ **FIGURE 14–5** *Local, Consolidated, and Virtualized Tape Drives*

application server is necessarily idle most of the time. One important advantage of client-server backup is that it consolidates tape drives in a few backup servers. As long as backup schedules can be staggered, a few tape drives connected to backup servers can meet the backup needs of many application servers.

Tape drives connected directly to backup servers cannot be shared, even though they may be co-located in a robotic media library enclosure. Connecting tape drives to storage networks, either directly or through **bridges,** has improved this situation considerably. Both hardware and software virtualizers for network-attached tape drives exist. These devices make drives available to any backup server on the network. Figure 14–5 illustrates local, client-server, and virtualized tape drive backup scenarios.

Software tape drive virtualizers negotiate control of network-attached tape drives among participating backup servers. Software tape drive virtualization is typically delivered as a backup manager feature. In essence, it *pools* tape drives, so that any backup server can use any available drive with appropriate characteristics (location, media type). Hardware tape drive virtualizers switch drive connections between different storage network ports to accomplish the same thing. In either case, if drives are co-located in a robotic media library, integrated data center-wide backup can run completely unattended.

CHAPTER SUMMARY

- Backup windows, impact on applications, tape and media utilization, and restore times are today's primary enterprise backup issues.
- The feature of virtual block storage that most directly affects backup is its ability to create snapshots of virtual devices and file systems. Snapshots enable consistent backups to be made while data continues to be used by applications.
- To make a consistent snapshot of data, applications using it must be paused or stopped, and the caches of file systems that manage it must be flushed.
- Split mirror snapshots stored on network-attached devices can easily be taken off-host for backup, eliminating impact on application performance.
- Copy-on-write snapshots conserve storage space, but it is more difficult to take them off-host, and impossible to avoid contention between backup and application for physical I/O resources.
- Incremental backup also plays a large role in minimizing the impact of backup on information service availability. Some backup managers are able to synthesize full backup tape sets from a baseline and one or more incremental backups.
- Block-level incremental backup, discussed in Chapter 16, makes incremental backup a practical reality for databases.
- Tape drive virtualization, delivered both by hardware and software vendors, is another important factor in enterprise backup flexibility and impact reduction.

The NetBackup Vault Option

Today, tape is the backup medium of choice, but there are some interesting trends on the horizon. Very low cost ATA disks have reduced the cost of disk backups substantially. VERITAS NetBackup™ already supports ATA disks as backup storage units. Under most circumstances, there is a performance advantage to using disks as backup media, particularly when data must be restored. But it is still risky to keep data on secondary disk systems for long periods.

The VERITAS NetBackup Vault Option eliminates this risk by automating the duplication and tracking of disk-based backup images to removable tape media. The Vault Option can also be configured to automatically expire disk backup images based on administrator-supplied criteria and reclaim the secondary disk space they occupy for further use.

CHAPTER 15

Experience is a hard teacher because she gives the test first, the lesson afterwards.

—VERNON SANDERS LAW

Files and Virtual Storage

In this chapter . . .

- How file systems exploit virtual storage capabilities
- File system and virtual device snapshots
- Cluster file systems and virtual storage

The concept of files is so integral to computing that it's difficult to imagine data processing without it. Files are used to structure virtually all persistent data, including operating system programs, libraries of executable functions, event logs, and operating parameters, as well as database containers.[1] Files are stored on block storage devices and access to them is controlled by software components called **file systems.**[2]

Nearly all computer system online storage is managed by file systems, because the file abstraction is much easier for applications and system soft-

1. One exception to this is database data stored without the aid of a file system in partitions of physical or virtual devices. As file systems become more database-aware, the advantages of physical device storage are diminishing, and this usage is decreasing.
2. The term *file system* is also used to denote the data structures within a range of block storage device capacity that is formatted and managed by file system software, as in "The volume contains an NTFS file system."

ware to deal with than the virtual block storage device abstraction. Whereas block storage devices are few in number, seldom changing in size, and long-lived, files are many in number, can easily be created and destroyed, and can grow and shrink by simple administrative or application action. The file paradigm is much more amenable to application data management. Appendix D contains a brief description of how file systems work.

VIRTUAL STORAGE AND FILE SYSTEMS

File systems can use virtual block storage to great advantage. At the most basic level, failure-tolerant virtual storage devices insulate file system data and metadata structures from storage device failure, making files more reliable (less likely to be destroyed) and more available (less likely to be inaccessible).

Similarly, placing a file system on a virtual device whose block addresses are striped across several disks or LUNs may improve application I/O performance in two ways:

- If the predominant I/O load is both random (with no discernible order to I/O requests) and heavy (with multiple I/O requests outstanding concurrently), concurrent requests will tend to be serviced by different physical devices, thus reducing queuing times compared to a single device.
- If the predominant I/O load consists of long streams of sequential data, as is common for graphic and scientific applications, individual requests tend to be broken into parts, each of which is serviced by a different physical device. With more resources working in parallel, requests complete faster, which in turn improves application throughput.

As long as a virtual device emulates a disk drive closely enough, the fact that storage is virtualized is transparent to the file system; no integration is required. Additional functionality is possible when a file system is aware of the advanced facilities provided by virtual storage.

VERITAS File System Performance

Manageability, resiliency, and, above all, performance are the primary file system selection criteria. Time after time, independent performance tests show the multiplatform VERITAS journaling file system (VxFS) outperforming other platform-specific file systems.

VxFSs achieve high performance through multiple techniques, including extent-based allocation, online defragmentation, and an automated performance tuning feature called *discovered direct I/O*. The latter feature is based on the observation that large writes are generally faster when performed directly (bypassing the File System cache), but smaller writes generally perform better when cached. Discovered direct I/O dynamically chooses an I/O technique–direct or cached—based on write request size. Storage administrators can set application-specific bounds on discovered direct I/O if necessary.

Changing Device Sizes

Creating a file system imposes a structure on the block storage space it occupies. Certain structures are located at well-known fixed block addresses. These structures describe other structures, such as the file system's unallocated space and its directories. By manipulating these structures, a file system creates, deletes, extends, truncates, moves, and copies individual files without interfering with other files it is managing.

Historically, file systems have organized fixed-size pools of storage, because that is the nature of physical disks. If files grew to occupy all of a file system's space, the only recourse was to install a larger device, format a file system on it, and move all data to the larger device. This procedure is time-consuming, disruptive to information services, and, like any operation infrequently performed by humans, error-prone.

Virtual block storage devices make it easier to accommodate file system growth, because a virtual device can grow in size, for example, by addition of a disk to a striped or concatenated array. If there were a way to make a file system aware that its storage device has grown, the awkward and disruptive procedure for increasing storage capacity could be simplified. Rather than effectively having to be replaced when more storage is required, such a file system could simply accommodate capacity growth in its underlying storage by adjusting its data structures to reflect the larger device. A conceptually similar (although more complex) procedure can accommodate reductions in storage device size.

Some file systems are virtual device-aware—they detect and respond to changes in virtual device capacity, either automatically or in response to administrative commands. File systems are able to detect capacity changes either because they are integrated with a virtualizer, or by querying virtual devices to determine their capacity, as when a file system first begins to run. A few older file systems cannot accommodate changing device capacity, and cannot use expanded virtual device capacity. This is usually because the file system's data structure design is predicated on a fixed device capacity (for example, fixed-length bitmaps with each bit representing a fixed number of blocks). As file systems evolve to accommodate virtual storage devices, this limitation is encountered less frequently.

File System Snapshots

Snapshot images of data at specific points in time can be used in several ways, the most important of which is backup (Chapter 14). A snapshot can be backed up while applications continue to modify the "live" file system. If the snapshot is a split mirror and the storage devices are connected

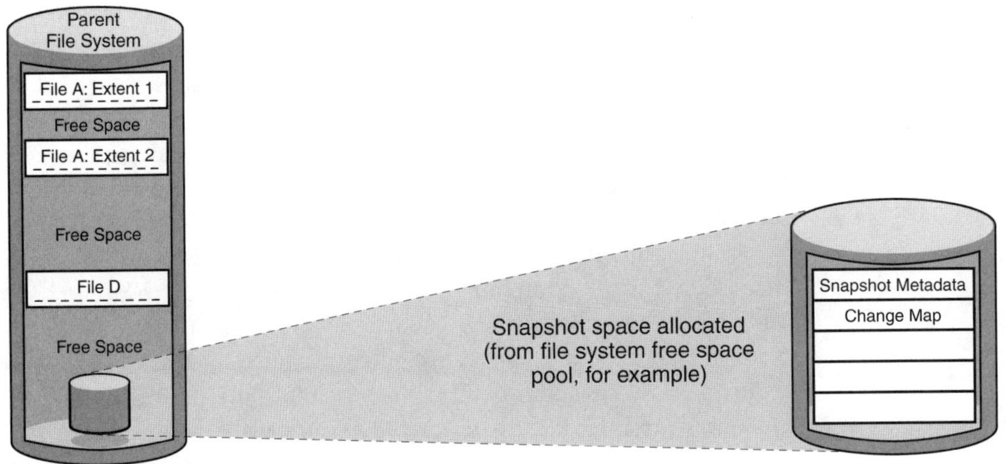

▼ **FIGURE 15–1** *File System Copy-on-Write Snapshot Initiation*

to a network, the backup can be taken "off-host" to a different server than the one processing live data.

Split mirror snapshots are point-in-time images of all virtual device contents. Copy-on-write snapshots can be implemented at either the virtual device or file system level, with file system implementations being more frequently encountered today. File system copy-on-write snapshots are closely related to virtual block storage, however, because they can result in requirements for file system expansion on short notice that can only be met by expanding device capacity, a capability that is not available with physical block storage devices.

One type of file system copy-on-write snapshot is a "file system within a file system." When a snapshot is initiated, the file system creates data structures that identify the snapshot and allocates storage space for a **change map.** Figure 15–1 illustrates a freshly initiated file system snapshot.

As Figure 15–1 suggests, a small amount of file system free space is allocated when a snapshot is initiated. The free space holds metadata describing the snapshot (so that multiple snapshots can be maintained concurrently) and a change map (initially empty) that describes file system updates made since snapshot initiation. The change map is gradually populated as files in the file system are updated.

Typically, application activity is suspended before file system snapshot initiation, so that the snapshot is consistent from an application point of view. Once a snapshot's data structures are initiated, its parent file system can again be used by applications. The snapshot is populated as applica-

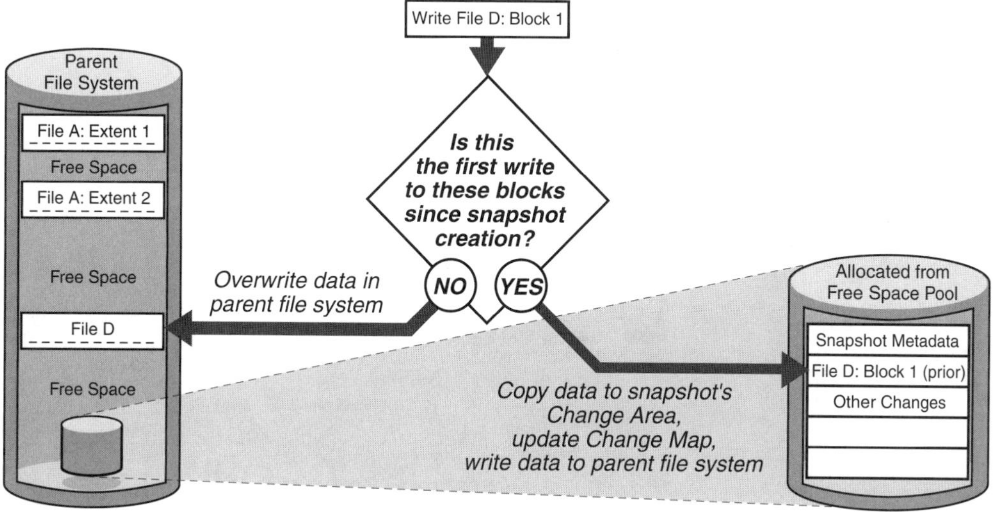

▼ **FIGURE 15–2** *Write to a File System with a Snapshot in Effect*

tions update files. The first time after snapshot initiation that a given block is written, the file system allocates space, copies the block's prior contents to it, and updates the change map. Figure 15–2 illustrates a file update in a file system using this type of copy-on-write snapshot.

As Figure 15–2 suggests, different code paths are followed depending on whether the target block has been modified since snapshot initiation. On the first write to a block after snapshot initiation, the file system allocates space and saves the block's prior contents. The change map is updated so that the block's prior contents can be quickly located, and the block is overwritten with the new data. Any subsequent update to an already-changed block is simply written to the block's original location.

Similar, although more complex, actions are performed when files are deleted, extended, or moved, and when directories are updated. The net result is that the snapshot's data structures enable presentation of the file system's image as of the instant of snapshot initiation.

The first update to a file system block after snapshot initiation takes two or three times as long to execute as an "average" write with no snapshot in effect, because of the space allocation and extra I/O needed to save the block's prior contents. Thus, with copy-on-write snapshots, average application write time is somewhat longer.

Copy-on-write snapshots can be mounted as read-only virtual file systems whose data can be read, for example, by backup or analysis software. As with writes, snapshot file system reads follow different paths

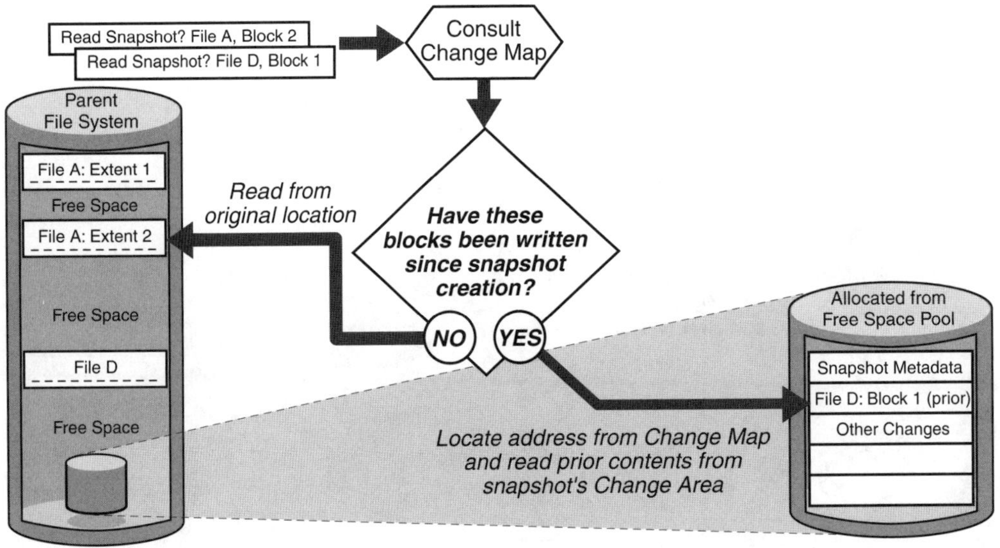

▼ **FIGURE 15–3** *Reading from a File System Snapshot*

depending on whether the requested blocks had been changed since snapshot initiation. Figure 15–3 illustrates reading data from one type of copy-on-write snapshot mounted as a virtual file system.

As Figure 15–3 indicates, application reads to a snapshot cause the change map to be consulted. If the requested block has not been changed since snapshot initiation, it is read from its original location in the parent file system. If it has been changed, the location of its saved prior contents is retrieved from the change map, and the file system reads these prior contents and returns them to the requester (e.g., backup).

Aside from a small fixed overhead, the space consumed by a copy-on-write snapshot is determined by the number of different blocks updated while the snapshot is in effect. Snapshot space requirements can therefore vary widely. Snapshot-capable file systems can automatically discard old snapshots, but it is always possible that a file system with active snapshots will suddenly need more storage space, and will rely on virtual storage device expansion to get it without disrupting application access to data.

VERITAS Quicklog Technology

Performance acceleration of VERITAS File Systems can be enhanced by placing the file system log, called the *intent log,* on a separate volume from the file system proper. Intent logs should be kept on striped and mirrored volumes for performance and availability reasons. This feature, known as Quicklog™, avoids the contention that can arise when both data and log information are written to the same storage devices.

Virtual Storage Device Snapshots

Copy-on-write snapshots can also be implemented at the virtual device level. These might be useful, for example, for databases using raw virtual partitions for their data storage. Again, if data in such a snapshot is to be consistent from an application point of view, applications using the parent device would have to be quiescent (paused in a way that guarantees no outstanding data activity) and file system or database cache would have to be flushed so that virtual device contents reflected the application's and data manager's view of persistent data state.

A virtual device snapshot is updated every time any block is written to its parent device, no matter what the block represents. Thus, while a file system snapshot records file system updates, a virtual device snapshot records the device operations that comprise those updates. For example, deletion of a file from a file system with a copy-on-write snapshot in effect would cause the blocks allocated to the file's data area to be added to the snapshot's change area so that the file's data would still be seen if it were accessed in the snapshot. With a virtual device snapshot, the directory block and free space map modifications resulting from the file's deletion would be recorded, but the file's data blocks would not be touched until they were reused (allocated to another file and written, for example), at which time their prior contents would be copied to the snapshot, so the deleted file's data would be preserved.

VIRTUAL STORAGE AND CLUSTER FILE SYSTEMS

Cluster volume managers (Chapter 11) create server-based virtual block storage devices that are accessible by all servers in a cluster. *Cluster file systems* enable concurrent access by all of a cluster's servers to file systems formatted on such virtual devices. From a file access standpoint, a cluster with a cluster file system behaves as though all applications were running on the same server. Clusters that run cluster file systems are called **shared data clusters.**[3]

3. Clusters that run only cluster volume managers can also fairly be called shared data clusters. In a shared data cluster that does not run a cluster file system, shared storage access obeys disk-like semantics, and database managers or applications are responsible for preserving data integrity by preventing concurrent accesses to storage from interfering with each other. For an excellent reference on shared data cluster technology, see *Shared Data Clusters* by Dilip M. Ranade, published by John Wiley & Sons; ISBN: 047118070X (July 19, 2002).

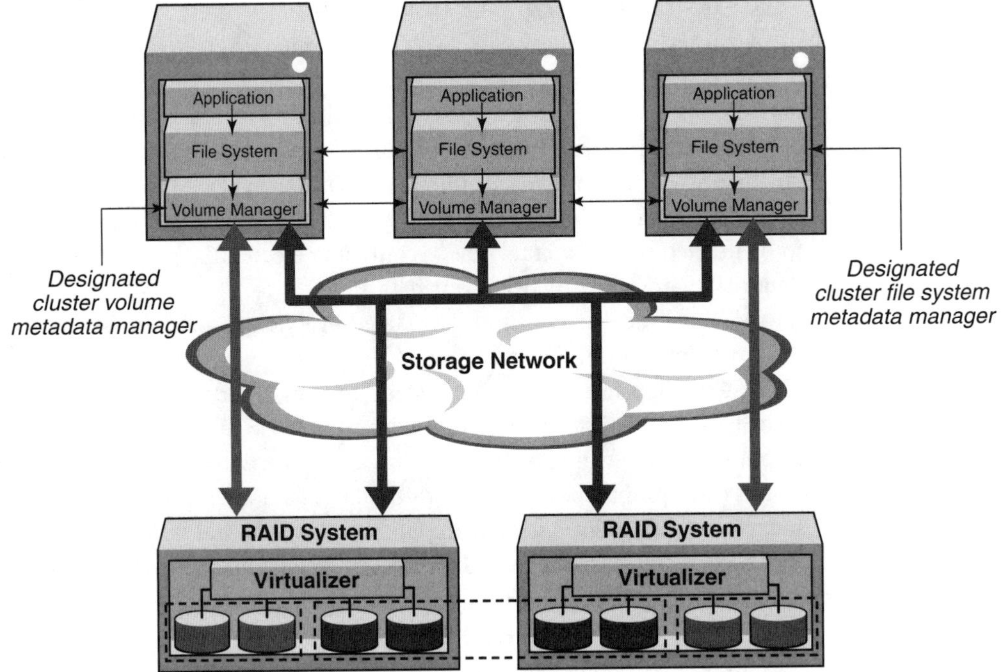

▼ **FIGURE FIGURE 15–4** *Cluster File System Based on Cluster Volumes*

The two most important advantages of a cluster file system are:

- ***Manageability:*** Shared data clusters are more easily managed than so-called shared nothing clusters, principally because any job that accesses data can be run on any of the cluster's servers with no failover or other reconfiguration. Manageability is also simplified because storage resources can be pooled and allocated as needed for data without regard for which of the cluster's servers "owns" the storage.
- ***Application scaling:*** Instances of compute-intensive applications can be run on several of a cluster's servers, because all can access the application's data. This is especially important for database applications (Chapter 16) that consolidate enterprise data and run multiple applications against it.

Figure 15–4 illustrates data access with a cluster file system. The cluster in this illustration uses a cluster volume manager (Chapter 11)[4]

4. Figure 15–4 illustrates a master-slave cluster volume manager, but the volume manager architecture is incidental to this discussion of file systems.

to provide virtual block storage that appears identical to all servers in the cluster at all times. Cluster file systems can be based on any type of virtual storage with this property.

The figure also indicates an advantage of server-based volume management—a cluster volume has been created from storage presented by two different RAID systems. The volume manager aggregates the capacity and performance of the LUNs presented by the RAID systems and, in addition, increases the number of survivable faults.

As Figure 15–4 suggests, cluster file systems follow a similar architecture. Cluster file systems have been implemented using a **distributed** or **symmetric architecture,** in which all servers update metadata, and coordinate their actions by distributed locking of data structures. Most implementations, however, use the **asymmetric** or **master-slave architecture** illustrated in Figure 15–4. In this architecture, all file system metadata changes (new directories or files, file extensions and deletions, property changes, and so forth) are made by the indicated servers, although they may be requested by any server in the cluster. The master-slave architecture is simple and robust, because metadata changes are all made from the same place, as they are with a single-server file system, but runs the risk of overloading the master server with metadata changes. Master-slave cluster file systems are best suited for applications with a high ratio of file access (reads and writes) to metadata changes (creates and deletes).

Figure 15–5 illustrates a cluster file system. The figure emphasizes the point that with a master-slave cluster file system architecture, all metadata requests (e.g., create file X.DAT) are sent to the master server. Data access requests (e.g., write file X.DAT), however, are made directly to storage devices by the server making the request.

Figure 15–5 also illustrates the need for a cluster volume manager—for a slave server to write directly to a physical storage device through a volume manager, the state of the virtual device of which it is a part must be valid. In other words, all virtual device state changes must become visible to all servers simultaneously.

Applications running on any of a shared data cluster's servers can create, extend, or delete files and directories in the cluster file system without regard for what applications on other servers are doing. The cluster file system coordinates application data and metadata requests across the cluster, and keeps the file system consistent.

If a server running a cluster file system fails, its applications restart on surviving servers, but in most cases the file system need not be restarted *because it is still running.* This minimizes what is typically the largest portion of application recovery time after a server crash— file system integrity checking. File system restart is only necessary when the

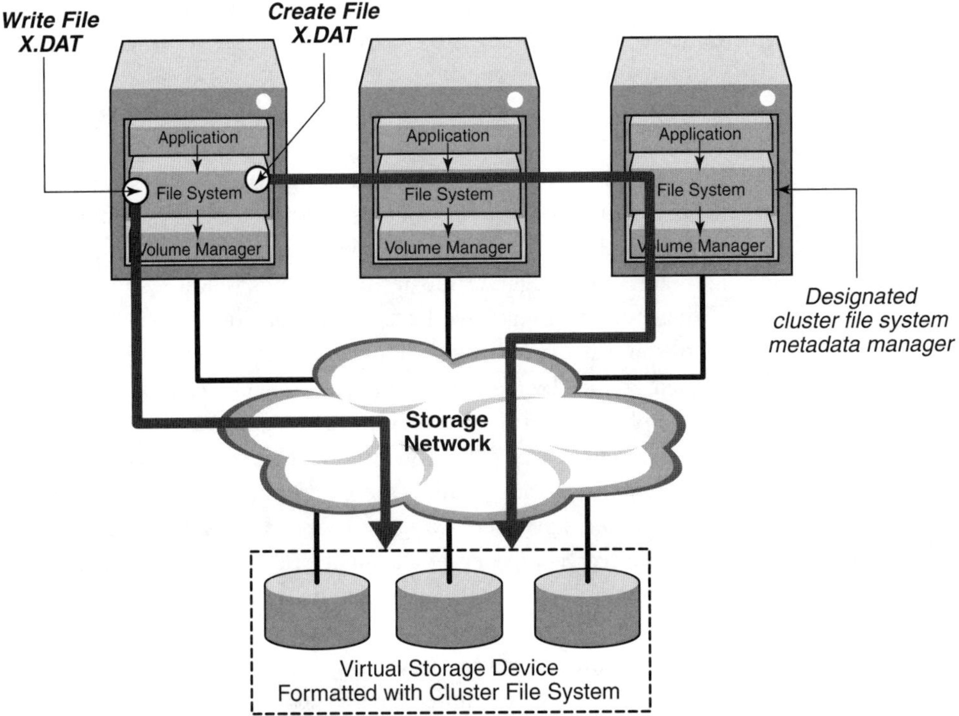

▼ **FIGURE 15–5** *Cluster File System Formatted on a Cluster Volume*

master server in a master-slave architecture fails. Even in this case, restart is automatic, and a (much faster) log replay replaces conventional file system integrity checking.

Cluster File System Benefits

Perhaps the greatest beneficiary of cluster file system technology is the system administrator. With a cluster file system, several administrative tasks are simplified or eliminated:

- Because all servers in a cluster can access the files in a cluster file system, consistency of reference data, application images, and libraries is automatic. All servers work from the same copy of control data and application files. Moreover, no storage space is required for additional copies of reference data.
- Failover is more flexible because it is not constrained by data accessibility—all servers in a shared data cluster have access to all files at

all times. Similarly, applications can be assigned to servers dynamically for load balancing or administrative purposes.

- Virtual storage (RAID systems and appliances) can be cost-justified more easily and used more effectively because all storage capacity is accessible simultaneously by all servers. Server-by-server capacity allocation is not required.
- Larger virtual devices with larger file systems improve application I/O load balancing. Cluster-wide I/O load can be distributed across more I/O resources.
- With fewer, larger file systems, managing individual data objects is easier for administrators, users, application developers, and backup.
- Adding a server to a cluster becomes easier, because its data organization is pre-defined by already-existing cluster file systems.
- Files and file systems can be managed from any server in a cluster.

All of these simplifications stem from the fundamental property of cluster file systems—from the management and application access standpoints, shared file systems and the data in them appear identical to all servers in a cluster.

Cluster File Systems and Applications

Most applications benefit from cluster file systems. Conventional, "cluster-unaware" applications can run from anywhere in a cluster. In multi-application clusters, overall I/O performance improves because larger file systems improve load balancing. Once a cluster file system is created, these benefits are automatic. No tuning is required.

Most transaction-oriented applications are **partitionable;** they consist of multiple concurrent execution threads that could run on different servers if they could coordinate their accesses to data. Multiple instances of such applications can run on different servers, using a cluster file system to coordinate their accesses to data. The instances balance client and data access load, thereby scaling beyond the capacity of any single server. The cluster file system does not balance I/O load per se, but by enabling shared data access, it enables application-level load balancing across server resources.

Cluster File Systems and System Crashes

If a cluster file system master server fails, surviving servers detect the failure and elect a replacement. Any application I/O that would conflict with I/O in progress from the failed server is blocked during this transition. Because slave servers do not update file system metadata directly, failure of a slave server does not require metadata repair. Recovery from slave server failure is therefore typically faster than recovery from master server failure.

With any state transition (e.g., a server leaving or joining the cluster), application I/O is suspended momentarily while the cluster file system revalidates its locks (to release any that had been held by an exiting server). When locks have been revalidated, applications can resume. To an application, some I/O requests stall imperceptibly; others (conflicting ones) stall momentarily, but otherwise the transition is transparent.

CHAPTER SUMMARY

- With the exception of some database data stored in *raw partitions*, nearly all of the persistent data used by computer systems today is organized by file systems.
- File systems organize the capacity of virtual and physical block storage devices into hierarchical trees of objects (files) that can easily be manipulated by applications, generally without regard for the actions of other applications. This is a much more convenient paradigm for applications than the virtual storage device.
- Ideally, file systems should interact with virtual storage devices that can change their capacity in order to make use of expanded capacity without requiring a system reboot or a reformatting of the entire file system.
- Some file systems include snapshot capability, which enables them to capture images of data at specific points in time for later backup or analysis. File system snapshots typically use the copy-on-write technique.
- File systems that maintain copy-on-write snapshots may experience sudden requirements for additional capacity. It is particularly important

VERITAS ServPoint NAS Software

ServPoint SAN appliance software virtualizes block storage devices from within the storage network. ServPoint NAS appliance software virtualizes file systems for clients over a TCP/IP network. ServPoint NAS appliance software turns conventional servers into very scalable "NAS gateways" to which a user's selection of storage devices can be connected. ServPoint NAS is based on VERITAS volume management, file system, clustering, replication, snapshot, and other technologies. ServPoint NAS appliance software uses the NFS and CIFS network file access protocols to provide file access services to clients. Client applications treat virtual file systems as though they were local.

ServPoint NAS appliances offer configuration flexibility—any storage device supported by the VERITAS™ Volume Manager can be used with an appliance. Clustering makes it possible to configure highly available multinode file servers. Replication technology makes it possible to configure a multisite disaster recovery configuration. Integration with the NDMP file backup protocol provides protection of data against device failure and application-induced corruption.

that these file systems be able to make use of expandable virtual storage devices.

- Cluster file systems enable applications running on different servers in a cluster to access the same data at the same time. Cluster file systems may use symmetric or asymmetric architecture. All instances of a symmetric cluster file system update metadata directly. With the asymmetric, or master-slave, architecture a designated master server performs all metadata updates.
- Cluster file systems (and volume managers) increase the ability of applications to scale by running multiple instances on different servers sharing access to the same data. They improve availability by making failover faster in the event of application server failure.

CHAPTER 16

It is a capital mistake to theorize before one has data.

—SIR ARTHUR CONAN DOYLE

Databases and Virtual Storage

In this chapter . . .

- Databases, transactions, logs, and virtual storage
- Using virtual storage with database backup
- Virtual storage and replication of database data

People work with data—contact lists stored on personal digital assistants (PDAs), budget spreadsheets, etc.—all the time. Small, simple sets of data with little or no relationship to other data can easily be stored in files.[1] If all data were simply structured, there would be little use for database managers.

But in an enterprise, data objects *are* interrelated. Billing records link to name and address records, order records affect inventory information, shipping instructions require credit verification, and so forth. Practically speaking, it is impossible to manage large and complex sets of data, such as bank records or production control data, in files. Files have no built-in mechanisms for reflecting relationships between data items, nor do they enforce semantics on individual data items.

1. In database contexts, files are often referred to as **flat files** because they impose no internal structure on data.

DATABASES

Databases managed by **database management systems** (**DBMSs** or **database managers**) address semantic and relationship requirements. Like file systems, database managers are a common point through which all applications access data. Unlike file systems, in that they impose structural relationships and semantic restrictions on the data they manage. Database managers perform four basic functions:

- ***Security:*** Database managers enforce access restrictions and guard against unauthorized access to data items.
- ***Organization:*** Database managers structure data so that developers don't have to implement logic to validate and interrelate data in every application that uses it.
- ***Integrity:*** Database managers enable multiple applications to access data at the same time without loss of integrity. If two applications attempt to modify the same data item at the same time, a database manager coordinates the modifications so that the net result makes business sense.
- ***Safety:*** Database managers include backup and restore facilities that are able to recover data to a consistent and up-to-date state after system crashes or physical disasters (as long as the virtual storage that holds the database is intact).

Most commercial database managers implement the **relational database model,** which represents each data item as a *row* (record) in a *table* (file). Applications use the standard **Structured Query Language** (SQL) to access relational database data. Because of the data integrity relational database managers provide, enterprises routinely store their most mission-critical data in relational

VERITAS™ Storage Foundation for Database and Applications

As more and more enterprise data is managed by databases, the management of database data becomes an increasing concern to system and database administrators. To improve the manageability of databases and their applications, VERITAS packages key technologies along with database-specific enhancements into database editions that improve database performance, availability, and manageability. VERITAS™ Storage Foundation for Database and Applications, which are available for Oracle, Sybase, and DB2, implement a specialized form of storage virtualization to enhance database I/O performance and data manageability.

The performance degradation that must be suffered in order to gain the improved data manageability of storing database data in container files has long been a dilemma for database administrators. VERITAS™ Storage Foundation for Database and Applications include a virtualization technology called *Quick I/O* that enables system administrators to manage database tables as though they were stored in files, but at the same time, provides the database manager with a direct volume interface that bypasses file system locking and caching. The result: the I/O performance of raw storage with the manageability of files—the best of both worlds for administrators.

databases. Doing everything possible to make databases both failure-proof and efficient is therefore a primary concern for storage architects.

A database failure is any sequence of events that results in data loss or unavailability. The two basic causes of database failure are human or application errors that lose or corrupt data in the database, and hardware, software, or environmental failure.

Human and Application Errors

Errors in a database can be caused by inadvertent or malicious user action, or by application bugs that corrupt data by performing actions that are syntactically correct but do not make business sense. In general, user errors cause "holes" of missing data in a structurally intact database, while application bugs tend to corrupt data items or relationships between them. The best safeguard against errors of either type is regular, well-managed backup, with copies transported promptly to safe locations to guard against environmental disasters.[2]

System and Environmental Failures

A server hosting a database can crash while databases are active. The challenge is to quickly restore application access to databases that are first of all consistent, and secondarily as current as possible under the circumstances.

Because of the structure they impose on data and the interrelationships among data items they maintain, database managers' protection techniques differ from the file system techniques discussed in Chapter 14. To understand these techniques, an appreciation of database *transactional* properties is helpful.

Database Transactions

A transaction is any set of database operations that comprise a single business action. For example, an accounting transaction might consist of:

▼ Reading a record to be debited and subtracting the debit amount from it

---

2. Compartmentalization of function is also key to protecting databases against human error. People should not be empowered to perform database operations not directly required by their job functions. Functional compartmentalization also protects against fraud and malicious abuse. Requiring collaboration by two or more individuals to perform actions that can destroy data reduces the ability of a lone disgruntled employee to attack enterprise data.

- Rewriting the (updated) debited record
- Reading the corresponding record to be credited and adding the amount deducted from the debited record to it
- Rewriting the (updated) credited record
- Writing a separate audit record that summarizes the business action

The operations comprising this transaction represent a single business action. If either the debit operations or the credit operations were not performed, the database would not reflect the business action (and therefore the state of the business) accurately. If the server executing this transaction were to crash after performing the debit operations but before the credit ones, funds would disappear. If it crashed after the credit but before the debit, funds would appear to have materialized from nowhere. Grouping the two into a transaction instructs a database manager to complete both sets of operations or neither, but never reflect the results of only one of them in the database.

Database managers enforce **transactional integrity** on database operations. This means that when a database is quiescent (not in use), either all operations that are part of any single transaction are reflected in the database or none of them is reflected, even if a crash occurred during transaction execution.

Database Manager Crash Recovery

When restarting after a crash, a database manager must allow for the possibility that a database disk image may contain some partially complete transactions that must be completed or "backed out" before applications can access the database. Database managers preserve transactional integrity across crashes by recording persistent *logs* of intended and completed actions. When recovering from a crash, a database manager **replays** its log to verify that completed transaction results are reflected in the database image and that all effects of incomplete transactions are reversed.

Figure 16–1 depicts the main recovery-related components of a database manager.

Database manager processes ("threads") read and write data from a shared **database cache.**[3] Files (indicated in Figure 16–1) are generally preferred over raw devices for database storage because of their manageability.

3. Each database management system has its own name for this memory pool. The essential common feature is that the pool is accessible by all the database manager processes or threads that read and write data in the database disk image.

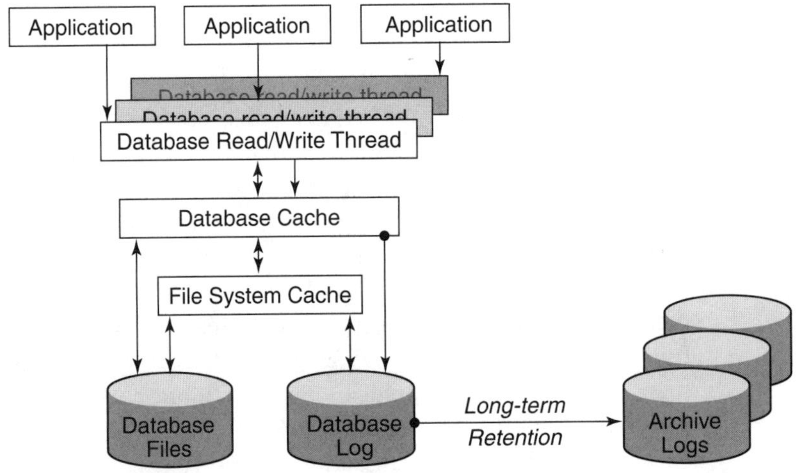

▼ **FIGURE 16–1** *Relational Database Manager Recovery*

The VERITAS™ Storage Foundation for Microsoft Exchange Server

Electronic mail has become critical to the conduct of almost all business, and the dominant mail system is Microsoft Exchange. Exchange administrators today find themselves faced with the same mission-critical uptime requirements that database administrators have been coping with for years. They urgently need manageability, availability, and recovery tools for their Exchange 2000 servers and databases.

To address this need, VERITAS developed Storage Foundation for Microsoft Exchange Server to combine Volume Manager and FlashSnap technologies with Exchange-specific features to manage and protect Exchange 2000 message databases. Storage Foundation for Microsoft Exchange Server provides rapid recovery through point-in-time snapshots of Exchange databases and transaction log files. In case of a failure, Exchange databases can be restored to the last prior snapshot, followed by automatic transaction log replay. For environments that require high availability, the Storage Foundation for Microsoft Exchange Server is fully compatible with both the VERITAS and Microsoft Cluster Servers.

In a sense, files are virtual storage containers for database data.

Database managers record changes in **database logs** before updating files. Database logs contain both data updates and the transaction context in which they occur. If a server running a database manager crashes, some committed updates may still be in cache, not yet **flushed** to persistent storage. All updates that are part of committed transactions, however, *are* recorded in the database log, which is written persistently as part of transaction commitment. Using this log, a database can be restored to a consistent state in which only committed transactions are reflected in it.

Log Archiving

Database managers typically *archive* logs when they fill. Collectively, **archive logs** comprise a long-term history of database updates. From a combination of a database backup and a complete set of archive logs, a database can be restored to a consistent state representing any point in its continuous history. A consistent, up-to-date database can be reconstructed by:

- Restoring a full database backup
- Replaying all archive logs in order against the restored backup
- Replaying the database log active at the time of failure

Database managers automate the recovery process, locating online logs and requesting that tapes containing archive logs be mounted for use. The same process that recovers from crashes can also recover from errors that corrupt a database by **rolling** the database **back** to a recovery point prior to the introduction of corruption.

Recovery from backup and logs may be the only option if a disaster incapacitates a data center. For the procedure to work, however, a database backup and a complete set of archive logs must be available at the recovery site. For up-to-date recovery, the active database log must also be mirrored or replicated at the recovery site.

One possible database recovery strategy is to establish a base point by making a full database backup, and then retain all archived logs from that point forward. Any database failure can be recovered by replaying enough archive logs. This would eliminate the adverse impact of backup on application availability and performance.

But rolling a database forward from logs takes time and requires media handling (if archive logs have been moved to offline media). A recovering database remains offline until all pertinent logs have been replayed. If a log is missing or unreadable, recovery may not be possible. For this reason, most installations back up important databases periodically and keep archive logs on mirrored or replicated storage. To enable up-to-date recovery, the active log must also be mirrored or replicated.

DATABASE BACKUP AND VIRTUAL STORAGE

Using files as virtual database storage improves data manageability. Files can easily be moved to balance I/O load, or extended when more table space is required. They can be backed up automatically and restored, either individually or in groups. Files introduce a complication, however, in that file systems typically cache updates to improve performance. File systems used for database storage must be configured to execute write requests synchronously (i.e., not indicating write completion to the database manager until data is actually on persistent storage) so that database manager dependencies on persistently stored data are met.

For a database backup to be useful, it must be possible to use it to restore a consistent database image—one that contains all transactions completed prior to the restore point and no others. A **cold backup** made while a database is stopped has this property, but results in a substantial interval of application outage. Backup while a database is in use is preferable, but it must be possible to recreate consistent database images from an online backup. Virtual storage has an important role to play in online database backup.

Online Database Backup

A database in use by applications can be backed up **logically** or **physically.** Logical online backup programs are supplied as part of the database manager, and have companion restore and recovery programs that are also database-aware. A logical online backup copies database objects rather than the contents of files that hold them. The disadvantage of logical database backup is its impact on application performance. Logical backup is essentially a long-running, resource-intensive application that affects large tracts of database data, and competes with other applications for database resources (processing, I/O bandwidth, storage device access, and cache occupancy).

A physical online backup is a copy of a database's container files or storage device contents made while the database is in use. Because these files are constantly being updated while the database is in use, they are likely to contain the results of partially complete transactions and, in addition, may contain individual **database pages**[4] that are inconsistent.

Database managers account for this possibility when they are put into **backup mode** prior to backup initiation. While a database is in backup mode, its database manager logs extra information about updates that can be used along with a backup to restore a consistent database. Restoring a database from a physical online backup requires:

- Restoration of database files
- Repair of inconsistent database pages
- Replay of logs to restore database transactional consistency to a desired recovery point

4. For I/O and space management efficiency, database managers request I/O in fixed-size *pages,* or sequences of consecutively numbered virtual device blocks, usually in the range of 2–8 kilobytes.

If the files of a large database are backed up while the database is in use, the frequency of pages needing repair is likely to be high, and restoration is likely to be time-consuming. If snapshots are available, however, one can be initiated immediately after the database is put into backup mode, and backed up while applications continue to process the "real" database image. A backup made from a snapshot may contain partial transactions or inconsistent pages, but the likelihood is much lower than if the database files being modified by applications are the backup data source.

Physical Online Database Backup

Figure 16–2 illustrates use of a split mirror snapshot for physical online database backup. The database represented in Figure 16–2 is stored on a three-mirror virtual device. To back this database up, an administrator would put the database into backup mode and split a mirror from the virtual device. The split mirror would be imported by the backup server, its file system mounted, and a backup made from it. No "backup window" is necessary as with file system backups. Container files in the snapshot could be backed up by a file-oriented backup manager.

If the virtual devices that hold a database are connected to a storage network, a second server (Server B in Figure 16–2) can import the split mirror and perform the backup, eliminating all impact on application performance. After the backup, however, when the split mirror is rejoined to its parent virtual device, resynchronization I/O *can* impact application performance. Resynchronization overhead can be minimized if changes made to a virtual device while a mirror is split are logged and the log is used to direct **fast resynchronization** during rejoin.

Physical online database backups can also be made from file system **copy-on-write snapshots** (Chapter 14). Copy-on-write file system snapshots can be mounted as though they were read-only file systems. Again, backup starts by suspending activity momentarily, putting the database into backup mode, mounting the snapshot, and reading backup data from it. As with split mirror snapshots, the backup is not necessarily consistent, but a combination of the backup and logs can be used to restore a consistent database at any desired recovery point. As with split mirror snapshots, a container file backup made from a snapshot might contain inconsistent data or pages, so database recovery includes repairing inconsistent pages. Database managers automate the steps of database recovery.

A database may also be stopped prior to backup, so that a snapshot can be made while it is in a consistent state. A backup made from such a snapshot is effectively a cold backup. It represents the database state at a single point in time, and recovery to that point in time is possible

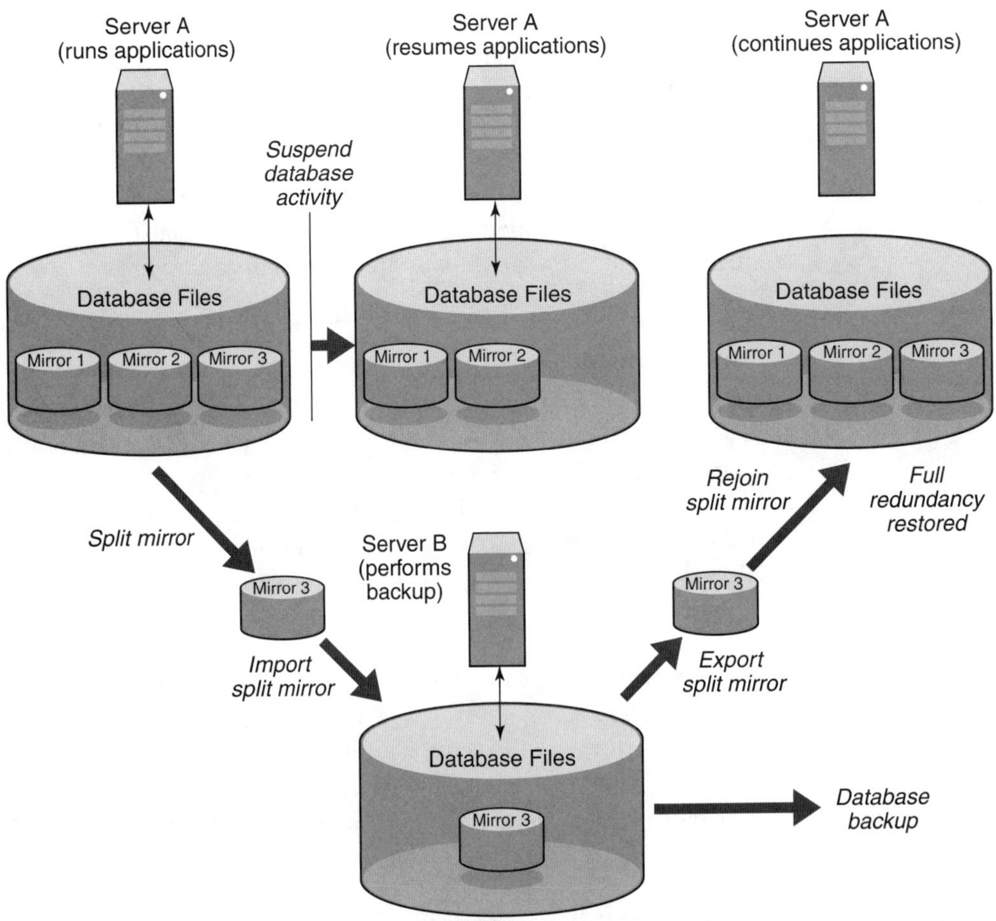

▼ **FIGURE 16–2** *Physical Online Database Backup on a Backup Server*

without log playback. The viability of this approach is limited by the time typically required to shut down database managers and the applications that use them, which can amount to several minutes.

Online database backups based on copy-on-write snapshots incur no resynchronization overhead. When a snapshot has served its purpose (been backed up), it can be deleted, and the space it occupied returned to a free space pool.

Overhead *is* incurred during the backup. Since a copy-on-write snapshot uses data in its parent file system or device, backup I/O competes with application I/O. Copy-on-write snapshot backups may not be the best choice for active databases.

Both split mirror and copy-on-write snapshot physical database backup techniques are based on underlying containers that can hold all database-related data. As long as it is stored on virtual devices or in file systems from which snapshots can be made, all database-related data, including control files, tables, indexes and other metadata, and logs are accessible to the backup manager without further administrator action.

INCREMENTAL DATABASE BACKUP

Increasing database sizes and rising availability demands are making full database backups untenable in many cases. As with file systems, databases can be backed up *incrementally,* copying only data that has changed since some previous backup. Both backup time and media can be saved when only changed data is copied. Like full backups, incremental database backups may be *logical* or *physical.*

Archive Logs

Archive logs are a simple form of logical incremental database backup. By restoring a full backup to establish a "baseline" and applying archive logs to it, a database can be recovered to any recovery point up to the end of the newest archive log.

As the number of archive logs grows, restore times and media handling both increase. For every situation, there is a point beyond which recovery from archive logs is intolerable. Incremental database backup strategies usually include periodic full backups to establish new baselines.

Logical Incremental Backup

Some database managers can perform logical incremental database backups while a database is in use. A logical incremental backup sends a stream of database elements whose contents have changed since the last backup to a backup manager, which writes them on tape. Database recovery can also be automated with this technique, because database manager restore utilities can recreate consistent database images from a baseline full backup and subsequent incremental backups. The disadvantage of incremental database backup is that it is resource intensive, because the database manager must identify and transfer all changed data elements selected for backup. The compensating advantage is selectivity—for example, individual tables can be backed up using this technique.

Physical Incremental Backup

Incremental backup of database container files is effectively a physical incremental database backup. But because any change to a file causes the entire file to be copied during incremental backup, file-based incremental backup is often effectively equivalent to full database backup. File system copy-on-write snapshot technology has been used to identify modified blocks within database files for selective *block-level incremental* backup. To restore from block-level incremental database backups, a backup manager must first restore the newest full backup, and then apply all newer block-level incremental backups in order to the restored baseline image.

Incremental database backups reduce both media consumption and backup times. One important advantage of shorter database backup times is that they enable backups to be made more frequently, shortening restore times and enabling recovery points that are closer to moments of failure (less lost data).

In general, restoring incremental backups requires more time and media handling than restoring full backups. Scheduling periodic full backups to establish new restore baselines limits media handling during a restore.

Block-Level Incremental Backup

VERITAS NetBackup™ implements block-level incremental backup (BLIB) technology as an option for database environments. VERITAS BLIB technology is unique in that it fully integrates block-level incremental backups with databases' own recovery managers.

BLIB is based on VERITAS™ File System copy-on-write snapshot technology. Copy-on-write techniques make the addresses of modified blocks available to NetBackup so that it can back up only those blocks. Compared with other techniques for discovering modified database blocks, the copy-on-write technique imposes very little overhead .

Another form of BLIB, called Delta File Technology, appears in VERITAS NetBackup Professional for protecting mobile computers' data. Delta File Technology identifies file blocks that have changed since the last backup and copies only those over the network. Minimizing network backup traffic is especially important for mobile computers that may be connected to their backup servers over relatively slow links.

RECOVERING DATABASES FROM BACKUPS

In a *complete* database recovery, all logged transactions are reapplied to the baseline database, so the result is a database image that reflects all transactions that had been committed at the instant of failure and none that had not. Complete recovery from database-corrupting errors is inappropriate, because it would reintroduce the corruption. Database recovery programs allow an administrator to halt log playback just prior to the incidence of a corrupting error. The recovery point is the last possible point in time or transaction prior to the corruption's occurrence.

Managing Database Logs

For fastest recovery, archive logs should be kept online and mirrored or replicated to the location where backups are stored. Administrators must balance between recovery point and resource consumption in determining how frequently to archive database logs. More frequent archiving reduces potential data loss, but consumes processing and I/O resources, possibly impacting application performance. Less frequent archiving reduces resource consumption, but increases the time between archive logs, possibly resulting in less current recovery points.

If a database and its current log are both destroyed by a disaster, data is necessarily lost, even if backup and log archiving procedures have been rigorously followed. Therefore, a vital part of complete database recovery is mirroring or replication of the current log to the recovery site. Most database managers are able to use enterprise network to *multiplex*, or make simultaneous local and remote log copies. Database manager multiplexing is usually slower than virtual storage techniques (mirroring and virtual device replication); the latter are generally preferred if available.

PROTECTING ONLINE DATABASES' DATA

Storage Redundancy

Recovery from a backup inherently implies database downtime. Failure-tolerant virtual storage eliminates several causes of downtime by enabling databases to ride through most hardware failures. For example, mirroring and parity RAID essentially eliminate disk drive failure as a cause of downtime.

Mirroring is sometimes perceived as expensive because it doubles storage device requirements. With disk drive cost decreasing, however, mirroring is increasingly attractive for its functional and performance benefits, especially in applications like banking and retail sales that have high update rates. Ideally, mirrored arrays should be configured using LUNs from different RAID systems and with multiple I/O paths to each device to maximize failure protection and I/O performance.

Parity RAID (RAID-5) consumes fewer devices than mirroring, but requires calculation and "extra" I/O every time an application writes data. It performs poorly in write-intensive applications. Parity RAID is most suitable for read-only or "read-mostly" database applications such as decision support.[5]

VERITAS and Parallel Databases

The VERITAS™ Storage Foundation Cluster File System HA includes the Cluster Volume Manager and Cluster File System that are prerequisites for shared data parallel databases, making it an ideal parallel database platform. High availability is delivered by the (included) VERITAS™ Cluster Server that provides cluster membership services to parallel databases using the VERITAS Low Latency Transport (LLT) and Global Atomic Broadcast (GAB) protocols. These protocols provide fast, reliable communications that keep cluster member servers synchronized by communicating state changes instantly and simultaneously throughout a cluster.

Virtual Storage for Parallel Databases

Some database managers (such as Oracle Real Application Cluster) are capable of accessing a single database image simultaneously from several servers in a cluster. Figure 16–3 shows database manager instances running on two servers using the cluster interconnect (usually Ethernet) to coordinate record access and keep the database consistent.

Such a *shared data* **parallel database** enhances information service availability and enables applications to scale beyond a single server. If one server fails, client requests are routed to surviving servers running the same applications and accessing the same database image. Surviving servers recognize the failure, release the failed server's locks, play back its log, and redistribute its client connections. Since the database itself remains in operation, full database recovery is not required.

Failure-tolerant virtual storage is a must for parallel database managers. RAID systems connected to a storage network provide shareable raw storage, but for manageability, including multiple access paths, online virtual device expansion, and coordination of multiple devices, a cluster volume manager such as is described in Chapter 11 is required. Cluster volume managers have unique advantages for parallel database systems:

- In small systems, server-based storage virtualization defers the high entry cost of a RAID system until database size and performance requirements justify it.

---

5. Some RAID systems have hardware assists for parity calculation and use cache to mitigate write overhead, making them somewhat more suitable for transaction processing. Parity RAID overhead compared to mirroring is inherent, however, and is difficult to totally eliminate. Moreover, parity RAID has no functionality comparable to mirror splitting.

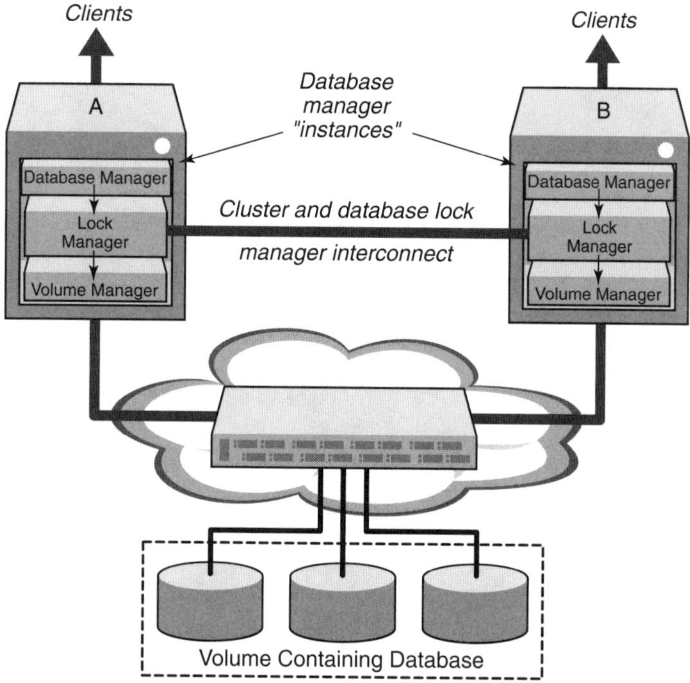

▼ **FIGURE 16–3** *Parallel Database Manager Use of a Cluster Volume Manager*

- In large systems, server-based virtualization complements RAID system virtualization, as illustrated in Figure 16–4, enabling higher capacity virtual devices and enhancing failure tolerance, by striping or mirroring across LUNs presented by two or more RAID systems and by supporting dynamic multipath access to storage devices.

Cluster file systems, using technology similar to that of cluster volume managers, enable shared image parallel database managers to use file-based storage. The technology allows a single file system to be mounted and accessed by multiple servers simultaneously. With file-based storage, a database can be expanded easily, backed up using file system backup managers, relocated while online, and so forth.

Cluster file systems offer an additional important benefit for shared image databases. During full recovery, one database manager instance must replay all instances' logs. Without a cluster file system, either logs must be copied, file systems containing them must be temporarily mounted on the recovering server, or a remote file access protocol such

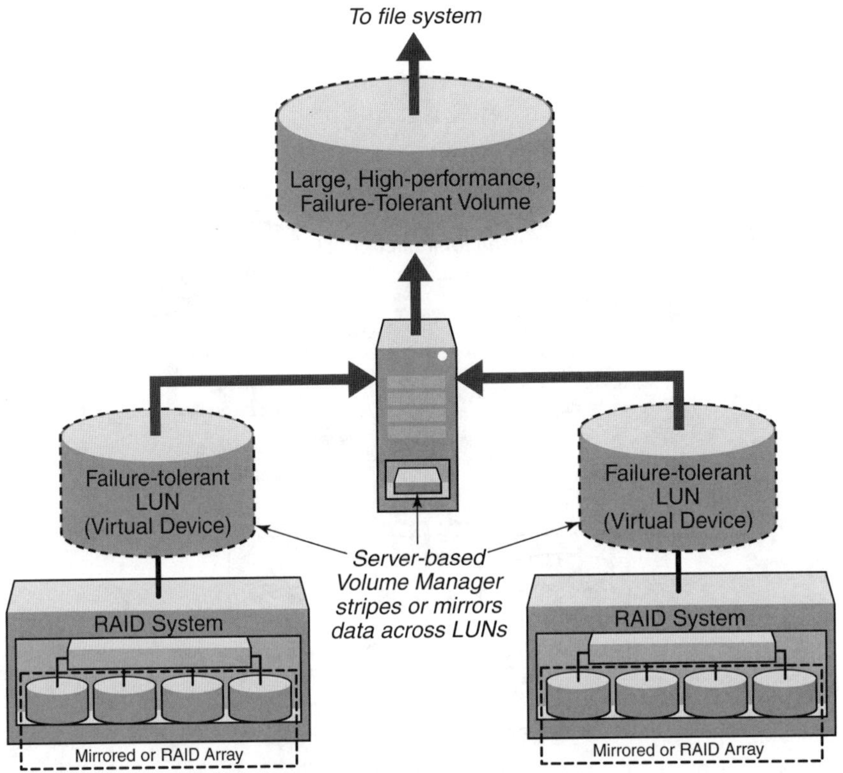

▼ **FIGURE 16–4** *Volume Manager Virtualization of RAID System LUNs*

as NFS must be used. With a cluster file system, all instances have immediate access to all logs. None of these is as simple (and therefore as robust during a stressful recovery) as a cluster file system through which all logs can be accessed automatically by any server in the cluster.

Finally, cluster file systems may allow all database manager instances to run from a single software image, simplifying software installation and maintenance. Where the technology is available, shared file system-based storage is generally preferable for parallel database performance, robustness, and manageability.

DATABASES AND VIRTUAL STORAGE REPLICATION

Because a database manager has so much information about the data it manages, more options are available for disaster recovery than with file-based applications. Like the backup-restore techniques on which they are based, database disaster recovery options require a baseline and a complete set of persistent logs at the recovery site. The usual techniques for moving database data and logs to a recovery site are mirroring and replication.[6] A database can be replicated by the database manager itself or by replicating the virtual storage that holds it.

There are three basic techniques for recovering databases from replicas:

- ***Replicated archive logs:*** Perhaps the simplest database disaster recovery technique is regular copying of archived logs to a recovery site, where they are applied to a *standby* copy of the database, usually under control of an automated script. This approach is simple to implement and administer; its main drawback is the recovery point—data can only be recovered to the end time of the newest available archived log. For applications that can tolerate loss of some data, this simple approach may be adequate.
- ***Database manager replication:*** Most database managers can replicate database objects in some form—procedures, log entries, or other. This capability is often used to distribute data among several locations that use portions of the data in it, or to replicate data from one type of database to another, but can also be used for recovery. Database manager replication is usually asynchronous, often with deliberate delays between main database updates and their reflection in replicas.[7]
- ***Virtual storage replication:*** Replication of virtual storage devices is a simple alternative to database manager replication that can automatically coordinate the replication of any number of databases and their ancillary application data between a data center and its disaster recovery site. Most information services maintain control files, program images, libraries, logs, and so forth, in files outside of their databases. Replication of a group of virtual storage devices automatically makes

---

6. Chapter 12 explains the differences between these two technology options. In essence, mirroring is useful over shorter distances or where application I/O latency is less critical, whereas replication is the preferred technique over long distances or where I/O latency is key to application performance.
7. This delay can be exploited to recover from human errors and rolling disasters (both of which propagate database corruption to replicas) by deliberately delaying updates to replicas for fixed periods. For example, if database updates are held for an hour before being applied to a replica, human and application errors detected within an hour of occurrence (as many are) are not reflected in the replica until an hour after they occur. If replication is stopped promptly, an as yet uncorrupted replica can be used to recover a corrupted primary database to a one-hour (or less) recovery point.

all of an application's data and program images, not just its databases, available at a recovery site.

Server-based virtualization is particularly advantageous for database storage replication because it can coordinate replication of any group of a server's virtual devices, no matter what physical storage they use. This allows database designers to configure the most appropriate storage devices for each type of data (tables, archive and current logs, control files and other ancillary data), and to start and stop coordinated replication of all of them with a single administrative action.

As Chapter 12 observes, a key property that makes virtual device replication useful for database recovery is **write order fidelity**—all writes to a group of virtual devices are executed in the same order on the replica at the recovery site. Without this property, a database replica could not be used for recovery, because it would not necessarily represent a previous state of the database and its logs.

Virtual device replicas containing databases can be used, however. The most obvious use is replication to mirrored virtual devices. A group of replicated devices can be quiesced, and a mirror can be split from the replica and used for backup or data analysis.

Volume Replicator and Databases

The VERITAS™ Volume Replicator (VVR) supports block storage replication for major database management systems such as Oracle, DB2, Sybase, and SQL Server. In addition to the disaster recovery advantages enumerated in the text, the simplicity of VVR means that storage administrators do not require in-depth database skills, as would be the case if a database-specific replication method were used. Once an administrator is familiar with the VERITAS™ Volume Manager and Volume Replicator, he or she can configure and manage replication for any application or data manager.

CHAPTER SUMMARY

- Database managers organize data independently of applications, and enforce both item-level and transactional semantics on it. Most databases in use today implement the relational database model.
- Database managers log updates, and periodically archive their logs. Archived logs aid in recovering a destroyed database, starting from a full backup.
- Copy-on-write and split mirror snapshots can both be used to capture a consistent database image so that a backup can be made while applications continue to use the database. Copy-on-write snapshots

have low creation and deletion overhead, but necessarily impact online database performance. Split mirrors require additional storage resources and resynchronization overhead, but can be moved "off host" to eliminate the impact of backup on application performance.

- Data mirroring and clustering are often employed to improve database and application availability because database data is typically of high value.
- Databases can be replicated for disaster recoverability using either database manager or virtual storage techniques. The favored technique for recovering from corruption is database manager replication, because it can be delayed so that corruption is not immediately reflected in the replica. For disaster recovery, virtual device replication is preferred because it enables all of an application's data, including multiple databases and ancillary files, to be replicated with low administrative effort.

PART 4

NETWORKS

There are three kinds of death in this world. There's heart death, there's brain death, and there's being off the network.

—GUY ALMES

CHAPTER 17

One of the greatest pains to human nature is the pain of a new idea.

—WALTER BAGEHOT

Interconnects for Virtual Storage

In this chapter . . .

- Characteristics of enterprise storage interconnects
- Storage network topologies
- Designing robust networks for virtual storage

A **storage interconnect** is the physical connection between servers and storage devices that enables the two to exchange data. The most common storage interconnects in server-class open systems are parallel SCSI and Fibre Channel. Parallel SCSI (Small Computer System Interface) connects storage devices *directly* to servers with no intervening infrastructure. Volume managers, RAID systems, and in-band storage network appliances all virtualize parallel SCSI-connected storage. Device addressing (16 per bus) and bus length (25 meters) limitations constrain parallel SCSI's usefulness in large and distributed systems.

Storage devices can also be connected to servers through a **storage network.** Most storage networks in use today are based on Fibre Channel technology, so the term *storage network* (and the acronym *SAN,* for storage area network) is often identified with Fibre Channel. Fibre Channel storage networks are almost always used to access block storage devices (disk drives and RAID system LUNs).

Parallel SCSI storage devices can be used in storage networks. Fibre Channel-to-SCSI **routers** connect parallel SCSI storage devices or server I/O adapters to storage networks, extending the useful lifetime of these components.

STORAGE NETWORKS AND FIBRE CHANNEL

Fibre Channel is a 1 gigabit per second or 2 gigabit per second (200 megabyte per second) storage network interconnect that can be configured in point-to-point, loop (known as Fibre Channel Arbitrated Loop or FC-AL), or fabric (a set of interconnected switches) topologies.

Point-to-point and fabric networks can be configured for full duplex (simultaneous bidirectional) data transfer for a maximum throughput of 400 megabytes per second. A loop shares a total of 100 or 200 megabytes per second of bandwidth among the devices it interconnects.

Multiple upper-level protocols (ULPs) can run simultaneously on a Fibre Channel network. Most storage access uses the **Fibre Channel Protocol** (FCP), a version of the SCSI-3 command set adapted for Fibre Channel network transport. IP (Internet protocol) is one ULP that can be used for cluster "heart beating" or LAN-free backup.

Storage networks require intelligent adapters at the server, intelligent switches in the network itself, and intelligent storage devices.

Server and storage device *bus adapters* (usually called host bus adapters, or HBAs) convert internal message and data representations to Fibre Channel Protocol for network transmission. HBAs are the interface between end components' internal I/O buses (e.g., PCI or Sbus) and the network.

A storage network *infrastructure* is the set of network components to which servers and storage devices connect. Fibre Channel loop infrastructures consist of *hubs* capable of interconnecting as many as 126 devices per loop. In a Fibre Channel loop, one device at a time can transmit data. Fibre Channel loops are primarily used to connect disk drives to RAID systems and to connect older storage devices to Fibre Channel fabrics.

A **switch** or **director**[1] is an active network component that shares high internal communication bandwidth among pairs of devices dynamically. In a switch with N ports, as many as N/2 pairs of devices can exchange data concurrently.

A Fibre Channel *fabric* is a set of interconnected switches. In a fabric, any port can communicate with any other port. Most Fibre Channel devices can connect directly to fabric ports. Some older devices connect only to loops, and must be bridged to a fabric through a hub.

Switches are the basic building blocks of storage network fabrics. **Inter-switch links** (ISLs) interconnect pairs of switch ports to create

---

1. The term *director* is commonly used to denote a larger, higher-performing, more resilient switch. Hereinafter, the term *switch* is used to denote both switches and directors, unless otherwise noted.

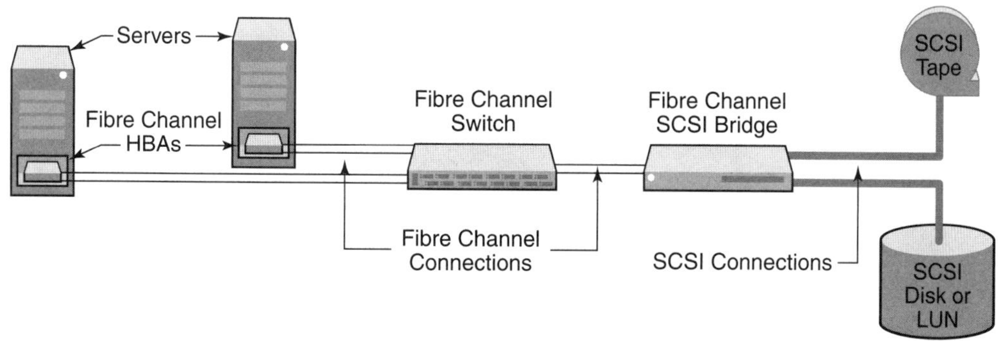

▼ **FIGURE 17–1** *Bridge (Router) in a Storage Network*

fabrics with hundreds of ports. Fabrics are often configured to isolate frequently intercommunicating devices' traffic to a single network segment.

Parallel SCSI and other devices can be connected to Fibre Channel networks via devices that are variously called bridges, gateways, or routers, as Figure 17–1 illustrates. The routers convert commands and data between Fibre Channel and parallel SCSI.

FIBRE CHANNEL STORAGE NETWORK TOPOLOGIES

The simplest Fibre Channel storage network topology that enables multiple servers to access common storage devices is the **loop** illustrated on the left of Figure 17–2. In a loop, one transmitting device and one receiving device can communicate at any instant. A switched fabric such as that represented on the right in Figure 17–2 can conduct multiple simultaneous communications between pairs of devices.

Fibre Channel switches can be connected into various fabric topologies. One simple Fibre Channel topology is a **ring** of two or more interconnected switches, as shown in Figure 17–3. In a ring topology, failure of one ISL makes the network into a **cascade.** All ports remain interconnected, so data can continue to flow.

Scaling of storage network rings is limited by the number of switch-to-switch "hops" required for devices to intercommunicate. As switches are added to these networks, devices must be located carefully to minimize the lengths of busy data paths.

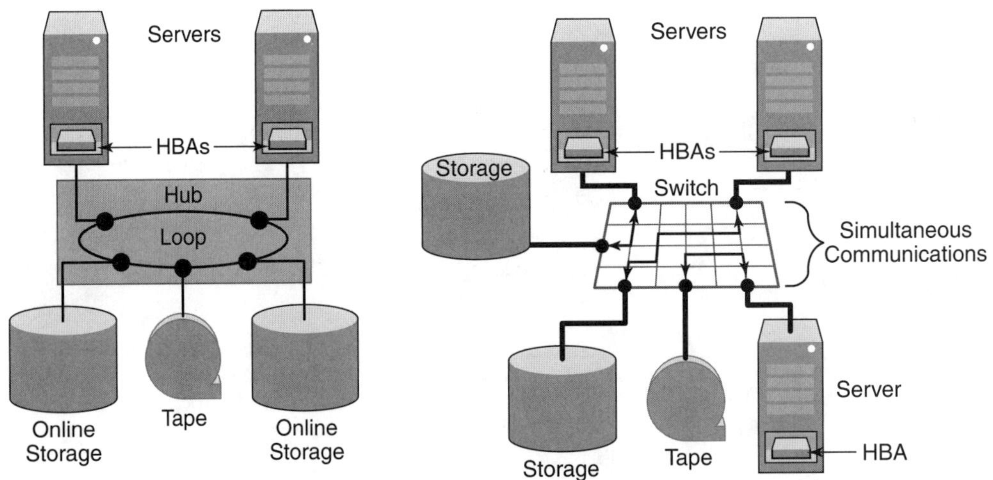

▼ **FIGURE 17–2** *Fibre Channel Storage Network Topologies*

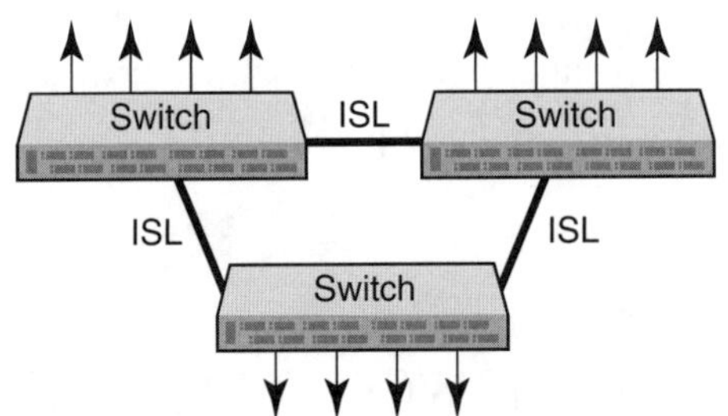

▼ **FIGURE 17–3** *Fibre Channel Ring Topology*

More complex fabrics enable larger, more resilient, and better performing networks. The partial mesh topology on the left in Figure 17–4 gives each switch two paths to any other switch, improving resiliency and performance over the ring topology.

The full mesh illustrated on the right in Figure 17–4 improves performance and resiliency over a partial mesh, but is expensive in terms of the number of ports consumed by ISLs, and can be complex to manage as switches are added.

The **core-edge** topology illustrated in Figure 17–5 is a partial mesh whose *core* switches primarily interconnect switches and whose *edge* switches primarily connect to servers and storage devices. Core-edge

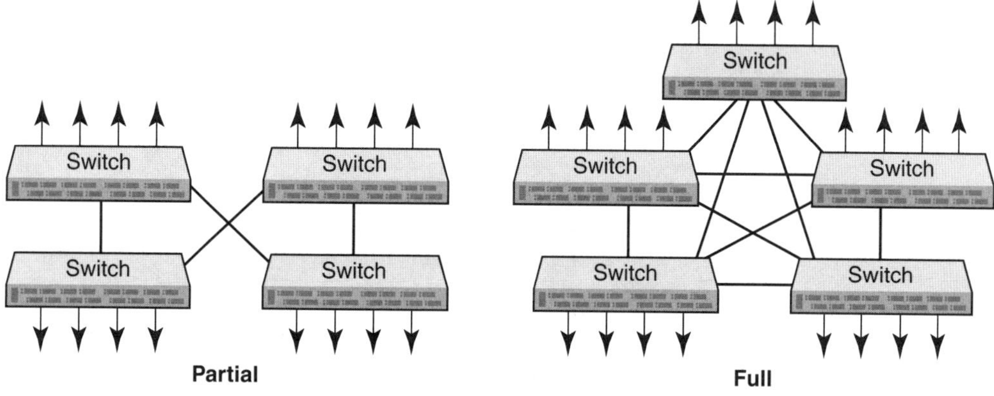

▼ **FIGURE 17–4** *Partial and Full Mesh Topologies*

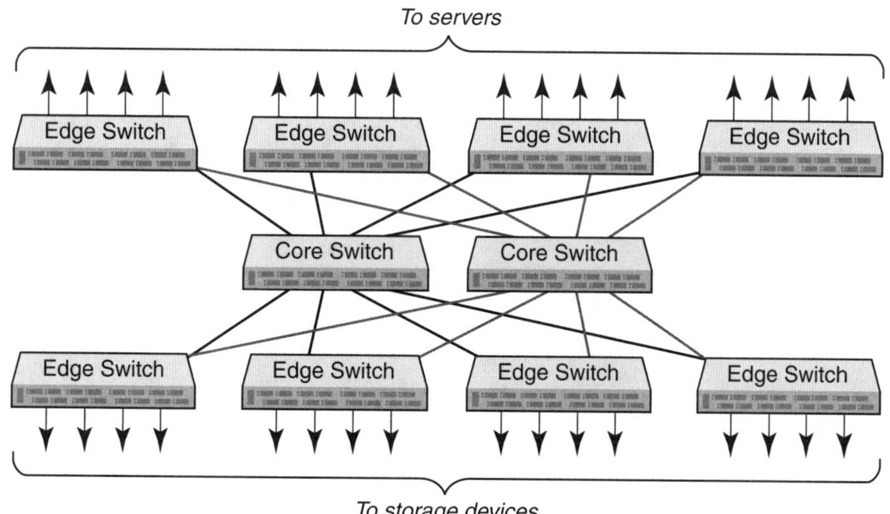

▼ **FIGURE 17–5** *Core-Edge Topology*

storage network design is similar to LAN design, which uses large switches at the core, and smaller ones at the edges.

Storage Network Redundancy

Whatever the topology, inter-switch connections should use double ISLs for resiliency and performance. For overall storage network resiliency, two

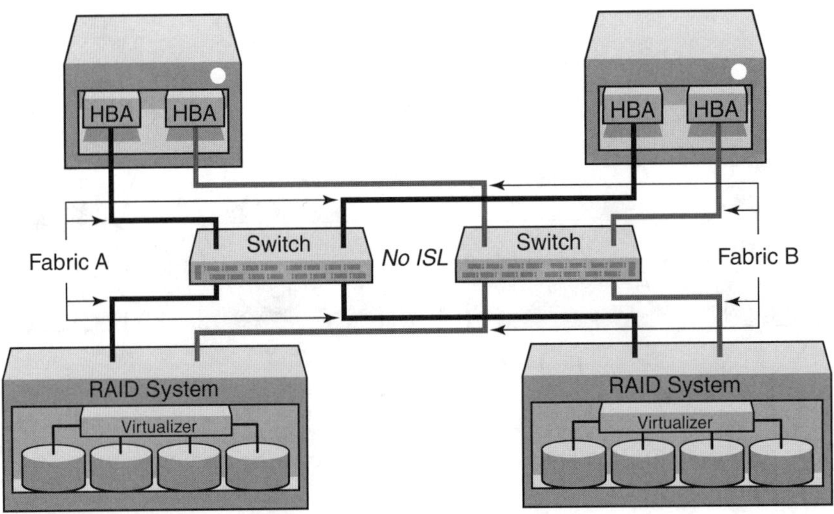

▼ **FIGURE 17–6** *Multifabric Storage Network*

VERITAS ™ Storage Manager Visualization

As storage network complexity increases, visualization becomes more challenging. VERITAS™ Storage Manager creates both physical and logical topology maps of a storage network. Of course, visualization must be based on a knowledge of components and interconnects. Storage Manager automatically discovers the addition or removal of components from a network.

Storage Manager is heterogeneous—it discovers and visualizes all major switches and storage devices, and displays maps of these components and connections between them. It can also produce this information in report form.

In addition to hardware, Storage Manager can discover and visualize software components such as volume managers, file systems, clusters, backup managers, databases, and Exchange environments.

separate fabrics should be configured, with each server and storage device connecting to corresponding switches on the two. The latter configuration, an example of which is shown in Figure 17–6, protects against HBA, cable, and switch failures and also improves fault containment.

This design provides fabric redundancy; even if an entire fabric fails, connectivity remains complete via the other. Both for resiliency and to minimize congestion, the temptation to interconnect everything should be resisted. It is usually preferable to create two unconnected fabrics with servers and storage devices connected to both.

Of course, connecting a device to two fabrics consumes two ports. Single-port HBAs consume two internal bus slots, which may be problematic for smaller servers. Some HBA modules contain two or more ports, but care should be taken when configuring these, because the

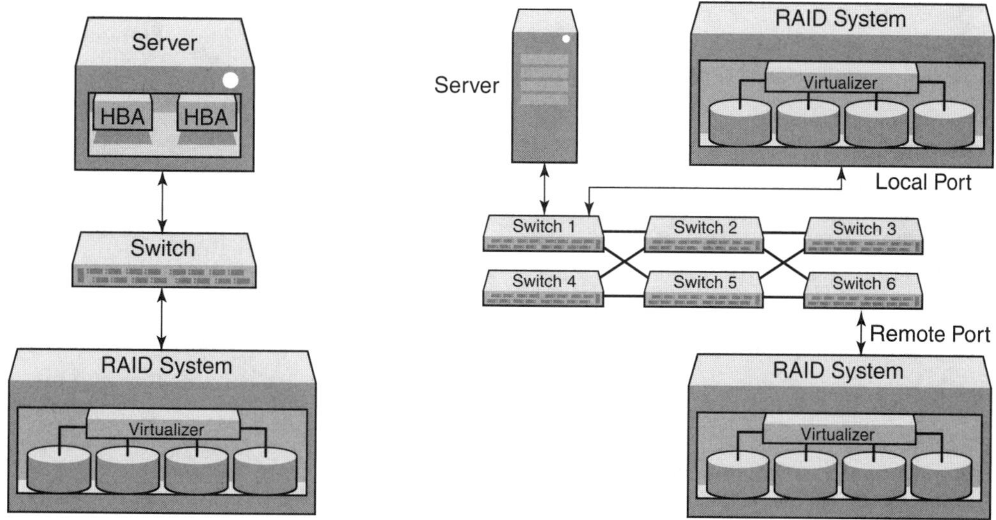

▼ **FIGURE 17–7** *Fabrics with Total and Partial Locality*

HBA's internal bus interface is a single point of failure. On servers with multiple internal buses, each HBA should be installed on a separate bus.

STORAGE NETWORK CONFIGURATION CONSIDERATIONS

Device Placement and Locality

Placement of devices that must intercommunicate is an important factor in network storage performance. **Locality** is a measure of the number of intercommunicating devices attached to the same switch in a fabric. A single-switch fabric has 100% locality, as the diagram on the left in Figure 17–7 illustrates.

Storage networks with high locality perform best. Two devices connected to the same switch pass frames directly to each other. When the devices are connected to different switches, frames are relayed over one or more ISLs. On a busy fabric, low locality may cause delays as frames are queued for transmission over an ISL.

The diagram on the right in Figure 17–7 illustrates a partial mesh fabric in which a server communicates with two storage devices. The server accesses the storage device connected to Switch 1 directly. To reach the storage device connected to Switch 6, data must pass through three switches (for example, Switches 1, 2, and 6). If a volume manager mirrored these two devices, application write performance would be bounded by the latency of communicating with the remote one. Locality of devices that intercommunicate frequently is important for I/O-intensive applications such as backup and databases.

Zoning and LUN Masking

In addition to its discovery and visualization capabilities, VERITAS™ Storage Manager supports active zone management from one central console for all popular storage network switches. Through its VERITAS Enabled™ program, VERITAS partnered with major switch vendors to exchange API information that has enabled the company to implement management functions from within Storage Manager.

The result is zone management from a SANPoint Control console that looks identical, no matter whether Brocade, Inrange, McData, or Qlogic switches are in use.

Similarly, VERITAS has partnered with storage device vendors to exchange LUN masking and binding API information. Again, this enables the storage administrator to monitor and control most RAID systems from the Storage Manager console, reducing vendor-specific skill requirements and minimizing the errors that can occur when unfamiliar management operations are performed under stress.

Zoning and Security

In a **flat Fibre Channel storage network,** all servers can access all storage devices. The ability of storage networks to interconnect many (possibly unrelated) servers and storage devices creates a need for security in the I/O path. Fibre Channel storage networks provide a basic level of access security by organizing devices into **zones** that are isolated from each other.

With **host-based zoning,** servers limit application access to specific storage devices. Cooperating switches create **fabric-based zones** to limit intercommunication to specific sets of devices or switch ports. RAID systems use *LUN masking* to divide LUNs into zones that limit LUN access to specific servers.

Figure 17–8 shows two disjoint zones implemented by two cooperating switches. Zones A and B each contain a server and a storage device. HBAs in each server and port adapters in each storage device connect to both switches for failure tolerance. The switches ports are designated as belonging to Zone A (indicated by triangles) or to Zone B (indicated by circles).

Administrators zone Fibre Channel networks to isolate incompatible devices from each other, and to isolate servers running operating systems that cannot coexist.

Fibre Channel and Distance

Fibre Channel uses *buffer credits* to control data flow. A transmitter can only send data when buffer credits are available. When buffer credits are exhausted, no data may be sent until more are extended. With enough

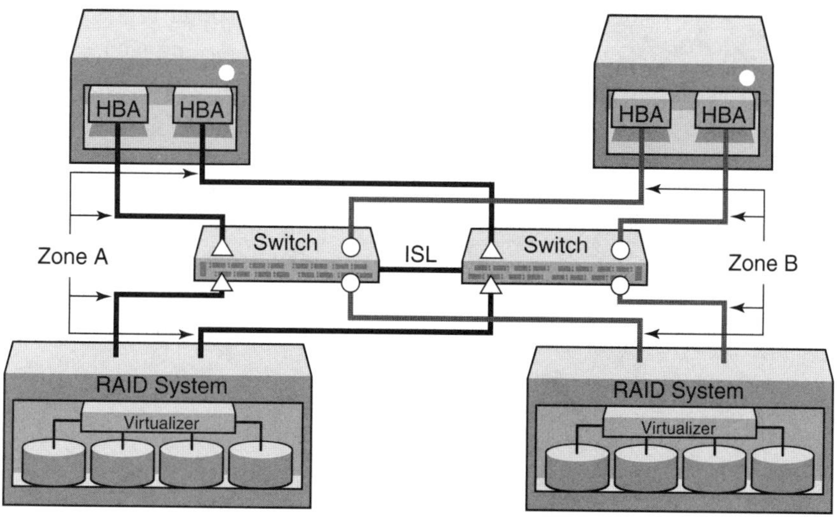

▼ **FIGURE 17–8** *Fibre Channel Port-Based Zoning*

buffer credits, a long-distance connection can be kept busy. Increasing the buffer size in a device and extending its buffer credit limit reduces latency over long distances.

Fibre Channel standards specify a maximum interconnect length of 10 kilometers, enabling the creation of campus-wide storage networks where fiber optic connections are available. Although this is a significant improvement over direct-attached storage, longer distances are required for metropolitan and wide area interconnection.

Several technologies are available for extending Fibre Channel interconnect distance. Connections of up to 80 kilometers can be created using long-wave GBICs and extended buffer credits. With **dense wave division multiplexing** (DWDM), connections can extend to over 100 kilometers. Fibre Channel frames can also be tunneled through TCP/IP networks using *Fibre Channel over IP* (FCIP) protocol. Chapter 18 discusses long-distance storage networks.

CHAPTER SUMMARY

- Storage networks represent an advance over direct connection of storage to servers in that they enable storage to be managed as a data center resource.

APIs and Storage Standards

Today, each storage network vendor implements unique APIs for active management functions such as zoning and LUN masking. In a heterogeneous storage network, these must be integrated and intensively tested one by one—a time- and resource-consuming process for vendors that delays product introductions.

To improve this situation, the Storage Networking Industry Association (SNIA) has undertaken a Storage Management Initiative (SMI) to create and promulgate open standard protocols for managing storage in a network. Based on already-existing CIM/WBEM standards, the SMI standard, code-named Bluefin, specifies mechanisms for storage object discovery and management. VERITAS is a founder of this initiative and, in fact, chairs the SNIA oversight committee; the company is fully committed to implementing compliant interfaces in its storage management solutions as the standard solidifies.

- Fibre Channel is the dominant storage networking technology today. Of the three available Fibre Channel topologies, switched fabrics are the most useful.
- Fibre Channel switches can be interconnected in multiple topologies with different complexity, efficiency, resiliency, and performance properties.
- For maximum performance, storage architects should strive to maximize locality when designing storage networks.
- The primary tool for Fibre Channel storage network security is zoning, implemented in cooperating switches, storage devices, or even by software in servers. Zones are disjoint sets of network addresses that represent devices allowed to intercommunicate.
- Emerging storage network interconnects include InfiniBand, FCIP, iFCP, and iSCSI. Appendix E discusses all of these technology developments.

CHAPTER 18

Information is the oxygen of the modern age. It seeps through the walls topped by barbed wire; it wafts across the electrified borders.

—RONALD REAGAN

Moving Virtual Data over Long Distances

In this chapter . . .

- Convergence of enterprise and storage networking
- Wide area storage network technologies
- Examples of converged networks

With the increasing importance of replicating data over long distances, enterprises' wide area networks are becoming an important part of the storage virtualization picture. Several technology options for replicating data over distance are readily available. More often than not, the question comes down to the cost of currency—how much an enterprise is willing to pay to keep its recovery site data replicas as close to the state of its main information services as possible. This chapter discusses options for moving replicated data over long distances at low latency.

NETWORK CONVERGENCE

Conventional wisdom holds that messaging networks should be optimized for many short-lived connections and short messages, while stor-

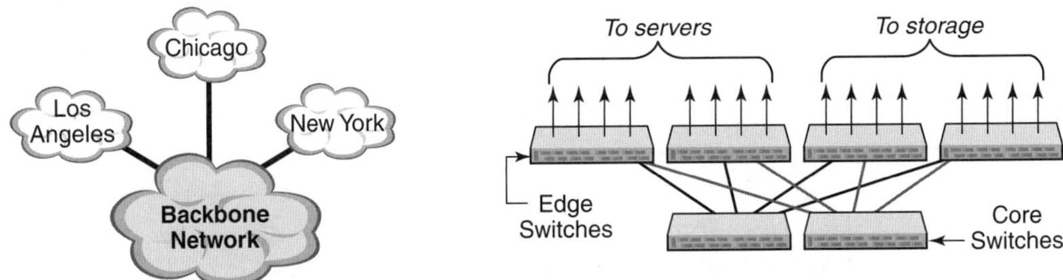

▼ **FIGURE 18–1** *Multicity Wide Area Network*

age networks should be optimized for relatively few long-lived connections and lengthy streams of data. With client-server backup and an increasing emphasis on long-distance mirroring and even longer distance replication, however, this disparity is no longer so clear.

As larger storage networks are deployed, storage and messaging networks are beginning to resemble each other topologically as well. Figure 18–1 represents an enterprise messaging network with a backbone interconnecting several regional segments (left), and a core-edge storage network topology (Chapter 17) in which the primary role of core switches is to interconnect the edge switches that attach devices to the network. The topologies of these networks (the components and their interrelationships without regard to size and performance) are very similar.

As enterprise network bandwidth increases and latency drops, transferring data between storage devices and widely separated servers becomes more practical. With adaptations of Fibre Channel technology, mirroring over distances of tens of kilometers is possible. Asynchronous replication makes it possible to support even very active file systems and databases over longer distances or more complex topologies with larger latencies. Carrying storage traffic over enterprise networks increases enterprise-wide storage management options in several ways:

- Storage and server consolidation
- Long-distance data distribution, backup, archiving, and vaulting
- Long-distance mirroring and real-time data replication
- **Stretch clusters** of widely separated servers

Figure 18–2 depicts an enterprise network consisting of LANs and SANs interconnected by a backbone. The figure shows how a unified enterprise network for storage and messaging makes all of these options possible. This diagram might represent a metropolitan network using

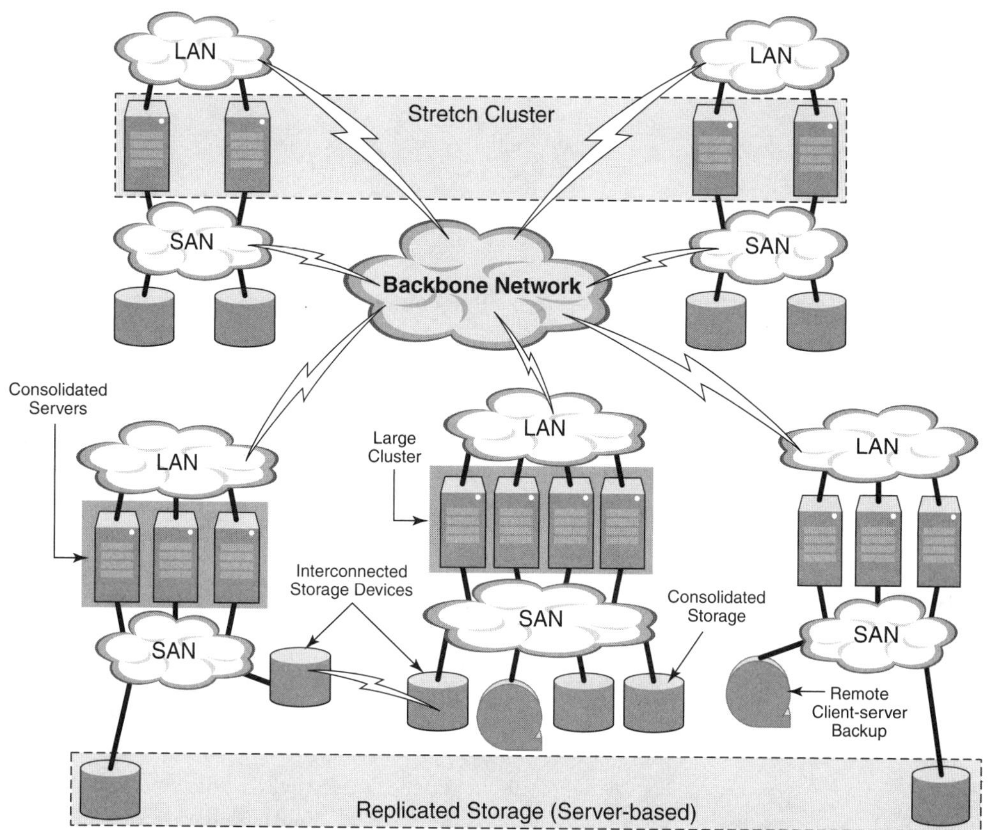

▼ **FIGURE 18–2** *Integrated Wide Area Messaging and Storage Networks*

Fibre Channel, Gigabit Ethernet, and DWDM, or a global network with Ethernet and Fibre Channel interconnected by TCP/IP-based services.

Enterprise Network Technologies

Wide area enterprise networks use a variety of technologies, including Gigabit Ethernet, Fibre Channel, ATM, and TCP/IP infrastructures. Both electrical and optical transmission media are used, with most new installations trending toward optical. Where dedicated optical connections, commonly called **dark fiber,** are available, **dense wave division multiplexing** (DWDM) can split a physical single fiber into many independent channels over which streams of data encapsulated by different protocols can flow. A DWDM path can support Fibre Channel, Ethernet, and other interconnects (e.g., FICON mainframe fiber interconnect) over tens of kilometers at full throughput.

WIDE AREA COMMUNICATIONS

Many factors, including routing, contending traffic, and upper-layer protocols, affect network performance. Today, storage access protocols are based on the assumption that data will nearly always arrive at its destination on the first transmission. Errors are extremely rare, so error recovery performance is secondary. Messaging protocols, on the other hand, assume that physical layers are unreliable, and usually have efficient built-in recovery.

Fiber Interconnects

There are two basic types of fiber optic cables.

- **Multi-mode fiber (MMF),** also called **short-wave** or *short-distance* **fiber**
- **Single mode fiber (SMF),** also called **long-wave** or *long-distance* **fiber**

Lower cost MMF cable is generally used within data centers or across small campuses. Maximum interconnect length depends on the upper-level protocol, the GBICs used,[1] and the data transmission speed. With MMF, low-speed protocols like FDDI can run over distances of up to 2 kilometers, but higher-speed ones like Fibre Channel and Gigabit Ethernet are limited to shorter distances (500 meters).

SMF uses laser signal generation, and has been used successfully over distances of 100 kilometers. Fibre Channel standards specify that with SMF, 10-kilometer connections are supported. Ultra-long-wave GBICs, high-quality cable, and large buffers[2] at the end points have all been used to extend this distance with acceptable performance. DWDM (discussed below) can extend storage network connections to over 100 kilometers at acceptable performance and error rates.

1. Gigabit Interface Converter—a module that converts between electrical signals produced by a data source and optical signals transmitted over a fiber and the reverse.
2. Fibre Channel protocols allow communicating devices to signal that they have buffer capacity available through a system of *buffer credits* used to enable or throttle message traffic.

Almost all new high-performance network installations use fiber optic connections for wide area voice and data communication. Compared to electrical media, fiber offers greater bandwidth, resiliency, noise immunity, and scalability, but stations connected to a fiber optic interconnect must be physically and protocol compatible. Since each protocol requires exclusive use of a connection, protocols cannot co-exist. Multiple protocols require investment in multiple optical connections. This can be prohibitively expensive for most enterprises. Dense wave division multiplexing (DWDM) technology fully exploits the bandwidth potential of a fiber optic connection, and makes multiple long-distance networks economically feasible.

DENSE WAVE DIVISION MULTIPLEXING

Fiber optic interconnects provided by a telecommunication carrier may be *lit* (provisioned by the carrier with a network protocol such as SONET or ATM) or *dark* (with no preconfigured network protocol).

Dense wave division multiplexing technology subdivides the bandwidth of a dark fiber into several independent *channels.* Each DWDM channel runs a protocol, such as Fibre Channel, ATM, or TCP/IP, independently of protocols running on other channels. For the (admittedly high) price of a single dark fiber, multiple messaging and storage networks can be extended over distances of up to 100 kilometers.

How DWDM Works

Optical networks send data by pulsing light sources on and off at precisely timed intervals. Data is encoded in the timing of pulses. DWDM multiplexes several modulated light pulse streams of different colors on a single dark fiber. Figure 18–3 illustrates the receiver of a **DWDM multiplexer,** which sends an incoming light signal through an optical splitter, dividing color bands into separate channels.

In Figure 18–3, each color band represents a channel, functionally equivalent to a dedicated physical connection. Traffic on one channel does not affect others. More of the dark fiber's bandwidth can be utilized by adding converters to a DWDM multiplexer. DWDM multiplexers typically accommodate between 16 and 64 channels, and typically support converters for FDDI, Gigabit Ethernet, ATM, Fibre Channel, FICON, and ESCON. Figure 18–4 illustrates DWDM multiplexing.

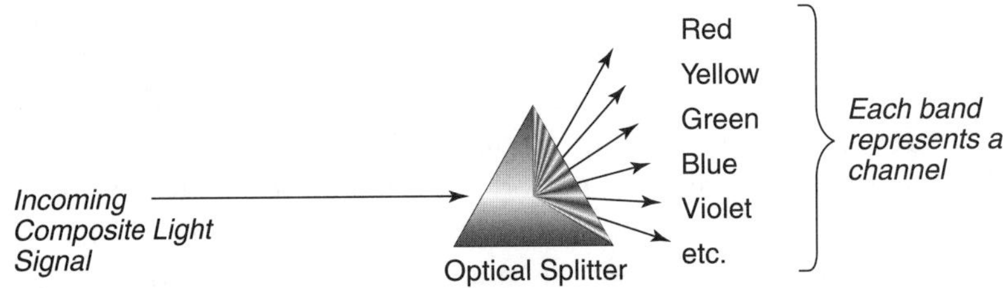

▼ **FIGURE 18–3** *Splitting Light into DWDM Channels*

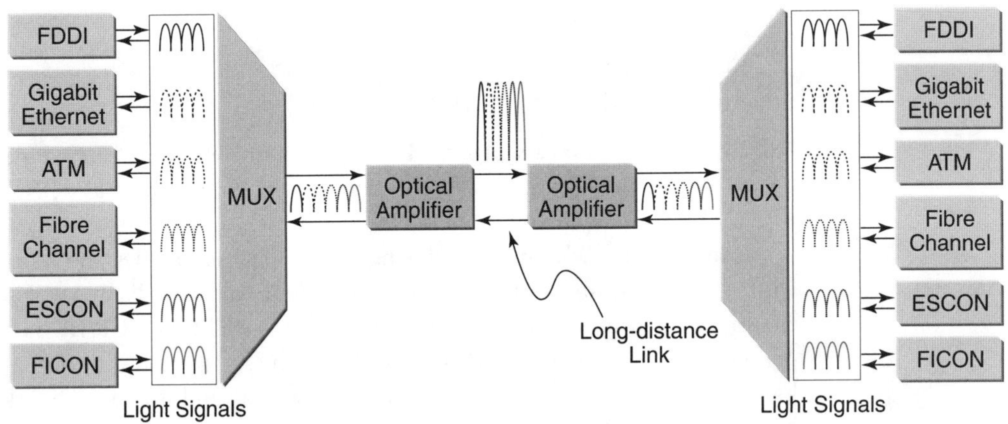

▼ **FIGURE 18–4** *DWDM Multiplexing*

Without DWDM, each protocol shown in Figure 18–4 would require its own fiber. With DWDM, a single fiber carries each protocol on a separate channel. DWDM requires dark fiber, so that the multiplexers can control the cable. DWDM can be configured in point-to-point, ring, and multidrop (open ring) topologies. Single-channel bandwidth typically ranges from 2.5 to 10 gigabits per second.

Figure 18–5 shows a DWDM physical network connecting Fibre Channel and Gigabit Ethernet devices to companion devices at other sites.

Dark Fiber and Failure Tolerance

The cost of dark fiber varies with location, type of service, distance, and proximity to other potential users (because carriers prefer to install fiber

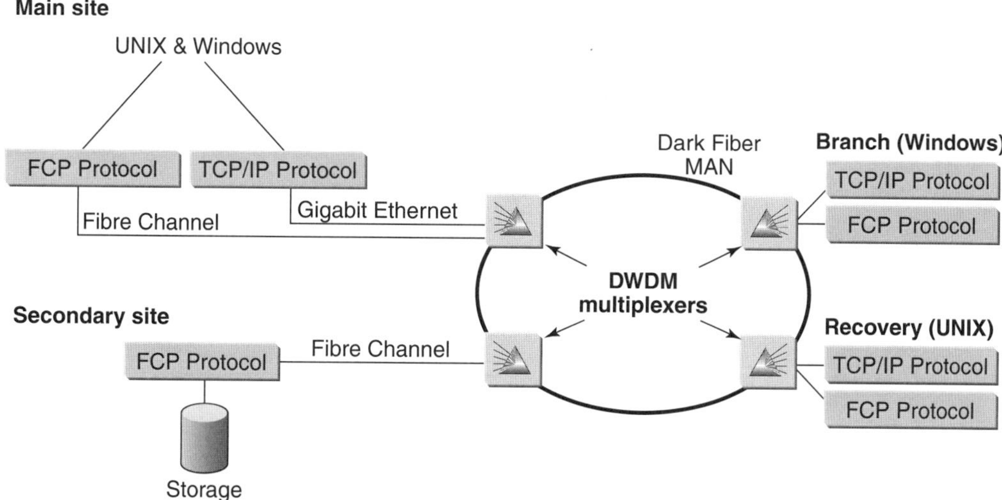

▼ **FIGURE 18–5** *Metropolitan Area DWDM Network*

where there are more potential customers). Although dark fiber cost is high, DWDM allows the user to amortize it over several networks. Moreover, DWDM users can self-provision bandwidth as required with no wait for carrier installation, up to the maximum number of channels supported by a DWDM multiplexer.

Running all enterprise communications over a single fiber would introduce a significant single point of failure. Redundant backbone networks should be configured for critical information services. Many network outages can be traced to failures of nonredundant components. Redundant connections should, in fact, be redundant, and not converge anywhere on their paths. This is particularly difficult (and important) to verify with carrier-provided connections. If, for example, a carrier trunks two external interconnects into a shared fiber, that fiber is a single element whose failure will cause a complete loss of network connectivity, despite the apparent redundancy.

With redundant wide area networks, the user, rather than the carrier, is typically responsible for connection failover. Some carriers provide *managed service packages* with managed DWDM redundant equipment and automatic failover included.

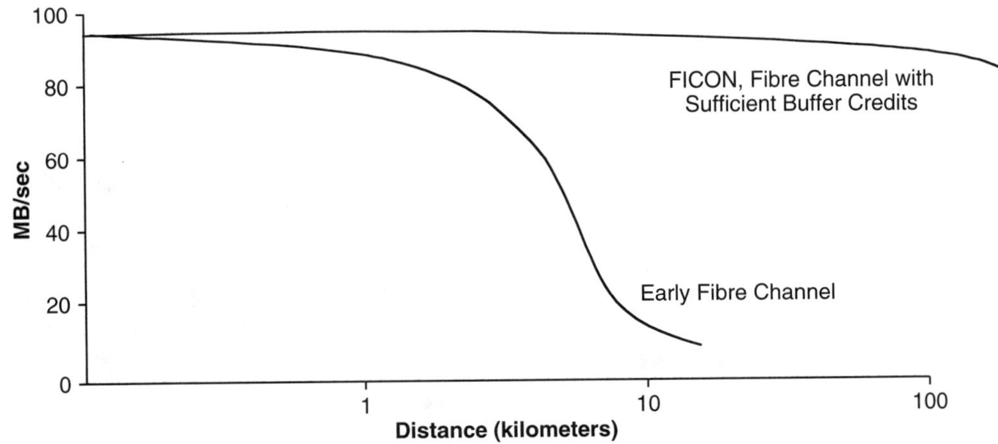

▼ **FIGURE 18–6** *Droop in Data Transfer Speed with Increasing Distance*

WIDE AREA STORAGE NETWORKS

For enterprise resiliency and other business purposes, it is useful—even critical—to extend storage networks across long distances. When data is sent across longer distances, propagation time increases, as do message latency and error rate. The decrease in effective data transfer rate with increasing distance is called **droop.** Droop is more problematic for storage access than for messaging because storage access protocols assume greater signal integrity. Figure 18–6 illustrates droop in older and newer long-distance Fibre Channel storage networks.

As Figure 18–6 suggests, Fibre Channel exhibits droop when end devices have insufficient frame buffering to keep a long interconnect full. Early Fibre Channel devices with few buffers drooped significantly at about 5 kilometers, and severely at 10 kilometers. Newer devices with more buffers enable communications over tens of kilometers with little or no droop. Adequate buffering allows successive frames to be sent over a long connection without waiting for responses.

Extending Storage Networks with FCIP

TCP/IP protocols assume that physical interconnects are unreliable, and that packets may be dropped in transit. This assumption has helped keep messaging network cost low by using software to overcome unreliable low-cost connections. Low cost makes TCP/IP an attractive option for storage networks. One mechanism for using TCP/IP in storage network applications is to *tunnel* storage traffic through a TCP/IP network using the Fibre Channel over IP (FCIP) protocol. FCIP is implemented by *FCIP bridges,* and sends individual Fibre Channel frames between two switches.

With an FCIP bridge, two Fibre Channel networks distant from each other can be merged into one, with a single name space, a single set of zoning rules, and so forth. In principle, server-based mirrored virtual devices with mirrors at two widely separated locations could be created. Caution must be exercised in configuring such devices, however, because the round-trip latency through a long-distance TCP/IP network is both greater and more variable than the latency through a pure Fibre Channel network. Moreover, there is processing overhead within the bridge when Fibre Channel frames are encapsulated for transmission. With I/O request latency to mirrored virtual devices determined by the write time of the most distant mirror, the performance degradation may be unacceptable. Asynchronous replication (Chapter 12) is usually more suitable for maintaining identical data images at widely separated locations interconnected by a TCP/IP network.

Though attractive from a cost and topology standpoint, TCP/IP requires too much protocol processing in software for storage-intensive applications. To overcome this, **TCP offload engines** (TOEs) are being developed. TOEs will use dedicated external processors to process TCP/IP protocol. In addition to enabling storage access over TCP/IP networks, TOEs are likely to improve messaging network performance.

Security

Security considerations inevitably arise when remote users connect to enterprise information services via the (inherently insecure) Internet. Virtual Private Networks (VPNs), which create encrypted "tunnels" through the Internet, are a useful technique for improving the security of long-distance networks, albeit at a cost in latency and processing overhead. Network security should encompass both an enterprise's own network proper and external access to information services. Securing remote sites requires not only mechanisms like VPNs, well-administered virus detection, and systematic backup, but also organizational policies that restrict information access appropriately.

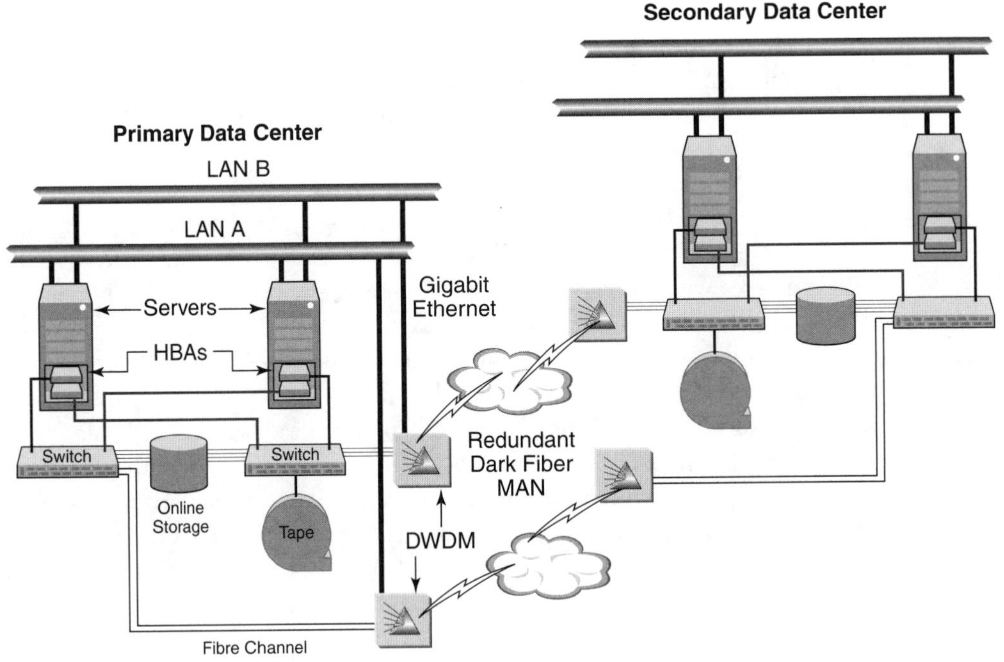

▼ **FIGURE 18–7** *Integrated Metropolitan Network*

INTEGRATED NETWORK EXAMPLES

Figure 18–7 shows a redundant two-site network using DWDM to interconnect Ethernet LANs and Fibre Channel storage networks at the two sites. Redundant storage and messaging networks are configured at both sites.

The extended storage network shown in Figure 18–7 has two unconnected fabrics, each consisting of a switch at each site interconnected to a companion switch at the other by DWDM. DWDM extends the radius of the redundant storage network fabrics, and also interconnects the two sites' messaging networks. Two dark fiber connections are configured for redundancy of the long-distance connection.

In this example, devices can be mirrored between the two sites because the storage devices at both sites are part of the same Fibre Channel network. The integrated storage network also allows either site to use tape resources at the other for backup.

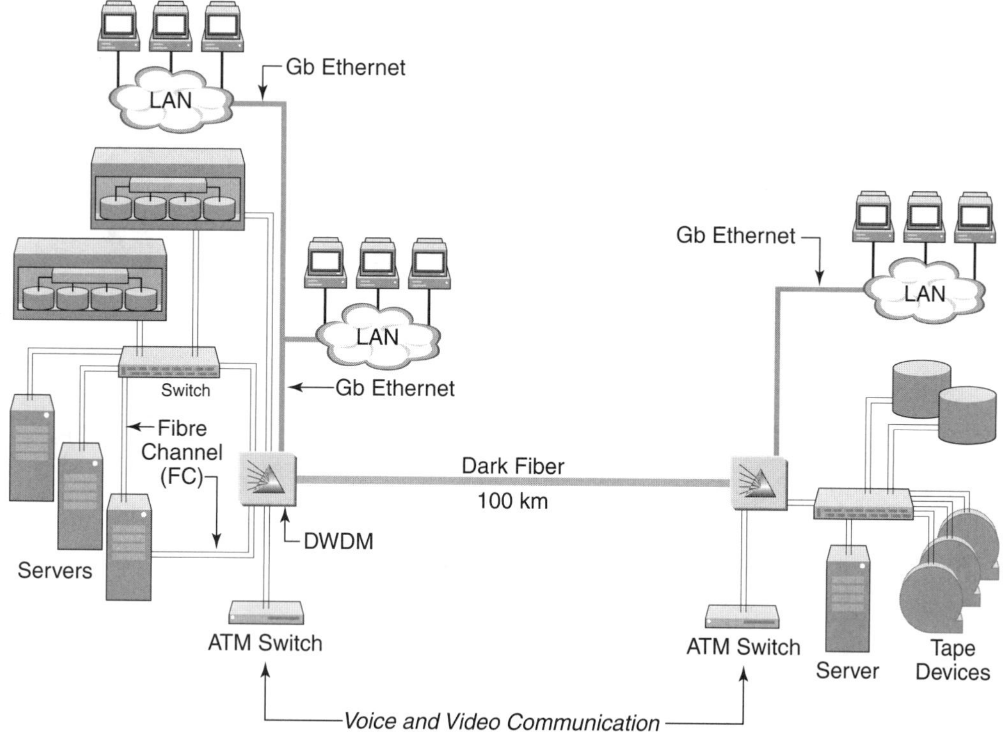

▼ **FIGURE 18–8** *Metropolitan Area Cluster over 100 Kilometers*

The example of Figure 18–8 builds on that of Figure 18–7 by increasing the distance between sites and adding ATM to the interconnects multiplexed by DWDM. A stretch cluster spans two sites 100 kilometers apart using DWDM to carry Fibre Channel, Gigabit Ethernet, and ATM communications between the two. Fibre Channel is used to access disk and tape storage, TCP/IP on Ethernet is used for messaging and cluster heartbeats, and ATM carries voice and video for the enterprise.

Finally, the example in Figure 18–9 shows TCP/IP-based storage access over arbitrary distances using FCIP. Remote servers access both storage local to them and centralized storage at one of the main data centers. FCIP routers connect the sites into a single storage network. In this configuration, care must be taken with propagation delays through the TCP/IP network, to which the tunneled FCIP traffic is subjected.

These three examples show how long-distance Fibre Channel, metropolitan area networking, TCP/IP, and ATM can converge to support messaging, storage access, and other communications for distributed enterprises.

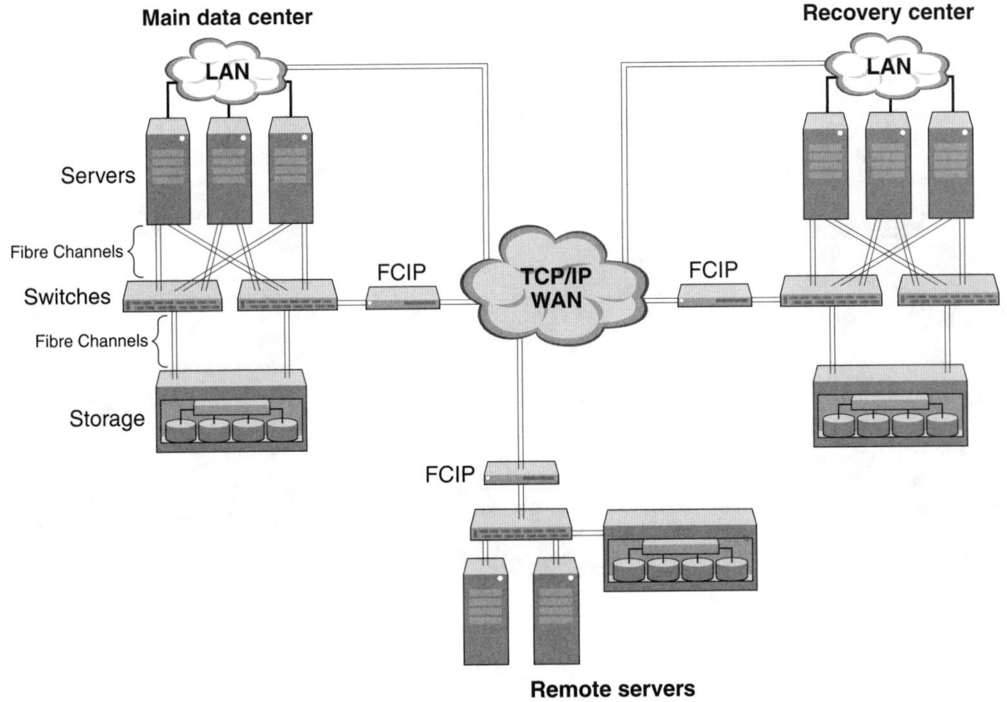

▼ **FIGURE 18–9** *Global Storage Network Using TCP/IP*

CHAPTER SUMMARY

- New network technologies such as FCIP and DWDM are starting to cause a convergence of messaging and storage networks into a single enterprise communication structure. Advanced storage functions previously available within the data center are able to span widely distributed data centers.
- With ultra-long-wave GBICs and sufficient end-point buffering, Fibre Channel connections can extend over as much as 80 kilometers, but I/O latency must be considered when using long-distance connections for storage virtualization techniques such as mirroring.
- The name dark fiber is used for fiber optic transmission cable that is not provisioned with a protocol. Dense wave division multiplexing (DWDM) devices subdivide the bandwidth available in a dark fiber into several channels, each of which can carry a separate protocol at full performance.

- DWDM can integrate local site networks into a single metropolitan area network with a radius of as much as 80 kilometers. Using DWDM, all of an enterprise's high-speed communications can be carried on a single dark fiber.
- For resiliency, DWDM connections should be configured in pairs, with each one carrying one half of an unconnected redundant interconnect. Again, when storage applications run over long distances, latency must be a design consideration.

CHAPTER 19

If it's there and you can see it—it's real. If it's not there and you can see it —it's virtual. If it's there and you can't see it—it's transparent. If it's not there and you can't see it—you erased it!

—SCOTT HAMMER

Another Type of Virtual Storage: HSM

In this chapter . . .

- Why HSM is a valid virtualization concept
- How HSM technology works
- HSM and backup strategies

A hierarchical storage manager (HSM) is software that identifies infrequently accessed files, moves ("migrates") their contents offline, and reclaims their online storage space for other uses. Application attempts to access migrated files cause the HSM to retrieve them transparently, making them appear to have been online all the time. In this sense, HSM virtualizes the files in a file system.

STORAGE HIERARCHIES AND HSM

HSM file virtualization is made feasible by the natural correlation between the cost and performance of storage technologies—more expensive

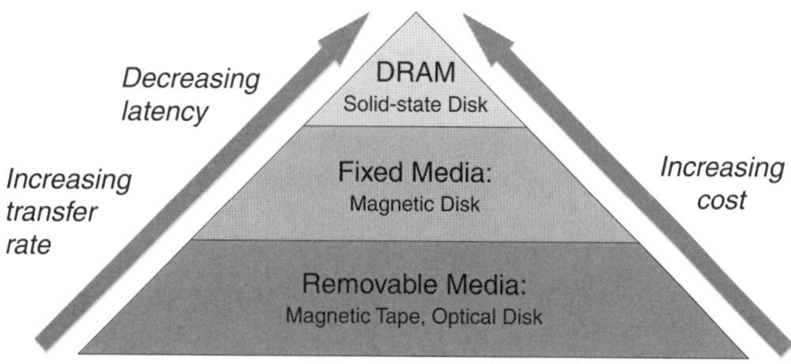

▼ **FIGURE 19–1** *Storage Technology Hierarchy*

storage delivers data at greater bandwidth or with lower access latency, or both. Figure 19–1 suggests this hierarchical relationship.

At the pinnacle of the hierarchy in Figure 19–1 is solid-state memory. Solid-state memory is expensive compared to disk storage, but has very low access latency and supports very high data transfer rates. Moving down the hierarchy, the cost per bit stored decreases, and typical access and data transfer times increase. One consequence of this hierarchy is the observation that data can be stored less expensively if one is willing to tolerate longer access times.

The storage *application* hierarchy illustrated in Figure 19–2 provides the motivation for HSM. Most applications are associated with data that is either:

- ***Active:*** frequently accessed in the daily conduct of business
- ***Recent historical:*** less frequently accessed, but still required online
- ***Archival:*** required to be retained, but rarely accessed

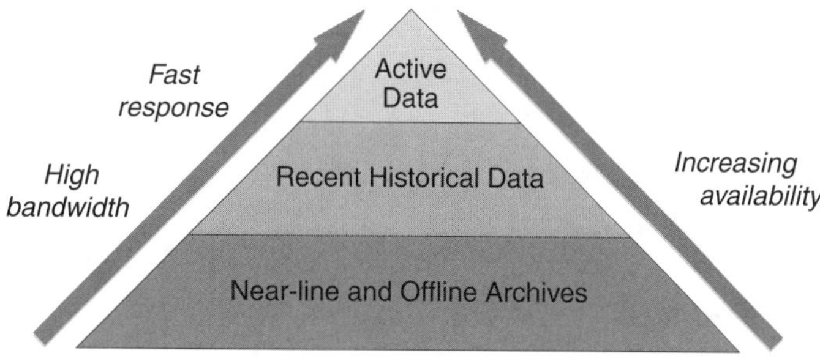

▼ **FIGURE 19–2** *Storage Application Hierarchy*

Intuitively, it seems to make economic sense to store infrequently accessed data on less costly storage, and pay the access time penalty on the rare occasions when it is accessed, provided that management cost does not increase. HSM virtualizes files so that their data can be moved up and down the storage hierarchy transparently to the applications that use it.

HSM automatic migration can also be used to store data according to business needs. Optical disks might be optimal for billing archives because these are typically accessed randomly in response to customer inquiries. Archived sales data might be better suited to tape, because it is typically accessed sequentially for analysis. Thus, HSM can both minimize a data center's average storage cost and segregate data by business criteria for optimal access performance or minimal management cost.

Online Data Usage

Several factors suggest that much of a typical enterprise's online data is "inactive" (seldom accessed). Data stored in online files may be inactive because:

- ***It is inherently inactive.*** Credit transaction records from prior months are not accessed unless someone inquires about past transactions. If no inquiries are made, prior months' data is never referenced, but must be online "just in case."
- ***Legal requirements demand it.*** Some highly regulated enterprises (e.g., nuclear power, medicine) are required to keep data available online for lengthy periods, even though it is only accessed if some legal issue arises.
- ***It is required to recover from failures.*** Most database managers maintain **archive logs** to enable a DBA to recover a database to almost any point in history by replaying logs against a backup image. Archive logs are normally kept online for administrative convenience, but are not accessed during normal operations.

The VERITAS™ Storage Migrator

Today, hierarchical storage management (HSM) is relatively rare in open systems (compared to its usage in mainframe environments). But increasing IT budget pressure and use of storage resource management (SRM) tools are making file access frequency more visible. CIOs are starting to ask whether HSM active storage management can migrate infrequently used data to less expensive storage. VERITAS addresses the demand for more effective UNIX and Windows storage utilization with the VERITAS Storage Migrator.

The VERITAS Storage Migrator enables the definition of flexible policies for determining which data is migrated when and to where. Migrated data remains in its original location until the space it occupies is required for other purposes, thus shortening average retrieval times. VERITAS NetBackup™ is aware of migrated files, and bypasses backing them up, saving backup time and media cost.

- ***Applications are designed to do so.*** Some applications create large numbers of files and access them infrequently (if at all) after creation. Applications might spawn millions of files that are not accessed between successive backups.
- ***It is simply forgotten.*** Users create files and forget about them for any number of reasons—testing, ad hoc reports, and so forth. Forgotten files are particularly challenging for administrators, because there is no systematic way to determine which of them could be safely moved offline.

Benefits of HSM

Whatever the reasons for inactive data, a hierarchical storage manager can move it transparently to offline storage, reclaiming online storage space for more active data and shortening backup times by eliminating unnecessary redundant copying. Shorter backup and restore times are obvious benefits of using HSM to prune inactive data. Properly configured, HSM delivers other benefits during normal operation:

- ***Reduced online storage requirements:*** Rather than requiring online storage for all of its online data, an enterprise can budget online storage for its active data plus a margin for the amount of inactive data likely to be retrieved.
- ***Reduced file system maintenance:*** Active file systems require frequent **defragmentation** to move files closer together and consolidate free space. Defragmentation can have a significant impact on application performance. With HSM fewer files are online, decreasing both the frequency and impact of file system defragmentation.
- ***Reduced offline media cost:*** With HSM, files that have migrated to offline media are not copied during backups. This reduces the amount of data copied during full backups, in turn reducing media cost. Reducing the number of redundant backup copies of inactive files can mean substantial expense (tape media) and capital (libraries) savings.
- ***Reduced management cost:*** Online and offline storage systems incur management cost whenever administrators set up and execute management procedures. If storage requirements grow more slowly, the time between upgrades can be increased, and less expense is incurred to install, configure, and allocate incremental storage. Similarly, less frequent defragmentation means less scheduling, and fewer tapes and libraries means less frequent library maintenance and less media handling.

Thus hierarchical storage management is worthy of consideration for several reasons. Its impact, however, is ultimately determined by how much of a data center's online data is infrequently accessed.

HOW HSM WORKS

File systems record metadata describing individual file properties, including the time that a file was last accessed (called *atime* in UNIX contexts). File systems update *atime* each time they open, read, write, extend, truncate, or otherwise change a file. HSM software uses *atime* to identify files that fit administrator-specified criteria for inactivity. When inactive files are identified, HSM software migrates them by:

- ***Copying*** the files to one or more alternate storage locations (tape, optical disk, or online storage) and cataloging those locations
- ***Reclaiming*** their online storage space, making it available for other purposes
- ***Modifying*** their online metadata to indicate that their contents have been moved

HSM software intercepts any subsequent application requests for migrated files, uses its catalog to locate their contents, and restores them to their original file systems. Restoration is functionally transparent to applications, but typically takes longer (seconds, or even minutes, depending on the technology) than accessing files that are already online (milliseconds).

In addition to minimizing online storage cost by aligning an enterprise's most expensive, highest performing storage with its most active data, HSM also reduces backup time, because it eliminates the need to back up the data for files that have been migrated to offline storage (metadata for such files is backed up so that the files can be identified and restored if necessary). Perhaps more

VERITAS NetBackup Storage Migrator™

It's a fact of life that Microsoft Exchange information stores grow. And yet, most old electronic mail messages are referenced seldom if at all. This suggests that hierarchical storage management could be very useful in Exchange environments.

Exchange information stores consist of private and public folders that store messages and file attachments. To help manage Exchange information stores, VERITAS offers VERITAS NetBackup Storage Migrator™ to monitor the information store and migrate attachments to secondary storage according to administratively defined policy. To Outlook users, migrated attachments are distinguishable from attachments that are still online. This distinction alerts users to expect longer access time, depending on the type of secondary storage used.

The VERITAS NetBackup for Storage Migrator™ is fully Microsoft certified for Exchange 2000 and 5.5 environments.

importantly, HSM reduces file system restore times by deferring restoration of migrated files' data areas until they are actually accessed.

HSM and File Access Performance

When an application *does* request a migrated file, retrieval from offline storage takes longer than direct access. HSM is thus a trade-off between storage cost, backup-restore benefits, and longer response time when seldom-accessed files are requested. Hierarchical storage managers typically have flexible migration policies that allow administrators to set the "rules" based on local requirements. Some support storing both primary and offline copies of files. These reduce backup times (because they need not be backed up), but still perform at disk speeds (because applications access the online copy). Online copies of such files are eligible for deletion when storage capacity is required by a file system.

HSM CAPABILITIES AND IMPLEMENTATIONS

Some HSM software uses companion backup software to store file contents. Other packages maintain their own offline storage pools. In either case, file metadata remains online, making it possible for HSM to be transparent to applications. Since metadata remains online, some management operations can be performed on migrated files. For example, changing a file's access permissions does not require access to the file's data, and can be done without retrieval.[1]

The crucial feature of HSM is that accessing migrated files is **functionally transparent** to applications. No application modifications are required when HSM software is installed. In some cases, modifications may be desirable. For example, it might be useful to run a script to retrieve migrated historical files prior to analysis runs that use them. But such procedures are optimizations rather than functional requirements.

HSM Policies

Hierarchical storage managers can be tuned by adjusting migration parameters or excluding certain files from migration. Administrators can typically adjust:

1. But moving a migrated file to an online directory that is excluded from migration *would* cause the file's contents to be retrieved.

- ***Inactivity time:*** Hierarchical storage managers typically use a separate inactivity threshold for each file system they virtualize. For example, file systems containing database archive logs might be configured to migrate promptly because archive logs are only required for disaster recovery. On the other hand, file systems containing graphical designs might have longer inactivity thresholds, because reuse of the files in them is less predictable.
- ***File size:*** Migrating small files does not reclaim much storage space, but does take time and consume resources. Different data centers and file systems have different needs, so each file system virtualized by HSM should normally have a unique size threshold for migration.
- ***System files, libraries, and executable images:*** These files might not be accessed for long periods, but should nonetheless remain online because when they are required response time is critical. Hierarchical storage managers typically exclude these files from migration by default, but allow an administrator to override the exclusion.
- ***Arbitrary named exclusions:*** Data centers may have online data that should not be migrated for reasons impossible for a hierarchical storage manager to detect. For example, automated recovery scripts that are only accessed when something goes wrong should nonetheless be online. Most HSM software allows administrators to exclude arbitrary lists of files and directories from migration.
- ***Groupings of like files:*** Some hierarchical storage managers enable administrators to co-locate certain files on offline media for convenient retrieval. For example, when a project phase is complete, files in its directories can all be migrated to the same offline storage media. Placing data contiguously on offline storage speeds retrieval of files that are likely to be retrieved together.

By combining HSM policies with file system and directory design, an administrator can create a managed storage environment to meet almost any application data requirements.

HSM Optimizations

Like most of information technology, implementing HSM is a balancing act. Setting migration policies balances the benefits of shorter backup times and reduced online storage cost against increased response time when migrated files are accessed. Some hierarchical storage managers include optimizations that improve the balance.

- ***Staging:*** When a file is migrated to offline storage there is no need to delete the online copy until its storage space is actually required. Some hierarchical storage managers "stage" files—copying them to offline storage, but retaining online copies until file system free space drops below a threshold.[2] When online space occupied by staged files is reclaimed, directory entries are updated to indicate that files have been migrated. The obvious benefit of staging is immediate retrieval when accessed by applications.
- ***File "slicing":*** Some applications and utility programs scan the first few bytes of data in files. For example, graphical user interfaces sometimes look for application signatures to determine which icon should represent a file in a screen display. Such applications would force retrieval of migrated files, even though they make no use of most of their data. To mitigate this impact, some hierarchical storage managers leave small "slices" of migrated files' data online. File slices, whose size is typically administrator specified, also improve perceived responsiveness with more conventional applications. Because a sliced file's first few bytes are actually online, initial response to application access requests is very fast; retrieval delays are seen only when data beyond the slice is accessed.

HSM Integration with Other Storage Management Components

HSM software is closely integrated with both file systems and backup managers. With respect to file systems, a hierarchical storage manager must be able to:

- ***Interpret*** file metadata in order to execute migration policies
- ***Modify*** location metadata for migrated files to indicate that they are not online, and must be retrieved from alternate locations when accessed by applications

HSM and backup software must cooperate to:

- ***Enable*** the hierarchical storage manager to determine the location of migrated objects from backup manager catalogs
- ***Back up*** extended metadata required for HSM

2. Of course, if a staged file is modified, copies on offline storage must be invalidated.

- ***Bypass*** migrated files during full backups
- ***Synchronize*** file system metadata for migrated files with the HSM database during restores

Ideally, a hierarchical storage manager would use the same media manager as backup so that the same offline storage devices and media pools can serve both purposes.

When data is migrated to offline storage and its online storage space reclaimed, offline copies become the *only* copies. Failure of media containing migrated data means that the data is lost. At the same time, one purpose of HSM is elimination of redundant copies of data. To balance these two objectives, hierarchical storage managers typically require that a file be stored on two or more separate offline media before deleting the online copy.

Storage Migrator and NetBackup

The two principal benefits of hierarchical storage migration are reduced online storage consumption and more efficient backups. For maximum efficiency, VERITAS integrates the Storage Migrator closely with the NetBackup product family (which includes VERITAS Backup Exec™) in several important ways.

The VERITAS NetBackup family is migration-aware. Migrated files are not recalled during a backup. Instead, NetBackup makes note of the files' migrated locations within the backup image so that they can be retrieved on demand if a full restore is performed.

Storage Migrator and NetBackup use the same Media Manager, allowing secondary storage devices and media pools to be shared between the two. This reduces backup hardware requirements, and makes it easy for NetBackup and Storage Migrator to access each other's media when required.

Finally, VERITAS™ NetBackup Global Data Manager can manage Storage Migrator operations, providing a universal data protection console for all enterprise needs.

Disaster Recovery with Backup and HSM

HSM affects backup strategies. The most important consideration is that with HSM, backup tapes no longer contain complete data. It is therefore important to carefully track backup copies and copies of corresponding migrated data. One useful strategy is to make two copies of all migrated data, one to remain at the data center, and the other to be taken to a vault or recovery site along with backup tapes. If a data center experiences total loss of data and media, backup copies of file systems virtualized by HSM can be restored, and inactive data retrieved when and if it is accessed.

Impact of HSM on a Data Center

HSM should improve both online storage management and disaster recoverability for most data centers, but benefits can be difficult to quantify prior to implementation. To assist in evaluation, some HSM vendors provide analytical tools that scan file systems and report the potential effect of HSM under different policies and activity assumptions. These tools estimate online storage space savings, file access times, and file sizes. Such tools can help administrators assess potential benefits of HSM, as well as predicting the effect of migration policy adjustments when HSM is in use.

A storage architect can take several steps to maximize the effectiveness of HSM:

- ***File system design:*** Enterprises typically organize file systems by application, database, user group, department, and so forth. When organizing file systems, it is also useful to consider backup, HSM, data replication, and failure tolerance policies. For example, a file system used solely to store database archive logs would logically have its own HSM policy, storage allocation policy, backup policy, and so forth.
- ***Choice of migration parameters:*** HSM's contribution to information service availability is a balance between retrieval overhead and recovery quality. If critical files are offline, application recovery takes longer. If too few files are migrated, file system restores take longer. Similar considerations apply to other migration policies. A storage architect using HSM to speed failure and disaster recovery should design policies that cause the files most critical to information service resumption to be restored first and in the most automated fashion.
- ***Location of HSM target data:*** HSM can simplify disaster recovery if migration targets are chosen carefully. Most hierarchical storage managers manage multiple copies of files. This facility can be used to automatically migrate files to both a local vault and a remote disaster recovery location. Files can be retrieved from the local vault when accessed by applications, while disaster recovery would use the remote copy.

Long-Term Data Storage

Both environmental conditions (e.g., humidity and temperature) and orientation (e.g., lying down or hanging) affect offline media readability. In addition, offline media formats change over time, and hardware to read older media may become unavailable or unserviceable. Vendors specify life expectancies for drives and media, as well as the environmental storage conditions that maximize readability and media life.

Because offline media inevitably age, however, hierarchical storage managers should include means for moving data from older media to newer with minimal manual involvement. Addition of new devices to a storage hierarchy and automated movement of managed data to them should be supported. *Device-to-device* data copying refreshes media and also allows obsolete files to be deleted in the same operation.

CHAPTER SUMMARY

- There is a cost-performance hierarchy of storage, with higher-performing devices having a higher cost per bit stored than lower-performing ones.
- Hierarchical storage management is motivated by the existence of the storage cost-performance hierarchy plus the observation that much of the data that is stored online is seldom accessed. This data can be moved to lower-cost storage, reducing the overall storage cost for a data center.
- Hierarchical storage managers use file system metadata to compare file access activity against administrator-defined policies and copy seldom-accessed files to lower-cost offline media. They modify online metadata to indicate that if a migrated file is accessed, it should be retrieved from its offline location. Migration and retrieval are transparent to applications.
- The primary benefits of HSM are reduced online storage requirements and shorter backup and restore times. HSM policies can be customized for each file system to optimize the benefits.
- Hierarchical storage managers must be closely integrated with file systems and backup managers, because all three must manipulate file metadata to provide correct and consistent views of online storage.
- HSM must be coupled with disaster recovery strategies, in particular, to insure that both backup and migrated data are available at recovery locations.
- Careful configuration of file systems, backup policies, and HSM parameters is required to obtain optimal benefit from hierarchical storage management.
- High-quality HSM software provides for long-term data storage in the form of automating migration of archived and migrated data between old and new storage media and devices with minimal human intervention.

PART 5

THE FUTURE

I have been over into the future, and it works.

—LINCOLN STEFFENS

This part incorporates ideas from a work by Dr. Paul L. Borrill, Ph.D., former Vice President and Chief Technology Officer of VERITAS Software Corporation.

CHAPTER 20

Science may be described as the art of systematic over-simplification.

—KARL POPPER

Challenges for Enterprise Storage

In this chapter . . .

- Complexity: the #1 enterprise storage challenge today
- Types of storage system complexity and their roots
- Present-day techniques for dealing with complexity

Much useful block storage virtualization technology has been developed and delivered to consumers. Today, virtual block storage offers a very usable set of technology capabilities:

- Virtualizing block storage aggregates online storage capacity and performance, increases deployment flexibility, and improves data availability by enabling physical storage failure tolerance.
- Block storage virtualization software may run in a RAID system, in a server or cooperating collection of servers, or in a network storage virtualization appliance or switch. In most enterprise systems, multiple levels of virtual storage can be advantageously combined.
- Advanced functions such as snapshots and online expansion enabled by virtual storage can be used to great advantage by backup, by file systems, and by database applications.
- Storage scaling, availability, performance, flexibility, and security are all enhanced substantially when clients and storage devices are connected to a storage network.
- One capability of virtual block storage that has become extremely important to enterprise resiliency is replication of virtual storage

device contents across long distances over connections of variable reliability and latency.

- Other forms of storage virtualization, such as cluster file systems, integrate with virtual block storage and extend its capabilities toward applications. Hierarchical storage management is another such extension of storage virtualization.

It is clear from its ubiquity in enterprise data centers that storage virtualization conveys significant benefits for enterprise data management. It is nonetheless appropriate to ask whether the job is finished—is virtual block storage as delivered today all it can be? How is virtualization technology likely to evolve in the future? To predict the future of virtual block storage, it is useful to understand the problems that today's incarnations of the technology do not solve.

COMPLEXITY: TODAY'S ENTERPRISE STORAGE CHALLENGE

Storage networks have enabled the construction of data center storage systems of unprecedented complexity. Enterprises routinely interconnect hundreds of servers and storage devices. Although the benefits of network storage—consolidation, utilization, performance, and resiliency—are undeniable, these same benefits create today's greatest challenge for the storage industry: managing the complexity they engender.

Sources of Storage System Complexity

Figure 20–1 represents the three main contributors to enterprise storage system complexity. The three lines in Figure 20–1 represent:

- ***Number of elements:*** The number of elements (e.g., storage devices, network components, clients, and data objects) in a storage system affects its complexity primarily by increasing the impact of repetitive tasks. It's harder to schedule firmware upgrades for a thousand disks than for ten; it's harder to back up a dozen file systems than one, and so forth.
- ***Number of connections:*** Connections increase complexity because they make it possible for actions taken on one part of a system to affect other parts in unexpected ways. For example, a Web response application that generates thousands of tiny network packets may bog

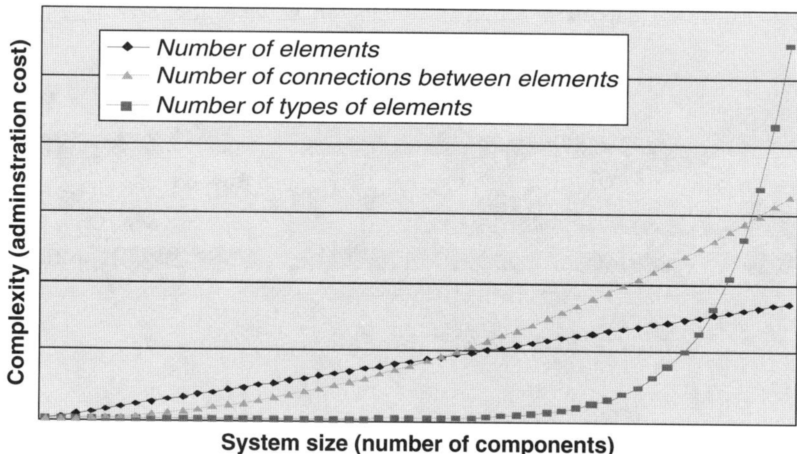

▼ **FIGURE 20–1** *Contributors to Storage System Complexity*

down a client-server backup because it adds just enough latency to the network backup stream to cause tapes to enter repositioning cycles. Another example: failure of a parallel SCSI disk drive may block the bus, causing other drives belonging to other arrays serving other applications on other servers to "fail."

- ***Number of types of elements:*** As storage interconnects have evolved from proprietary to standards based over the last two decades, the storage industry has evolved to be one of independent suppliers. Today, the average enterprise storage system contains components delivered by different vendors, who cooperate at different levels. Moreover, technology evolves so rapidly that installed storage systems are continually changing, with new components added and old ones removed, primarily for business reasons. The result is a huge industry-wide interoperability matrix, with component vendors in a constant race to keep hardware, firmware, and software compatible with an ever-increasing list of complementary products as they incorporate new features and functions.

Each of these factors increases storage system complexity in a different way as discussed in the paragraphs that follow. Whatever the source of the complexity, however, it is the user who bears the cost, largely in the form of administration.

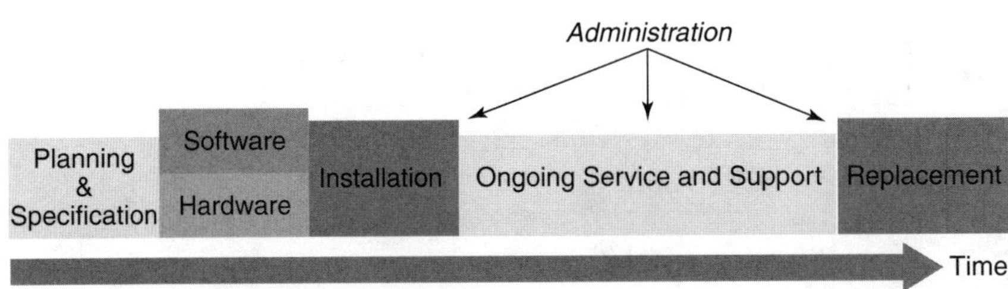

▼ **FIGURE 20–2** *Total Cost of Storage Ownership*

The Cost of Complexity: Administration

As storage system size and complexity increase, more administrators and administrators with higher skill levels are required to install, configure, debug, tune, back up, upgrade, and maintain storage and data. Figure 20–2 represents the components of lifetime storage cost. In each phase of a storage system's life, greater complexity means greater cost, whether it is more components to specify, purchase, and install, or more interactions to troubleshoot and upgrade, or more intricate replacement strategies.

Storage system complexity becomes an even larger factor during disaster recovery, when administrators are subjected to extraordinary stress. Too much information results in cognitive overload and suboptimal performance. Storage system administrative information overload comes from poor encapsulation, nonintuitive abstractions, and, most of all, exposed complexity. Design and process simplicity and human-computer interaction can increase chances for a quick return to normal operation without stress-induced errors.

Storage system component developers tend to assume that all system administrators are highly skilled. In fact, administrators often lack the training, skills, and motivation to comprehend and actively manage complex systems. To be sure, expert system administrators do exist, but storage system architectures and tools must be designed for the great majority, not the exceptional few.

Storage system complexity (and the administrative cost it implies) may ultimately become the limiting factor on the size, performance, and utility of enterprise information services. The sections that follow discuss how storage system size, interconnection, and diversity affect complexity, and therefore cost, in different ways.

System Size

The number of elements in a distributed storage system affects management complexity primarily by changing the magnitude of routine management tasks. Scheduling and executing device replacement, firmware and software upgrades, backups, and so forth become increasingly complex as the numbers of devices, upgrades, and so forth increase. Because system size increases management complexity primarily through repetition of operations, Figure 20–1 models it as a linear function of size (number of components).

Interconnection

The number of connections between elements in a storage system affects management complexity in a slightly different way. In small systems, additional connections between elements actually simplify management, as, for example, dual access paths to storage devices, or shareable storage in a cluster. For larger systems, however, particularly those whose storage is connected to a network, interconnections play a role in management that is both larger and harder to automate. Inadvertently adding a storage device to the wrong network zone can result in puzzling behavior: Why don't servers recognize the device and configure it? Why have Web response times doubled since accounts receivable's database was migrated to a faster RAID system? Interconnection issues such as these increase management complexity and cost in two ways:

- More applications and subsystems can be affected by systems changes. A change to a self-contained system affects only the behavior of that system. A change to a large distributed system may affect components, subsystems, and applications that appear on the surface to be completely unrelated to it.
- Side effects of change are more difficult to diagnose and remedy. In a small, self-contained system, adverse side effects are easily discerned and traced to root causes. In a large distributed storage system, it may be difficult to relate problematic behavior to a cause, or to predict the effect a proposed change might have on overall system behavior.

In small systems, more interconnections have little impact, and may actually simplify administration, for example by providing more availability options. For larger systems, however, interconnections cause complexity to grow faster than the number of components, because each new component adds at least one and probably more connections to other components.

Diversity

The third contributor to storage system management complexity is *diversity*—the number of different *types* of components a system contains. Components may be diverse because they come from different vendors, because they are different models from the same vendor, or because they are acquired at different times. Annual product changes are common in the storage industry, whereas most users still plan for storage component lifetimes in the three- to five-year range.

Diversity problems are similar to interconnection problems; seemingly simple and straightforward changes cause bizarre and inexplicable behavior in apparently unrelated parts of a system. Problems stem from difficult-to-predict factors like incompatible firmware revisions for the same model adapter or RAID system. More experienced administrators carefully verify interoperability before making storage network changes of any kind, but like interconnection complexity, dealing proactively with diversity takes time and effort, requires highly skilled administrators, and is not particularly amenable to automation (at least with today's technology).

As with interconnections, component diversity is not much of a problem for small systems. Small systems are typically acquired from one vendor, and even though they may contain components from multiple sources, they are typically qualified as built. Even large systems are often delivered by groups of vendors who qualify and support each others' components. Typically, it is only as a storage system grows very large or has been in place for some time that component diversity becomes a factor.

After a year or two of operation, distributed storage systems often contain disk drives, RAID systems, network switches and other components of different models acquired at different times, possibly from different vendors. Storage purchases are fundamentally motivated by capacity needs, with I/O performance and availability as secondary factors. Keeping diverse components working reliably together inevitably becomes an administrative responsibility. "Working reliably together" is a function of both the components and the interconnections between them, and therefore becomes an even larger contributor to complexity cost than interconnection by itself, as Figure 20–1 suggests.

The cost of diversity is the main reason that vendors qualify components with their systems, and why integrators qualify entire configurations that work together. It is why conservative users tend to prefer homogeneous systems, or systems supported by a single vendor, to heterogeneous ones configured from "best of breed" components with the user ultimately responsible for support.

DEALING WITH STORAGE SYSTEM COMPLEXITY

The success of storage networks has made storage system complexity a fact of data center life. The benefits of storage networks outweigh the cost of complexity to the extent that vendors have developed design techniques to deal with it and users have developed administrative procedures to exploit these techniques. Storage system design approaches to managing complexity include:

- ***Component encapsulation:*** Aggregating components and encapsulating them into larger elements reduces the number of "things" that must be managed. For example, RAID systems and other virtualizers aggregate disk drives into arrays presented as virtual devices, which become the managed elements. File systems and directories encapsulate large numbers of files. Perhaps the best example of encapsulation is the network-attached storage (NAS) "appliance" that aggregates disk drives, servers, file systems, network connections, and protocol stacks into a single managed element—the file server.
- ***Connectivity aggregation:*** In many cases, connectivity aggregation is a result of encapsulation. RAID systems and in-band network appliances reduce interelement connectivity. A hundred or more disk drives in a RAID system may be presented on a few network connections, with no connection between drives and other parts of the system. Another important aggregation of connectivity is the trend to more ports in storage network switches. More ports in a single switch means fewer switches and inter-switch links (ISLs) to install and manage, reducing both component and connectivity complexity. The connectivity of a storage system can be reduced significantly by these and other forms of connectivity aggregation.
- ***Management coverage:*** Component vendors provide tools with which to manage their components. Although these tools are a business necessity for the vendor, they can be almost more of a problem than a solution to users, who are forced to develop skills to manage every component in their storage networks. Moreover, users must develop further (largely undocumented) skills to make vendors' management tools work effectively together (diversity complexity). To simplify the user task, component vendors are broadening the scope of their storage management tools to manage components supplied by other vendors as well as their own.

User responses to the challenge of storage system complexity are partly adoption of the tools and techniques provided by component vendors and partly good operational practices. User techniques for managing storage network complexity include:

- ***Consolidation:*** Co-locating very large amounts of storage with skilled administrators increases management efficiency. Not only are there economies of scale (for example, packaging, environmental control, and pooling), but administrators' proficiency inevitably increases as they perform storage administrative tasks more frequently and become more familiar with the systems they manage.
- ***Tool standardization:*** Even as vendors develop more heterogeneous management tools, users are pressuring them to standardize even further and manage more storage network components more comprehensively from a single console. Storage industry efforts to standardize component management protocols are aiding in attempts to universalize storage management, so that, for example, RAID system and volume manager virtual devices can be managed identically.
- ***Availability management:*** If a storage system fails, its client information services are disrupted. Virtual storage systems configured to tolerate and recover from most failures without disrupting client operations are clearly preferable. Failure-tolerant virtual storage, along with robust administrative procedures, reduces the consequences of component failures and therefore the complexity of management. Administrative procedures like prompt replacement of failed components and proactive management of software patches and upgrades can improve system availability significantly.
- ***Homogenization:*** Complete computer system homogeneity is impractical in large and distributed enterprises. Best-in-class hardware, software, and service strategies differ from application to application. Nevertheless, conservative users often standardize on one or two vendors for each type of component to reduce diversity complexity. Where homogeneous system components are impractical, multiplatform storage management software can reduce complexity by reducing dependencies on particular hardware components.
- ***Training:*** As more enterprises recognize storage management as a distinct administrative specialty on a par with system and network management, more storage administrators are being formally trained and even certified in their profession. Storage management has evolved from an afterthought for system administrators to a learned-by-experience specialty, to a recognized profession for which formal training is available.

Though simplifying administration (and therefore helping to contain administrative cost), these techniques (with the possible exception of encapsulation) do not fundamentally alter the root causes of storage system complexity: number of components, number of interconnections, and degree of diversity. With current storage system architectures, complexity can easily increase faster than system size, as Figure 20–1 suggests. For the most part, the abovementioned techniques attempt to cope with complexity as it exists, rather than reduce it by altering its root causes.

Techniques that address the roots of complexity can dramatically simplify storage system deployment and increase resiliency by reducing complexity, particularly when systems are disrupted by major failures or disasters.

STORAGE VIRTUALIZATION AND COMPLEXITY

Block storage virtualization is the one technique in wide use today that actually deals with the root causes of complexity. From a complexity point of view, block storage virtualizers essentially encapsulate complexity, reducing the number of system components that must be managed.

Encapsulation can be viewed as creating abstractions at a system's natural boundaries. The abstraction presented at each boundary allows administrators to focus on essential behavior rather than details of layers below or requirements of layers above. Thus, for example:

- Virtual block storage devices can have larger capacity than disk drives, survive disk drive and path failures, and grow to meet increasing requirements for storage. The virtual block storage device is a more useful abstraction for managing physical storage capacity than the disk drive (which itself is an abstraction as Chapter 2 describes).
- File systems can be formatted, populated, defragmented, and backed up with no awareness of the properties of the virtual devices on which they reside. The file system is a more natural and useful abstraction for managing files than the virtual storage device.
- Applications abstract the data in files or databases into entities that are relevant to users. Word processor users deal with documents, graphic designers deal with images or clips, and so forth, without regard to the properties of the file system or storage device in which they are stored.

Of course, encapsulation doesn't stop disk drives from failing or users from erroneously deleting documents. What it does do, however, is allow administrators to concentrate on managing each aspect of a storage system at the most appropriate layer, and ignore other layers until *their* attributes are being managed.

All types of storage virtualization—RAID systems, volume managers, network virtualization appliances and switches—increase storage system complexity by adding both connectivity and diversity to a system. The complexity they add is offset by encapsulation (virtualization), however.

CHAPTER SUMMARY

- Network storage, while delivering important benefits for enterprise information services, has resulted in a quantum increase in storage system complexity that is reflected in administrative cost that grows faster than the storage system.
- Storage management complexity and cost result from system size (number of components), component interconnections, and diversity of components.
- Both vendors and users are developing techniques for dealing with storage system complexity. By and large, these techniques deal with complexity as it is rather than addressing its root causes—size, connectivity, and diversity.
- Storage virtualization encapsulates storage devices into larger aggregates that are more easily managed. This approach is nearly alone among solutions available today in dealing with root causes of complexity rather than coping with it as it exists.

CHAPTER 21

It is the last lesson of modern science, that the highest simplicity of structure is produced, not by few elements, but by the highest complexity.

—RALPH WALDO EMERSON

Virtual Storage for the Future

In this chapter . . .

- Limitations of today's model for virtual block storage
- Storage objects: a new concept for coping with large amounts of data
- How storage objects may change the nature of virtualization

As discussed in Chapter 20, block virtualization is unique among today's techniques for dealing with storage management complexity in that it addresses root causes rather than attempting to "manage around" them. This chapter suggests additional techniques for reducing storage management complexity that may be developed and used in the future.

THE POPULARITY OF BLOCK STORAGE VIRTUALIZATION

Block storage virtualization is attractive because it improves the quality of online storage service. With virtualization, storage resources can perform better, store data more reliably, provide advanced functions like snapshots, and, when physical storage is connected to a network, be deployed more flexibly across an entire data center.

While all of these properties are valuable, another important property of virtual storage has undoubtedly contributed heavily to the technology's rapid and wide acceptance—virtualization leaves the basic disk drive paradigm for online storage unaltered. When block storage is virtualized in the network or by a RAID system, the entire server-based I/O "stack"—device drivers, file systems, database managers, backup software, and so forth—works unmodified just as it would if storage were not virtualized. Server-based volume managers are inserted into the I/O stack between device drivers and file systems, but leave the stack otherwise unaltered. Virtualization improves the important qualities of block storage devices used throughout commercial data processing without requiring application or environmental modifications.

Why Virtualization Is Widely Adopted

Of course, the reason that emulating the disk drive paradigm is so popular is its universal applicability. Since the first standards were introduced nearly two decades ago, the SCSI block storage device has become the universal behavioral model for online storage devices.[1] Although it remains prudent to test storage devices to ensure that they work in a given environment, it is generally true that one block storage device can replace another with little or no perturbation to the I/O stack. This simple but profound fact has, to a large extent, made possible the independent storage industry, and has changed many enterprises' storage buying patterns from system vendor dominated to "best of breed" purchasing of major storage components from vendors of choice.

Limitations of the Block Storage Device Model

The SCSI disk drive model (and its Fibre Channel Protocol, or FCP, derivative) that has remained essentially intact for nearly twenty years was conceived at a time when computer systems were far simpler than they are today. In the mid-1980s, storage networks, RAID systems, clusters of cooperating servers, low-cost gigahertz microprocessors, very low-cost raw disk storage, and ubiquitous networks were all yet to be invented. Computer systems were designed around a central processor, with storage and other devices occupying **peripheral** positions. The key characteristics of the SCSI disk drive model that result from this heritage are:

1. The major exception, of course, is the *count-key-data* disk model used with mainframe computers.

- ***Master-slave architecture:*** A SCSI disk drive is a slave to an *initiator* (a host I/O bus adapter, or HBA) that issues commands to which the drive responds. These commands read and write data, and also set and obtain information about drive properties, status, and state changes. Though workable for a single-server system, this mode of operation is less suitable for storage devices connected to a network, and has in fact evolved into a more networklike model for network storage devices with facilities like Fibre Channel worldwide naming and the Simple Name Server (SNS).
- ***Device addressing:*** Parallel SCSI is designed for connecting eight or sixteen devices to a bus, including initiators. The design limits growth in two ways. First, bus arbitration priority is determined by a device's bus address. As more devices are connected to a bus, they must be configured so that low-priority devices are not "starved" by higher-priority ones. This requires administrative skill and effort. The second limitation is in the device naming scheme. With at most fifteen target devices connected to a bus that radiates from a server, the SCSI *bus-target-LUN* addressing scheme is adequate. With storage connected to a network, however, a device's name must be independent of the address at which servers "see" it. A more networklike address-independent naming scheme is required. Again, Fibre Channel standards have evolved to accommodate this networklike requirement.
- ***Security:*** Parallel SCSI was conceived for deployment inside a physical security boundary (the computer room). With one server controlling all storage, a maximum of sixteen devices on a bus, and a maximum bus length of 25 meters, there is little to fear from "rogue" devices. This assumption is not valid for storage networks, particularly those extended with the long-distance communication technologies described in Chapter 18. Unauthorized devices, "man in the middle" attacks, and denials of service all become possible, and protection against them is required. Moreover, with dozens of servers connected to a storage network, destructive server malfunctions can corrupt data belonging to other servers. Fibre Channel protocols have made some progress in this area with device log-ins and network zoning, but again, more networklike architectures in which storage devices act as peers providing dynamically definable services to authenticated clients would be more appropriate.
- ***Flat data address space:*** A SCSI disk drive can store data persistently in a fixed number of individually addressable blocks of fixed capacity (usually 512 bytes). Again, this model works well when a single server is "in charge"—a file system can manage the block space, creating dynamic subdivisions (files) that are convenient for application

use. With storage devices connected to a network, however, this model is limiting; each potential client must be granted or denied access to the entire device. As a result, all servers that access a given storage device must cooperate with each other on some level. Shared nothing clusters provide primitive cooperation; shared data clusters' volume managers and file systems (Chapter 11) cooperate more closely for more dynamic data sharing. Clearly a more flexible data model would be preferable for networked storage devices that serve multiple clients (application servers).

- ***Data attributes:*** Aside from capacity, the "flat" block address space presented by a SCSI disk drive has only one significant attribute—*write protection*—either all of the blocks on a SCSI disk can be overwritten by a client or none of them can. Again, with storage devices connected to a network and accessible by multiple servers, a richer set of storage attributes applied with finer granularity would be more appropriate.

The Status Quo

Storage systems have evolved to deliver the benefits enabled by connecting storage to the network. Some of the required properties have been implemented in the networks and storage devices themselves (e.g., zoning, LUN masking, device log-in); others have been implemented at the file system level in both server-based cluster file systems and NAS appliances (e.g., finer granularity for data object addressing, properties, and security). The result is the complex, but workable network storage architectural models for enterprise computing that are illustrated in Figure 21–1.

Both the SAN and NAS enterprise storage architectures illustrated in Figure 21–1 deliver important benefits:

- ***Capacity pooling:*** Data center storage capacity can be pooled, virtualized, and allocated to servers or groups of servers. With increased management protocol standardization (e.g., the SNIA's *Bluefin* storage management initiative), it is becoming possible for storage management applications to "look inside" RAID systems to determine individual LUN properties for coordinated policy-based management of diverse physical and virtual devices.
- ***Data access scaling:*** Cluster file systems (Chapter 11) and parallel database managers (Chapter 16) whose instances run in multiple servers coordinate their access to common pools of data (file systems or databases) to allow application processing capacity to grow beyond the capability of a single server.

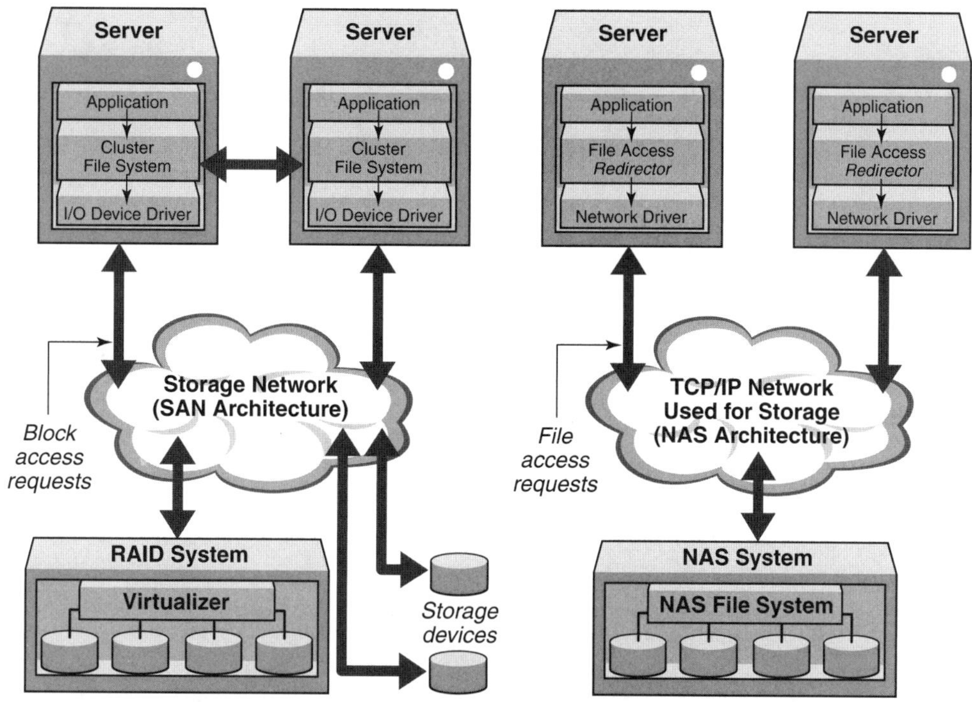

▼ **FIGURE 21–1** *Today's Enterprise Storage Network Architectures*

The combination of standards and advances in vendors' management tools is extending and simplifying central management of diverse storage devices across a data center and beyond. So what's wrong with this picture? Does enterprise virtual storage have to evolve at all? Are there important additional benefits to be derived from changes in the conventional virtual device/data manager models of enterprise storage illustrated in Figure 21–1?

OBJECTS: THE FUTURE OF VIRTUAL STORAGE?

Speculation about the future is exactly that—speculation. But not all speculation is uninformed. Examining the "pain points" in current enterprise storage systems is likely to lead to accurate predictions about where change will occur in the future. A look at the division of function in current distributed enterprise storage systems can be instructive in this regard.

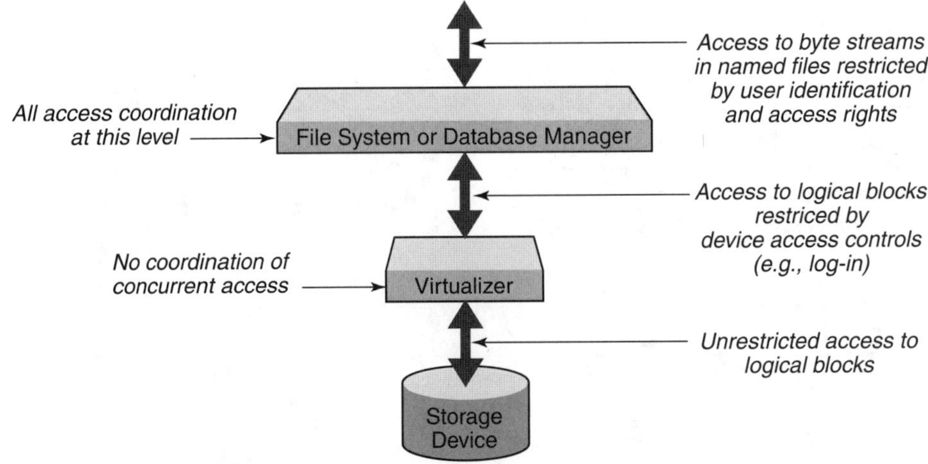

▼ **FIGURE 21–2** *Functional I/O Stack for Online Storage Access*

In today's storage systems, the physical or virtual block storage device presents a large (hundreds of gigabytes) flat block space of fixed capacity[2] to any and all clients that can authenticate and connect to it. All responsibility for controlling and coordinating access to data objects stored on these devices rests with file systems or database managers that run in application servers or in NAS appliances. Figure 21–2 illustrates this division of function.

To properly reproduce conventional (single-server) data sharing semantics, cluster file system and database manager instances must signal their intentions to modify data and metadata using *distributed locking* techniques. Distributed lock managers have one thing in common—they work by exchanging network messages among cooperating servers. Cluster file systems and parallel database managers that use these techniques must synchronize all of their actions. With today's technology, these managers must be **homogeneous** (run on identical platforms). NAS appliances support heterogeneous clients, but they, too, must communicate locking information with their clients. In essence, storage devices don't have enough information available to them to manage data sharing, so NAS appliances, file systems, and database managers must cooperate to do it.

2. It is true that virtualization designs allow the capacity of virtual devices to expand and contract, but the anticipated frequency of change is very low, and is ignorable for the purposes of this argument.

Because this cooperation occurs at such a high level in the I/O path, it results in significant message traffic between the cooperating servers, which in turn limits scaling.

Today, the microprocessors and cache within a single disk drive are more powerful than many of the data center mainframes of the 1980s. Given that the capabilities and economics of storage devices have changed so dramatically over the last two decades, it is worth exploring the conventional split of function in the I/O path (Figure 21–2), and, in particular, asking whether complexity could be reduced and scaling improved by partitioning distributed storage system function in some other way.

Today's storage systems are structurally oriented; designs are predicated on seldom-changing components, connections, and data locations. With the vastly more powerful components available today, would it be possible for future storage systems to be designed more along functional lines (like today's peer networks) and thereby exhibit better scaling, less complexity, and, coincidentally, greater resiliency?

Object Storage Devices

Not surprisingly, academic research has focused on this question, and has developed interesting alternative storage architectures. This research, which is migrating into the industrial arena both in the form of **object storage device (OSD)** standards and in work being conducted in major storage companies, is rooted in the observation that there are five quintessential functions in the path between applications (clients) and data stored on virtual devices in a storage network:

- ***Name resolution:*** Conversion between the symbolic names by which applications refer to files and the representations of files' metadata and data locations on virtual storage devices
- ***Authentication:*** Validating that clients are actually what or who they represent themselves to be
- ***Capacity management:*** Subdividing virtual devices' flat block address spaces into dynamic objects (files) that are convenient for applications to deal with
- ***Data access control:*** Ensuring that only authenticated clients are able to access managed data objects, and only in authorized ways (e.g., for reading only)
- ***Block address conversion:*** Converting between the file block addresses used in application read and write requests and the virtual device block addresses at which data is stored

Of these, the first two are completely operating system-specific. Each operating system platform has its own way of naming and organizing files and its own rules for permitting or denying access to specific applications and users. The third, fourth, and fifth of these functions, however, are generic (common across all platforms) and occur frequently during system operation. Common operations that occur frequently are always candidates for offloading to devices designed specifically to perform them optimally (NAS appliances are an extreme example of this). Intuitively, it seems likely that distributed system scaling might be improved by distributing block storage capacity management, data access control, and block address conversion among the storage devices in a network.

This is in fact the premise of object storage device technology. Object storage devices contain "mini file systems" that allocate and manage the devices' flat block address spaces. Clients' read and write commands to object storage devices refer to blocks within named objects. The devices themselves create and delete these objects dynamically in response to client control commands. In essence, an object storage device is a virtual file server. Its clients are file system-like entities running in application servers that manage name spaces and control user access to files. Two other key components, a central **object manager** and an **access token mechanism,** are required to implement a distributed storage system based on object storage devices.

Figure 21–3 illustrates a distributed storage system based on object storage devices. As the figure suggests, a server-based *object storage client* (analogous to a conventional file system) communicates with the system's central object manager to determine storage object locations and to gain the right to access objects on behalf of applications or users. The object storage client (which might well store its own persistent metadata structures in storage objects) is responsible for validating applications' access rights to files and for sending file names to the object manager, which makes the objects accessible by clients.

The object manager makes an object accessible to a client by sending unique access tokens to both client and object storage device. These tokens enable object storage devices to validate requests coming from clients of which they may have no prior knowledge.[3] Thus, with an object storage

3. This discussion of object storage access tokens is greatly simplified. The access token concept is an outcome of academic research, not of standards activity. Tokens have additional features such as automatic revocation in case of client failure or timeout. Object storage access protocols also allow for both request and data encryption to enable their use on insecure networks.

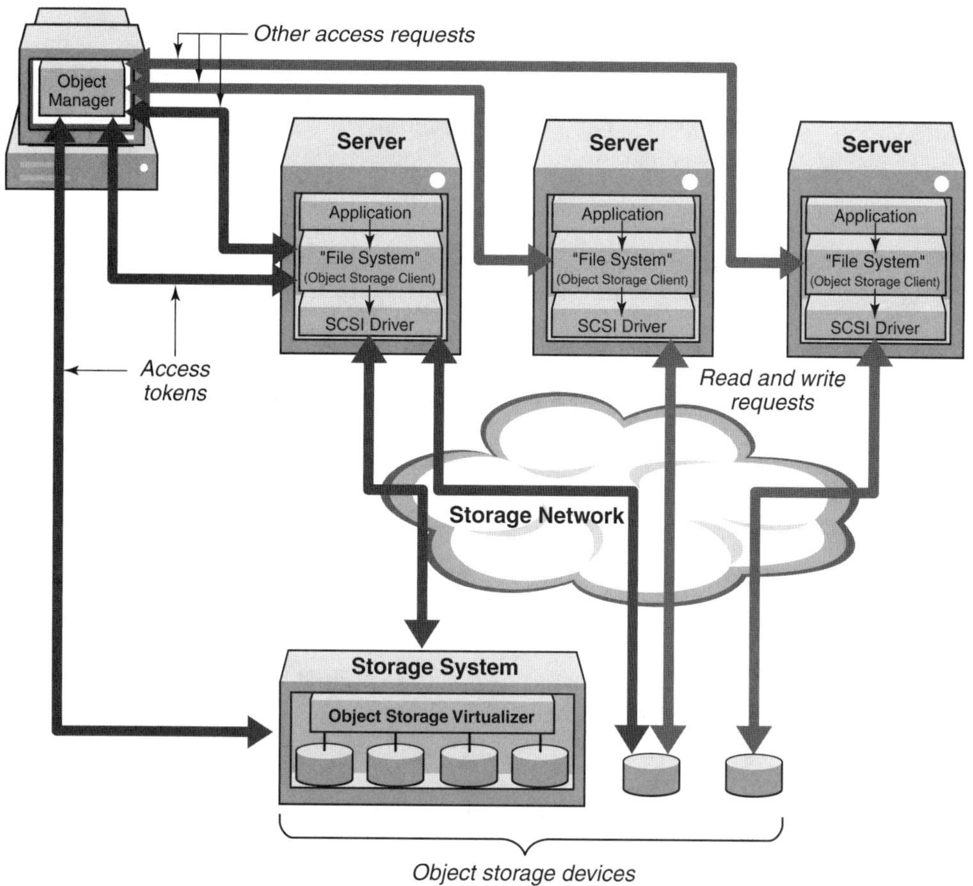

▼ **FIGURE 21–3** *An Object Storage Device Network*

device-based system, application servers need not cooperate as closely as the servers in a conventional cluster.

Armed with the network address of the device that contains its object and with an access token, a client can make read and write requests directly to the object storage device. The read and write path from storage device to client is therefore short, and the object manager is not a bottleneck in it.

Direct access between devices and clients is reminiscent of out-of-band block storage virtualization (Chapter 10) and has a similar benefit—improved scaling. With this architecture, clients, storage devices, or network capacity can be added to a data center independently of each other to increase processing power, storage capacity, or I/O bandwidth and request performance to meet data center needs.

Separating Object Storage Concepts

Object storage devices are defined in a relatively recent proposed SCSI standard for an *object device type.* The proposed standard specifies commands for creating, extending, and deleting objects, and for reading and writing the data in them. Object attributes similar to those of files (e.g., creation date, size, date last accessed, etc.) are defined, as are commands to set and retrieve their values.

Like SCSI disk drives, object storage devices are an abstraction, and, as Figure 21–3 suggests, could be implemented either in disk drive firmware, by RAID-like systems, or by network storage appliances using conventional persistent storage devices. The latter approaches enable failure-tolerant object-based data storage, although RAID-like systems do not automatically provide anything like long-distance replication of virtual device contents for disaster recovery. A related problem (solved for conventional storage by volume managers but reintroduced by object storage devices) is that of virtual devices made by aggregating other virtual devices, as, for example, a virtual device that mirrors data on two LUNs presented by different RAID systems.

When delivered commercially, object storage devices promise to improve data center storage system scaling and to reduce large system complexity by "flattening" the I/O stack. But they also pose unique challenges that must be met if they are to become prevalent in enterprise data centers. To explore these challenges, it is helpful to summarize the basics of object storage devices:

- Object storage devices manage disklike block address spaces and present a file system-like object interface to clients.
- Clients (file system-like components running in servers) create, extend, and delete filelike objects, and read and write data in them. The file system's role is reduced to managing an operating system-dependent file name space and controlling client access to objects presented as files.
- A central object manager translates between object identifiers and the network addresses of devices on which the objects are stored, and grants client access to objects.
- Clients write and read data directly to and from storage devices. This shortens the I/O path, relative to a NAS appliance, for example. The object storage devices themselves execute I/O requests atomically, although clients are responsible for maintaining the integrity of data within an object.

- Object storage device protocols include a system of access tokens meted out by the object manager. Access tokens accompany client requests to object storage devices and provide validation of a client's right to make a given request.

The strengths of object storage devices are distribution of work, short I/O path (direct from client to storage device), and dynamic access security provided by the token system. The weaknesses are the central object manager (which must somehow be made resilient) and the inability of objects to span multiple storage devices (for improved performance, availability, or resiliency) without some external support. The question arises as to whether a compromise approach is possible—whether the advantages of object storage devices can be combined with today's virtualization techniques to achieve bottleneck-free virtual storage with the full capabilities of today's solutions.

It is tantalizing to imagine a generation of cooperating object storage appliances (perhaps based upon blade servers) that manage physical storage in the form of conventional disk drives and present a network of objectlike virtual devices to application servers. Cooperation among these appliances might take the form of replicating object spaces to remote appliances, thus solving the problem of storage resiliency to disaster. Individual appliances might accommodate more or larger objects by the addition of storage capacity, much as today's RAID systems and network storage appliances do.

USING OBJECTS TO REDUCE STORAGE COMPLEXITY

Moving data object awareness into storage devices raises the interesting prospect of attaching storage quality of service parameters to data objects rather than to the block address spaces in which they reside. Instead of formatting a file system on a mirrored or striped virtual device, one can imagine creating mirrored, striped, or replicated objects as business requirements indicate, and storing ordinary objects on ordinary storage, all within the same file system. Because it would manage storage capacity internally, an object appliance could provide per-object quality of storage service in response to client demands. Such object storage appliances might be capable of changing an object's quality of storage in response to client demands (e.g., moving an object from simple to mirrored storage when it becomes mission critical).

Using Object Storage Devices in the Near Term

Moving responsibility for storage quality from the virtual device layer of the I/O stack to the file system layer is a profound and far-reaching change that will probably take a long time to enter the mainstream. But this is not to say that the object storage device concept could not be useful in the near term.

One way to use object storage device technology in the relatively near future might be to use storage objects as the components of complex virtual storage devices. For example, a server-based volume manager might create two 100-gigabyte objects on different object storage devices, mirror writes to them, and present them as a 100-gigabyte virtual block storage device. Similarly, if a set of four object storage appliances all have internal redundancy (as would clearly be possible with the device illustrated on the left of Figure 21–3), a volume manager could create a striped mirrored virtual device by creating objects of one-fourth the required capacity on each of the devices and striping data across the four objects.

These examples closely resemble how virtualization implementations of all types work today. They create logical subsets of device capacity (variously called *subdisks, logical disks, plexes,* and so forth), and combine these subsets by mirroring writes between them, striping data across them, or using parity RAID algorithms with them. When conventional disks and LUNs are used in this way, the virtualization software is the only enforcement of these logical boundaries. In RAID systems, in-band network virtualization appliances, and server-based volume managers, this is a negligible problem because the virtualization software is engineered, tested, and executed as a coherent unit. Out-of-band network-based virtualization, however, relies on cooperation among different virtualization component implementations (Chapter 10) running on servers that are not necessarily cooperating in any way except for these components. Certain rare client failure modes, or the introduction of rogue servers into a storage network, could cause inadvertent or malicious corruption of data belonging to other servers. By contrast, the token-based data access protocols of object storage technology could provide security for out-of-band block storage virtualization. Object storage devices themselves could evaluate the legitimacy of requests before executing them. This would surely increase out-of-band virtualization technology's viability, particularly in environments of heterogeneous noncooperating platforms.

Using Object Storage Devices in the Longer Term

The standards to enable object storage devices exist, at least in draft form.[4] The emergence of server and appliance-based block virtualizers able to utilize object storage devices, should it occur, might popularize the technology and create an installed base of object storage devices. If the technology does, in fact, become popular, there will be greater motivation for file system and database manager developers to explore whether object storage could be used to advantage by their products.

One can envision *storage-aware* file systems that allocate directories or even individual files according to storage quality properties specified either by policy or as individual files are created. Alternatively, file systems themselves could manage storage quality properties, for example, creating two or more objects on different devices for files specified as critical, and so forth. Carrying the concept further, file systems could also automatically allocate critical files on devices whose object spaces were replicated at remote locations, or they could replicate the objects themselves.

Today, data replication is primarily based on virtual devices that contain large numbers of files. The coarse granularity of replication makes it most suitable for disaster recovery. If individual files and directories could be replicated with similar survival semantics, other applications for replicated data might present themselves.

Storage System Evolvability

A system's evolvability is its ability to adapt as its environment changes over long periods of time. Current storage system architectures are static and structurally oriented rather than dynamic and functionally oriented. They are not automatically evolvable without extensive administrative action to reconfigure virtual devices, start and stop replication, and so forth, and then take the corresponding file system actions to make use of the reconfigured storage. More to the point, today's concept of a file system is structural—it is inextricably associated with a (physical or virtual) storage device. The file system is formatted on the device, and that's where it stores the data it manages. If the device is virtual, its capacity may change, or part or all of it may move to different physical storage devices, but the virtual device is the one and only place where the file system stores data for its entire lifetime.

---

4. In the lexicon of storage standards, a draft is usually regarded as a sufficiently stable base for vendors to invest in implementation. It is not uncommon for actual standards to lag commercial implementations, sometimes by a year or more.

If, however, a file system "understood" object storage devices, it could become effectively a catalog of pointers to objects. With such an architecture, it would be relatively easy for individual files to reside at different locations on a network. If a file system manages replicas, then the concept of a file's "location" takes on a new meaning. With suitable instrumentation it should be possible for a file system to make a policy decision to assign a "home" or "main" location to an object based on usage information, perceived threats, changes in criticality, or arbitrary administrative directive. Similar policies could govern the number of replicas of an object, the quality of storage on which they were stored, and other object attributes.

One can carry this further, and imagine "policy engines" that integrate backup and restore functionality with awareness of data object replicas. With today's storage and data object paradigms, when a file is copied, the copy effectively becomes a new object. As a result, huge amounts of storage are consumed with redundant files that are neither synchronized nor accurately cataloged as point-in-time versions of a base object. If file systems delivered their value by tracking the state of object replicas rather than by allocating storage capacity, it might be possible to deliver a dramatically improved quality of storage service, both in terms of availability and performance, essentially using resources that are already being expended today.

This is not to reiterate the old data processing adage that periodically predicts the end of tape storage. For ultra-secure vaulting, easy transportation, and long-term archive retention, it is certain that tape storage media or something like it will be a part of information handling for the foreseeable future. But tape media are not optimal for recovering lost or destroyed data quickly, especially individual files. It would be far more effective to use an online data replica of known location and vintage to recover from a failure, disaster, or user error, or to reverse data corruption by "falling back" to a version representing a point in time at which data was known to be uncorrupted.

The essence of these examples is the repartitioning of the critical functions listed earlier in this chapter so that storage devices manage data objects and client I/O requests to them. In this proposed paradigm, today's file systems are replaced by components that manage sets of objects to deliver today's file system functionality with significantly more automated policy-based management than is the case today. Of course, at the time of publication, all of this is speculation. There are certainly other foreseeable paths that virtual storage and enterprise-wide data management could follow in the future. Moreover, this high-level look at "endgame" capabilities necessarily glosses over much hard work and attention to detail, both in technology and in market awareness, that would have to happen. Nonetheless, the vision of globally virtualized "data from a plug in the wall" remains a tantalizing one, and provides a lofty goal for developers to aim for and for users to demand.

Conclusion

In a sense, policy-based management of data objects in a distributed storage network is the "punch line" of this and the preceding chapter. By associating knowledge about a data object (e.g., its size, modifiability, creation time, etc.) with the data object itself, and by morphing today's monolithic data management into the management of sets of objects distributed throughout a storage network, today's "I/O stack" can be simplified, and the roots of storage management complexity can be attacked in a fundamental way by policy-based automation tools that deal with abstract objects rather than the details of their representation on storage media.

CHAPTER SUMMARY

- Block storage virtualization reduces complexity by encapsulating it so that properties germane to each layer of a storage system can be managed at that layer, without cognizance of details related to other layers.
- Block storage virtualization delivers value, but at least one important reason why it was so widely adopted so quickly is that it does not change the online data storage paradigm—applications and data managers access virtual storage without alteration pretty much as they would access physical storage.
- The introduction of storage networks has strained the "SCSI disk drive" paradigm in several important ways, including multiclient access and the need for security in the data path as storage moves to a network. The worst of these strains have been dealt with, but the question of whether it is time to rethink the basic block storage access paradigm arises nonetheless.
- Object storage device technology repartitions the functions of the I/O stack, taking advantage of low-cost intelligence at the device level to migrate certain functions conventionally associated with file systems into storage devices.

- Object storage device technology repartitions function, but also introduces protocols that enforce the limitation of client access to storage to authorized objects. These protocols could also be applied to improve the robustness of out-of-band block storage virtualization in today's storage paradigm.
- Although file systems and database managers are unlikely to take advantage of object storage devices in the near future, server and network appliance-based block virtualizers could probably use them to advantage. This, plus the existence of standards, may be sufficient to cause data manager developers to look at how their products could take advantage of object storage device technology.
- Managing files and directories as device-based objects "flattens" the I/O stack, and introduces possibilities for dramatically improving the automation of storage and data management in several ways. This presents developers with an opportunity to attack a root cause of storage management complexity.

APPENDIXES

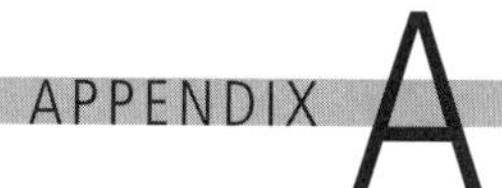

A Summary of Block Storage Virtualization Techniques and Implementations

Table A–1 compares the intrinsic properties of the seven RAID models described by the Berkeley researchers in 1988 and 1989. Intrinsic properties of a RAID model are properties implied by the check data mechanisms and block address conversion algorithms it uses. Thus, for example, the performance of a parity RAID array executing small writes is low compared with that of a single disk because keeping the array's check data up to date implies that each user write must be accompanied by a series of overhead reads and writes to recompute and update the corresponding check data. Many RAID implementations mitigate undesirable intrinsic performance characteristics, principally through the use of nonvolatile cache to defer writes. The semantics of such techniques are a fascinating subject that is beyond the scope of this book.

In Table A–1, I/O performance is shown both in terms of *large I/O requests,* which measure relative ability to transfer data, and *random I/O request rate,* which measures relative ability to satisfy I/O requests, because each RAID Level has different intrinsic performance characteristics relative to these two metrics. Each RAID Level's particular strong points are highlighted in the table by shading.

RAID Type	Common Name	Description	Relative Cost (Disk Drives)	Relative Data Availability	Large Read Data Transfer Speed[1]	Large Write Data Transfer Speed	Random Read Request Rate	Random Write Request Rate
0	Block Address Striping	User data distributed across the devices in the array. No check data.	N	lower than single disk	very high	very high	very high	very high
1	Mirroring	User data duplicated on N separate devices. (N is usually 2.) Check data is second copy (as in Figure 8–8).	N	higher than RAID Level 3, 4, 5; lower than RAID Level 2, 6	higher than single disk (up to 2x)	slightly lower than single disk	up to Nx single disk	similar to single disk
"0+1"	Striped Mirrors	User data striped across M separate pairs of mirrored devices. Check data is second copy (as in Figure 4–1).	$2M$	higher than RAID Level 3, 4, 5; lower than RAID Level 2, 6	much higher than single disk	higher than single disk	much higher than single disk	higher than single disk
2		User data striped across N devices. Hamming code check data distributed across m devices. (m is determined by N).	$N+m$	higher than RAID Level 3, 4, 5	highest of all listed types	highest of all listed types	approximately 2x single disk	approximately 2x single disk
3	RAID 3, Parallel Transfer Disk Drives with Parity	Sychronized disk drives. Each user data block distributed across all data disk drives. Parity check data stored on one disk.	$N+1$	much higher than single disk; comparable to RAID 2, 4, 5	highest of all listed types	highest of all listed types	approximately 2x single disk	approximately 2x single disk
4		Independent devices. User data distributed as with striping. Parity check data stored on one disk (as in Figure 7–7).	$N+1$	much higher than single disk; comparable to RAID 2, 3, 5	similar to disk striping	slightly lower than disk striping	similar to disk striping	significantly lower than single disk
5	RAID 5, "RAID"	Independent devices. User data distributed as with striping. Parity check data distributed across devices (as in Figure 7–8).	$N+1$	much higher than single disk; comparable to RAID 2, 3, 4	slightly higher than disk striping	slightly lower than disk striping	Slightly higher than disk striping	significantly lower than single disk; higher than RAID level 4
6	RAID 6	As RAID Level 5, but with additional independently computed distributed check data.	$N+2$	highest of all listed types	slightly higher than RAID Level 5	lower than RAID Level 5	slightly higher than RAID Level 5	lower than RAID Level 5

▼ **TABLE A–1** *Theoretical Summary Comparison of Common Forms of RAID Technology*

1. The Data Transfer Speed columns reflect only I/O performance inherent to the RAID model, and do not include the effect of other features, such as cache.

	Volume Manager	Embedded RAID System	External RAID System	SAN Infrastructure
Inherent Cost	Lowest. No specific hardware required. Some server operating systems include basic volume management.	Moderate. RAID system uses server enclosure and power system. Some server enclosures provide bays for a few disk drives.	Highest. RAID system includes enclosure, power, and cooling for controllers and disk drives. Often configured with complete redundancy.	Moderate to high. No specific storage hardware required. Requires virtualization server, which may be an appliance, a block address conversion server, or an enhanced switch.
Performance (Mirrored Array)	High. Short request execution times due to shortest command and data path. Server processor upgrades increase RAID performance as well.	High. Short request execution times due to short command and data path. Usually include specialized hardware for high throughput.	High. Slightly longer request execution times due to longer command and data path. Usually include specialized hardware for high throughput.	High. Slightly longer request execution times due to longer command and data path.
Performance (Parity RAID Array)	Low. Parity and address conversion computations detract from application performance.	Typical capabilities. Hardware assist for parity computation and nonvolatile cache.	Typical capabilities. Hardware assist for parity computation, nonvolatile cache, and cache mirroring.	Lower. Usually lack specialized hardware assists for parity computation.
Growth Potential	Highest. Limited by server disk connection and addressing capability. Can revirtualize very large virtual disks presented by RAID systems.	Lowest. Limited by the disk drive connection limits of the embedded RAID system.	High. Limited by the disk drive's connection limits of the RAID system. Usually possible to connect multiple RAID systems to a single server.	Highest. Limited by number of ports that can belong to a single virtualization domain. Can revirtualize very large virtual disks presented by RAID systems.
Protection against Disk Failure	Typical capabilities. Striping, parity RAID, *n*-way mirroring (with striping).	Typical capabilities. Striping, parity RAID, mirroring (with striping).	Typical capabilities. Striping, parity RAID, *n*-way mirroring (with striping).	Typical capabilities. Striping, parity RAID, *n*-way mirroring (with striping).
Protection against Control Software Processor Failure	Control software runs on the server, so this is equivalent to server failure.	Equivalent to server failure.	Typical capabilities. Paired RAID systems connected to the same disk drives. Transparent and nontransparent fail over to alternate hosts.	Typical capabilities. Clusters of appliances, block address conversion servers, or redundant switches.
Protection against Server Failure	Provided if storage devices are connected to alternate servers (e.g., through a SAN) and volume manager is cluster-aware.	Requires disk drives connected to two mutually aware RAID systems in different servers, and RAID system-specific cluster support.	Comparable to server-based virtualization, because external RAID systems typically emulate disk drives.	Inherently capable of switching ports on which virtualized devices are presented to connect them to alternate servers.
Protection against Application Failure	Typical capabilities. Split mirror snapshots, fast resynchronization.	None.	Typical capabilities. Split mirror snapshots, fast resynchronization. Business continuance volumes.	Typical capabilities. Split mirror snapshots, fast resynchronization.

▼ **TABLE A–2** *Summary Comparison of Different Virtualization Implementations*

APPENDIX B

Other Forms of RAID

RAID Level 6

In 1989, the researchers who published "A Case for Redundant Arrays of Inexpensive Disks"[1] published another paper entitled "Disk System Architectures for High Performance Computing,"[2] in which a sixth RAID model offering protection against *two* concurrent disk failures was described. This model became known as *RAID Level 6.* For large arrays, RAID Level 6 provides much higher data availability than mirroring at modest incremental raw storage cost. It is complex to implement, however, and has a larger inherent write penalty than parity RAID, and so has fallen into disuse.

RAID Levels 0+1, 1+0, and 10

The terms ***RAID Level 0+1, RAID Level 1+0,*** and ***RAID 10*** are sometimes used to denote disk arrays in which user data is both mirrored and striped across multiple devices. This book avoids all of these terms, using instead the phrases *striped array of mirrored virtual devices* and *mirrored array of striped virtual devices* for these types of disk arrays. While cumbersome, these phrases leave no room for ambiguity about which form of virtualization occurs first.

Table A–1 on page 298 compares the cost, data availability, and I/O performance of the seven common RAID Levels.

1. http://www-2.cs.cmu.edu/~garth/RAIDpaper/Patterson88.pdf
2. http://sunsite.berkeley.edu/TR/UCB:CSD-89-497

What Ever Happened to RAID 3?

As described in "A Case for Redundant Arrays of Inexpensive Disks," the devices comprising a RAID Level 3 array would rotate synchronously. Each block of user data would be split across all but one of them, and the remaining one would contain parity. Strict interpretation of this proposal would have required specialized disk drives, I/O buses, and disk controllers, which would have been prohibitively expensive. In practice, RAID Level 3 systems were typically approximations of the ideal implemented with conventional hardware components.

As Table A–1 asserts, RAID Level 3 intrinsically performs well with large sequential I/O requests. This is because each large data transfer is divided among an array's disk drives, which read or write concurrently to complete it faster. RAID Levels 4 and 5 can deliver nearly equal performance for large sequential I/O requests, however. Moreover, cache has become ubiquitous in RAID systems (and in other layers of the I/O stack as well), masking individual device I/O latencies to some extent.

These factors have combined to diminish the motivation for specialized RAID Level 3 systems, which *only* perform well with large sequential I/O loads, in favor of more generally applicable parity RAID systems.

APPENDIX C

Gather Writing and Scatter Reading

Sophisticated I/O systems can combine requests for multiple data stripes into a single request, even when the data is to be delivered to nonconsecutive memory addresses. Figure C–1 illustrates this.

Figure C–1 illustrates Disk A from the example of Figure 8–4. If an application writes the entire file at once, then Segments 000 and 001, and Segments 010 through 013 will be written to consecutive blocks on Disk A. Most I/O systems include hardware that allows nonconsecutive areas of application memory to be logically "gathered" for writing to consecu-

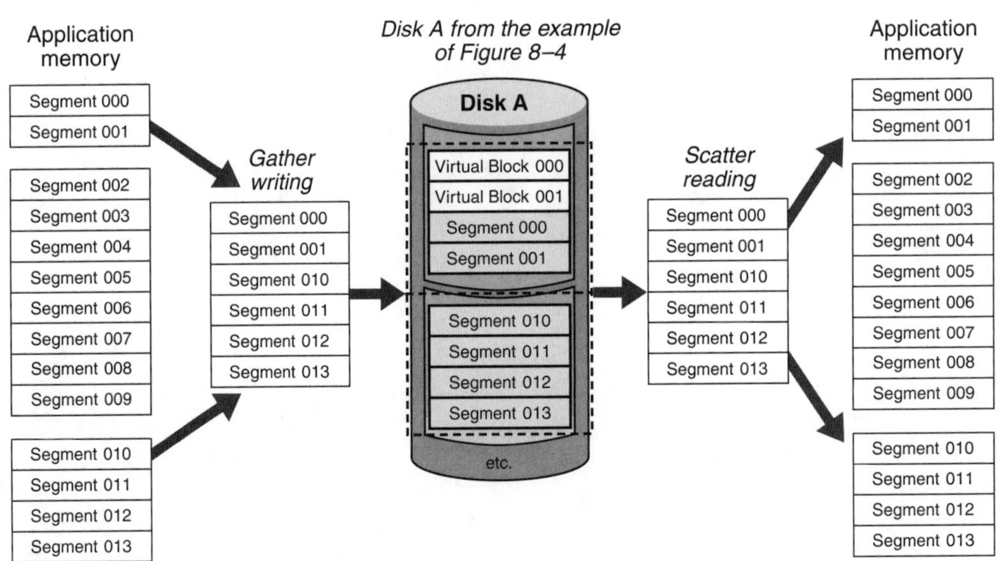

▼ **FIGURE C–1** *Gather Writing and Scatter Reading*

tive disk blocks in a single request. This is called *gather writing,* because noncontiguous blocks of memory are gathered together for delivery to contiguous disk blocks. Systems that support gather writing also support the converse capability—delivery of consecutive disk blocks to nonconsecutive application memory areas as they are read from the disk. This is called *scatter reading.*

Scatter reading and gather writing improve performance by:

- Eliminating most of the separate I/O commands that control software must issue to satisfy an application request
- Eliminating "missed" disk revolutions caused by the time required to issue these additional requests (e.g., requests 4–6 in the example of Figure 8–4)

Scatter-gather capability is sometimes implemented by processor memory management units and sometimes by I/O interface ASICs.[1] It is therefore usually available with both server-based and RAID system-based virtualizers.

1. Application-specific integrated circuits, such as the single-chip SCSI and Fibre Channel interfaces found on some computer main boards.

APPENDIX D

A Brief Overview of File Systems

THE NATURE OF FILE SYSTEMS

The file concept is so integral to computing that it's difficult to imagine data processing without files. Paradoxically, the file systems that implement the file paradigm often go unnoticed precisely because files are so ubiquitous, and so inseparably intertwined with all facets of data processing.

Files are used to structure all kinds of persistent data, including operating system programs, libraries of executable functions, event logs, and operating parameters, as well as containers for databases. Files are stored on block storage devices and access to them is controlled by software components called *file systems.*[1]

Over time, integration between operating systems and file systems has increased; today, file systems are nearly an integral part of most operating systems, used for all data access and management except at the very beginning of operating system loading. As they begin to run, operating systems use files to determine things like:

- Which modules to load into memory for execution
- The system's startup operating mode (e.g., graphical or text console, network enabled or not, etc.)

1. The term *file system* is also used to denote a consecutive range of numbered blocks on a block storage device that is formatted and managed by a file system software component, as in "The volume contains an NTFS file system."

Once operating systems are running, file systems continue to be useful, for example, for:

- Storing encrypted credentials against which user and remote computer log-ins are validated
- Storing application program images ready for loading and execution
- Holding parts of executing programs that have been temporarily suspended ("paged" or "swapped" out)
- Logging exceptional events such as network or I/O errors for later problem analysis and resolution
- Logging "normal" events such as log-ins and file access attempts, for security and other auditing purposes

As applications run, they, too, use files for a variety of purposes:

- Holding configuration parameters that define operating modes
- Logging events that occur during execution
- Storing libraries of functions shared among several applications
- Storing the data they process

File systems are literally the lingua franca of electronic data storage. Developers have realized that one mechanism can organize all persistent data, no matter what its nature, and the modern file system is it.

What File Systems Do

To understand why file systems have become so pervasive, it is useful to consider the services they provide. Chapter 2 discusses the *virtual disk drive* abstraction—the representation of the storage capacity of a disk drive as a fixed set of consecutively numbered blocks of the same size. Block storage virtualization extends this abstraction across multiple disk drives. This abstraction isolates system software from differences in storage device technology; to system software, all devices behave identically, no matter what their internal characteristics. But the abstraction is not convenient for applications. It is much more convenient for applications to deal with data items that:

- Can vary in size (e.g., can grow as more data is written to them or be truncated as data in them is discarded)
- Can be created and deleted freely with little overhead, and, most important, with no human intervention

- Can be easily identified and located in a population of millions of similar items sharing the same physical or virtual pool of raw storage capacity
- Can have access to them limited to designated applications or users

These are properties of computer system files, the data abstraction provided by file systems. A file system organizes the set of numbered blocks exported by a virtual device and provides its clients with:

- A data access paradigm that allows an application to treat a file as though it were an entire storage device reserved for the application's exclusive use
- A naming scheme (almost always hierarchical) that allows an arbitrary number of files to be identified and located using names that are convenient for application use and easily recognizable by humans
- Access controls that prevent unauthorized users and applications from reading or writing data in specific files
- Space allocation mechanisms that allow applications to freely allocate and remove files from a single pool of storage capacity (a virtual device) without regard for the activities of other applications
- A set of operations that allow applications and users to manipulate either entire data items (e.g., create, delete, extend, truncate, change ownership, etc.) or the storage space within them (e.g., read and write streams of bytes at specific locations within a file)

The "data items" are, of course, files as they are known in today's computing environments. The hierarchical naming scheme is nothing more than a tree structure of directories in which files are logically located for user and application convenience.

File System Data Organization

A file system inevitably has a *root,* or fixed starting point from which searches for files begin. The root contains several *top-level* directories, and may also contain some files. Each top-level directory may contain both subdirectories and files. Subdirectories may contain files and subdirectories of their own. For the vast majority of applications, the maximum depth of a directory tree is not an obstacle.

Directories provide a convenient means of organizing files by application or usage, making it intuitively easy for humans and applications to locate a single file among millions as long as something is known about

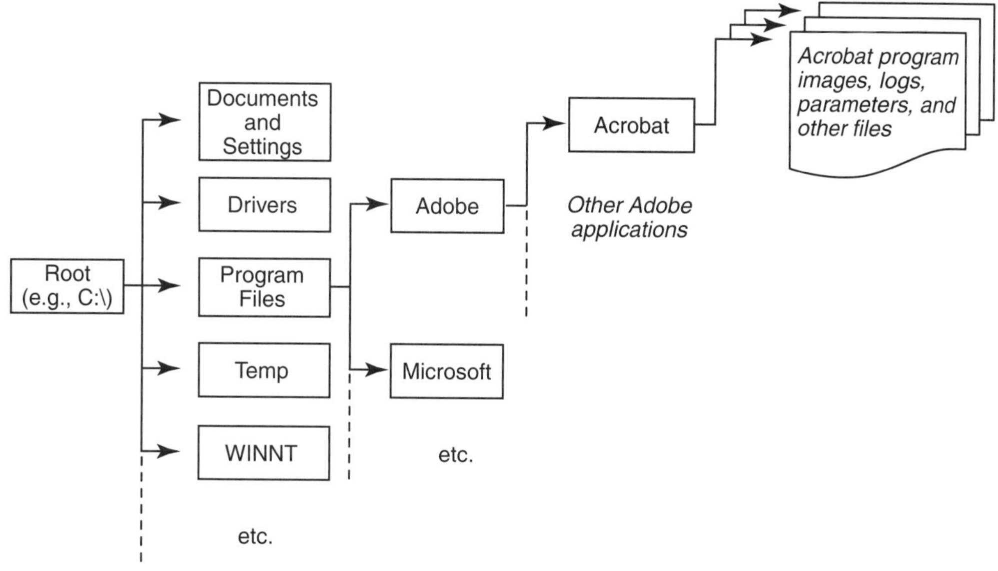

▼ **FIGURE D–1** *A Hierarchical File System Directory Structure*

it. For example, in Windows[2] operating systems, program images and other files associated with the operating system are typically stored in a directory called **WINNT.** Installing an application typically creates a subdirectory in another directory called **Program Files.** Thus, for example, a Windows system on which Adobe Acrobat[3] is installed typically has a subdirectory called **Adobe,** in which all applications from Adobe Systems are organized. The **Adobe** directory has a subdirectory of its own called **Acrobat** in which files related to the Acrobat application are stored. Figure D–1 illustrates this structure.

The leaf nodes of trees such as that illustrated in Figure D–1 consist of data structures that describe the location of the virtual disk blocks that comprise a file's data storage area.[4] These structures describe file data locations in terms of virtual device block locations. For example, a structure might indicate that file blocks 0–99 are located at virtual device

2. Windows is a registered trademark of Microsoft Corporation.
3. Acrobat is a registered trademark of Adobe Systems, Incorporated.
4. In file systems used with the UNIX operating system, these structures are called *inodes.*

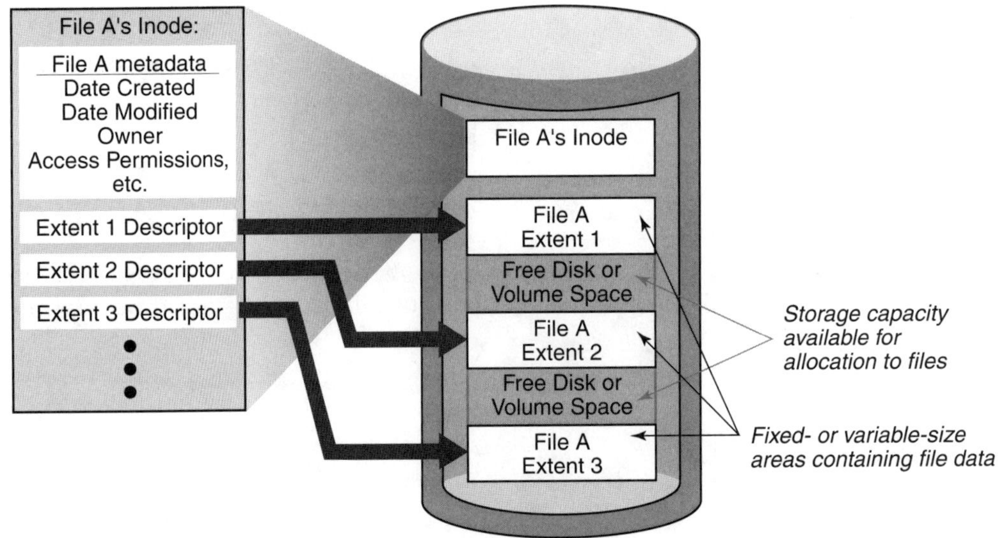

▼ **FIGURE D–2** *Block-Based File System Typical of UNIX Systems*

blocks 10,246–10,345. With this indirect structure, it is easy to visualize how files may be created, extended, moved, truncated, and deleted simply by manipulating block numbers.

For a file system to manage a single pool of space organized as a changing number of files of changing size, it must also keep a record of space in the pool that is *not* allocated to any file. A typical file system manages a free space pool, removing blocks from it when they are consumed by file creation or extension, and returning blocks to it when a file is truncated or deleted.

File System Space Allocation

File systems typically manage the space they occupy as **allocation units,** or **file system blocks,** each consisting of a consecutively numbered sequence of virtual device blocks.

UNIX file systems, for example, use on-disk data structures called *inodes* to describe files. An inode contains administrative data about a file, as well as *descriptors* that indicate which virtual disk blocks are occupied by the file's data. Figure D–2 illustrates how a file system might describe a file.

As Figure D–2 suggests, each of the file's descriptors indicates a consecutive range of virtual disk block numbers. When an application makes an I/O request specifying file data addresses, the file system uses these descriptors to convert them to virtual disk block addresses and makes device I/O requests to store or retrieve data.

How File Systems Do Their Work

File systems use part of the capacity they manage to store information about files—their names, access permissions and other attributes, and the location of their data within the virtual device. This descriptive information is called *metadata.*

Figure D–2 illustrates that it is the file system that gives meaning to individual blocks of storage. The block containing File A's inode is just like any other block. It is only recognized for what it is because the file system's algorithms locate it during a search for File A. Similarly, the blocks that contain File A's data only contain File A's data because the file system's data location algorithms convert descriptors in File A's inode into device block addresses to which I/O requests can be directed. It is only the file system that imputes meaning to otherwise indistinguishable blocks of disk storage.

File Systems and Data Integrity

File systems organize and manage virtually all types of persistent data used by computer systems. They use part of the storage capacity of the virtual devices on which they are formatted to hold metadata structures that describe the location and attributes of files. Computer systems rely utterly on the correct functioning of their file systems. If file system metadata is erroneous:

- Users or applications may gain access to files for which they have no authorization.
- Data may be "lost" from files, or the random contents of unallocated space may be treated as file data.
- Entire files may "disappear"—be impossible to locate—even though their contents are intact on disk storage.
- Blocks of storage may be allocated to two or more files, with obvious disastrous consequences for applications.

Thus, it is absolutely imperative that file systems maintain metadata integrity. File system metadata must be correct, no matter what happens to the computer on which the file system is running or the underlying virtual storage it uses.

HOW FILE SYSTEMS FAIL AND RECOVER

Reflection should also make it clear that in the course of maintaining metadata integrity, a file system must perform many *atomic* sequences of I/O operations. An atomic sequence of operations is one for which all of the operations must occur for correct overall system operation. For example, to create a file, a file system must:

- Remove blocks for both metadata and data from its free space pool. This requires updating the file system's metadata to indicate that the allocated blocks are no longer part of the free space pool.
- Populate the newly allocated blocks with file metadata (and possibly application data as well) and write them to disk storage.
- Link the metadata blocks into the directory structure so that the file can be located by users and applications. This requires that directory metadata be both read and written.

For the file to be correctly allocated so that it can subsequently be found and used by applications, all of these operations must be performed correctly and completely. Partial execution of the sequence can lead to a corrupt file system. For example, if a file system rewrites its free space data structures to indicate that space has been allocated, but fails to complete the other operations, the space is simply lost—it is neither part of a file nor available as free space to be used for other purposes. If, on the other hand, the file system were to link the new file's metadata blocks into its directory structures before updating free space metadata, there is a chance that the same blocks could be allocated twice, with obvious disastrous consequences.

File System Metadata Consistency Techniques

File system metadata is necessarily complex; most updates are actually sequences of I/O operations that must be executed atomically if metadata is to remain consistent. Atomic metadata update sequences are perhaps the single biggest challenge to file system structural integrity, because computers can crash at any time, including during execution of these sequences. Crashes may leave metadata partially updated, and therefore potentially inconsistent. File systems are designed to minimize the impact of system crashes, and to repair metadata if necessary when they restart after crashing.

To minimize the impact of crashes on metadata consistency, file system designers adopt two general strategies:

- ***Metadata redundancy:*** Real file system metadata structures are considerably more complex than the example of Figure D–2 suggests. In part, this is because they are designed to be redundant, expressing the same information in more than one form. One major reason for metadata redundancy is consistency—if a piece of metadata is destroyed, it is often possible for a file system to recreate it, or use different metadata to achieve its ends. For example, most file systems have some kind of metadata structure that indicates which of its blocks are in use and which are free. Obviously, such a structure makes space allocation fast. If this metadata structure is destroyed, it is still possible for a file system to identify free space by scanning other data structures, but it may take longer.
- ***Careful writing:*** File systems are carefully designed so that every metadata update leaves on-disk structures in a state that results in minimal structural damage if the update is interrupted or followed by a system crash. Thus, for example, when storage capacity is allocated, free space metadata is typically updated before the allocated space is used or linked into other structures. If a crash occurs between these two operations, the allocated but unlinked space may be "lost," but no data files are lost or destroyed.

The goal of these strategies is not to preserve file system metadata consistency at all costs—that would be too onerous. Instead, the goal is to enable the file system to restore metadata integrity within a reasonable amount of time after crash recovery.

File System Recovery Techniques

A computer can crash at any time, leaving a file system's on-disk metadata in disarray. In recovering from a crash, the file system must detect and repair any metadata inconsistencies on its virtual storage. The conventional technique for doing this is to scan all metadata, searching for inconsistencies. UNIX operating systems include a system utility program called the file system checker or **fsck** that performs this function. In Windows systems, a program called **chkdsk** performs the equivalent function. Both of these programs scan file system metadata for inconsistencies, and make repairs as necessary.

Repairs make use of metadata redundancy to restore consistency. In some cases, repair cannot be accomplished, because, for example, a system crashed before a sequence of metadata operations completed. For example, after recovery from a failure, a file system cannot complete a file creation if naming and attribute information are not persistently stored at the instant of a crash, and are therefore no longer available. What a file system *can* do is detect that space had been allocated but not used for any purpose recorded in file system metadata. This space can be restored to the free space pool, making it available for other postrecovery purposes, and avoiding shrinkage of the file system's available storage capacity. File system transactions in progress at the time of the crash are effectively nullified.

Although revalidation of file system metadata after crashes is an absolute necessity for data integrity, in a large file system containing millions of files it can literally take hours to accomplish. This is a problem for availability, because applications cannot be allowed to use files until file system integrity has been completely verified. Verifying the integrity of a large file system can result in lengthy crash recovery.

Cache and File System Metadata Integrity

Organizing data into files exacts a toll in system overhead. Creating a file may require several dozen disk accesses to locate and allocate the optimal free space, write metadata, and link it into existing directory structures. This overhead comes largely in the form of I/O requests, many of which are *serialized* (i.e., not allowed to occur concurrently) by careful writing techniques.

A busy enterprise computer system's file system might be performing dozens of metadata transactions at the same time. It's easy to imagine this activity being detrimental to application performance, because it absorbs some I/O capacity that applications might otherwise use. Moreover, reading or writing a disk takes time—typically a few milliseconds. A file system request that requires 50 disk accesses can take up to half a second, which becomes part of application response time.

The impact of metadata access on application performance was recognized relatively early in the history of file systems. To minimize it, most file systems *cache* metadata, and write updates to persistent storage *lazily*, after they have taken effect from the standpoint of applications and users. The result is markedly improved system performance. Application actions that affect file system metadata are accomplished by recording updates in a private cache. The updates are made permanent by writing them at low priority, effectively using gaps in application I/O streams.

Of course, almost all server-level cache is *volatile* (i.e., its contents are lost when the system crashes). If hundreds or thousands of metadata updates are cached but not yet written to disk when a system crashes, verification of file system metadata during recovery is that much more challenging. Entire file system transactions, including new file creations, old file deletions, and existing file extensions, might have been recorded only in cache. If a system crashes while its file system is in this state, files can be "lost," and deleted files can mysteriously reappear after recovery. For this reason, file systems that cache metadata updates, but do not have a mechanism for making metadata changes persistent, are unsuitable for managing critical enterprise data.

Logging: Fast Recovery and Improved Integrity

Some file systems implement a compromise strategy that minimizes the impact of metadata updates on application performance while limiting the potential impact of a system crash on file system recovery time: They log their intention to update metadata prior to actually performing the updates. The intent log is written to persistent storage before any file system data structures are actually updated.

With such a file system, each application request that requires file system metadata updates (e.g., when a file or directory is created, extended, or deleted) causes a representation of all the metadata updates necessary to complete the transaction to be written to a nonvolatile *log* before any metadata is actually modified. Thus, at any point in time a file system log is essentially an indicator of which metadata might be inconsistent after a crash.

When recovering after a system crash, a logging file system reads its log and verifies that all transactions indicated in it have been completed. It does this by checking its metadata against the log and completing any incomplete transactions. Because the number of file system transactions pending at any instant typically affects a tiny fraction of a large file system's metadata, replaying a log is normally *much* (orders of magnitude) faster than running **fsck** or **chkdsk** against the entire file system. Log playback instead of full file system metadata checking enables a file system to be used sooner after a crash, which in turn enables database recovery to start earlier, and ultimately increases application availability.

Obviously, a file system's log is key to data integrity in the event of a system crash. It is therefore prudent to use failure-tolerant storage to store it. Moreover, a file system log can (and should) be located on a separate virtual storage device than the file system's data area so that a failure of one virtual device does not destroy both the file system and the ability to recover it from its log.

FILE SYSTEM ADMINISTRATION WITH VIRTUAL STORAGE

As application data grows and otherwise changes over time, *reorganization* of the storage space it occupies is inevitably required. For example:

- As files are created and deleted, a file system's storage space becomes *fragmented,* leading to inefficient allocation, wasted space, and poor performance.
- As files and databases outgrow the storage capacity of a file system, they require larger storage devices.
- To balance I/O load, avoid impending device failures, and so forth, files and file systems must sometimes be relocated to alternate virtual storage devices.

Most of data storage reorganization amounts to moving data items from one place to another. Moving data *en bloc* can be counter to business requirements to maximize application availability, so file systems that can be administered while they are in use are a definite advantage. The following sections discuss three important file system administrative functions—defragmentation, file system expansion, and snapshot creation—that can be performed while a file system is mounted for use by applications.

Defragmentation

As applications run, files are created, extended, truncated, and deleted, continually allocating and freeing storage space. Over time, the storage space occupied by a file system becomes *fragmented,* as the right side of Figure D–3 illustrates, with files and small block ranges of free space intermixed. When a file system is in this condition, applications' file creation requests may fail, even though there is adequate free space to fulfill them. Even if noncontiguous space can be allocated, the overhead of accessing fragmented files reduces application I/O performance.

One way to eliminate fragmentation is to copy all files to an alternate empty file system in rapid succession. The resulting space allocation is as optimal as the file system's space allocation algorithms can make it, and free space is to be contiguous. This technique, of course, requires an "extra" virtual storage device whose capacity is equal to the size of the source file system. An alternative technique is to back up a fragmented file system, delete all files in it, and restore the backup. Again, new files are created in an empty file system in rapid succession, and the resulting allocation is likely to be optimal.

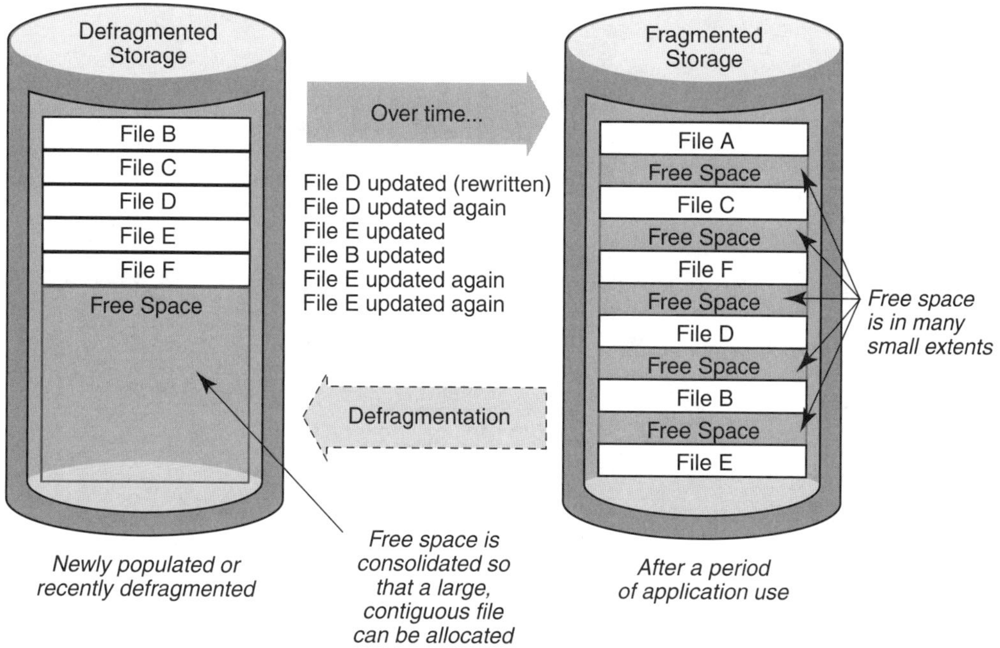

▼ **FIGURE D–3** *File System Fragmentation and Defragmentation*

Both of these techniques require that file systems be out of service for lengthy periods. This is generally unacceptable to critical applications. A preferable alternative is a file system that can defragment itself while it is in use by systematically moving files between ranges of virtual disk blocks to consolidate free space. File movement is transparent to applications, which access files identically before, during, and after they are relocated. Defragmenting a file system makes its files and directories contiguous, as the left side of Figure D–3 illustrates. Free space is consolidated in a small number of block ranges, making space allocation easier.

Moving a file that is not being used is easy—the file is copied and the original deleted. Moving a file that is being accessed by applications is more of a challenge. Figure D–4 illustrates one technique for moving files that are in use by applications.

To move a file that is in use, a file system first allocates destination space. It then locks and copies ranges of file blocks (extents). Metadata is updated to reflect new data locations as each block range is copied, and the moved block range is unlocked for application access. If an application accesses blocks that are being copied, its I/O request stalls until the

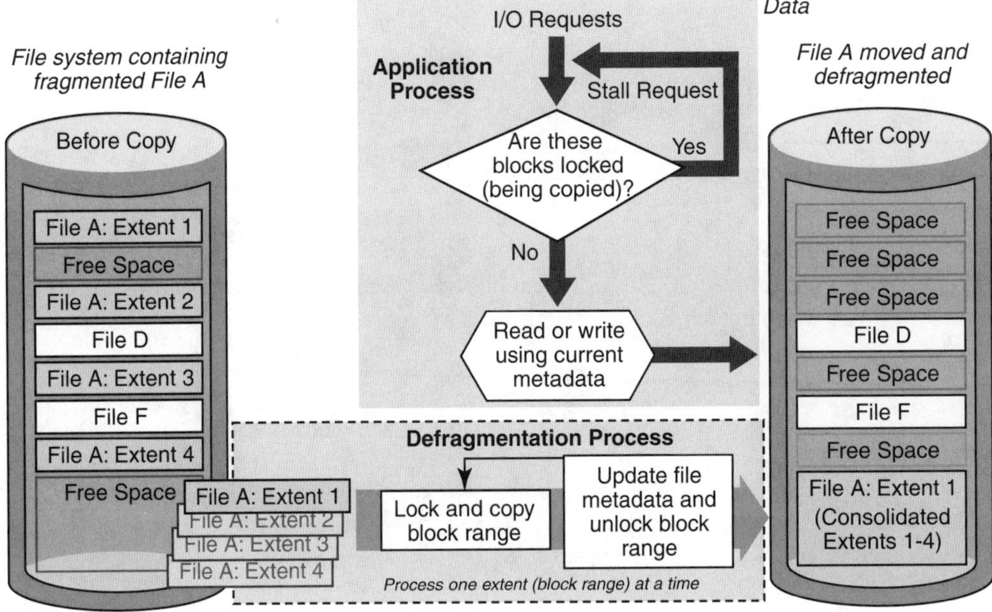

▼ **FIGURE D–4** *Moving an Open File*

move is complete. If the file system attempts to copy blocks that are being used by an application, *its* I/O stalls until the blocks are released.

Online Expansion

With rapid, unpredictable growth in online data, *storage capacity expansion* becomes a file system requirement. A file system's needs may outgrow its virtual storage device's capacity because it supports more users or applications, or because its store of historical data grows over time. Until storage virtualization technology became common, storage devices had fixed capacity, so when a file system needed more space, the only alternative was to move it to a larger storage device.

Unlike a disk drive, a virtual storage device *can* grow, through the addition of raw capacity and (possibly) reassignment of virtual block addresses to different LBAs. Growth of a virtual storage device, however, is of little value unless:

- ▼ The operating system controlling the virtual device can recognize the growth.
- ▼ The file system on the device can reorganize to use the additional space.

Operating systems have evolved from being unable to accommodate changing storage device capacities, to requiring a reboot to recognize a change in device capacity, to being fully capable of recognizing and responding to the fact that the capacity of a storage device has changed.

File systems have historically been limited in their ability to accommodate changing storage device capacities because their data structures are inflexible. For example, when a file system is created, it organizes a little of the capacity of its virtual device into root data structures, and the remainder into a pool of unallocated space. It is common to use a bitmap to manage free space, with each bit representing a number of consecutive blocks.

Although this technique is efficient, it does not accommodate changes in storage device capacity. If a file system runs low on free space, a new file system must be formatted on a larger storage device (with a larger free space bitmap) and files copied to it. In other words, the result of such a file system running low on space is application downtime while the file system is moved to a larger device. Other file system data structures may also be device-capacity dependent, either because they are proportional to device capacity like the free space bitmap in this example, or because they use fixed block addresses that depend on device capacity [for example, a data structure stored in the last (highest addressed) block of a storage device].

File systems whose data structures are based on a fixed storage device capacity must be moved even if their storage devices are virtual, and capable of online capacity expansion. Even though a device's capacity can expand, the file system cannot take advantage of that expansion, and must be reformatted for the larger device. This is usually done by making a full backup, deleting all files from the file system, reformatting it to use the larger device, and restoring the backup to the larger file system. Obviously, applications cannot use the file system while this is being done, and the larger the file system, the longer the period of outage.

If a file system is to expand to make use of an expanded storage device, its space management data structures must accommodate expansion. Thus, if a file system is to be able to make use of expanded virtual device capacity, it must have flexible space management mechanisms.

For an excellent reference on file system architecture, see *UNIX Filesystems: Evolution, Design, and Implementation* by Steve D. Pate, published by John Wiley and Sons; ISBN: 0-471-16483-6 (Jan. 2003).

APPENDIX E

Developments in Storage Network Technology

Several emerging storage networking technologies promise to further enhance information services. Use of TCP/IP networks for storage access will enable storage to be located thousands of kilometers from servers. Within the computer room, InfiniBand promises to increase inter-server communication speed, enabling higher-performing clusters and parallel databases.

Fibre Channel Enhancements

Like most computer-related technologies, Fibre Channel is evolving rapidly. Recently introduced enhancements include:

- A 2-gigabit data rate for switches, directors, HBAs, and storage devices
- New standards for routing, zoning, and ISLs that enhance interoperability

Enhancements expected in the future include:

- 10-gigabit data transfer speed
- Autonomous regions
- Bridging over other wide area interconnects such as ATM and SONET

These enhancements will increase Fibre Channel storage network performance and enable greater separation between devices for wide area clustering, remote backup, and remote mirroring and replication.

InfiniBand

Server I/O buses (e.g., PCI) are located within the server enclosure, and bridge between I/O interconnects and memory controllers over distances

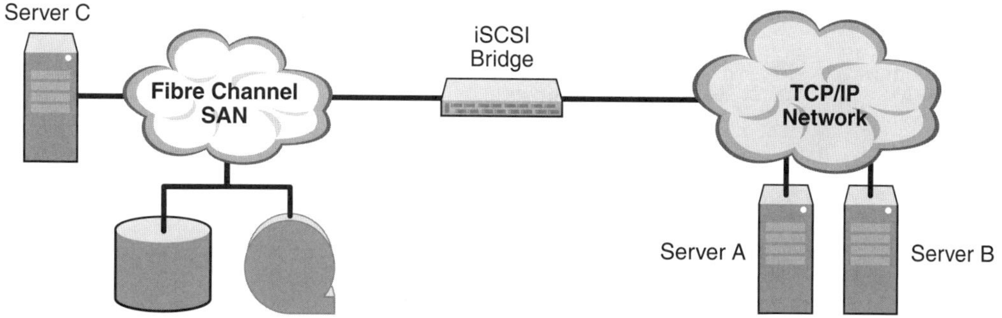

▼ **FIGURE E–1** *Wide Area Storage Network Using iSCSI over TCP/IP*

of inches. InfiniBand is designed to replace these buses with an external network architecture that enables an I/O bus to extend for up to about 100 meters. InfiniBand uses 2.5-gigabit-per-second connections that can be configured in 10-gigabit and 30-gigabit bundles, and supports low overhead memory-to-memory transfers. Point-to-point and switched fabric topologies can be configured.

InfiniBand is expected to be an inter-server interconnect to which Fibre Channel and gigabit Ethernet networks will attach. InfiniBand is expected to be an important enabler for application clusters and parallel databases because it enables ultra-low latency messaging between servers.

iSCSI (Block Storage Access Using TCP/IP)

iSCSI is a TCP/IP ULP that sends SCSI block data access commands over TCP/IP networks. iSCSI components include HBAs, RAID systems, and switches that interconnect servers and storage devices. One anticipated effect of iSCSI is lower storage networking cost, making the technology available to smaller systems. iSCSI technology will also enable remote servers to back up with Fibre Channel-based disk and tape devices directly, as Figure E–1 illustrates, without the use of a backup server.

FCIP

FCIP tunnels Fibre Channel protocols through TCP/IP networks, connecting widely separated Fibre Channel *SAN islands* into a single storage network, as Figure E–2 illustrates. FCIP *gateways* tunnel Fibre Channel frames by encapsulating them in TCP/IP packets. Storage networks

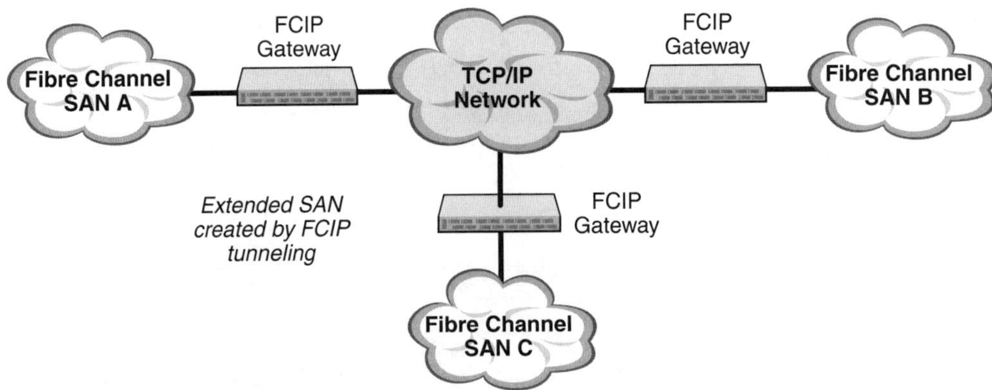

▼ **FIGURE E–2** *Wide Area Storage Network Using FCIP to Connect SAN Islands*

interconnected by FCIP share a common Fibre Channel name and address space.

FCIP enables Fibre Channel storage networks to extend beyond 100 kilometers, for example, for remote mirroring and extended backup and restore.[1] FCIP interconnects local, campus, or metropolitan SAN islands into global storage networks, much as LAN segments are interconnected.

iFCP

An alternative to FCIP tunneling is to base the entire storage network on TCP/IP protocols. Figure E–3 illustrates *iFCP gateways* that connect Fibre Channel servers and storage devices to a TCP/IP network. This technology is useful for reducing storage network cost, thereby making the technology practical for a broader range of systems.

1. However, the latency of sending data over a 100-kilometer TCP/IP network may be unacceptable for application responsiveness.

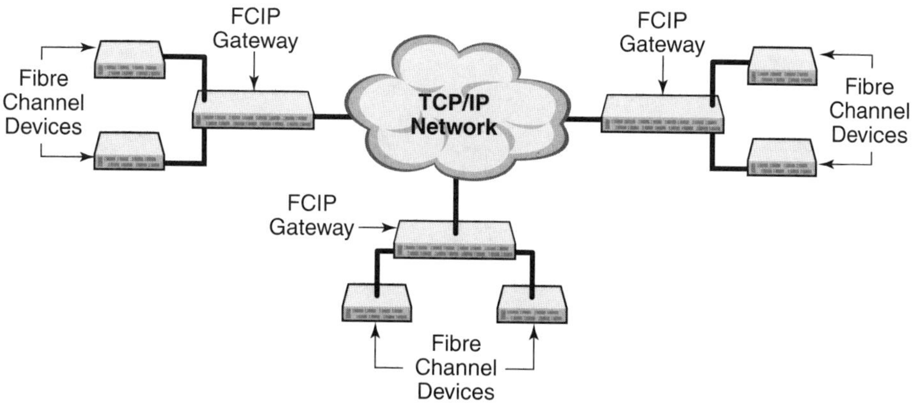

▼ **FIGURE E–3** *Wide Area Storage Network Using iFCP to Connect Fibre Channel Devices to a TCP/IP Network*

APPENDIX F

The Nature of Availability

This appendix on the nature of availability is adapted from work by Evan Marcus, principal engineer in the VERITAS Product Operations department. The author is grateful for Evan's framing the topic in this way, and for permission to adapt the formulation for this book.

AVAILABILITY: ORDINARY AND HIGH

Historically, the most important reason for virtualizing online storage has been to improve its availability. One source[1] defines *availability* as:

> ***availability*** *n: the quality of being at hand when needed.*

Online storage is *available* if it is at hand for use when required. This definition is at the same time simple and profound. It is simple because anyone can relate to it. Storage is available if applications can read and write data when they have to. The definition is profound because it expresses a requirement. According to it, storage devices can be serviced when applications are not using them without loss of availability.

This definition suggests a fundamental principle of available system design—storage should be configured to maximize the likelihood that it will be available when needed. There is little reason for mirrored storage on laptop computers. Mission-critical server applications, on the other hand, usually require online storage that is essentially unbreakable. Storage architecture may be defined as assessing availability requirements and configuring equipment and procedures that meet them.

1. http://www.dictionary.com

The Availability Continuum

This definition of availability oversimplifies two important factors:

- ***Performance:*** "At hand" may not be a binary state. Virtual storage systems are often designed so that component failures leave the system functional, but with reduced performance.
- ***Function:*** Some failures may leave virtual storage partially functional. For example, a network-attached storage device may continue to serve files, even though failed communications prevent it from making remote backups.

The same dictionary, in fact, recognizes this in a secondary definition of availability:

> ***availability:*** *<system> The degree to which a system suffers degradation or interruption in its service to the customer as a consequence of failures of one or more of its parts.*[2]

The storage architect's challenge is to balance I/O performance and availability requirements against cost constraints to construct storage systems that best meet enterprise needs.

High availability is one of information technology's most cherished, and yet least well-defined concepts. The term is regularly used to describe computer systems and components in the sense of:

- ***Goals, rather than results:*** Promoters of highly available systems typically do not assert that their systems will be "at hand when needed," but that they are designed to withstand certain component failures. For example, RAID systems are typically designed to withstand disk, power and cooling, external interface, and cache failures, but not to meet specific data availability or performance goals.
- ***Relativity to an implicit norm:*** Highly available systems are positioned as being more available than (usually unnamed) systems of "ordinary" availability. A hint about the roots of this usage may be found in the same online dictionary:

  > ***high*** *adj 1: greater than normal in degree or intensity or amount.*[3]

2. Ibid.
3. http://www.dictionary.com/cgi-bin/dict.pl?term=high (citing WordNet ® 1.6, © 1997 Princeton University)

In other words, "high" typically does not refer to a specific level, but to one that is relatively great. A RAID system may be highly available compared to a disk system without RAID, but not as highly available as two RAID systems coordinated by a server-based volume manager.

An Alternative Definition

Storage virtualization enables the construction of storage systems that can tolerate and recover from a wide variety of failures and disasters. In designing a virtual storage system, storage architects must think in terms of system and enterprise requirements. The result should be a level of availability implied by a design that is expected to meet or exceed the requirements for which the storage system is implemented.

Design Parameters for High Availability

In designing highly available storage, there are two critical parameters:

- How often must the system be available? (What is its *duty cycle*?)
- What are the consequences if the system is not available?

Figure F–1 uses a two-dimensional graph to position four well-known highly available systems relative to these five considerations:

- ***Flight control system:*** Airlines try to maximize equipment utilization, so an airplane's control system has a relatively high (although not continuous) duty cycle. The consequences of failure can be severe, so this application is positioned high and to the right in Figure F–1.
- ***Vital sign monitor:*** A hospital's vital sign monitor typically has a medium duty cycle, with potentially severe failure consequences (patient death), but less so than an airliner flight control system (mass death).
- ***Drone flight control system:*** A drone aircraft, as used in military operations, may fly only once. The duty cycle of its control system is therefore relatively low. The consequences of failure are typically a failed mission, which may be less severe than those of the preceding examples.
- ***Internet gaming:*** Internet gaming has become very popular, particularly in Asia. Online gaming services typically operate around the clock. The consequences of failure of these systems, however, are purely financial, and for individual users, are quite low.

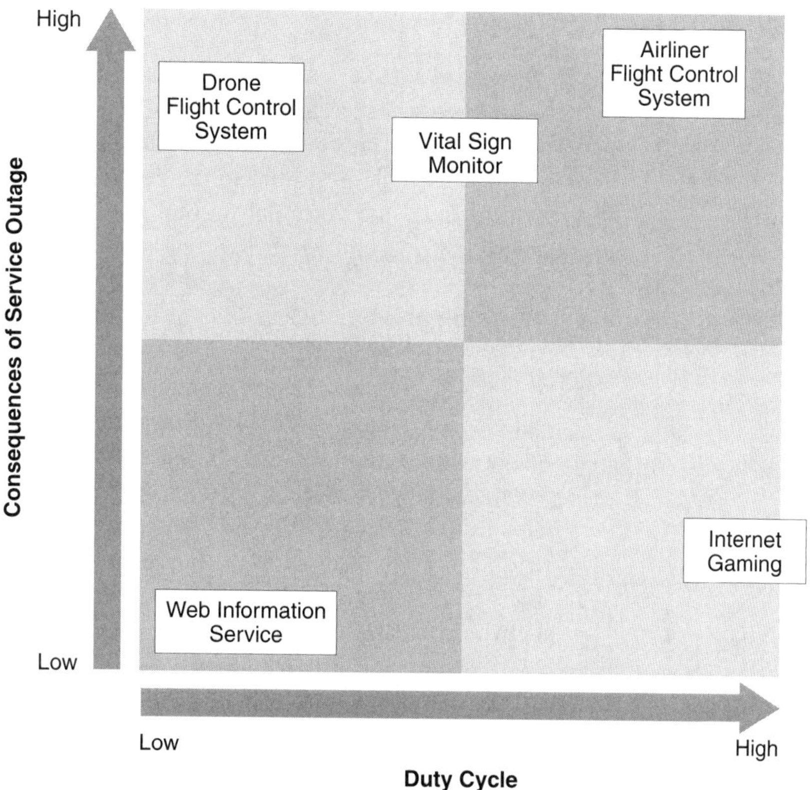

▼ **FIGURE F–1** *Highly Available System Design Considerations*

- ***Web information service:*** Low-value Web information services are used infrequently for short periods. The consequences of outage are low—users will typically resort to alternatives or forgo the service.

All of these systems might use virtualization to make their storage highly available. Their usage might be quite different, however, because duty cycles and the consequences of failure differ. For example, it is worth almost any cost to provide continuous reliable data to airliners' control systems. An Internet gaming server's storage design, on the other hand, would typically give more attention to performance.

"NINES" OF AVAILABILITY

Discussions of virtual storage availability often mention the number of "nines" offered by different technologies. One hears of three (99.9%), four (99.99%), or five nines (99.999%) of estimated uptime. These percentages, shown in Table F–1, refer to the percentage of time during which a system is operational. Although "nines" are an interesting way to express availability, they ignore some essential factors:

- ***The time at which downtime occurs is significant.*** An outage that stops users from working is more costly than one that merely inconveniences them. An inconveniencing outage is more costly than one (like a disk failure in a RAID array) that is undetectable. For example, a RAID system might experience a single thirty-minute outage to replace a failed cache during the course of a year, for an apparently respectable 99.994% uptime.[4] But if the outage occurs during a year-end closing, it is much more significant than if it can be scheduled for a relatively quiet period. Uptime percentage does not distinguish between the two.

▼ TABLE F–1 *Percentage of Downtime per Year ("The Nines")*

Percentage Uptime	Downtime per Year[5]	Downtime per Week
98%	7.3 days	3.3 hours
99%	3.65 days	1.7 hours
99.9%	8.75 hours	10.1 minutes
99.99%	52.5 minutes	1 minute
99.999%	5.25 minutes	6 seconds
99.9999%	31.5 seconds	0.6 second

4. Based on a 100% duty cycle of 8760 hours/year. 8759.5 ÷ 8760 – 0.99994.
5. Assuming a 100% duty cycle, or required in-service time.

- ***The number of outages may be as significant as total downtime.*** One thirty-minute outage per year might be inconvenient, but thirty one-minute outages over the same period can be considerably more disruptive.

Some component suppliers specify uptime percentages for their products. Though useful, these are not indicative of overall information service uptime. The number of components in a system, the interconnections and interactions among them, and external factors make calculating uptime impossibly complex.

Glossary of Terminology

This glossary defines terminology used in this book and in other information services contexts. Some of the definitions have been created by the author, while others are reproduced by permission from the online dictionary maintained by the Storage Networking Industry Association (SNIA), whose contribution is gratefully acknowledged. The definitions contributed by the SNIA are reproduced without alteration, and are set in gray boxes. The online dictionary from which they are drawn can be found at http://www.snia.org/dictionary. It is updated regularly as technology evolves, and the terminology used to describe it adapts to the evolution. Definitions that are not identified as SNIA contributions are the responsibility of the author.

access path
CONTEXT [**Storage System**]
The combination of host bus adapter, logical unit number, route through the host-storage interconnect, controller, and logical unit used by a computer to communicate with a storage device. Some configurations support multiple access paths to a single device. *cf.* multipath I/O

access token mechanism
The mechanism used by object storage devices to determine the validity of client requests. An object manager returns an access token to a client as part of granting access to an object. At the same time, it notifies the object storage device that it has given out an access token. When the client accesses the device, its access token is found to be valid and its request is honored.

active-active (components, controllers)
CONTEXT [**Storage System**]
Synonym for dual active components or controllers.

active-active (redundant system)
A type of system with redundant components in which the redundant components are installed and powered, but do no work until they are required to replace the function of failed components with which they are redundant.

active-passive (redundant system)
A type of system with redundant components in which the redundant components share in the workload when the entire system is functional.

actuator
A component of a disk drive that moves one or more read-write heads relative to spinning media for the purpose of reading or overwriting particular blocks of data on the media.

administrator
A person charged with the installation, configuration, and management of a computer system, network, storage system, database, or application.

agent
A software component that provides an interface between a client and the services of a server. Agents are generally used to enable interoperation between clients and servers that were not designed to be aware of each other.

aggregation
The virtualization of two or more storage devices so that they behave as a single device.

allocation unit
The fixed-size unit of storage capacity used by a file system or database management system for internal allocation. An allocation unit is usually expressed in storage device blocks (also of fixed capacity).

alternate path restore
CONTEXT [Backup]
The process of restoring files to a different directory than the one from which they were backed up.

API
Acronym for Application Programming Interface.

application programming interface
An interface used by an application program to request services. Abbreviated API. The term API is usually used to denote interfaces between applications and the software components that comprise the operating environment (e.g., operating system, file system, volume manager, device drivers, etc.)

archive log
A saved copy of a segment of a database log. Archive logs can be used to reconstruct a correct database state at any point in time over an entire database generation.

array
(1) Two or more storage devices managed by a common body of array management software. (2) A RAID or RAIT system. This book uses the first definition exclusively.

asymmetric (file system architecture)
An architecture for cluster file systems in which one server, called the master server, writes all metadata changes (create and delete files and so forth) to the virtual device that holds the file system. In an asymmetric file system architecture all other servers that mount the file system request that changes be made by the master server.

asynchronous replication
A form of data replication in which completion of I/O operations is signaled to applications before receipt of data is acknowledged by target locations. Asynchronous replication generally results in better application performance than synchronous replication, but introduces the risk that target location replicas can be "out of date."

atomic operation
An indivisible operation that, from an external perspective, occurs either in its entirety or not at all. For example, database management systems that implement the concept of business transactions treat each business transaction as an atomic operation on the database. This means that either all of the database updates that comprise a transaction are performed or none of them are performed; it is never the case that some of them are performed and others not. RAID arrays must implement atomic write operations to properly reproduce single-disk semantics from the perspective of their clients. Atomic operations are required to ensure that component failures do not corrupt stored data.

authentication

CONTEXT [Network]

The process of determining what principal a requestor or provider of services is or represents.

CONTEXT [Security]

A security measure designed to establish the validity of a transmission, message, or originator, or a means of verifying an individual's authorization to receive information.

authorization

CONTEXT [Network]

The process of determining that a requestor is allowed to receive a service or perform an operation. Access control is an example of authorization.

CONTEXT [Security]

The limiting of usage of information system resources to authorized users, programs, processes, or other systems. Access control is a specific type of authorization. Authorization is formally described as controlling usage by subjects of objects.

automatic backup

CONTEXT [Backup]

A backup triggered by an event (e.g., a schedule point, or a threshold reached) rather than by human action.

automatic failover

Failover that occurs without human intervention.

automatic swap

The substitution of a replacement unit (RU) in a system for a defective one, where the substitution is performed by the system itself while it continues to perform its normal function (possibly at a reduced rate of performance). Automatic swaps are functional rather than physical substitutions, and do not require human intervention. Ultimately, however, defective components must be replaced in a physical hot, warm, or cold swap operation. *cf.* cold swap, hot swap, warm swap, hot spare

availability

The amount of time that a system is available during those time periods when it is expected to be available. Availability is often measured as a percentage of an elapsed year. For example, 99.95% availability equates to 4.38 hours of downtime in a year ($0.0005 \times 365 \times 24 = 4.38$) for a system that is expected to be available all the time. *cf.* data availability, high

availability cluster

Synonym for failover cluster.

average response time

The average of the response times for a large number of service requests.

backup client

A computer system that controls data that must be backed up by and restored from a separate backup server.

backup mode

A mode of database operation in which hot database manager backups are run. When a database manager is in backup mode, sufficient information is logged to reconstruct a consistent database to be reconstructed even though the backup does not represent a point-in-time image of database data.

backup server

A computer system that performs backups and restores for other computer systems, receiving the data to be backed up over an enterprise or storage network.

backup window

The interval during which data must remain unaltered so that a consistent backup copy can be made.

block device
block storage device

A disk drive-like abstraction implemented by virtualization software. Block storage devices are like disk drives in that they contain numbered blocks of storage capacity that can be read and persistently written in any order. They are unlike disk drives in that their storage capacity can be enlarged or reduced, they can survive failures of the physical devices on which they are based, and they have special properties such as the ability to produce snapshots of their contents.

block-level incremental backup
An incremental backup in which the copied objects are virtual device blocks that have changed since some prior backup. Block-level incremental backup is particularly useful with databases that use container files for data storage.

block virtualization
block storage virtualization
block storage device virtualization
The implementation of an ideal behavioral model for a block storage device. Block virtualization may be implemented by a RAID system, a server-based volume manager, or a network storage appliance.

bridge
A storage network component used to connect one or more devices whose communication protocols are different from those of the network. A storage network bridge converts between the protocols and data formats used on the network and those expected by the devices.

business continuity
Continuation of some or all of an enterprise's operations in the event of unforeseen events, including disasters that have a negative effect on the enterprise's ability to operate.

cascade topology
A Fibre Channel storage network topology in which there are two end switches or directors, each of which is connected to exactly one other switch or director. All remaining switches in a cascade topology are connected to exactly two other switches.

causality
The principle that if two processes in a computer system are permitted to proceed concurrently, neither can be dependent on the completion of the other. Causality is used in some data replication implementations to determine which replica I/O operations can proceed concurrently with each other and which must be delayed until others complete.

CDB
Acronym for command data block.

change map
A data structure associated with some copy-on-write snapshots. A change map contains the locations of blocks that have changed since the moment of snapshot initiation and the locations of private data areas used to hold the prior contents of changed blocks.

check data
Information derived by performing some computation on a fixed set of user data that can be used to determine whether the user data is valid, and, in some cases, to reconstruct it if it is partially destroyed. Cyclic redundancy checks, error correction codes, mirrors, and RAID parity are all forms of check data.

C-H-S (addressing)
Synonym for cylinder-head-sector addressing.

CIFS
Acronym for Common Internet File Services.

client-server (architecture)
An architecture for distributed computer systems in which some computers (the servers) deliver services to other computers (the clients) over a network. File and database servers are two of the most common uses of client-server architecture.

cluster

A collection of computers that are interconnected (typically at high-speeds) for the purpose of improving reliability, availability, serviceability and/or performance (via load balancing). Often, clustered computers have access to a common pool of storage, and run special software to coordinate the component computers' activities.

clustering

The employment of cluster technology to solve data processing problems.

cluster manager

The software component that manages interactions among the servers comprising a cluster. Cluster managers are responsible for monitoring resource and application service group status, and for conducting failover according to predefined policies.

cold backup

A backup of a set of data made while the data is not in use by applications.

command data block

The SCSI protocol's data structure by which an initiator conveys I/O and control commands to a target device.

Common Internet File Services

A file access protocol used to access files stored on network attached storage devices.

container file

A file used as a data container by a database management system. Database managers organize the block storage capacity in container files just as they organize the raw block storage capacity presented by disk drives or LUNs. *cf.* raw

control software

Software that virtualizes storage devices. Control software may run in a server (usually called a volume manager), in a RAID system's control processor, or in a storage appliance or other network virtualization device.

copy-on-write (snapshot)

A snapshot of a virtual block storage device or file system in which changes to the device or file system made after the snapshot is initiated cause the data being changed to be sequestered in a changed data area for future retrieval. When a copy-on-write snapshot is mounted for use, unmodified data is read from its original virtual device location. Modified data is read from the changed data area.

core-edge topology

A Fibre Channel storage network topology in which core switches interconnect edge switches and each other. Edge switches' primary function is to connection storage devices and servers to the network.

core switch

A switch in a Fibre Channel core-edge topology storage network whose primary function is to interconnect other switches.

crash consistency

A property of database and file system replicas that enables them to be restored to a consistent (although not necessarily completely current) state when they are mounted after an unrecoverable failure of the master database or file system.

cylinder

The set of tracks on all of a disk drive's recording surfaces that have the same nominal radius (whose blocks are at the same nominal distance from the disk drive's center of rotation).

cylinder-head-sector addressing

A form of addressing data stored on a disk in which the cylinder, head/platter combination, and relative sector number on a track are specified. Abbreviated C-H-S addressing. *cf.* block addressing

dark fiber

An optical fiber used for point-to-point data communications that does not include a preconfigured protocol or signaling convention. Dark fiber can be used to implement any protocol by the addition of compatible conversion devices at each end, or it can be configured to carry multiple protocols concurrently by the addition of a dense wave division multiplexer at each end.

data currency
data freshness
The difference between the point in time to which operational data is restored after a disaster, and the time at which the restoration is complete. For example, if it takes two days to restore a backup that is four days old at the time of the disaster, the data currency is six days—restored data is six days out of date.

data replication
The copying of updates to a set of data to remote storage devices as the updates occur. Updates to database, file, or virtual block storage devices can be replicated. Replication can be synchronous, with updates being copied in lockstep, or it can be asynchronous, with copying of updates being allowed to lag by a bounded amount. Replication differs from mirroring in that it is designed to deal with high-latency and unreliable network connections.

data sharing
Coordinated simultaneous access of data by two or more clients. Disks, virtual block storage devices, file systems, and files may all be shared by multiple applications running on the same or different application servers. Data sharing requires coordination of client accesses so that data's functional correctness is preserved when multiple clients read or update data simultaneously.

database cache
A cache used by a database manager to improve database access performance. A database cache is a common memory pool accessible by both the application interface threads and read/write threads of the database manager.

database file
Synonym for container file.

database log
A log in which a database manager records events and data that might be of significance to recovery or roll-back.

database manager
Synonym for database management system.

database management system
A suite of data management software that organizes data independently of applications, imposes syntactic and semantic constraints on it, and maintains transactional integrity. Abbreviated DBMS.

database page
A fixed number of consecutively numbered blocks used by database managers as the unit in which I/O requests are made and storage space is managed.

DBMS
Acronym for database management system.

defragmentation
The movement of the data areas of files within a file system for the purpose of consolidating fragmented files and unallocated space. Defragmentation usually improves access performance by reducing the amount of overhead I/O required to locate file blocks in a file system.

degraded operation interval
The period of time during which a system operates in a degraded fashion after recovery from a failure or disaster. Abbreviated DOI. During a degraded operation interval, a system may operate at reduced performance and/or with increased susceptibility to a second failure.

dense wave division multiplexing
A technique for transmitting data over optical fiber in which multiple streams of data (possibly formatted using different protocols) are transmitted by modulating light streams of different wavelengths.

deployment
The process of placing a set of storage resources into service.

director
An enterprise-class switch, typically with built-in redundant components for internal failure tolerance. Directors typically include more ports (64+) than switches (8+).

disk array
An array of disks.

disk system
A storage system whose persistent storage devices are disk drives.

distributed (file system architecture)
Synonym for symmetric file system architecture.

DOI
Acronym for degraded operation interval.

downtime
Synonym for recovery time.

droop
In optical data transmission, a decrease in effective data transfer rate that results from increasing the distance over which data is transmitted.

dual active (components)
A pair of components, such as the controllers in a failure tolerant storage subsystem that share a task or class of tasks when both are functioning normally. When one of the components fails, the other takes on the entire task. Dual active controllers are connected to the same set of storage devices, improve both I/O performance and failure tolerance compared to a single controller. Dual active components are also called active-active components.

duty cycle
The percentage of time during which a system is actively performing its function. A system that serves users for 8 hours a day during 5 workdays per week has a duty cycle of 23.8% (40 of 168 hours).

DWDM
Acronym for dense wave division multiplexing.

DWDM multiplexer
A multiplexer that accepts multiple inputs, converts them to modulated optical signals of different base wavelengths, and transmits them concurrently on a single dark fiber.

edge switch
A switch in a Fibre Channel core-edge topology storage network whose primary function is to connect storage devices and servers to the network.

fabric-based zoning
A form of zoning implemented by cooperation of the switches and directors that comprise a Fibre Channel storage network.

failback
The restoration of a failed system component's share of a load to a replacement component. For example, when a failed controller in a redundant configuration is replaced, the devices that were originally controlled by the failed controller are usually failed back to the replacement controller to restore the I/O balance, and to restore failure tolerance. Similarly, when a defective fan or power supply is replaced, its load, previously borne by a redundant component can be failed back to the replacement part.

failover
The automatic substitution of a functionally equivalent system component for a failed one. The term failover is most often applied to intelligent controllers connected to the same storage devices and host computers. If one of the controllers fails, failover occurs, and the survivor takes over its I/O load.

failover cluster

A cluster whose sole purpose is to increase application availability by enabling failover from one server to another.

failover management software

Software that automates and manages the failover of a set of applications from one server to another within a cluster.

failover server

In a cluster, a server that is designated to restart an application service group if the service group's primary server fails.

failure

A malfunction of a system or a component in a system that impedes the system from performing its intended function or renders it unable to perform entirely.

failure tolerance

The ability of a system to continue to perform its function (possibly at a reduced performance level) when one or more of its components has failed. Failure tolerance in disk systems is often achieved by including redundant instances of components whose failure would make the system inoperable, coupled with facilities that allow the redundant components to assume the function of failed ones. *cf.* failure, fault

fast resynchronization
fast mirror resynchronization

A form of mirrored array resynchronization in which entries in a log of changed blocks are used to determine which blocks need to be recopied to a split mirror that is being rejoined.

fault

Synonym for failure.

FCP

Acronym for Fibre Channel Protocol.

Fibre Channel Protocol

A Fibre Channel Upper Layer Protocol that maps the commands, messages, and data transfer conventions of the SCSI protocol to Fibre Channel transport protocols.

file access client

A software component that runs in an application server and issues file I/O commands to a file server on behalf of applications or data managers.

file server

A server in a client-server architecture whose primary function is to respond to client requests for file access services (create, delete, open, close, read, write, etc.). A file server that is designed specifically and exclusively for the purpose of serving files is sometimes called a network-attached storage device (NAS device).

file system

(1) A suite of software programs that collectively implement a file abstraction for computer system applications.
(2) A virtual storage device that has been formatted by file system software to store and retrieve files.

file system block

Synonym for allocation unit.

flat Fibre Channel storage network

A Fibre Channel storage network in which all devices are able to intercommunicate. A flat Fibre Channel storage network does not implement zoning.

flat file

A file whose data has no structural relationships with data in other files. The term flat file is often used to contrast with databases, which do maintain structural relationships among the data objects they store. *cf.* container file

flush

(transitive verb) To write to persistent storage. Typically used in connection with data managed by file systems and database managers to denote the process of writing data that has been updated in cache to persistent storage.

footprint

Presence. A virtualizer is said to have a footprint in a storage network device if one or more of its software components runs in that device. For example, an out-of-band storage network virtualizer necessarily has a footprint in each participating application server.

frozen image

A physical or virtual copy of a set of data (usually the contents of one or more virtual devices or file systems) as it appeared at some single point in time. Snapshots of data are frozen images. Frozen images of file systems or virtual block storage devices are useful for making consistent backups.

full backup

A backup that contains a copy of all the data in a file system or database.

functional transparency

A property of changes made to a component in a system. If a change to a component is functionally transparent, other components cannot detect that the change has been made by virtue of a change in the operation of the subject component. (Detection of functionally transparent changes by altered performance or reliability may be possible.) From a file system and database manager standpoint, a change from a physical storage device to a virtualized one is functionally transparent.

GBIC

Acronym for gigabit interface converter. *cf.* GLM

geometry

The characteristics of a disk that relate to how data blocks are laid out on media surfaces. Geometry includes the number of tracks, surfaces, and the number of blocks per track in each recording zone. For compatibility with client software, virtual block storage devices present geometries, although these are typically arbitrary, and do not relate to physical data block locations.

gigabaud link module

A transceiver that converts between electrical signals used by host bus adapters (and similar Fibre Channel devices) and either electrical or optical signals suitable for transmission. Abbreviated GLM. Gigabaud link modules allow designers to design one type of device and adapt it for either copper or optical applications. Gigabaud link modules are used less often than gigabit interface converters because they cannot be hot swapped. *cf.* gigabit interface converter

gigabit interface converter

A transceiver that converts between electrical signals used by host bus adapters (and similar Fibre Channel and Ethernet devices) and either electrical or optical signals suitable for transmission. Abbreviated GBIC. Gigabit interface converters allow designers to design one type of device and adapt it for either copper or optical applications. Unlike gigabaud link modules (GLMs), GBICs can be hot swapped, and are therefore gradually supplanting the former type of transceiver. *cf.* gigabaud link module

GLM

Acronym for gigabaud link module. *cf.* GBIC

HBA

Acronym for host bus adapter.

heterogeneity

An architectural or physical difference in two storage system components that affects their ability to be commonly used or managed. Heterogeneity is encountered in operating system block storage device formats, storage device interconnect types, disk drive types, and so forth. Some systems are designed to cope with heterogeneity, for example, file servers can provide their services to heterogeneous clients as long as the clients implement the appropriate network file access protocols. Other systems are restricted to homogeneous components, as, for example, clusters, which are normally able to incorporate only systems of the same architecture and operating system release level. *cf.* homogeneity

hierarchical storage management
A technique for managing the block storage space occupied by large numbers of files by moving less-frequently accessed files to (presumably lower-cost) secondary storage and reclaiming the primary storage space they occupy for other use. Abbreviated HSM. Hierarchical storage management moves, or *migrates*, files in such a way that they can be recalled transparently (as if they were still in their original locations) when applications access them.

hierarchical storage manager
A software suite that performs hierarchical storage management.

high availability
The ability of a system to perform its function continuously (without interruption) for a significantly longer period of time than the reliabilities of its individual components would suggest. High availability is most often achieved through failure tolerance. High availability is not an easily quantifiable term. Both the bounds of a system that is called highly available and the degree to which its availability is extraordinary must be clearly understood on a case-by-case basis.

homogeneity
The property of being alike in all material respects, and therefore amenable to common control or management. The servers that comprise a cluster must normally be homogeneous, meaning that all must run the same version of the same operating system, but need not be alike in nonmaterial respects, such as processor model or memory complement. *cf.* heterogeneity

host-based zoning
A form of zoning implemented by software that runs in servers connected to a Fibre Channel storage network.

host bus adapter
A device that provides an interface between a computer's internal I/O bus and an external I/O bus or storage network.

hot backup
A backup of a set of data made while the data is in use by applications. Hot backups may be made from snapshots that freeze an image of the data while applications continue to update it, or they may be "fuzzy," and not represent a consistent data state. In order for data to be restorable to a consistent state from a fuzzy backup, a log of data updates made while the backup was in progress is required.

HSM
Acronym for hierarchical storage management.

in-band (virtualization)
A form of block storage virtualization in which the virtualization metadata is managed by the same array management software that performs block address translation for I/O requests. Volume managers and RAID systems are examples of in-band virtualizers. *cf.* in-band (virtualization) [cross reference should probably be out-of-band virtualization]

incremental backup
A form of backup in which only data objects that have changed since some prior backup are copied. Individual data objects can be restored from incremental backups, but restoring an entire file system or database requires both a baseline full backup and a complete sequence of incremental backups.

information processing
information processing service
Synonyms for information service.

information service
A service related to the handling and processing of information. Abbreviated IS. Information services are typically provided by departments that are specifically responsible for that function. These are often called IS departments.

Usage note: information services departments are typically responsible for deploying information technology.

information technology
A collective term for equipment, software, and other facilities used to process computer information, or to provide information services.

inter-switch link
In a Fibre Channel storage network, a point-to point link used to interconnect E-ports on two switches or directors.

I/O path
Synonym for access path.

I/O software stack
I/O stack
The collection of server software components that process an application's I/O request. The I/O stack typically consists of file system, volume manager, and one or more I/O device drivers. In database applications, a database manager is added to the stack.

IS
Acronym for information services.

ISL
Acronym for inter-switch link.

IT
Acronym for information technology.

LBA
Acronym for logical block address.

locality
In a Fibre Channel storage network, the percentage of devices that are connected to the same switch as other devices with which they communicate.

log
A persistent record of an action taken or contemplated stored on a different virtual device from the one on which the action is taken. A log can be used in conjunction with an out-of-date frozen image of a set of data to reconstruct a more up-to-date image, or to reverse the effect of selected actions on the data, restoring it to an image that was valid at an earlier time.

logical (database) backup
A database backup in which the objects copied are database objects rather than the underlying storage objects.

logical block
A block of fixed capacity on a virtual block storage device in which data can be stored. Addressed with a logical block address (LBA).

logical block address
A number that uniquely identifies a logical block on a disk drive or virtual block storage device.

logical unit
A virtual storage device presented by a physical storage device over a network or I/O bus. Abbreviated LUN. (The acronym LUN actually stands for logical unit number, but is universally used to refer to logical units as well as the numbers by which they are addressed.)

logical volume manager
Synonym for volume manager.

long-wave fiber
Synonym for single-mode fiber.

loop topology
A Fibre Channel storage network topology that uses the arbitrated loop (FC-AL) protocols to intercommunicate between devices connected to each other in a loop. In an FC-AL loop topology, one pair of devices at a time can intercommunicate. Fibre Channel loop topology networks are used primarily to connect low-cost devices, such as disk drives, to initiators.

LUN
Acronym for logical unit (number).

LUN masking
A technique used by storage appliances and RAID systems to selectively limit the set of clients to which to which LUNs are presented. LUN masking is a form of storage network security.

mapping
The conversion between virtual device block addresses and block addresses on physical storage devices or LUNs.

master-slave (file system architecture)
Synonym for asymmetric file system architecture.

mean time between failures
A statistical measure of reliability. Abbreviated MTBF. The mean time between failures is the average interval between device failures in a large population of devices operating under identical circumstances.

mean time to repair
A statistical measure of reliability. Abbreviated MTTR. The mean time to repair is the average time required to restore a failed device to operational status, either by repairing it or replacing it. In the context of virtual storage arrays, mean time to repair a failed storage device includes the time required to restore the data on the repaired or replacement device to a state consistent with the remainder of the array.

mesh topology
A Fibre Channel storage network topology in which there are multiple connections between switches and directors.

metadata
Data that describes data. In disk arrays, metadata consists of items such as array membership, member extent sizes and locations, descriptions of logical disk drives and partitions, and array state information. In file systems, metadata includes file names, file properties and security information, and lists of block addresses at which each file's data is stored.

metadata server
A server that manages virtualization metadata for one or more address translation instances. Metadata servers are typically embedded in volume managers, RAID system control software, and in in-band appliance control software. Out-of-band virtualizers typically rely on external metadata servers.

metadata management appliance
A component of an out-of-band storage virtualizer that manages the metadata used for address translation between virtual objects and the physical objects used to instantiate them. Metadata managers are typically integrated with other components in in-band virtualizers. In out-of-band virtualizers, they are usually implemented in separate appliances that provide services to distributed address translation components running in the virtual storage clients.

migration
The act of copying data objects from one storage device to another. Hierarchical storage managers use migration to copy files from primary to secondary (usually tape or optical disk) storage, releasing primary storage capacity for other purposes, and modifying file system metadata to indicate that file data can be located using a catalog, and that the file's primary storage space can be *purged*, or reallocated for other purposes. Volume managers and other virtualization control software also use migration to move segments of virtual storage capacity between physical devices to balance load or to protect against gradually failing devices.

mirror
(1) A complete copy of a virtual block storage device's storage capacity, usually on a separate set of storage devices from other copies.
(2) The process of block virtualization by making two or more identical copies of the block address spaces of one or more striped or concatenated disks or LUNs.

mirrored device
A virtual block storage device implemented with mirroring technology.

mirroring
A storage virtualization technique in which two or more complete copies of a block storage device's storage capacity are kept in synchronization.

MMF
Acronym for multi-mode fiber.

MTBF
Acronym for mean time between failures.

MTTR
Acronym for mean time to repair.

multi-mode fiber
A low-cost optical fiber used to implement links that transmit data over distances of up to one kilometer.

mutual consistency
A state of a replicated data object in which user actions on any replica have identical results.

NAS
Acronym for network-attached storage. Persistent data storage that is connected ("attached") to its clients via a network. Abbreviated NAS. The term network-attached storage is almost always used to denote a class of storage devices that organize data in files and use file access protocols (CIFS and NFS) to communicate with clients.

network-attached storage device
A storage device that organizes data in files and uses file access protocols (CIFS and NFS) to communicate with clients.

network file access protocol
A network communication protocol used to transmit file access requests between clients and file servers that hold the requested data.

Network File System (protocol)
A client-server file network access protocol originally developed by Sun Microsystems Computer Corporation and commonly implemented for UNIX operating systems (although other implementations exist for other server platforms. Abbreviated NFS. The IETF is responsible for the NFS standard.

network interface card
An I/O adapter that connects a computer or other type of node to a network. Abbreviated NIC. A NIC is usually a circuit module; however, the term is sometimes used to denote an ASIC or set of ASICs on a computer system board that performs the network I/O adapter function. The term NIC is universally used in Ethernet and **token ring** contexts. In Fibre Channel contexts, the terms adapter and NIC are used in preference to host bus adapter. *cf.* adapter, host bus adapter, I/O adapter

network partition
A failure of a communication network that results in a set of servers being partitioned into disjoint subsets within which servers can intercommunicate with each other, but not with servers in other subsets.

NFS
Acronym for Network File System.

NIC
Acronym for Network Interface Card.

object manager
A server that provides its clients with a correspondence between names and object storage device address/object identifier pairs.

object storage device
A disk-like random access persistent storage device that organizes its physical storage capacity into a varying number of objects of varying size and attributes. Functionally, object storage devices resemble file systems except in that they identify objects by number instead of by name.

one-copy serializability
The concurrent execution of a set of actions on replicated data such that the results on each replica are equivalent at every stage to serial execution of the same set of actions on nonreplicated data.

OSD
Acronym for object storage device.

out-of-band (virtualization)
A form of block storage virtualization in which the virtualization metadata is managed by some entity other than the entity that performs block address translation for I/O requests. *cf.* in-band (virtualization)

parallel database
A database managed by several cooperating instances of a database manager.

parity RAID
A form of RAID in which blocks of redundant check data are created by computing the exclusive or (**XOR**) of several blocks of user data. A parity RAID array protects against the failure of any single one of its disks.

partition
(1) A form of storage virtualization in which a set of consecutively numbered blocks on a physical or virtual storage device is presented to data managers and applications as a storage device.
(2) A property of applications that allows them to be subdivided and run on multiple servers concurrently.

path
Synonym for access path.

persistence
Durability through adverse circumstances. In information technology contexts, the term is most often used to denote stored data that can survive loss of power to the device that holds it. Data stored on a magnetic disk or tape is persistent, because it survives a power outage to the disk or tape drive, while data stored in dynamic random access memory (DRAM) is not, because if the DRAM loses power, its contents are not preserved.

physical (database) backup
A database backup in which the database's underlying storage (virtual devices or container files) contents are copied.

policy processor
A microprocessor built into a disk drive, RAID system, or storage appliance that is used to control the device's overall operation.

purging
The removal of a file's data blocks from primary (disk) storage, leaving only the file's descriptive metadata. The file metadata that remains on primary storage enables a hierarchical storage manager to locate the purged data blocks for retrieval when the file is accessed by an application.

RAID
(1) Acronym for Redundant Array of Inexpensive Disks.
(2) Acronym for Redundant Array of Independent Disks.

RAID array
Synonym for disk array.

RAID system
A storage system capable of using RAID techniques to virtualize disk storage.

RAIT
Acronym for Redundant Array of Inexpensive Tape (drives).

raw device
raw partition
A block storage device or partition whose storage capacity is managed directly by a database manager without an intervening file system layer. *cf.* container file

reclamation
The process by which a hierarchical storage manager frees space within a file system by removing data blocks from HSM migrated files. Also used to describe the clearing of voided space from HSM managed offline storage media by copying valid data from one tape or disk cartridge to another while discarding voided files.

recovery point
The point in time represented by a restored backup of operational data used to recover an information service after a failure or disaster.

recovery point objective
A desired recovery point. Abbreviated RPO. Recovery point objectives are used to perform cost-performance analysis of recovery technology alternatives.

recovery time
The time required to restore operation of an information service after a failure or disaster.

recovery time objective
A desired recovery time. Abbreviated RTO. Recovery time objective is determined both by the type of outage (e.g., failed disk, crashed system, etc.) and the recovery strategies (e.g., RAID, multiple I/O paths, clustering, redundant network, etc.).

redeployment
The reuse of a set of storage resources that had previously been used for another purpose. Online storage is often redeployed when it is replaced by newer technology.

Redundant Array of Independent Disks
An array of disk drives or other block storage devices that is virtualized by any of several forms of control software. Abbreviated RAID.

Redundant Array of Independent Tapes
An array of tape drives that is virtualized by any of several forms of control software. Abbreviated RAIT.

Redundant Array of Inexpensive Disks
The original meaning of the acronym RAID. Coined by researchers at the University of California at Berkeley in the late 1980s.

relational database manager
A database manager that organizes data in records called rows, each consisting of one or more fields, called columns. A relational database manager is capable of relating rows to each other based on the contents of designated columns.

remote data access
The use of data by a client that is remote from the data's storage location. In this context, *remote* typically means beyond the maximum length of conventional I/O bus or storage network end-to-end links.

replay
The reading of a file system or database log during recovery from a crash or disaster and using the log's contents to ensure that the file system or database contains only complete transactions.

replication
Synonym for data replication.

replicator
A device or software component that performs replication.

rescan
The process by which a computer discovers which storage devices are accessible to it on an I/O bus or storage network. Rescanning is typically necessary whenever a device is added to or removed from a network.

response time
The time between the issuance of a request for service and the completion of the request's execution. Response time includes both queuing time while awaiting resources to process the request and execution time once the request is removed from the queue and execution begins. In an I/O system context, applications typically stall for the response time after issuing I/O requests, so response time is critical to application performance.

restorative downtime
A period of information service outage that is required to restore full system capability after a failure or disaster. Restorative downtime occurs after information service recovery, and can usually be scheduled for administrative or

operational convenience. Its purpose is to permit repair or replacement of failed redundant components, thereby restoring a system to full redundancy.

resynchronization
The restoration of a disk array's contents after some damage to the array's contents has been repaired. The damage may be in the form of a disk or path failure, or may result from administrative action, such as splitting a mirror. Array contents are resynchronized by executing algorithms that utilize the array's redundant check data to reconstruct user data.

retrieval
The automatic returning of a file's data blocks to their original location by a hierarchical storage manager when the file is accessed by an application or user. Also known as caching.

revectoring
The transparent substitution of a block on a disk for another one. Revectoring is used by disk drive firmware to present the appearance of defect-free media when defects that make recording of data in certain blocks impossible are present.

ring topology
A Fibre Channel storage network topology in which each switch or director is connected to exactly two other switches.

roll-back
The process of restoring a set of data files or a database to its state at a defined point in time by starting from a (possibly corrupt) image of the data and removing the effects of any partially complete transactions. A log containing "before images" of data modified by transactions is replayed, and for incomplete transactions, the "before images" of data overwrite the contents of the database. Roll-back is typically used to eliminate the effects of faulty applications or erroneous transactions.

roll-forward
The process of restoring a set of data files or a database to a defined recovery point by starting from an image of the data captured at an earlier point in time and applying updates read from logs. Roll-forward may be used to restore a database destroyed by a disaster by first restoring a backup of the database and then reading updates made to the database since the time of the backup from transaction and archive logs and re-applying them in order to the restored database image.

router
A storage network component that is capable of translating between network addresses and rerouting network traffic to translated addresses. Some routers also convert between network communication media, as between Fibre Channel and TCP/IP.

RPO
Acronym for recovery point objective.

RTO
Acronym for recovery time objective.

SAN appliance
Synonym for virtualization appliance.

scalability
The ability to accommodate growth in one dimension and provide proportional growth in another. For example, a storage system is scalable if its capacity can grow without sacrificing availability or performance.

scaling
Scalable growth.

servo (information)
servo (pattern)
Permanently recorded patterns on recording media surfaces that help read/write heads position themselves more precisely with respect to data.

shared data cluster
A cluster in which applications running on two or more servers can access the same data concurrently. A shared data cluster requires a cluster file system, cluster volume manager, or parallel database, as well as storage devices that are simultaneously accessible by all servers that share data.

shared nothing cluster
A cluster in which each storage device is accessed by one server at a time. The right to access shared nothing clusters' storage devices can be passed from server to server, but this is a time-consuming operation, typically performed only during application failover.

short-wave fiber
Synonym for multi-mode fiber.

single mode fiber
A type of optical fiber used to transmit data over distances of up to ten kilometers. Single mode fiber is generally more costly than the multi-mode fiber used in shorter distance applications.

slave (instance)
slave (server)
In an asymmetric cluster volume manager or file system, a server or instance that is not responsible for making metadata updates.

slice
A copy of the first few data blocks of a file that is left on primary storage after a hierarchical storage manager has purged the rest of the data blocks to reclaim space for more active data. The size of a slice is typically configurable by administrative action, and may range to gigabytes.

SMF
Acronym for single mode fiber.

snapshot
A physical or virtual image of the contents of a virtual block storage device or of a file system as they exist at a single point in time. Snapshots are usually made at times when data is consistent, as, for example, when applications are quiescent and data manager caches contain no unflushed data.

snapshot virtual device
A virtual storage device representing a point-in-time snapshot of another virtual storage device. A snapshot virtual device is typically used (for example, by backup), or held for a time (for example, snapshots kept to guard against application data corruption), and then discarded. Snapshot virtual devices are instantiated by server-based virtualizers.

source (device)
A virtual storage device whose contents are replicated to one or more target devices.

split mirror (snapshot)
A snapshot created by removing a mirror from a mirrored virtual device and mounting the removed mirror as an independent virtual device. The contents of a split mirror snapshot must be resynchronized with its volume when the two are rejoined.

SQL
Acronym for Structured Query Language.

staging
(1) Synonym for retrieval. The copying of file data blocks back to primary storage by a hierarchical storage manager.
(2) A more proactive intelligent means of retrieving multiple files in an optimized manner.

storage appliance
A storage network component dedicated to responding to I/O requests from clients by managing and accessing storage devices connected to it.

storage client
An entity that uses storage and I/O services. Application servers connected to a storage network are storage clients.

storage device
Any device that holds data persistently for retrieval or updating on demand. Storage devices may be physical, as disk drives and tape drives, or virtual, as LUNs presented by RAID systems or storage appliances.

storage network
A network whose primary purpose is intercommunication between storage devices and application servers, or between groups of storage devices.

storage system
A computer system whose primary function is the persistent storage and delivery on demand of data.

storage virtualizer
A device or body of software that virtualizes storage. Server-based volume managers, RAID systems, and network storage appliances all virtualize storage in some form.

store-and-forward (transmission)
A form of multistep data transmission in which intermediate routers or switches receive data, store it momentarily, and forward it on to the next step in the communication path.

stretch cluster
A cluster in which some of the servers or storage devices are separated from others by distances of hundreds of meters or more.

stripe
In a striped mapping, any set of corresponding ranges of disk or LUN block addresses on all devices included in the mapping whose lengths are equal to the stripe depth, and whose starting block addresses are a multiple of the stripe depth.

stripe depth
In a striped mapping, the number of consecutive virtual block addresses that correspond to consecutive block addresses on a single disk or LUN.

stripe size
The product of stripe depth and stripe width. The stripe size is the amount of data contained in a stripe.

stripe width
The number of devices in an array with striped block address translation.

striped mapping
striping
A form of virtual block address translation in which fixed-size ranges of virtual device block addresses correspond to ranges of block addresses on several disks or LUNs in a regular rotating pattern.

Structured Query Language
An ANSI standard programming language for accessing data in relational databases.

switch
A storage network infrastructure device that interconnects storage clients (e.g., application servers), storage devices, and other switches. The distinguishing characteristics of a switch are the ability to establish and break momentary connections between pairs of devices and the ability to maintain multiple connections between pairs of devices simultaneously.

switch port
The point at which a storage client or storage device connects to a switch.

symmetric (file system architecture)
An architecture for cluster file systems in which all servers that mount a file system make metadata changes (create and delete files and so forth) by writing directly to the virtual device that holds the file system.

synchronous replication
A form of data replication in which completion of I/O operations is not signaled to applications until receipt of data is acknowledged by target locations. Synchronous replication can impact application performance, but avoids the risk of "out-of-date" target location replicas.

synthetic full backup
A full backup created by combining an older full backup with one or more incremental ones.

tape drive virtualization
The pooling of tape drives so that any drive from a pool can be assigned to satisfy a backup server's request for a tape drive. Tape drives may be virtualized by cooperating software modules running in each of the backup servers with access to the pool, or by hardware components in a storage network that assigns tape drives on demand to respond to network addresses that are "owned" by servers.

target (device)
A virtual storage device to which data updates made to a source device are replicated.

TCP offload engine
A specialized integrated circuit designed to perform a significant part of the processing required to interpret TCP/IP packets. Abbreviated TOE. TOEs reduce the server processing overhead of TCP/IP communication.

TOE
Acronym for TCP offload engine.

track
The set of storage blocks on a single disk surface that are at the same distance from the disk's center.

transaction
A collection of operations on data that has business significance as a unit. The operations that comprise a transaction must be performed in their entirety for the data on which they operate to accurately reflect a business state. Database management systems implement transactional semantics for application-defined sets of database operations.

trunking
The aggregation of several physical network connections into one logical connection for the purpose of increasing the available bandwidth between two end points. Trunking has the beneficial side effect of improving the availability of the connection between the two points because if one of the physical interconnects fails, communication can continue using the remaining ones.

ULP
Acronym for Upper Level Protocol.

upper level protocol
Any message and data transfer protocol that is designed to be carried on a Fibre Channel transport.

user data parity
Parity check data created by computing the exclusive or (**XOR**) of several blocks of user data in a RAID array.

virtual block storage device
Synonym for block storage device.

virtual disk drive
A virtual storage device whose behavior is sufficiently similar to that of a disk drive that it can be used interchangeably with a physical disk drive by data managers and applications.

virtual private network
A logical channel within a TCP/IP network within which data is encrypted so that it is private to the nodes participating in the logical channel.

virtual storage device
An abstraction implemented in software whose behavior is sufficiently similar to that of a physical storage device that applications and data managers can use it as such.

virtual volume
volume
Synonyms for virtual block storage device.

virtualization appliance
virtualization engine
A storage appliance that virtualizes storage. The term is commonly applied to devices that perform block storage virtualization.

volume manager
Application server-based block virtualization control software.

VPN
Acronym for virtual private network.

write order fidelity
write ordering
write sequencing
The process of executing writes in a fashion that preserves the integrity of the data structures. Write sequencing, in a replication environment, must always be maintained. That is, all write operations on primary data structures must be executed in the same sequence on the target.

ZDR
Acronym for zoned data recording.

zone
(1) A set of port or device addresses in a storage network that are permitted to intercommunicate.
(2) A set of adjacent tracks on a disk drive, all of which are formatted to contain the same number of blocks.

zoned data recording
A technique for recording data on disks in which outer tracks (whose length is greater) are formatted to hold more blocks than inner tracks. Groups of adjacent tracks are organized as zones, with each zone having the same number of blocks formatted on all of its tracks.

zoning
A technique used in Fibre Channel storage networks to limit the set of attached devices with which other devices can communicate. Zoning is most often implemented in switches, but can also be implemented by server-based software. The technique is comparable to LUN masking.

Index

Note: A *b* following a page number indicates a boxed sidebar, a *t* following a page number indicates tabular material, and an *f* following a page number indicates a figure.

A

Abstraction, intelligent disk drives and, 26
Access token mechanism, 286
Active redundant components, 63–64
Actuators, 21, 21*f*
Adapters, bus/host bus
  in Fibre Channel storage network, 234, 235*f*
  multifabric storage networks and, 238–239
Addressing data, 22, 22*f*
Agents, use of application programming interfaces and, 189
Aggregation
  connectivity, storage system complexity affected by, 275
  storage capacity, 4. *See also* Block storage virtualization
    in server-based volume manager virtualization, 114
Algorithms, for virtual-to-logical address conversion, 72, 73–74, 78–79, 79*f*, 124
Allocation units, file system, 308
APIs. *See* Application programming interfaces
Appliances
  RAID, failure of, mirroring and RAID limitations and, 68–69
  virtualization
    in-band virtualization by, 125, 126*f*
    replication and, 162–165, 162*b*, 163*f*, 164*f*
Application errors, in database, 214
Application I/O throttling, 174
Application programming interfaces (APIs), 188–189
  storage standards and, 242*b*
  zoning/LUN masking and, 240*b*, 242*b*
Application scaling. *See also* Scaling
  cluster file systems and, 206
Application servers
  block storage virtualization and, 8–9, 106, 108, 113–118, 113*f*, 114*f*, 116*f*
  failure of
    clustering and, 110, 111*f*, 139
    mirroring and RAID limitations and, 69
  RAID system for, 109–112, 110*f*, 111*f*
  replication and, 162
Applications
  availability of
    shared data clusters and, 143
    shared nothing clusters and, 142–143
  cluster file systems and, 209
  hierarchical storage management (HSM) transparent to, 260, 261
  performance of
    backup windows affecting, 187
    copy-on-write snapshots and, 194
    virtual storage device replication affecting, 168–173
  requirements for, clustering and, 139
  virtual block devices and, 6
Archive logs, 216–217
  database recovery and, 217, 223, 227
  hierarchical storage management (HSM) and, 258
  incremental backup and, 221
  replicated, 227
Arrays, 29, 30, 30*f*
  degraded, 65
  logical units (LUNs) and, 34–35, 35*f*
  mirrored, 38, 38*f*
    multidevice, 40–41, 41*f*
    multiway, 41–42
  partitioning, 77
  RAID, 30, 30*f*. *See also* RAID system
    writing data to, 93, 94*f*
  in tape drive virtualization, 7
Asymmetric (master-slave) architecture, 146–147, 146*f*, 206*f*, 207–208, 208*f*, 281
  in SCSI disk drive model, 281
Asynchronous replication, 169, 171–173, 172*f*, 173*f*
  recovery points and, 53
  switching to synchronous replication and, 171*b*
ATA channels
  virtualized I/O interfaces and, 20
  virtualized RAID systems and, 106
atime, HSM software using, 260

ATM, 247
example of integrated network using, 253, 253*f*
Atomic sequences, metadata integrity and, 310
Authentication, 285
Availability, 50–61, 322–327
of components, 51–56
continuum of, 323–324
data center destruction and, 58–61, 59*t*, 60*b*
degraded operation interval and, 53–54, 55*f*
data center destruction and, 59, 59*t*, 60
single disk failure and, 57, 57*t*, 58
high, 62–70, 323–324, 325*f*. *See also* Highly available systems
design parameters for, 324–325, 325*f*
versus ordinary, 56–61, 57*t*, 59*t*, 322–325
mirroring and, 66, 67*f*, 68–69
"nines" of, 326–327
outage types and, 55–56
parity RAID and, 67, 68–69, 68*f*
RAID and, 65–69, 67*f*, 68*f*
recovery points and, 52–53, 53*f*, 54*t*
data center destruction and, 58, 59*t*, 60
single disk failure and, 56, 57*t*, 58
recovery time and, 51–52, 51*f*, 54*t*
data center destruction and, 59, 59*t*, 60
single disk failure and, 57, 57*t*, 58
restorative/planned downtime and, 54–55, 55*f*
data center destruction and, 59, 59*t*, 60
single disk failure and, 57, 57*t*, 58
server-based volume manager virtualization and, 116–117
shared nothing clusters and, 142
single disk failure and, 56–58, 57*t*
storage system complexity and, 276
virtualization affecting, 4, 50–61, 62–70, 324, 325
Availability cluster configuration, 122
Availability Manager (VERITAS), 60*b*, 159*b*
Average response time, block address striping affecting, 89

B

Backup, 185–198
cold, 189, 190*f*, 219–220
consistent data for, 189
contemporary issues in, 185–187
database/database managers and, 213, 217–222, 220*f*
incremental, 196, 221–222
logical
incremental, 221–222
online, 218
online, 218–219
physical
incremental, 222, 222*b*
online, 219–221, 220*f*
recovering database from, 217, 222–223
hierarchical storage management (HSM) and, 263–264
disaster recovery with, 264
hot, 188, 189, 190*f*
incremental, 195–196
off-host, with split mirror snapshots, 190, 191*b*
tape drive virtualization and, 7, 9–10, 196–198, 196*b*, 197*f*
versus data replication, 153
virtual block storage device replication for, 157
Backup Exec (VERITAS), 60*b*
Backup mode, database, 218. *See also* Backup, database/database managers and
Backup servers, 185
Backup windows, 186, 187
block storage virtualization and, 188–195, 188*b*, 190*b*, 192*b*, 193*f*, 195*f*
techniques for minimizing, 195–196
Bare Metal Restore (VERITAS), 187*b*
Bidirectional replication, 165–166, 166*f*
BLIB. *See* Block-level incremental backup
Block address conversion, 33–34, 33*f*, 109, 285
in out-of-band storage network virtualization, 132, 133
Block address striping, 4, 31*b*, 32, 33*f*, 41, 41*f*, 77–79, 77*f*, 79*f*, 298*t*
applications for arrays with, 80, 80*f*
device failure and, 80–81, 81*f*
I/O performance and, 86–92, 92*f*
data transfer-intensive applications and, 90–91, 90*f*
I/O request-intensive applications and, 86–89, 87*f*, 88*f*, 89*f*
with mirroring, 98–101, 99*f*, 100*f*
with mirroring, 98–101, 99*f*, 100*f*, 298*t*
failure tolerance and, 100–101
object storage devices and, 290
parity RAID and, 80–83, 81*f*, 82*f*
server-based, 80, 80*f*
storage network-based, 80
Block-level incremental backup, database, 196, 222, 222*b*
Block storage
file/file system access characteristics differentiated from, 11*t*
virtualization of, 3, 3*f*, 5–6, 123–125. *See also* Block storage virtualization
Block storage replication, 157–159, 159*f*
alternatives in, 160–165
asynchronous, 169, 171–173, 172*f*, 173*f*
characteristics of, 168–181
disaster recovery and, 173–176, 176*f*, 177*f*
initial synchronization for, 177–178, 178*f*
for point-in-time copy creation, 179–180
RAID system, 161–162, 161*f*
server-based, 158, 159*f*, 160–161, 160*f*, 161*f*

setting up, 177–180, 178*f*, 179*b*
storage network, 162–165, 162*b*, 163*f*, 164*f*
synchronous, 169, 169–171, 171*f*
timing of, 168–169, 170*f*
Block storage virtualization, 3, 3*f*, 5–6, 123–125. *See also* Virtual block devices
advantages of, 269–270, 279–280
backup and, 185–198
complexity and, 277–278
components of, 123–125, 124*f*
conventional, 105–119
failure tolerance in, 37–49. *See also* Failure tolerance
file/file system, 6, 199–211. *See also* File/file system virtualization
administration and, 314–317
advantages of, 200
architecture of, 12–14, 13*f*
implementation of, 10–14, 11*t*, 12*f*
future of, 279–294
implementations of, 106–109
iSCSI over TCP/IP and, 319, 319*f*
limitations of, 280–282
locating user data on, 71–84
objects/object storage devices and, 283–289, 287*f*
performance of, 85–101. *See also* I/O performance
popularity of, 279–283
by server-based volume managers, 106, 108, 113–118, 113*f*, 114*f*, 116*f*
advantages of, 116–118
limitations of, 118
by storage network appliances, 106, 108–109, 120–136. *See also* Storage network virtualization
switch-based, 129*b*
techniques and implementations of, 297, 298*t*, 299*t*
universality and, 280
within RAID system, 5, 8, 106, 107, 109–112, 110*f*, 111*f*
advantages of, 107, 110–112
limitations of, 112
BMR. *See* Bare Metal Restore
Bridges
FCIP, 251
in storage network, 235, 235*f*
in tape drive virtualization, 197
Buffer credits, 240–241, 250*f*
Bus adapters
in Fibre Channel storage network, 234, 235*f*
multifabric storage networks and, 238–239
Bus-target-LUN addressing scheme, in SCSI disk drive model, 281

C

C-H-S (cylinder, head, sector) addressing, 22, 22*f*
disk media defects and, 25
logical block addressing and, 22–23, 24*f*, 25
Cache, file system metadata integrity and, 321–323
Capacity, virtualization affecting, 4
in file system, 201, 316–317
management and, 285
in RAID system, 112
in server-based volume manager virtualization, 114–115
Capacity pooling, 282
Cascade, Fibre Channel ring topology and, 235, 236*f*
Causality, 176, 177*f*
CDB. *See* Command Data Block
Change maps, file system snapshots and, 202–204, 202*f*, 203*f*, 204*f*
Channels, in DWDM, 247
Check data, parity RAID, 29, 31, 32*f*, 33, 43*f*, 44, 46–49, 47*f*, 48*f*
Client footprint, in out-of-band storage network virtualization, 134
Client-server architecture, 11
Client-server backup, 185–186, 186*f*
Cluster file system, 205–210, 206*f*. *See also* Clusters
applications and, 209
benefits of, 206, 208–209
parallel databases and, 225–226
system crashes and, 209–210
Cluster File System (VERITAS), 118*b*, 224*b*
Cluster manager instances, 139
Cluster Server (VERITAS), 142*b*, 148*b*, 224*b*
Cluster Volume Manager (VERITAS), 118*b*, 148*b*, 224*b*
Cluster volume managers, 145–149, 146*f*
architectural concepts for, 146–148, 146*f*, 147*f*, 207
cluster file systems and, 206–208, 206*f*, 208*f*
data access and, 148
distributed model for, 147–148, 147*f*, 207
master-slave model for, 146–147, 146*f*, 206*f*, 207–208, 208*f*
for parallel databases, 224–225, 225*f*, 226*f*
server crashes and, 148–149, 209–210
Clustering, 139–144, 140*f*
benefits of, 139–140
Clusters, 139, 140*f*. *See also* Cluster file system
availability, 122
data access and, 148
models for, 142–144, 143*f*, 144*f*
failover, 110, 111*f*, 139
server, 69
shared data, 142, 143–144, 144*f*, 205
storage virtualization for, 144–149, 146*f*, 147*f*
shared nothing, 142, 142–143, 143*f*
stretch, 244
virtual storage and, 140–141, 141*f*
virtual volumes for, 118*b*
Cold backup, snapshots and, 189, 190*f*, 219–220
Command Data Block (CDB), 79

Communication reliability, data replication and, 152
Complexity
database replication and, 155
in-band virtualization and, 126*f*, 127*f*, 130–131
storage system, 270–274, 271*f*
cost of (administration), 272, 272*f*
diversity and, 274
interconnections and, 273
management of, 275–277
objects in reduction of, 289–293
sources of, 270–271, 271*f*
system size and, 273
virtualization and, 277–278
Components
availability of, 51–56
of block storage virtualization, 123–125, 124*f*
cost of in-band virtualization, 132
diversity of, storage complexity and, 274
encapsulation of, storage system complexity affected by, 275
redundant, high availability and, 63. *See also* Highly available systems
active and passive, 63–64
reducing cost of, 64–65
relocation capabilities and, 64, 64*b*
Concatenation, 40–41, 41*f*, 72–74, 73*f*, 75*f*
capacity affected by, 74, 74*b*
characteristics of, 74
I/O performance and, 75–76, 75*f*, 88–89, 88*f*
Concise expression, by database manager, 154–155
Configuration
flexibility of, in server-based volume manager virtualization, 116, 117
storage network virtualization and, 121, 121*f*, 239–241, 239*f*, 241*f*
Connection outages, replication and, 174–175
Connections, number of, storage complexity and, 270–271, 271*f*
Connectivity aggregation, storage system complexity affected by, 275
Consolidation (storage)
in RAID system, 111
storage system complexity and, 276
Container files, backup of, 196
Controllers, RAID
embedded, 299*t*
failure of, 69
external, 299*t*
block storage virtualization and, 106
failure of, 68–69
Cooling systems, failure of, mirroring and RAID limitations and, 68
Copy-on-write snapshots
backup using, 192–194, 192*b*, 193*f*
with replication, 194–195, 195*f*
block-level incremental backup using, 222, 222*b*
file system, 202–205, 202*f*, 203*f*, 204*f*
physical online database backup using, 219–220
virtual device, 205
Copy Service Option (VERITAS), 39*b*, 41*b*
Core-edge topology, Fibre Channel, 236–237, 237*f*
Corruption, data. *See* Data, corruption/integrity of
Costs
of disk storage, 20
virtualization affecting, 4
of diversity, 274
of highly available systems
factors affecting, 62
minimizing, 64–65
management, storage network virtualization and, 122–125, 123*f*, 124*f*
of parity RAID, 43–44
of split mirror snapshots for backup, 191–192
Cylinder, 21, 22, 22*f*
Cylinder, head, sector (C-H-S) addressing, 22, 22*f*
disk media defects and, 25
logical block addressing and, 22–23, 24*f*, 25

D

Dark fiber
examples of integrated network using, 252–253, 252*f*, 253*f*, 254*f*
failure tolerance and, 248–249
Dark fiber connections, 245
Dark fiber optic interconnects, 247
Data
addressing, 22, 22*f*
corruption/integrity of
database managers and, 213
file systems and, 309, 310–313
human/application error causing, 69
replication and, 173–176, 176*f*, 177*f*
inactive, hierarchical storage management (HSM) and, 257–259
locating, 71–84. *See also* Data access
block address striping and, 77–79, 77*f*, 79*f*
applications for arrays with, 80, 80*f*
parity RAID and, 80–83, 81*f*, 82*f*
concatenation and, 72–76, 73*f*, 75*f*
partitioning and, 76–77, 76*f*
sharing. *See* Data sharing
Data access. *See also* Data availability; I/O performance
block storage versus file/file system access characteristics, 11*t*
with cluster volume managers, 148
models for, 142–144, 143*f*, 144*f*
control of, 285
remote, file access protocols and, 11
virtualization affecting, 4
Data access scaling, 282

Data analysis, virtual block storage device replication for, 157
Data attributes, in SCSI disk drive model, 282
Data availability, 50–61. *See also* Data access
  components and, 51–56
  continuum of, 323–324
  data center destruction and, 58–61, 59*t*, 60*b*
  degraded operation interval and, 53–54, 55*f*
    data center destruction and, 59, 59*t*, 60
    single disk failure and, 57, 57*t*, 58
  high, 62–70, 323–324, 325*f*. *See also* Highly available systems
    design parameters for, 324–325, 325*f*
    versus ordinary, 56–61, 57*t*, 59*t*, 322–325
  mirroring and, 66, 67*f*, 68–69
  "nines" of, 326–327
  outage types and, 55–56
  parity RAID and, 67, 68–69, 68*f*
  RAID and, 65–69, 67*f*, 68*f*
  recovery points and, 52–53, 53*f*, 54*t*
    data center destruction and, 58, 59*t*, 60
    single disk failure and, 56, 57*t*, 58
  recovery time and, 51–52, 51*f*, 54*t*
    data center destruction and, 59, 59*t*, 60
    single disk failure and, 57, 57*t*, 58
  restorative/planned downtime and, 54–55, 55*f*
    data center destruction and, 59, 59*t*, 60
    single disk failure and, 57, 57*t*, 58
  server-based volume manager virtualization and, 116–117
  shared nothing clusters and, 142
  single disk failure and, 56–58, 57*t*
  virtualization affecting, 4, 50–61, 62–70, 324, 325
Data center
  destruction of
    database recovery from backup and logs and, 217, 223
    failure tolerance and, 58–61, 59*t*
    file recovery with hierarchical storage management (HSM) and backup and, 264
  hierarchical storage management (HSM) affecting, 264–265
Data clusters, shared, 142, 143–144, 144*f*
  storage virtualization in, 144–149, 146*f*, 147*f*
Data currency, 52, 53*t*
Data layout, disk drive, 21–22, 21*f*, 22*f*
Data managers, server-based volume manager virtualization and, 117–118
Data recovery points, 52–53, 53*f*, 54*t*
  data center destruction and, 58, 59*t*, 60
  single disk failure and, 56, 57*t*, 58
Data recovery time, 51, 51*f*
  data center destruction and, 59, 59*t*, 60
  single disk failure and, 57, 57*t*, 58
Data recovery time objectives, 51–52, 51*f*, 54*t*
Data redundancy, RAID and, 33, 37
  mirroring for, 4, 31, 31*b*, 37–42, 38*f*
  parity for, 31, 31*b*, 32, 32*f*, 42–49, 43*f*
Data replication, 151–167
  alternatives to, 153
  application performance and, 168–173
  archive log, for database recovery, 217, 223
  asynchronous, 169, 171–173, 171*b*, 172*f*, 173*f*
    recovery points and, 53
  bidirectional, 165–166, 166*f*
  database, 153, 154–155, 155*f*, 217, 223, 226–228
  disaster recovery and, 152, 158, 159, 165–166, 166*f*, 173–176, 176*f*, 177
  file, 154, 156, 157*f*
  forms of, 153–154
  initial synchronization for, 177–178, 178*f*
  mirroring and, 152–153
  for point-in-time copy creation, 179–180
  RAID system, 161–162, 161*f*
  to remote locations, 152–153, 243–255
    dense wave division multiplexing and, 247–249, 248*f*, 249*f*
    enterprise network technologies and, 245–246
    examples of integrated network and, 252–253, 252*f*, 253*f*, 254*f*
    FCIP and, 250–251
    fiber interconnects and, 246–247
    recovery time objectives for, 52
    remote convergence and, 243–246, 244*f*, 245*f*
    security and, 251
    in server-based volume manager virtualization, 115
    wide area communications and, 246–247
    wide area storage networks and, 250–251, 250*f*
  setting up, 177–180, 178*f*, 179*b*
  storage network, 162–165, 162*b*, 163*f*, 164*f*
  synchronous, 169, 169–171, 171*f*
  virtual block storage device, 157–159, 159*f*
    alternatives in, 160–165
    characteristics of, 168–181
Data reuse, virtual block storage device replication for, 157
Data sharing
  file access protocols and, 11–12
  file system virtualization architecture and, 13, 14
  in shared data cluster, 142, 143–144, 144*f*
Data snapshots. *See* Snapshots
Data storage. *See also under* Storage
  long-term, hierarchical storage management (HSM) and, 265
Data striping, 4, 31*b*, 32, 33*f*, 41, 41*f*. *See also* Block address striping
Data transfer-intensive applications, block address striping and, 90–91, 90*f*
Database cache, 215–216, 216*f*

Database logs, 216, 216*f*
archiving, 216–217
in database recovery, 217, 223
Database management systems/database managers, 213–217. *See also* Databases
backup and, 217–222, 220*f*
incremental, 196, 221–222
logical
incremental, 221–222
online, 218
online, 218–219
physical
incremental, 222, 222*b*
online, 219–221, 220*f*
recovering database from, 217, 222–223
human and application errors and, 214
log archiving and, 216–217
parallel, shared data clusters used by, 143
replication and, 227
shared nothing clusters used by, 143
system and environmental failures and, 214
recovery from, 215–216, 216*f*
transactions/transactional integrity and, 214–215
Database pages, online database backup and, 218, 219
Database replication, 153, 154–155, 155*f*, 217, 223, 226–228
Database scaling, shared nothing clusters and, 143
Databases, 212–229. *See also* Database management systems/database managers
errors in, human and application, 214
failure/failure recovery and, 214, 215–216, 216*f*
online
backing up, 218–221
logical, 218
physical, 218, 219–221, 220*f*
protecting data in, 223–226, 225*f*, 226*f*
storage redundancy and, 223–224
parallel, virtual storage for, 224–226, 225*f*, 226*f*
recovering from backup, 217, 222–223
relational model for, 213–214
storage redundancy in, 223–224
transactions in, 214–215
DBMSs. *See* Database management systems/database managers
Defective block substitution, disk virtualization and, 25, 26*f*
Defragmentation, file system, 314–316, 315*f*, 316*f*
hierarchical storage management (HSM) affecting need for, 259
Degraded array, 65
Degraded operation interval (DOI), 53–54, 55*f*
data center destruction and, 59, 59*t*, 60
single disk failure and, 57, 57*t*, 58
Delayed replication, by database manager, 154
Delivery speed. *See also* I/O performance
virtualization affecting, 4
Delta File Technology, 222*b*
Dense wave division multiplexing, 241, 245–246, 247–249, 248*f*, 249*f*
examples of integrated network using, 252–253, 252*f*, 253*f*
Descriptors, file, 308–309
Device addressing, in SCSI disk drive model, 281
Device block address conversion, 33–34, 33*f*, 109, 285
in out-of-band storage network virtualization, 132, 133
Device combination, by virtualization, storage management and, 4–5
Device failure protection, with split mirror snapshots, 190–191
Device naming, in SCSI disk drive model, 281
Director. *See also* Switch
in Fibre Channel storage network, 234
Directories, 306–307, 307*f*
Dirty region logging, 39*b*
Disaster recovery
clustering and, 140
data replication and, 152, 158, 159, 165–166, 166*f*, 173–176, 176*f*, 177*f*
database manager, 214, 215–216, 216*f*, 226–228
file system, 310–313
with hierarchical storage management (HSM) and backup, 264
storage system complexity and, 272
Discovered direct I/O, 200*b*
Disk array, 29, 30
logical units (LUNs) and, 34–35, 35*f*
RAID, 30, 30*f*. *See also* RAID system
writing data to, 93, 94*f*
Disk capacity, 21. *See also* Capacity
Disk drive data layout, 21–22, 21*f*, 22*f*
Disk drive virtualization, 1, 5. *See also* Disk virtualization
result of, 20*f*
Disk drives, intelligent, 26, 27*f*
Disk failure (single disk), failure tolerance and, 56–58, 57*t*
Disk media defects, 25, 26*f*
Disk storage
advantages of, 19–20
data layout and, 21–22, 21*f*, 22*f*
virtualization of. *See* Disk virtualization
Disk storage cost, 20
virtualization affecting, 4
Disk system, 29, 30. *See also* RAID system
Disk virtualization, 3, 3*f*, 5–6, 19–27
advantages of, 19–20
disk drive data layout and, 21–22, 21*f*
disk media defects and, 25, 26*f*

logical block addressing and, 22–26, 23*f*
RAID and, 29
result of, 20*f*
zoned data recording and, 23–24, 25*f*
Distributed architecture, 147–148, 147*f*, 207
Distributed file system virtualizer, 12–13, 13*f*
Distributed locking techniques, 284
Distribution (publication), data replication and, 151
Diversity, storage complexity and, 274
DMP. *See* Dynamic multipathing
DOI. *See* Degraded operation interval
Downtime
restorative/planned, 54–55, 55*f*
data center destruction and, 59, 59*t*, 60
single disk failure and, 57, 57*t*, 58
types of, 55–56
Droop, 250, 250*f*
Duty cycle, high availability and, 324, 325*f*
DWDM. *See* Dense wave division multiplexing
DWDM multiplexer, 247
Dynamic multipathing, 114, 116, 117*b*

E

Elements, number of, storage complexity and, 270–271, 271*f*
Embedded RAID controllers/systems, 299*t*
block storage virtualization and, 106
failure of, mirroring and RAID limitations and, 69
Encapsulation, component, storage system complexity affected by, 275
Enterprise Administrator (VERITAS), 118*b*
Enterprise network technologies, 245–246
Enterprise storage challenges, 269–289
complexity and, 270–274, 271*f*
management of, 275–277
objects in reduction of, 289–293
storage virtualization and, 277–278
Environmental failure, databases and, 214
Error correction code (ECC), 21, 21*f*
Exclusive OR (XOR), 44, 46–49, 47*f*, 48*f*
block address striping and, 81, 81*f*
I/O performance and, 93, 94*f*, 97, 98*f*
small writes and, 93–95, 96*f*
Executable images, hierarchical storage management (HSM) policies and, 262
External RAID controllers/appliances, 299*t*
block storage virtualization and, 106
failure of, mirroring and RAID limitations and, 68–69

F

Fabric, Fibre Channel, 234, 236, 237*f*
redundancy and, 237–239, 238*f*
Fabric-based zones, 240
Failover
cluster file systems and, 208–209
VCS, 142*f*, 148*b*
VERITAS Volume Replicator and Availability Manager in automation of, 159*b*
Failover clusters, 110, 111*f*, 139
Failover server, shared nothing clusters and, 142
Failure tolerance, 33, 37–49. *See also* Disaster recovery
availability and, 50–61
in highly available versus ordinary systems, 56–61, 57*t*, 59*t*
in server-based volume manager virtualization, 116–117
cluster file systems/volume managers and, 148, 207–208, 209–210
dark fiber and, 248–249
database, 214, 215–216, 216*f*
degraded operation interval (DOI) and, 53–54, 55*f*
data center destruction and, 59, 59*t*, 60
single disk failure and, 57, 57*t*, 58
downtime types and, 55–56
file system, 310–313
mirroring and, 4, 31, 31*b*, 37–42, 38*f*
in highly available system, 66, 67*f*, 68–69
parity and, 31, 31*b*, 32, 32*f*, 42–49, 43*f*
in highly available system, 67, 68–69, 68*f*
recovery points and, 52–53, 53*f*, 54*t*
data center destruction and, 58, 59*t*, 60
single disk failure and, 56, 57*t*, 58
recovery time and, 51–52, 51*f*, 54*t*
data center destruction and, 59, 59*t*, 60
single disk failure and, 57, 57*t*, 58
replication and, 173–176, 176*f*, 177*f*
restorative/planned downtime and, 54–55, 55*f*
data center destruction and, 59, 59*t*, 60
single disk failure and, 57, 57*t*, 58
server-based volume manager virtualization and, 116–117
shared nothing clusters and, 142
single disk failure and, 56–58, 57*t*
striped block addressing and, 80–81, 81*f*
striped mirrors versus mirrored stripes and, 100–101
Fallback mode, for replication, 174–175
Fan failure, mirroring and RAID limitations and, 68
Fast mirror resynchronization, 40, 41*b*, 191, 191*b*
physical online database backup and, 219
Fast Resync (VERITAS), 39*b*, 41*b*
FCIP. *See* Fibre Channel over IP
FCIP bridges, 251
FCP. *See* Fibre Channel Protocol
Fiber interconnects, 246–247
Fiber optic connections, 247
Fibre Channel over IP (FCIP), 241, 250–251, 319–320, 320*f*
example of integrated network using, 253, 254*f*, 320*f*

Fibre Channel Protocol (FCP)
- enhancements to, 318
- out-of-band virtualization and, 135–136
- for storage network, 234
- virtualized I/O interfaces and, 20
- virtualized RAID systems and, 106

Fibre Channel storage networks, 233, 234–235, 235*f*
- distance and, 240–241, 250–251, 250*f*
- enhancements to, 318
- examples of, 252–253, 252*f*, 253*f*, 254*f*
- redundancy and, 237–239, 238*f*
- topologies of, 235–239, 236*f*, 237*f*, 238*f*
- zoning and, 240, 240*b*, 241*f*

Fibre Channel-to-SCSI routers, 233, 235, 235*f*

File access clients, file system virtualization and, 12

File access performance, hierarchical storage management (HSM) and, 261

File access protocols, 10–12
- virtualization of files and, 12

File/file system access characteristics, block storage differentiated from, 11*t*

File/file system virtualization, 6, 199–211. *See also* File systems
- administration and, 314–317
- advantages of, 200
- architecture of, 12–14, 13*f*
- cluster file systems and, 205–210, 206*f*, 208*f*
  - parallel databases and, 225–226
- device size changes and, 74*b*, 201
- HSM (hierarchical storage management) and, 6, 256–266. *See also* Hierarchical storage management
- implementation of, 10–14, 11*t*, 12*f*
- snapshots and, 201–205, 202*f*, 203*f*, 204*f*

File migration, virtualization and, 6
- in hierarchical storage management (HSM), 256–266. *See also* Hierarchical storage management
- in server-based volume manager virtualization, 115, 116–117, 117*b*

File replication, 154, 156, 157*f*

File Replicator (VERITAS), 156*b*

File segments, block address striping and, 90–91, 90*f*

File servers, 11

File size, hierarchical storage management (HSM) policies about, 262

File "slicing," optimizing hierarchical storage management (HSM) and, 263

File system blocks, 308, 308*f*

File system snapshots, 201–205, 202*f*, 203*f*, 204*f*

File System (VERITAS), 74*b*, 200*b*
- capacity change awareness and, 74*b*
- virtual backup to disk and, 192*b*

File systems, 199–200, 304–317
- administration of with virtual storage, 314–317
- data organization and, 306–308, 307*f*
- defragmentation of, 314–316, 315*f*, 316*f*
- design of, hierarchical storage management (HSM) effectiveness and, 265
- evolution of object storage devices and, 291–293
- failure/recovery of, 310–313
- function of, 309
- hierarchical storage management (HSM) integration and, 263
- maintenance of, hierarchical storage management (HSM) affecting, 259
- metadata integrity and, 309, 310–313
  - cache and, 312–313
  - logging and, 313
- nature of, 304–309
- online expansion and, 316–317
- purpose of, 305–306
- recovery techniques of, 311–312
- space allocation and, 308–309, 308*f*
- storage-aware, 291

File virtualization, 6. *See also* File/file system virtualization

Files
- in database, 212
  - virtual storage and, 217–218
- fragmentation/defragmentation of, 314–316, 315*f*, 316*f*

FlashSnap (VERITAS), 186*b*, 188*b*, 191*b*

Flat data address space, in SCSI disk drive model, 281–282

Flat Fibre Channel storage network, zoning and, 240, 241*f*

Flat files, 212

Flexibility, network, storage network replication and, 164

Flushing cache, database manager crash recovery and, 216

Four-mirror arrays, 42

Frozen images, 188. *See also* Snapshots

G

GAB. *See* Global Atomic Broadcast protocol

Gateways
- FCIP, 319, 320*f*
- iFCP, 320, 321*f*

Gather writing, 302–303, 302*f*

Geometry, disk drive, C-H-S addressing and, 22–23

Global Atomic Broadcast protocol, 224*b*

H

HBA. *See* Host bus adapters

Hierarchical storage management (HSM), 6, 256–266
- benefits of, 259–260
- capabilities and implementation of, 261–265
- data center affected by, 264–265

disaster recovery and, 264
file access performance and, 261
integration with other storage management components and, 263–264
long-term data storage and, 265
online data usage and, 258–259
optimization of, 262–263
policies of, 261–262
storage hierarchies and, 256–260, 257*f*
techniques of, 260–261
Highly available systems, 62–70, 323–324, 325*f*
cost of
factors affecting, 62
minimizing, 64–65
design parameters for, 324–325, 325*f*
failure tolerance of
data center destruction and, 58–61, 59*t*
disk drive failure and, 56–58, 57*t*
mirroring and, 66, 67*f*, 68–69
parity RAID and, 67, 68–69, 68*f*
RAID and, 65–69, 67*f*, 68*f*
redundant components in
active and passive, 63–64
relocation capabilities and, 64, 64*b*
virtual storage and, 65–69, 67*f*, 68*f*
Homogenization, storage system complexity and, 276
Host-based zoning, 240
Host bus adapters
in Fibre Channel storage network, 234, 235*f*
multifabric storage networks and, 238–239
Hot backup, snapshots and, 188, 189, 190*f*
Hot relocation, 64*b*
Hot spares, relocation and, 64*b*
Hot swapping, restorative downtime and, 55
HSM. *See* Hierarchical storage management
Hubs, in Fibre Channel storage network, 234

I

I/O interfaces
path failure and, 68
virtualized, 20
I/O load balance/imbalance
cluster file systems and, 209
concatenation and, 88–89, 88*f*
parity device bottleneck and, 81–83, 82*f*
I/O paths
with cluster volume managers, 145
in in-band storage network virtualization, 131–132
in out-of-band storage network virtualization, 134
in server-based volume manager virtualization, 114, 116, 117*b*
I/O performance
backup windows affecting, 187
characteristics of, 86
cluster storage access models and, 142–144, 143*f*, 144*f*, 148
database virtualization and, 213*b*
discovered direct I/O and, 200*b*
file system virtualization and, 200
server-based volume manager virtualization and, 117
storage network device placement and locality affecting, 239–240, 239*f*
virtualization affecting, 4, 85–101
block address striping and, 86–92, 92*f*
data transfer-intensive applications and, 90–91, 90*f*
with mirroring, 98–101, 99*f*, 100*f*
request-intensive applications and, 86–89, 87*f*, 88*f*, 89*f*
concatenated arrays and, 75–76, 75*f*, 88–89, 88*f*
file system virtualization architecture and, 14
mirrored arrays and, 42
with block address striping, 98–101, 99*f*, 100*f*
parity RAID and, 93–97, 98*f*, 112
large writes and, 96–97, 96*f*
small writes and, 93–96, 96*f*
writing data to RAID array and, 93, 94*f*
replication and, 168–181
I/O request-intensive applications, block address striping and, 86–89, 87*f*, 88*f*, 89*f*
I/O software stack, volume manager virtualization and, 113, 113*f*
I/O throttling, application, 174
IBM's Storage Tank, 12
iFCP, 320, 321*f*
In-band network storage virtualization, 9, 12*b*, 106, 108–109, 123–125, 124*f*, 125–132, 126*f*, 128*f*
advantages of, 129–130
limitations of, 130–132
RAID system replication and, 162
storage networks and, 128
infrastructure and, 129
replication and, 162, 163*f*
Inactivity time, hierarchical storage managers determining, 262
Incremental backup, 195–196
of databases, 221–222
block-level, 196, 222, 222*b*
Independence
server
with RAID replication, 162
with storage network replication, 164
storage, with server-based replication, 160
InfiniBand, 318–319
Infrastructure, storage network, 234, 299*t*
in-band virtualization and, 129
Infrastructure intelligence, storage networks and, 122–123
Inodes, 308

Integrity, data. *See* Data, corruption/integrity of
Intelligence, infrastructure, storage networks and, 122–123
Intelligent disks, 26, 27*f*
Intent log
file system recovery and, 313
in VERITAS Quicklog, 204*b*
Inter-switch links, in Fibre Channel storage network, 234–235
Interconnects, 233
fiber, 246–247
storage complexity and, 271, 271*f*, 273
for virtual storage, 122, 233–242
configuration considerations and, 239–241, 239*f*, 241*f*
device placement and locality and, 239–240, 239*f*
Fibre Channel storage networks and, 233, 234–235, 235*f*
distance and, 240–241
examples of, 252–253, 252*f*, 253*f*, 254*f*
topologies of, 235–239, 236*f*, 237*f*, 238*f*
redundancy and, 237–239, 238*f*
zoning and security and, 240, 240*b*, 241*f*
Interface ASICs, path failure and, 68
Interleaving (parity), 82–83, 82*f*
Internet, long distance network security and, 251
Internet protocol, on Fibre Channel network, 234
iSCSI, 319, 319*f*
ISLs. *See* Inter-switch links

J

Journaling file system (VERITAS), 200*b*

L

Latency, data replication and, 152
LBA. *See* Logical block addressing
LDM. *See* Logical Disk Manager (Windows)
Legacy, configuration flexibility of server-based volume managers and, 116
Libraries, hierarchical storage management (HSM) policies and, 262
Lit fiber optic interconnects, 247
LLT. *See* Low Latency Transport protocol
Locality, 239–240, 239*f*
Log archiving, 216–217
database recovery and, 217, 223, 227
hierarchical storage management (HSM) and, 258
incremental backup and, 221
replication and, 227
Log overflow, resynchronization and, 178–179, 179*b*
Logical block addressing, 22–26, 23*f*
C-H-S addressing and, 22–23, 24*f*, 25
mapping of virtual device block addresses and, 71
Logical Disk Manager (Windows), 107*b*
Logical disks, 290
Logical incremental backup, 221–222
Logical online database backup, 218
Logical units (LUNs), 8, 34–35, 35*f*
masking, 112, 117
zoning and, 240, 240*b*
in RAID system, 109, 111
in volume manager virtualization, 113–114
Long-distance replication. *See* Remote data replication
Long-term data storage, hierarchical storage management (HSM) and, 265
Long-wave/long-distance fiber, 246
Loop, Fibre Channel, 234, 235, 236*f*
Low Latency Transport protocol, 224*b*
LUN masking, 112, 117
zoning and, 240, 240*b*
LUNs. *See* Logical units

M

Manageability, cluster file systems and, 206
Managed service packages, 249
Management costs
clustering affecting, 140
hierarchical storage management (HSM) affecting, 259
virtualization affecting, 4–5
storage network, 122–125, 123*f*, 124*f*
Mapping, 71
Master-slave architecture, 146–147, 146*f*, 206*f*, 207–208, 208*f*, 281
in SCSI disk drive model, 281
Mean time between failures (MTBF), 65–66
Mean time to repair (MTTR), 66
Mesh topology, Fibre Channel, 236, 237*f*
Messaging network, storage networks and, 243–245, 244*f*, 245*f*
Metadata, 309
integrity of, 309, 310–313
cache and, 312–313
logging and, 313
recovery techniques and, 311–312
redundancy of, 311
updating
with cluster volume managers, 145
in distributed architechture, 147*f*, 148, 207
master-slave architecture, 146–147, 146*f*, 206*f*, 207, 208*f*
consistency techniques and, 310–311
logging and, 313
Metadata managers
hierarchical storage management (HSM) migrated files and, 261
storage network virtualization and, 106
out-of-band storage networks and, 132–133, 133*f*, 134, 135

Metadata servers, file system virtualization and, 12
Metropolitan area networking, 252–253, 252*f*, 253*f*
Migration, file virtualization and, 6
  in hierarchical storage management (HSM), 256–266. *See also* Hierarchical storage management
  in server-based volume manager virtualization, 115, 116–117, 117*b*
Mirrored arrays, 38, 38*f*. *See also* Mirroring/mirrors
  for database, 223
  multidevice, 40–41, 41*f*
  multiway, 41–42
Mirrored virtual device, 31. *See also* Mirroring/mirrors
Mirroring/mirrors, 4, 31, 31*b*, 37–42, 38*f*, 298*t*
  archive log, for database recovery, 217, 223
  availability and, 66, 67*f*, 68–69
  with block address striping, 98–101, 99*f*, 100*f*, 298*t*
    failure tolerance and, 100–101
  for database protection, 223
  object storage devices and, 290
  recovery points and, 53
  recovery time objectives and, 52
  remote, 153
  splitting, for point-in-time data snapshots, 38–40, 39*b*, 40*f*
    backup using, 189–192
    file system, 202
    physical online database backup using, 219, 220*f*
  versus data replication and, 152–153
Multi-mode fiber (MMF), 246
Multidevice mirrored arrays, 40–41, 41*f*
Multifabric storage network, 237–239, 238*f*
Multipathing, dynamic, 114, 116, 117*b*
Multiplexing, 223
  dense wave division, 241, 245–246, 247–249, 248*f*, 249*f*
    examples of integrated network using, 252–253, 252*f*, 253*f*
Multiway mirrored arrays, 41–42

N

N + 1 redundancy, 64
N-way mirrors, snapshots and, 39*b*
Name resolution, 285
NAS architecture, for storage network, 282, 283*f*, 284–285
NetBackup (VERITAS), 60*b*, 187*b*, 222*b*
NetBackup Shared Storage Option (VERITAS), 10
NetBackup Storage Migrator (VERITAS), 260*b*
NetBackup Vault Option (VERITAS), 198*b*
Network cables, path failure and, 68
Network failure, clustering and, 139
Network file access protocols, 10–12
Network file copies, versus data replication, 153
Network flexibility, storage network replication and, 164
Network sharing, with server-based replication, 160
Network storage appliances
  block virtualization and, 5, 9, 106, 108–109
  replications and, 162–165, 162*b*, 163*f*, 164*f*
Network storage-based striping, 80
Network storage virtualization, 9, 106, 108–109, 120–137, 282–283, 283*f*
  configuration considerations and, 121, 121*f*, 239–241, 239*f*, 241*f*
  device placement and locality and, 239–240, 239*f*
  Fibre Channel storage networks and, 233, 234–235, 235*f*
    distance and, 240–241, 250–251, 250*f*
    enhancements to, 318
    examples of, 252–253, 252*f*, 253*f*, 254*f*
    topologies of, 235–239, 236*f*, 237*f*, 238*f*
  in-band, 9, 12*b*, 106, 108–109, 123–125, 124*f*, 125–132, 126*f*, 128*f*
  interconnects for, 233–242
  iSCSI over TCP/IP and, 319, 319*f*
  management cost and, 122–125, 123*f*, 124*f*
  new technologies and, 318–320, 319*f*, 320*f*, 321*f*
  out-of-band, 9, 12*b*, 106, 109, 123–125, 124*f*, 132–136, 133*f*
  redundancy and, 237–239, 238*f*
  replication and, 162–165, 162*b*, 163*f*, 164*f*
  security and, 240, 240*b*, 241*f*, 251
  server-centric, 120–121, 121*f*
  versus server-based virtualization, 131*b*
  zoning and, 240, 240*b*, 241*f*
"Nines" of availability, 326–327
Nodes, 139. *See also* Clusters

O

Object manager, 286
Object storage client, 286, 287*f*
Objects/object storage devices, 283–289, 287*f*
  advantages and disadvantages of, 289
  separating object storage concepts and, 288–289
  for storage complexity reduction, 289–293
  types of, 288
Off-host backup, with split mirror snapshots, 190, 191*b*
Off-host processing, data replication and, 151–152
Offline media cost, hierarchical storage management (HSM) affecting, 259
Offload engines, TCP, 251
Online data
  hierarchical storage management (HSM) of, 258–259, 258*b*
  storage capacity expansion and, 316–317
Online database
  backing up, 218–221
    logical, 218
    physical, 218, 219–221, 220*f*

protecting data in, 223–226, 225*f*, 226*f*
storage redundancy and, 223–224
Online storage requirements, hierarchical storage management (HSM) affecting, 259
OSD. *See* Objects/object storage devices
Out-of-band network storage virtualization, 9, 12*b*, 106, 109, 123–125, 124*f*, 132–136, 133*f*
advantages of, 134
cluster volume managers and, 138, 145
limitations of, 135–136
object storage devices and, 290
RAID system replication and, 162
storage network replication and, 163, 164*f*
Outage time, 33, 37–49. *See also* Failure tolerance
availability and, 50–61. *See also* Availability
in highly available versus ordinary systems, 56–61, 57*t*, 59*t*
degraded operation interval (DOI) and, 53–54, 55*f*, 57, 57*t*
data center destruction and, 59, 59*t*, 60
single disk failure and, 57, 57*t*, 58
downtime types and, 55–56
mirroring and, 4, 31, 31*b*, 37–42, 38*f*
parity and, 31, 31*b*, 32, 32*f*, 42–49, 43*f*
recovery points and, 52–53, 53*f*, 54*t*, 56, 57*t*
recovery time objectives and, 51–52, 51*f*, 54*t*, 57, 57*t*
restorative/planned downtime and, 54–55, 55*f*
data center destruction and, 59, 59*t*, 60
single disk failure and, 57, 57*t*, 58
single disk failure and, 56–58, 57*t*
Overhead, low, virtual block storage device replication and, 158

P

Parallel database, virtual storage for, 224–226, 225*f*, 226*f*
replication and, 226–228
Parallel database managers, shared data clusters used by, 143
Parity device bottleneck, 81–83, 82*f*
Parity RAID, 31, 31*b*, 32, 32*f*, 42–49, 43*f*
array sizes and, 44, 45*f*
availability and, 67, 68–69, 68*f*
bottlenecks and, 81–83, 82*f*
for database protection, 224
hardware cost of, 43–44
I/O performance and, 93–97, 98*f*, 112
large writes and, 96–97, 96*f*
small writes and, 93–96, 96*f*
writing data to RAID array and, 93, 94*f*
interleaving and, 82–83, 82*f*
limitations of, 44–49, 45*f*
object storage devices and, 290
striping and, 80–83, 81*f*, 82*f*
Parity RAID check data, 29, 31, 32*f*, 33, 43*f*, 44, 46–49, 47*f*, 48*f*
Partitioning, 76–77, 76*f*
cluster file systems and, 209
Passive redundant components, 63–64
Path failure, mirroring and RAID limitations and, 68
Performance. *See* I/O performance
Persistent data storage, 2
magnetic disk for, 19–20
Physical incremental backup, 222
Physical online database backup, 218, 219–221, 220*f*
Planned/restorative downtime, 54–55, 55*f*
data center destruction and, 59, 59*t*, 60
single disk failure and, 57, 57*t*, 58
Plexes, 290
Point-in-time data snapshots. *See* Snapshots
Point-to-point Fibre Channel, 234
Policy processor, for RAID system, 11, 109–110, 110*f*
Power failure, mirroring and RAID limitations and, 68
Powered (VERITAS), 128*b*
Processor, for RAID system, 109–110, 110*f*
Provisioning, storage network virtualization and, 121, 121*f*
Publication (distribution), data replication and, 151

Q

Quick I/O, 213*b*
Quicklog (VERITAS), 204*b*

R

RAID, 28–36, 297, 298*t*, 299*t*, 300–301. *See also specific aspect* and RAID system
cluster file systems and, 209
distinguishing features of, 33–35
high availability and, 63, 65–69, 67*f*, 68*f*
history of, 30–32
logical units (LUNs) and, 34–35, 35*f*
server-based, 29
striping of, 80, 80*f*
striping data and, 31*b*, 32, 33*f*, 80–83, 81*f*, 82*f*, 298*t*. *See also* Striping
techniques and implementations of. , 297, 298*t*
virtualization concepts and, 33–35, 109–113
RAID appliances, failure of, mirroring and RAID limitations and, 68–69
RAID array, 30, 30*f*
writing data to, 93, 94*f*
RAID controllers, failure of, mirroring and RAID limitations and, 68–69
RAID Level 0, 31*b*, 32, 80, 298*t*. *See also* Striping
RAID Level 0+1, 1+0, and 10, 299*t*, 300
RAID Level 1, 31, 31*b*, 298*t*. *See also* Mirroring
RAID Level 3, 81, 298*t*, 301
RAID Level 4, 31*f*, 32, 298*t*. *See also* Parity RAID
RAID Level 5, 31*f*, 32, 83, 298*t*. *See also* Parity RAID
for database protection, 224
RAID Level 6, 298*t*, 300

RAID levels, 31–33, 31*b*, 298*t*, 300–301
RAID system, 29, 30, 30*f*, 109–112, 110*f*, 111*f*, 299*t*. *See also* RAID
  block storage virtualization in, 5, 8, 106, 107, 109–112, 110*f*, 111*f*
    advantages of, 107, 110–112
    limitations of, 112
  clusters/cluster file systems and, 141, 141*f*, 209
  failure tolerance in, 37–49
    mirroring for, 4, 31, 31*b*, 37–42, 38*f*
    parity for, 31, 31*b*, 32, 32*f*, 42–49, 43*f*
  high availability and, 63
  object storage devices and, 290
  for parallel databases, 224–225, 225*f*
  performance and, 93–97, 98*f*, 112
  replication with, 161–162, 161*f*
  resilient virtual storage with, 28–30, 30*f*
RAID system replicators, 161–162, 161*f*
RAIT (redundant array of independent tapes), 7
Random access, with magnetic disk storage, 20
Read-writeback synchronization, 39*b*
Recovery points, 52–53, 53*f*, 54*t*
  data center destruction and, 58, 59*t*, 60
  single disk failure and, 56, 57*t*, 58
Recovery time, 51, 51*f*
  data center destruction and, 59, 59*t*, 60
  single disk failure and, 57, 57*t*, 58
Recovery time objectives, 51–52, 51*f*, 54*t*
Redeploying of storage capacity, 4. *See also* Block storage virtualization
Redirection of workload, redundant components and, 64, 64*b*
Redundancy
  metadata, 311
  storage, database protection and, 223–224
  storage network, 237–239, 238*f*
Redundant array of independent disks. *See* RAID
Redundant array of independent tapes (RAIT), 7
Redundant components, high availability and, 63. *See also* Highly available systems
  active and passive, 63–64
  reducing cost of, 64–65
  relocation capabilities and, 64, 64*b*
Redundant data, RAID and, 33, 37
  mirroring for, 4, 31, 31*b*, 37–42, 38*f*
  parity for, 31, 31*b*, 32, 32*f*, 42–49, 43*f*
Redundant wide area networks, 249
Relational database model, 213–214
Reliability, of magnetic disk storage, 20
Relocation of redundant components, 64, 64*t*
  hot, 64*b*
Remote data access, file access protocols and, 11
Remote data replication, 152–153, 243–255. *See also* Replication
  dense wave division multiplexing and, 247–249, 248*f*, 249*f*
  enterprise network technologies and, 245–246
  examples of integrated network and, 252–253, 252*f*, 253*f*, 254*f*
  FCIP and, 250–251
  fiber interconnects and, 246–247
  recovery time objectives for, 52
  remote convergence and, 243–246, 244*f*, 245*f*
  security and, 251
  in server-based volume manager virtualization, 115
  wide area communications and, 246–247
  wide area storage networks and, 250–251, 250*f*
Replication, 151–167
  alternatives to, 153
  application performance and, 168–173
  archive log, for database recovery, 217, 223
  asynchronous, 169, 171–173, 172*f*, 173*f*
    recovery points and, 53
  bidirectional, 165–166, 166*f*
  database, 153, 154–155, 155*f*, 217, 223, 226–228
  delayed, by database manager, 154
  disaster recovery and, 152, 158, 159, 165–166, 166*f*, 173–176, 176*f*, 177*f*
  file, 154, 156, 157*f*
  forms of, 153–154
  initial synchronization for, 177–178, 178*f*
  mirroring and, 152–153
  for point-in-time copy creation, 179–180
  RAID system, 161–162, 161*f*
  to remote locations, 152–153, 243–255
    dense wave division multiplexing and, 247–249, 248*f*, 249*f*
    enterprise network technologies and, 245–246
    examples of integrated network and, 252–253, 252*f*, 253*f*, 254*f*
    FCIP and, 250–251
    fiber interconnects and, 246–247
    recovery time objectives for, 52
    remote convergence and, 243–246, 244*f*, 245*f*
    security and, 251
    in server-based volume manager virtualization, 115
    wide area communications and, 246–247
    wide area storage networks and, 250–251, 250*f*
  setting up, 177–180, 178*f*, 179*b*
  storage network, 162–165, 162*b*, 163*f*, 164*f*
  synchronous, 169, 169–171, 171*f*
  virtual block storage device, 157–159, 159*f*
    alternatives in, 160–165
    characteristics of, 168–181
Replicators. *See also* Replication
  RAID system, 161–162, 161*f*
  server-based, 160, 160*f*
  virtual device, 157

Request execution time, block address striping and, 92, 92*f*
Rescanning, capacity change awareness and, 74
Response time, average, block address striping affecting, 89
Restorative/planned downtime, 54–55, 55*f*
  data center destruction and, 59, 59*t*, 60
  single disk failure and, 57, 57*t*, 58
Restore from backup
  recovery points and, 53
  recovery time and, 52, 187
Resynchronization, 39*b*, 40, 40*f*
  fast, 40, 41*b*, 191, 191*b*
    physical online database backup and, 219
  log overflow and, 178–179, 179*b*
  split mirror, 191, 191*b*
Retrieval, file, in hierarchical storage management (HSM), 261
Revectoring/revectoring table, disk virtualization and, 25, 26*f*
Ring topology, Fibre Channel, 235, 236*f*
Robustness, in-band virtualization and, 127*f*, 131
Roll back, database, 217
Root, file system, 306, 307*f*
Rotation, in data location, 22
Routers, Fibre Channel-to-SCSI, 233, 235, 235*f*
Row, in relational database model, 213
RTOs. *See* Recovery time objectives

S

SAN. *See* Storage Area Network
SAN appliance, in-band virtualization by, 125, 126*f*
SANPoint Foundation (VERITAS), 147*b*
Saturation, of striped array, I/O performance and, 92
Scaling
  cluster file systems and, 206
  data access, 282
  file system virtualization architecture and, 14
  in-band virtualization and, 131
  shared nothing clusters and, 143
  storage network replication and, 164–165
  storage network rings and, 235
Scatter reading, 302–303, 302*f*
SCSI
  characteristics of, limitations of block storage device model and, 280–282
  out-of-band virtualization and, 135, 136
  storage networks and, 233
  virtualized I/O interfaces and, 20
  virtualized RAID systems and, 106
Security
  database managers and, 213
  in-band virtualization and, 130
  long distance networks and, 251
  out-of-band virtualization and, 135–136
  in RAID system, 112
  in SCSI disk drive model, 281
  in server-based volume manager virtualization, 117
Seeking, in data location, 22
Segments (file), block address striping and, 90–91, 90*f*
Selection, in data location, 22
Selectivity, in database replication, 155
Server-based block storage device replication, 158, 159*f*, 160–161, 160*f*
Server-based RAID, 29, 30*f*
  striping of, 80, 80*f*
Server-based virtualization. *See* Server-based volume managers
Server-based volume managers, block storage virtualization and, 106, 108, 113–118, 113*f*, 114*f*, 116*f*
  advantages of, 108, 116–118
  applications of, 114–115
  database recovery and, 228
  limitations of, 118
  versus network-based virtualization, 131*b*
Server-centric storage virtualization, 120–121, 121*f*
Server independence
  RAID system replication and, 162
  with storage network replication, 164
Servers
  block storage virtualization and, 8–9, 106, 108, 113–118, 113*f*, 114*f*, 116*f*
  cluster volume managers and, 145
    in master-slave architecture, 146, 146*f*
  failure of
    clustering and, 110, 111*f*, 139, 148–149, 209–210
    databases and, 214, 215–216, 216*f*
    mirroring and RAID limitations and, 69
  in out-of-band storage network virtualization, limitations in, 135
  in storage network, 122, 123*f*
Servo patterns, 21, 21*f*
ServPoint NAS Appliance Software (VERITAS), 162*b*, 210*b*
Shared data clusters, 142, 143–144, 144*f*, 205
  manageability of, 206
  storage virtualization in, 144–149, 146*f*, 147*f*
Shared nothing clusters, 142, 142–143, 143*f*
Shared Storage Option (VERITAS), 196*b*
Sharing, data
  file access protocols and, 11–12
  file system virtualization architecture and, 13, 14
  in shared data cluster, 142, 143–144, 144*f*
Short-wave/short-distance fiber, 246
Single mode fiber, 246
"Slicing" (file), optimizing hierarchical storage management (HSM) and, 263
SMF. *See* Single mode fiber
SMI. *See* Storage Management Initiative

Snapshot virtual device, 189, 192–193, 193*f*
Snapshots, 39, 188–189, 188*b*
backup and, 186*b*, 188–195, 188*b*
consistent data for, 189, 190*f*
physical online database, 219, 220*f*
with replication, 194–195, 195*f*
split mirror, 189–192
cold backup and, 189, 190*f*, 219–220
copy-on-write
for backup, 192–195, 192*b*, 193*f*, 195*f*
with replication, 194–195, 195*f*
block-level incremental backup using, 222, 222*b*
file system, 202–205, 202*f*, 203*f*, 204*f*
physical online database backup using, 219–220
virtual device, 205
file system, 201–205, 202*f*, 203*f*, 204*f*
periodic replication for creation of, 179–180
for physical online database backup, 219–221, 220*f*
split mirror, 38–40, 39*b*, 40*f*
for backup, 189–192
file system, 202
for physical online database backup, 219, 220*f*
VERITAS FlashSnap for, 186*b*, 188*b*, 191*b*
virtual storage device, 205
SNIA. *See* Storage Networking Industry Association
Software testing, virtual block storage device replication for, 157
SONET, 247
Source devices, in virtual block storage device replication, 157, 159*f*
Source to target, data replication and, 152
bidirectional, 165–166, 166*f*
Split mirror snapshots, 38–40, 39*b*, 40*f*
for backup, 189–192
for physical online database backup, 219, 220*f*
SQL. *See* Structured Query Language
SSO. *See* Shared Storage Option
Stability, of magnetic disk storage, 20
Staging, optimizing hierarchical storage management (HSM) and, 263
Standardization tool, storage system complexity and, 276
Standby copy, of database, 227
Storage access protocols, out-of-band storage network virtualization and, 135
Storage administrator. *See also* System administrator
training, 276
Storage appliances
failure of, mirroring and RAID limitations and, 68–69
network, block virtualization and, 5, 9, 106, 108–109
Storage application hierarchy, 257–259, 257*f*
Storage area network, 233, 282, 283*f*, 299*t*
Storage-aware file systems, 291
Storage capacity, virtualization affecting, 4
in file system, 201, 316–317
hierarchical storage management (HSM) and, 259
management and, 285
in RAID system, 112
in server-based volume manager virtualization, 114–115
Storage checkpoints, 192*b*
Storage client, RAID system for, 109–112, 110*f*, 111*f*
Storage consolidation
in RAID system, 111
storage system complexity and, 276
Storage costs
management of. *See* Management costs
virtualization affecting, 4
Storage devices
networked, 122, 123*f*
placement of, 239–240, 239*f*
partitioning, 76–77, 76*f*
replicating. *See* Block storage replication
size changes in, file system virtualization and, 201
Storage Foundation (VERITAS), 75*b*
Storage Foundation Cluster File System (VERITAS), 148*b*, 224*b*
Storage Foundation for Database and Applications (VERITAS), 213*b*
Storage Foundation for Microsoft Exchange Server (VERITAS), 216*b*
Storage Foundation–Volume Manager (VERITAS), 39*b*
Storage hierarchies, 256–260, 257*f*. *See also* Hierarchical storage management
Storage independence
with server-based replication, 160
with storage network replication, 164
Storage interconnects, 233
for virtual storage, 233–242
Storage Management Initiative (SMI), 242*b*
Storage management tools, storage system complexity and, 275
Storage Manager (VERITAS)
visualization and, 238*b*
zoning and LUN masking and, 240*b*
Storage Migrator (VERITAS), 258*b*
Storage network, 122–123, 123*f*, 233
block storage virtualization and, 9, 120–137, 282–283, 283*f*. *See also* Storage network virtualization
in-band virtualization and, 128
configuration considerations for, 239–241, 239*f*, 241*f*
device placement/locality and, 239–240, 239*f*
Fibre Channel, 233, 234–235, 235*f*
distance and, 240–241, 250–251, 250*f*
enhancements to, 318
examples of, 252–253, 252*f*, 253*f*, 254*f*

redundancy and, 237–239, 238*f*
topologies of, 235–239, 236*f*, 237*f*, 238*f*
infrastructure of, 234
long-distance, 240–241, 250–251, 250*f*
management costs and, 122–125, 123*f*, 124*f*
messaging networks and, 243–245, 244*f*, 245*f*
new technologies in, 318–320, 319*f*, 320*f*, 321*f*
replication and, 162–165, 162*b*, 163*f*, 164*f*
security and, 240, 240*b*, 241*f*, 251
sharing, with server-based replication, 160
zoning and, 240, 240*b*, 241*f*
Storage network appliances, block storage virtualization and, 5, 9, 106, 108–109
Storage network-based striping, 80
Storage network infrastructure, in-band virtualization and, 129
Storage network virtualization, 9, 106, 108–109, 120–137, 282–283, 283*f*
configuration considerations and, 121, 121*f*, 239–241, 239*f*, 241*f*
device placement and locality and, 239–240, 239*f*
enhancements to, 318
Fibre Channel storage networks and, 233, 234–235, 235*f*
distance and, 240–241, 250–251, 250*f*
enhancements to, 318
examples of, 252–253, 252*f*, 253*f*, 254*f*
topologies of, 235–239, 236*f*, 237*f*, 238*f*
in-band, 9, 12*b*, 106, 108–109, 123–125, 124*f*, 125–132, 126*f*, 128*f*
interconnects for, 233–242
iSCSI over TCP/IP and, 319, 319*f*
management cost and, 122–125, 123*f*, 124*f*
new technologies and, 318–320, 319*f*, 320*f*, 321*f*
out-of-band, 9, 12*b*, 106, 109, 123–125, 124*f*, 132–136, 133*f*
redundancy and, 237–239, 238*f*
replication and, 162–165, 162*b*, 163*f*, 164*f*
security and, 240, 240*b*, 241*f*, 251
server-centric, 120–121, 121*f*
versus server-based virtualization, 131
zoning and, 240, 240*b*, 241*f*
Storage Networking Industry Association (SNIA)
Storage Management Initiative (SMI) of, 242*b*
virtualization taxonomy of, 2–3, 3*f*
Storage redundancy, database protection and, 223–224
Storage replication log, asynchronous replication and, 179*b*
Storage Replicator (VERITAS), 60*b*, 156*b*
Storage system complexity, 270–274, 271*f*
cost of (administration), 272
diversity and, 274
interconnections and, 273
management of, 275–277
objects in reduction of, 289–293
sources of, 270–271, 271*f*
system size and, 273
virtualization and, 277–278
Storage systems, evolution of object storage devices and, 291–293
Storage Tank (IBM), 12
Storage technology hierarchy, 256–257, 257*f*
Storage virtualization. *See also* specific type
advantages of, 3–5
block, 3, 3*f*, 5–6, 105–119, 123–125
complexity and, 277–278
iSCSI over TCP/IP and, 319, 319*f*
clusters and, 140–141, 141*f*
shared data clusters, 144–149, 146*f*, 147*f*
complexity and, 277–278
database, 212–229
recovery and, 227–228
definition of, 2–3
disk, 3, 3*f*, 5–6
disk drive, 1, 5
file/file system, 6, 199–211
administration and, 314–317
forms of, 2–3, 3*f*
high availability and, 62–70, 324, 325. *See also* Highly available systems
HSM (hierarchical storage management), 6, 256–266
implementation of, 8–14
interconnects for, 233–242
introduction to, 1–15
network, 9, 106, 108–109, 120–137, 282–283, 283*f*
configuration considerations and, 121, 121*f*, 239–241, 239*f*, 241*f*
interconnects for, 233–242
new technologies and, 318–320, 319*f*, 320*f*, 321*f*
objects/object storage devices and, 283–289, 287*f*
for storage complexity reduction, 289–293
tape drive, 7, 9–10, 196–198, 196*b*, 197*f*
utilization issues and, 187
tape library, 8, 10
tape media, 6–7
techniques of, 5–8, 297, 298*t*, 299*t*
Storage virtualizers, 13, 13*f*
Store and forward switching point, in-band virtualization and, 131–132
Stretch clusters, 244
Stripe, 77*f*, 78, 79*f*
Stripe depth, 77*f*, 78
Stripe size, 77*f*, 78
Stripe width, 77*f*, 78, 79*f*
Striping, 4, 31*b*, 32, 33*f*, 41, 41*f*, 77–79, 77*f*, 79*f*, 298*t*
applications for arrays with, 80, 80*f*
device failure and, 80–81, 81*f*
I/O performance and, 86–92, 92*f*

data transfer-intensive applications and, 90–91, 90*f*
with mirroring, 98–101, 99*f*, 100*f*
request-intensive applications and, 86–89, 87*f*, 88*f*, 89*f*
with mirroring, 98–101, 99*f*, 100*f*, 298*t*
failure tolerance and, 100–101
object storage devices and, 290
parity RAID and, 80–83, 81*f*, 82*f*
server-based, 80, 80*f*
storage network-based, 80
Structured Query Language, 213
Subdisks, 290
Switch, in Fibre Channel storage network, 234, 234–235, 235*f*
Switch virtualization, 129*b*
Symmetric (distributed) architecture, 147–148, 147*f*, 207
Synchronization
hierarchical storage management (HSM) and, 264
initial, for replication, 177–180, 178*f*
parity RAID limitations and, 45
read-writeback, 39*b*
Synchronous replication, 169, 169–171, 171*f*
switching to asynchronous replication and, 171*b*
Synthetic full backup, 196
System administrators
cluster file system technology and, 208–209
hierarchical storage management (HSM) policies and, 261–262
server-centric storage virtualization and, 120–121, 121*f*
storage complexity and, 272
System crashes. *See* Failure tolerance; Servers, failure of
System files, hierarchical storage management (HSM) policies and, 262
System size, storage complexity affected by, 273

T

Table, in relational database model, 213
Table lookups, for block address conversion, 71–72
Tape drives, virtualization of, 7, 9–10, 196–198, 196*b*, 197*f*
utilization issues and, 187
Tape library virtualization, 8, 10
hierarchical storage management (HSM) and, 259
Tape media virtualization, 6–7
hierarchical storage management (HSM) and, 259
Target devices, in virtual block storage device replication, 157, 159*f*
TCP/IP networks, 282, 283*f*
examples of, 253, 254*f*, 319*f*, 320*f*, 321*f*
extending storage networks and, 250–251
FCIP using, 319–320, 320*f*
iFCP using, 320, 321*f*
replication on, 159*b*
sSCSI using, 319, 319*f*
TCP offload engines, 251
Three-mirror arrays, 41–42
Throughput, block address striping and, 91–92, 92*f*
TOEs. *See* TCP offload engines
Tool standardization, storage system complexity and, 276
Top-level directories, 306
Tracks, 21, 21*f*
Training, storage administrator, 276
Transactional integrity, 215
Transactions, database, 214–215

U

Universality
of magnetic disk storage, 20
popularity of virtualization and, 280
in RAID system, 111
of virtual block storage device replication, 159
UNIX operating system
device partitioning and, 77
file system recovery techniques in, 311
space allocation by, 308–309, 308*f*
Upper-level protocols, Fibre Channel storage network and, 234
User data. *See also* under Data
locating, 71–84
block address striping and, 77–79, 77*f*, 79*f*
applications for arrays with, 80, 80*f*
parity RAID and, 80–83, 81*f*, 82*f*
concatenation and, 72–76, 73*f*, 75*f*
partitioning and, 76–77, 76*f*
User data parity, 31, 32, 32*f*. *See also* Parity RAID

V

VCS. *See* VERITAS Cluster Server
VERITAS software. *See specific program*
Virtual block devices, 5–6, 29. *See also* Block storage virtualization
implementation of
in application server, 8–9
in RAID system, 8, 112
in storage network, 9
performance of, 85–101. *See also* I/O performance
Virtual block storage. *See* Block storage virtualization
Virtual block storage device replication, 157–159, 159*f*
alternatives in, 160–165
asynchronous, 169, 171–173, 172*f*, 173*f*
characteristics of, 168–181
disaster recovery and, 173–176, 176*f*, 177*f*
initial synchronization for, 177–178, 178*f*
for point-in-time copy creation, 179–180
RAID system, 161–162, 161*f*
server-based, 158, 159*f*, 160–161, 160*f*, 161*f*

setting up, 177–180, 178*f*, 179*b*
storage network, 162–165, 162*b*, 163*f*, 164*f*
synchronous, 169, 169–171, 171*f*
timing of, 168–169, 170*f*
Virtual block striping, 4, 31*b*, 32, 33*f*, 41, 41*f*. *See also* Block address striping
Virtual device block addresses
conversion of to physical storage, 33–34, 33*f*, 109, 285
in out-of-band storage network virtualization, 132, 133
mapping of to logical block addresses, 71
Virtual device failure, protection against with split mirror snapshots, 190–191
Virtual device migration, 6
in server-based volume manager virtualization, 115, 116–117, 117*b*
Virtual device replicator, 157
Virtual device snapshots, 205
Virtual disk drives, 1
Virtual Private Networks, 251
Virtual storage. *See* Virtualization
Virtual storage availability, 50–61. *See also* Availability
components of, 51–56
data center destruction and, 58–61, 59*t*, 60*b*
data recovery time and, 51–52, 51*f*, 54*t*
data center destruction and, 59, 59*t*, 60
single disk failure and, 57, 57*t*, 58
degraded operation interval and, 53–54, 55*f*
data center destruction and, 59, 59*t*, 60
single disk failure and, 57, 57*t*, 58
in highly available system, 62–70, 324, 325. *See also* Highly available systems
limitations of, 68–69
mirroring and, 66, 67*f*, 68–69
parity RAID and, 67, 68–69, 68*f*
versus ordinary system, 56–61, 57*t*, 59*t*
outage types and, 55–56
recovery points and, 52–53, 53*f*, 54*t*
data center destruction and, 58, 59*t*, 60
single disk failure and, 56, 57*t*, 58
restorative/planned downtime and, 54–55, 55*f*
data center destruction and, 59, 59*t*, 60
single disk failure and, 57, 57*t*, 58
server-based volume manager virtualization and, 116–117
shared nothing clusters and, 142
single disk failure and, 56–58, 57*t*
storage complexity and, 276
virtualization affecting, 4, 50–61, 62–70, 324, 325
Virtual storage device snapshots, 205
Virtual volumes, 5
Virtualization. *See also specific type*
advantages of, 3–5, 279–280
block/block storage, 3, 3*f*, 5–6, 105–119, 123–125
complexity and, 277–278
iSCSI over TCP/IP and, 319, 319*f*
clusters and, 140–141, 141*f*
shared data clusters, 144–149, 146*f*, 147*f*
database, 212–229
definition of, 2–3
disk, 3, 3*f*, 5–6
disk drive, 1, 5
file/file system, 6, 199–211
administration and, 314–317
forms of, 2–3, 3*f*
future of, 279–294
high availability and, 62–70, 324, 325. *See also* Highly available systems
HSM (hierarchical storage management), 6, 256–266
interconnects for, 233–242
introduction to, 1–15
network, 9, 106, 108–109, 120–137, 282–283, 283*f*
configuration considerations and, 121, 121*f*, 239–241, 239*f*, 241*f*
interconnects for, 233–242
new technologies and, 318–320, 319*f*, 320*f*, 321*f*
objects/object storage devices and, 283–289, 287*f*
for storage complexity reduction, 289–293
tape drive, 7, 9–10, 196–198, 196*b*, 197*f*
utilization issues and, 187
tape library, 8, 10
tape media, 6–7
techniques of, 5–8, 297, 298*t*, 299*t*
universality and, 280
Virtualization appliances
in-band virtualization by, 125, 126*f*
replication and, 162–165, 162*b*, 163*f*, 164*f*
Virtualization engine, in-band virtualization by, 125, 126*f*
Virtualization parameter management, in out-of-band storage network virtualization, 132–133
Visualization, VERITAS Storage Manager and, 238*b*
Volume Manager (VERITAS), 7*b*
capacity change awareness and, 74*b*
dynamic multipathing and, 117*b*
hot relocation and, 64*b*
migrating data and, 117*b*
RAID layouts of, 31*b*
replication resource sizing and, 179*b*
Volume Manager for Windows (VERITAS), 107*b*
Volume managers, 29, 299*t*
cluster, 145–149, 146*f*
architectural concepts for, 146–148, 146*f*, 147*f*, 207

cluster file systems and, 206–208, 206*f*, 208*f*
data access and, 148
distributed model for, 147–148, 147*f*, 207
master-slave model for, 146–147, 146*f*, 206*f*, 207–208, 208*f*
for parallel databases, 224–225, 225*f*, 226*f*
server crashes and, 148–149, 209–210
server-based, 5, 8–9, 106, 108, 113–118, 113*f*, 114*f*, 116*f*
advantages of, 108, 116–118
applications of, 114–115
limitations of, 118
versus network-based virtualization, 131*b*
Volume Replicator (VERITAS), 60*b*, 158*b*, 159*b*
synchronous-asynchronous switching and, 171*b*
Volumes, virtual, 5
resynchronization of, 39*b*
VPNs. *See* Virtual Private Networks
VSR. *See* VERITAS Storage Replicator
VVR. *See* VERITAS Volume Replicator
VxFSs. *See* VERITAS journaling file system

W
Wide area communications, 246–247
Wide area storage networks, 250–251, 250*f*
FCIP and, 319–320, 320*f*
iFCP and, 320, 321*f*
iSCSI and, 319, 319*f*
redundant, 249
Window of exposure, with parity RAID arrays, 45
Windows operating system
device partitioning and, 77
file system recovery techniques in, 311
storage virtualization and, 107*b*
Windows Logical Disk Manager, 107*b*
Write order fidelity, 165, 175–176, 176*f*, 228
Write performance, of large parity RAID arrays, 46
Write protection, in SCSI disk drive model, 282

X
XOR (exclusive OR), 44, 46–49, 47*f*, 48*f*
block address striping and, 81, 81*f*
I/O performance and, 93, 94*f*, 97, 98*f*
small writes and, 93–95, 96*f*

Z
Zoned data recording (ZDR), 23–24, 25*f*
Zoning, 240, 240*b*, 241*f*